The Great War in Irish Poetry

The Great War in Irish Poetry

W. B. Yeats to Michael Longley

FRAN BREARTON

OXFORD
UNIVERSITY PRESS

OXFORD
UNIVERSITY PRESS

Great Clarendon Street, Oxford OX2 6DP
Oxford University Press is a department of the University of Oxford.
It furthers the University's objective of excellence in research, scholarship,
and education by publishing worldwide in

Oxford New York

Athens Auckland Bangkok Bogotá Buenos Aires Calcutta
Cape Town Chennai Dar es Salaam Delhi Florence Hong Kong Istanbul
Karachi Kuala Lumpur Madrid Melbourne Mexico City Mumbai
Nairobi Paris São Paulo Singapore Taipei Tokyo Toronto Warsaw

and associated companies in Berlin Ibadan

Oxford is a registered trade mark of Oxford University Press
in the UK and certain other countries

Published in the United States
by Oxford University Press Inc., New York

© Fran Brearton 2000

The moral rights of the author have been asserted
Database right Oxford University Press (maker)

First published 2000

British Library Cataloguing in Publication Data

Data available

Library of Congress Cataloging in Publication Data

Data available
ISBN–0–19–818672–X

1 3 5 7 9 10 8 6 4 2

Typeset by Kolam Information Services Pvt. Ltd, Pondicherry, India
Printed in Great Britain
on acid-free paper by
T. J. International Ltd,
Padstow, Cornwall

For my parents, with love

Preface

The Great War has left a legacy which is both disturbing and compelling. In the preface to his Great War memoir, *Undertones of War*, Edmund Blunden writes: 'I must go over the ground again'. It is a ground which, even after the event, is 'thickly and innumerably . . . strewn with the facts or notions of war experience'. The imaginative return to the subject of the war is, for Blunden, less a deliberate undertaking than it is an almost involuntary compulsion, one which is destined to continue until his death. That sense is one which reverberates throughout the twentieth century. The more tangible effects of the Great War on social and political structures are still very much in evidence; so too is its sometimes intangible presence in the cultural life of the century. Far from being displaced in memory by subsequent horrors—notably the far greater death toll of the Second World War—the Great War has become to some extent, at least in the western world, a paradigm for all war in the twentieth century, an imaginative ground which is reinvented time and time again.

The compulsion to 'go over the ground again', to 'revisit' the Great War, is central to Irish poetry this century, but its centrality is rarely acknowledged. Anyone who writes about the cultural effect of the Great War does so now in Paul Fussell's shadow. The extent to which his 1975 study, *The Great War and Modern Memory*, has influenced contemporary thinking about the Great War is almost incalculable. Nevertheless, the case of Ireland falls outside the scope of his analysis, and it does so for several important reasons. Fussell explores the notion of the 'literary war' in England. Its 'literariness' is, in some ways, the war's dominant characteristic. The privileged and prominent place the work of the Great War poets and memoirists holds in English culture has, as a consequence, also led to perceptions of the Great War as in some senses a unique and aberrant event, something which seems to occur outside the bounds of conventional history.

If this view is deceptive in relation to English literature and history, fed only by the high literary profile of its soldier poets, in Ireland such deception is, practically speaking, impossible. Ireland's Great War literature is not primarily by combatants, and in contradistinction to the English tradition of war poetry, it is not a tradition whose strengths are most in evidence between 1914 and 1918. Irish involvement in the Great War was extensive, but Ireland was also a country with divided loyalties that was on the verge of civil war when the Great War broke out, and which dissolved into civil war at its close. Even if one accepts the view, commonplace in England since the Great War and shared by many of the soldier poets, that war writing is, first and foremost, experiential writing, the notion of what constitutes war experience cannot be restricted in Ireland to something which occurs away from the 'Home Front'. Consequently, Ireland's Great War literature cannot be seen either in isolation from the social, political, and cultural issues which pre- and post-date the years 1914–18, or as belonging only to those years. That it requires a different framework from the one consolidated by Fussell in relation to the English tradition is at least one reason for its neglect.

This book considers the impact of the Great War on the imaginations of six poets, only two of whom—W. B. Yeats and Robert Graves—wrote during the Great War itself, and yet all of whom reveal in their work an underlying, and sometimes overt, fascination with the images and events of the Great War. With the exception of Robert Graves, none of the poets here discussed has first-hand experience of combat, but all of them have written and forged their aesthetic theory and practice in wartime: Yeats in the Great War, the Anglo-Irish War, and the Civil War; Louis MacNeice in the Second World War; Derek Mahon, Michael Longley, and Seamus Heaney in the Northern Irish 'Troubles'. Robert Graves, spectacularly, wrote and published through all these events, though he is popularly associated primarily with the Great War, only occasionally with the Second World War, and not at all with the Irish wars in the twentieth century.

In the cases of Yeats and MacNeice, my contention is that their engagement or fascination as writers with the subject of the Great War has often been either misrepresented or underestimated. To re-evaluate this engagement is not only to illuminate repressed or complex areas of Irish history and culture, it is also to shed new light on these two poets' influence on recent Northern Irish poetry. Robert Graves's inclusion in a study of Irish poetry might seem rather more arbitrary. He is not claimed here as an 'Irish poet' but his position is instructive in relation to Yeats and MacNeice since one might say that for Graves the reverse situation holds true. His high-profile association with the Great

War, notably through *Goodbye to All That*, and his status as one of the longest-serving soldier poets on the Western Front, have problematized, at times wholly obscured, his relations to Ireland and to Irish letters. For all three, the misrepresentations have their roots in the ambiguous place the Great War holds in Irish memory, in the dominance, in critical thinking, of English understanding and mythologies of the Great War, and in the sometimes reductive versions of literary history consequent upon these two things.

For several reasons, the second part of this study focuses on contemporary Northern Irish poetry. The fallout in Ireland from the world wars has been particularly divisive: partition after the First World War; the Republic's neutrality as against Northern Ireland's participation in the Second World War. Remembrance of the Great War, in which men from all parts of Ireland participated, is an issue which reverberates in both the Republic and Northern Ireland. But, as will be seen, the complex and competing mythologies that emerged in Ireland have given that issue different resonances north and south of the border. In addition, events in Northern Ireland over the last thirty years have brought different pressures to bear on poets in the North, pressures which have encouraged, or certainly given a new dimension to, the fascination with the Great War. They have also helped to determine the strong influence of Yeats, Graves, MacNeice, and other poets of both world wars, on the Northern poets considered here. In choosing, therefore, to follow this particular Northern trajectory, I do not wish to imply that the Great War has not exerted a fascination on the imaginations of writers in the Republic of Ireland. Rather it is the case that the experience of the Republic of Ireland in the post-Second World War era in determining the forms of imaginative preoccupations with the Great War differs from that of the North and, for pragmatic reasons, falls largely outside the bounds of this study.

In a recent poem, 'The War Graves', Michael Longley, echoing Edmund Blunden, writes: 'There will be no end to clearing up after the war'. It is a phrase which resonates both literally and metaphorically. The landscape of the Western Front still yields up, year after year, the debris of the Great War, a debris which continues to claim its casualties. The traumatic upheavals in Irish history in the war years, upheavals which continue to have violent repercussions, make the war, even if obliquely, an imaginative ground to which Irish writers return again and again. Far from being an activity confined to the generation who experienced the war, it is perhaps the peculiarity of the Irish case that aspects of Great War history have been told, sometimes for the first time, through the imaginations of writers who never experienced the Great War. The sense of writing in a century which has also been a closed circuit of violence—its end in its beginning—has been heightened by their experience of Northern Ireland.

When Irish writers engage with the subject of the Great War, their engagement reverberates in, and revises aspects of, Irish political and cultural history. In that sense, although my concern is with the ways in which the Great War has been imagined in Irish poetry, the subtext to this study is the extent to which those imaginings have themselves struggled with reductive mythologies of history, and have at times become casualties of competing versions of the literary canon. The work of all six poets discussed here disrupts various assumptions about Irish history in relation to the Great War. Their work has also caused, or at least should cause, some canonical confusion in both England and Ireland. Poetry in Ireland offers a challenge to reductive perceptions of the Great War. Its refusal, in many cases, to subscribe to those perceptions may also partially account for the fact that the significance of the Great War in Irish poetry has been, on the whole, unrecognized, misrepresented, or misunderstood.

Acknowledgements

This book began as research undertaken while I was a doctoral student at the University of Durham. I owe an incalculable debt to Professor Michael O'Neill for his help, encouragement, and patience in supervising this research. I am also grateful to staff in the English department at Durham, particularly Mark Sandy, Sean Burke, Patricia Waugh, and Gareth Reeves, for their advice and support.

A number of people have generously shared ideas and information, and offered helpful suggestions, and I am much indebted to them. They include (amongst others) Ian Firla, Patricia Horton, Keith Jeffery, Edna Longley, Gillian McIntosh, Bernard McKeown, Scott Masson, and Tony Needham. I am grateful to Roy Foster for his valuable advice on Chapter 2. I have profited greatly from discussions with Michael Allen and Patricia Horton in writing Chapter 6. Eamonn Hughes has read and advised throughout with tireless generosity. I am also grateful to Peter McDonald for his advice and encouragement, particularly in the final stages of this project.

The English department at University College Scarborough offered both a friendly and a rigorously critical environment for completion of the book. My thanks go to Martin Arnold, Lucy Bending, and Matthew Pateman.

I am grateful to the following for permission to quote copyright material: A. P. Watt Ltd on behalf of Michael B. Yeats for poems and prose extracts by W. B. Yeats; David Higham Associates, for poems by Louis MacNeice; Carcanet Press Ltd, for poems by Robert Graves; The Gallery Press, for poems by Derek Mahon; Faber and Faber Ltd, for poems by Seamus Heaney; Michael Longley, for permission to quote from his poems. Part of Chapter 5 appeared in the *Irish Review* (Winter/Spring 1997). A shorter version of Chapter 8 appeared in *Critical Survey* 10/1 (1998).

F.B.
Belfast, September 1999

Contents

Abbreviations

MacNeice, *CP*	Louis MacNeice, *The Collected Poems of Louis MacNeice*, ed. E. R. Dodds (London: Faber, 1966)
MacNeice, *PWBY*	Louis MacNeice, *The Poetry of W. B. Yeats* (1941; 2nd edn., London: Faber, 1967)
Yeats, *AV*	W. B. Yeats, *A Vision* (1937; 2nd edn., London, Macmillan, 1962)
Yeats, *CP*	W. B. Yeats, *Collected Poems* (London: Macmillan, 1950)
Yeats, *E & I*	W. B. Yeats, *Essays and Introductions* (Dublin: Gill and Macmillan, 1961)

Part I

The Art of War

CHAPTER ONE

Ireland in the Great War: Literature, History, Culture

I have turned my face
To this road before me,
To the deed that I see
And the death I shall die.

Padraic Pearse[1]

The road that takes us back from the fight,
The road we love, it is straight and white,
And it runs from the battle, away, away.

Patrick MacGill[2]

I

On 11 November 1998, eighty years after the Armistice, the Irish president, Mary McAleese, and the British sovereign, Queen Elizabeth II, commemorated the Irish dead of the First World War in a ceremony at Messines in Belgium. Messines, near Ypres, is, significantly, the place where Irish soldiers from the 36th (Ulster) Division and the 16th (Irish) Division fought side by side in 1917. President McAleese unveiled a new monument to the Irish soldiers—an Irish round tower built by workers from both sides of the Irish border. The memorial was seen to provide a common ground for both republicans and unionists: those who attended included DUP, Fianna Fáil, SDLP, Fine Gael, Labour, and Alliance members. The event marked, for many, a new stage in Irish politics, an outward manifestation of a sea change in political attitudes and, therefore, in attitudes towards the Irish war dead. This was the first

---

[1] 'Renunciation', *Rogha Dánta: Selected Poems,* ed. Dermot Bolger (Dublin: New Island Books, 1993), 45.
[2] 'The Dawn', *Soldier Songs,* (1917), repr. in *The Navvy Poet: The Collected Poetry of Patrick MacGill* (Dingle, Co. Kerry: Brandon, 1984), 95.

official recognition by the Republic of Ireland's president at a Remembrance Day ceremony of the sacrifice made by soldiers from the twenty-six counties in the Great War; it was also the first occasion on which North and South together commemorated the Great War casualties from both unionist and nationalist traditions, either side of the border.

The commemoration did not mark the end of a process whereby neglect of the memory of Ireland's war dead has been redressed; it marked only an official beginning, and its terms indicated that there is still some way to go. Eighty years may seem an unduly long time to wait for that beginning. The facts and figures concerning Irish involvement in the Great War, even in a conservative estimate, one which does not take into account first- and second-generation Irishmen who enlisted outside Ireland, are daunting. Around 150,000–200,000 Irishmen volunteered for the British Army between 1914 and 1918. As far as is known, at least 35,000 were killed in the war, almost 3 per cent of the eligible male population in Ireland.[3] Even without the conscription that pushed that percentage up in Britain, the scale of Irish suffering is immense. Yet while these figures would seem to be able to speak for themselves, they have not done so.

Irish involvement in the Great War was, and has remained, a problematical subject precisely because the issue was entangled from the beginning with Irish domestic politics. The issues surrounding Irish participation in the Great War are so contentious, and so heavily politicized that the war itself, in the interests of security, has subsequently been excluded, sidelined, or misrepresented in versions of Irish political history. The Irish problem dominated British politics in the immediate pre-war years. Ulster's resistance to the Third Home Rule Bill led to a stalemate which, it seemed, would be resolved only through civil war. While the democratic process appeared to make Home Rule an inevitability, Ulster Unionism's resistance to it was not easily dismissed. Between 1912, the signing of the Ulster Covenant, and 1914, the Ulster

---

[3] If first- and second-generation Irishmen are taken into account, the number serving is much higher—approaching half a million. These numbers are in addition to the Irish already serving in the Regulars when war broke out. The casualty figures are controversial. Other estimates have placed the number of dead as around 49,000, though as Patrick Casey points out, the evidence for such a figure is untrustworthy. Terence Denman suggests 35,000 as more accurate, and Patrick Casey, in a search through *Soldiers died,* has so far recorded over 30,000 names, also estimating the total to be in the region of 35,000. See Patrick Casey, 'Irish Casualties in the First World War', *Irish Sword,* 20/81 (Summer 1997), 193–206.

Volunteer Force was formed, a paramilitary body 100,000 strong, de-
signed to resist Home Rule, with force if necessary. From 1913, a militia
was correspondingly formed in Dublin, of the Irish National Volun-
teers, to protect Home Rule. Ulster was described, in 1914, as 'an armed
camp'.[4] As Paul Fussell points out, 'It was not that "war" was entirely
unexpected during June and July of 1914. But the irony was that trouble
was expected in Ulster rather than in Flanders.'[5] On 25 May 1914, the
Third Home Rule was passed by the Commons, awaiting Royal Assent,
and an Amending Bill offered which allowed the electorate in six of
Ulster's counties an opt-out clause for a period of six years. The Lords
returned the Bill, proposing instead the exclusion of all nine Ulster
counties indefinitely. The situation deadlocked. In late July 1914, with
no agreement in sight, the politicians concerned debated partition op-
tions in a desperate, last-ditch attempt to avoid civil war in Ireland. The
outbreak of the Great War interrupted that political process, and it was
never resumed on the same terms. Four and a half years later, and after
the Easter Rising, the political landscape in Ireland looked rather differ-
ent. Fussell, in *The Great War and Modern Memory*, asks us to picture a
'situation potent with theatrical possibilities', the Cabinet meeting of 24
July 1914:

the map of Ireland [was] spread out on the big table. 'The fate of nations,' says
John Terraine, 'appeared to hang upon parish boundaries in the counties of
Fermanagh and Tyrone.' To them, enter Sir Edward Grey ashen-faced, in his
hand the Austro-Hungarian ultimatum to Servia: *coup de théâtre*.[6]

At this point, the Irish story, as it exists in English consciousness, comes
to a temporary close, shunted off-stage by events of greater magnitude.
For the British, the outbreak of the First World War served one
enormously useful purpose—it appeared to diffuse a domestic issue
which had threatened the peace and stability of the nation. Asquith
wrote, as Austria moved troops to the Serb frontier on 25 July 1914,
'This will take the attention away from Ulster, which is a good thing'.[7]
Sir Edward Grey also affirmed that 'the one bright spot' in all this was the
unexpected diffusion of the Irish issue, that it was 'not a consideration

---

[4] Kathleen Isherwood, quoted in Paul Fussell, *The Great War and Modern Memory*
(London: OUP, 1975), 25.
[5] Ibid. 24.
[6] Ibid. 25.
[7] Quoted in Peter Vansittart, *Voices from the Great War* (1981; London: Pimlico,
1998), 11.

among the things we have to take into account now'.[8] In 1966, A. J. P. Taylor still expounds a view which was common to British politicians in 1914: 'Before the war Ireland had been near to civil conflict', but once war against Germany was declared, 'Virtually all Irishmen rallied enthusiastically to the cause of Belgium', and 'both Roman Catholic and Protestant enlisted in the British army'.[9]

Taylor's cause and effect sequence—the needs of Belgium inspired a sacrifice which in turn resolved domestic disputes—is optimistic, but wrong. It is a version of events which assumes that the Irish question could be, and was, put on hold in the face of a greater emergency. The cause and effect is rather that Irish soldiers were encouraged to enlist precisely because they had been so close to civil war: what took place, as far as many Irish politicians were concerned, was not a suspension of hostility, but a transference of it. In reality, far from resolving political disputes, the Great War, as Alvin Jackson argues, 'fully exposed the tensions within Irish politics'.[10] Almost two years later, the events of Easter 1916 did not create divisions in a unified Irish Front in Flanders; Easter 1916 both exploited, and was a consequence of, divisions inherent in Irish participation in the war that were apparent, if elided, at its outbreak in 1914.

Keith Jeffery suggests that, in a sense, the Great War 'did not matter to Ireland', that there was 'a collective lack of engagement with the conflict'.[11] The European stage might have been the stage on which the Irish drama was, in part, played, but the European war itself was not the dominant theme. Churchill proclaimed in a famous speech in 1922:

Great Empires have been overturned. The whole map of Europe has been changed.... The modes of thought of men, the whole outlook on affairs, the grouping of parties, all have encountered violent and tremendous changes in the deluge of the world. But as the deluge subsides and the waters fall short

[8]   Quoted in Thomas Hennessey, *Dividing Ireland: World War I and Partition* (London: Routledge, 1998), 46.

[9]   *The First World War: An Illustrated History* (London: Penguin, 1966), 146. Taylor's reading of the situation here also reverberates in his later suggestion that 'There have been periods when Ireland had virtually no history at all', and that 'The moment its history is renewed it becomes yet another chapter in the story of Ireland's liberation from Great Britain' ('Distressful Country', review of *Political Violence in Ireland: Government and Resistance since 1848* by Charles Townshend, *Observer*, 12 Feb. 1984).

[10]   'Unionist History (I)', *Irish Review*, 7 (Autumn 1989) 63.

[11]   'The Great War in Modern Irish Memory', in T. G. Fraser and Keith Jeffery (eds.), *Men, Women and War*, (Dublin: Lilliput Press, 1993), 152.

we see the dreary steeples of Fermanagh and Tyrone emerging once again. The integrity of their quarrel is one of the few institutions that has been unaltered in the cataclysm which has swept the world.[12]

If England, with its many imperial responsibilities, was only intermittently concerned with Ireland and Irish affairs, Ireland, as F. S. L. Lyons points out, was always preoccupied with England.[13] Churchill assumed, from a profoundly Anglocentric point of view, that the outbreak of the Great War brought down the curtain on the Irish problem. In 1919, from this perspective, the drama began again with the Anglo-Irish War that had been expected in 1914. But for Ireland, the Great War was part of its continuing quarrel; it neither postponed it, nor resolved it, nor, as events in 1916 were to show, suppressed it. In England, Fussell suggests, 'the Great War was perhaps the last to be conceived as taking place within a seamless, purposeful "history" involving a coherent stream of time running from past through present to future'.[14] It is not conceived, retrospectively, in these terms in Ireland. On the contrary, the war mattered, and matters, to Ireland, not, as for Churchill, or, more generally, English consciousness, because it entailed a break with the past, the destruction of pre-war institutions, but because it played a part in a history whose main themes and 'institutions' existed long before the Great War and continued long after it was over.

By mid-September 1914, the Home Rule Bill was placed on the statute-book, together with an Act suspending its operation for one year, or for the duration of the war, whichever was longer. Far from the factors behind civil conflict disappearing, they were compounded by the outbreak of war. The principle of partition may have been conceded by both sides in the dispute; the question of borders remained unresolved. As a consequence, recruitment in the Great War was, for Irish politicians, a political tool, one which, they hoped, could be manipulated in ways which might affect the Irish question after the war. In practice, even with the Home Rule Bill on the statute-book, both unionists and nationalists were left hanging in 1914, with the potential to gain or lose over the coming months.

On 3 August 1914, John Redmond, leader of the Irish Party, and the Irish National Volunteers, volunteered Irish troops for garrison duty in

---

[12]   Quoted in Tom Nairn, *The Break-Up of Britain: Crisis and Neo-Nationalism* (2nd edn., London: Verso, 1981), 223.

[13]   *Culture and Anarchy in Ireland 1890–1939* (1979; Oxford: OUP, 1982), 16.

[14]   *The Great War and Modern Memory*, 21.

Ireland, stating their willingness to work with the Ulster Volunteer Force, with the idea of freeing the British troops for service in France. After Royal Assent was given to the Home Rule Bill, he went a stage further, and encouraged enlistment of the Irish National Volunteers in the British Army, believing that a policy of imperial loyalty would best serve the ends of Irish independence. In August 1914, negotiations were likewise under way regarding the UVF, a ready-made force which Kitchener wanted for his new army. By 3 September, Edward Carson announced to the Ulster Unionists that 'our duty is clear...And under these circumstances, knowing that the very basis of our political faith is our belief in the greatness of the United Kingdom, and our Empire, to our Volunteers, I say without hesitation: Go and help save your country.'[15]

Broadly speaking, then, one might say that Irish National Volunteers and members of the UVF enlisted in the British Army in 1914 for the purposes for which they had been formed—to defend or resist Home Rule. To put it in these terms is, of course, to deny the fissures that opened up in nationalist and unionist positions—the southern unionist response to war differed from the northern unionist response; nationalists split over the issue of enlistment—as it is also to attribute domestic political motivation to each and every Irishman who fought. For many the issue was no more complicated by domestic politics than it was for their English counterparts. (If anything, evidence suggests that their approach, in the south of Ireland at least, may be seen as more pragmatic and less 'politicized' than that of the English or Ulster volunteers.)[16] The

[15]   Quoted in Thomas Hennessey, *Dividing Ireland*, 72–3. Hennessey's study provides a detailed analysis of the pre-war Home Rule crisis, and the enlistment debate in Ireland in 1914.
[16]   Bernard Shaw pointed out, when suggesting ways of encouraging recruitment in Ireland, that the trenches were almost certainly a safer place to be than the Dublin slums, and that the wives left behind would receive a separation allowance. ('Open Letter, 1918', in Seamus Deane (gen. ed.), *The Field Day Anthology of Irish Writing* (Derry: Field Day, 1991), ii. 513). The point is not as flippant as it might sound—it was a consideration to the extent that, when the Easter Rising took place, 250 soldiers' wives in Enniscorthy complained they were unable to collect their allowance from the Post Office held by the rebels. See Pauline Codd, 'Recruiting and Responses to the War in Wexford', in David Fitzpatrick (ed.), *Ireland and the First World War* (Dublin: Trinity History Workshop, 1986), 20. Sean O'Casey, in *The Silver Tassie*, parodies the ruthless domestic economics behind enlistment. Mrs Heegan's first concern, when her son overstays his leave, and it is pointed out to her that 'On active service [desertion] means death at dawn' is: 'An' me governmental money grant would stop at once' (*Collected Plays*, ii (London: Macmillan, 1949), 18).

pro-Belgium and anti-German propaganda which encouraged enlist-
ment to such a large extent in England in the first months of the war
had its effect in Ireland as well. Although the war was seen by
a discerning few from an early stage as the most propagandist war in
history, the desire to support fellow Catholics in Belgium and fight for
'the freedom of small nations' had an obvious, and largely uncom-
plicated appeal for some, as did the desire to protect the British Empire
against a military aggressor for others. As Terence Denman points out,
of the 95,000 Irishmen who had joined up by February 1916, over half of
them had no stated Volunteer connections.[17]

Yet the war has been, and to some extent still remains, a taboo subject
in Ireland, marginalized by history in the south and heavily politicized in
the north, and however uncomplicated their motives might have seemed
to participants in the Great War, the fact remains that the 'cultural
legacy' of the war is, as Keith Jeffery notes, 'comparatively limited'.[18]
The most likely reason for that limited cultural legacy is the extreme
cultural confusion existing within the restrictions of the fairly rigid
ideologies which came to dominate on either side of the border, and
a growing awareness of the gaps opening up between individual motiva-
tion, political determinants, and actual combatant experience. This was
particularly pertinent in the south of Ireland, where the Irish National
Volunteer, however straightforward and politically validated his motives
might have seemed in 1914, found the goalposts effectively changed by
the 1916 Rising and its aftermath. It was also true, in a different way, for
unionist volunteers in the north, whose actions were politically validated
as a demonstration of loyalty to the extent that their personal experience
was written out of history.

Almost as soon as Irishmen enlisted in the British Army in 1914,
attempts were made to predetermine the roles which their involvement
in the war played in Irish affairs; the soldier went to fight, in other words,
under a weight of expectation of which he could quite feasibly be
oblivious. Those leaders who encouraged Irish participation projected
a sense of certainty of purpose (and hence, one assumes, the supposed
inevitability of some kind of reward). The certainties as manifested by
the Ulster Unionist Party on the one hand and Redmond's Irish Party on

---

[17] *Ireland's Unknown Soldiers: The 16th (Irish) Division in the Great War, 1914–1918* (Dublin:
Irish Academic Press, 1992), 36.
[18] 'The Great War in Modern Irish Memory', 152.

the other were incompatible with each other; they seem, therefore, at this distance, illogical, in that despite their incompatibility they tended towards the same action—Irish participation in 'England's' war. Theoretically, both the Ulster and the Irish National Volunteers enlisted in loyal support of Britain's war aims; in reality, the leaders of both sides volunteered their troops in an attempt to influence British policy. The 'opponent' in each case, paradoxically, was England; the way to victory over England, whether through the granting or rejection of Home Rule, was perceived as being by means of a competitive and public demonstration of loyalty. The old Irish nationalist cry of 'England's difficulty is Ireland's opportunity' took on an unexpected twist in Redmond's offer of what turned out to be cannon fodder to consolidate the Irish Party's position at Westminster; for Ulster Unionists, England's difficulty was Ulster's opportunity to demonstrate how valuable an asset the Province was to the Empire, a point which Westminster had been in danger of forgetting. Irish volunteers in the British Army had, therefore, whether they themselves knew it or not, special interests. But, as has been pointed out, the mistake Irish politicians made, which could not have been foreseen by either Carson or Redmond, was that in the Great War, the nature of trench warfare was such that all special interests were expendable.[19]

John Redmond, in his recruiting speech, encapsulated most of the 1914 myths about the nature of the Great War, the future of Ireland, and the purpose of Irish involvement. But the speech is problematical because it also contains within it all the contradictions which would eventually undermine those myths:

The Empire is engaged in the most serious war in history. It is a just war, provoked by the intolerable military despotism of Germany. It is a war for the defence of the sacred rights and liberties of small nations, and the respect and enlargement of the great principle of nationality. Involved in it is the fate of France, our kindred country, the chief nation of that powerful Celtic race to which we belong

That the Empire could be engaged in a just war was, for some Irish nationalists, a contradiction in terms: James Connolly complained in 1915 that the supposed war for civilization was in fact 'a war upon a nation [Germany] whose chief crime is that it refuses to accept

---

[19] See Gillian McIntosh, *The Force of Culture: Unionist Identities in Twentieth-Century Ireland* (Cork: Cork University Press, 1999), ch. 1.

a position of dependence'.[20] The parallel with Ireland is obvious. Redmond's suggestion that Irish nationalists would be fighting for the principle of Irish nationality is not quite the same thing as fighting for the right to an Irish nation. Redmond concluded his declaration:

I … appeal to our countrymen of a different creed, and of opposite political opinions, to accept the friendship we have so consistently offered them, to allow this great war, as to which their opinions and ours are the same, to swallow up all the small issues in the domestic government of Ireland which now divide us; that, as our soldiers are going to fight, to shed their blood, and to die at each other's side, in the same army, against the same enemy, and for the same high purpose, their union in the field may lead to a union in their home, and that their blood may be the seal that will bring all Ireland together in one nation, and in liberties equal and common to all.[21]

The appeal is potentially, and unconsciously, divisive. The 'race to which we belong' is a Celtic and Catholic one. Ulster Protestants are not part of that 'race'; they are also cast as the guilty party, since they have refused 'friendship'. The issues which have presumably led them to refuse that friendship are, in Redmond's terms, small domestic issues, doubtless deserving of Churchill's post-war impatience. And the reasons for fighting belong to Irish nationalism, not unionism, despite Redmond's attempt to project them onto all the volunteers—'the same high purpose' being 'the rights and liberties of small nations'. He also subscribes to the view shared by British politicians, and perpetuated throughout the century, that Irish Catholics and Protestants, if they fought and died together, would unite a divided country. That belief was put forward for different reasons and at different times by both north and south. It is perhaps the dominant myth of the war in Ireland, and the one which has least basis in fact. Lt. Col. H. C. Bernard, before the Battle of the Somme, thought that 'The Ulster and the Irish divisions, shoulder to shoulder in France, should consolidate the home front afterwards, despite the Easter Rebellion'.[22] The reality, however, was that dying together on the fields of Flanders was not quite the same as living together at home: it is, as Charles Sorley puts it, 'easy to

[20] 'A War for Civilisation', in Deane (gen. ed.), *Field Day Anthology of Irish Writing*, iii. 730.
[21] 'Declaration issued by Mr Redmond on behalf of the Irish Party', 17 Sept. 1914, ibid. ii. 345.
[22] Quoted in Tom Johnstone, *Orange, Green and Khaki: The Story of the Irish Regiments in the Great War 1914–1918* (Dublin: Gill and Macmillan, 1992), 236.

be dead'.[23] As Keith Jeffery points out, 'the sombre truth remains that the nationalist and unionist Irish casualties of the Great War became more divided in death than they had ever been in life'.[24] The reminder that both Catholic and Protestant gave their lives in the war is still put forward in the hope that it might, of itself, bridge political divides. But as the 1998 Armistice commemorations indicated, inclusive remembrance of the war dead is not a cause but a consequence of a less confrontational home front. The ceremony at Messines may be seen as a contribution towards the peace process in Ireland, but it was also, first and foremost, a product of that peace process.

Whatever else Ulster Unionists may have been fighting for on the Western Front, they were not fighting for the right of self-government for small nations such as Ireland, or in defence of the Celtic race. Carson's recruitment speech encouraged them to fight for their place within the British Empire, and the security of that empire, to demonstrate their loyalty to the union. Their readiness to fight the British Army and resist Home Rule indicates, from the unionist perspective, a loyalty to the concept of empire over and above loyalty to a British, not an imperial, parliament. To then support British (imperial) war aims, aims which had little to do with the principle of nationality, is not an alteration of that position but a reaffirmation of it. As the *Belfast Newsletter* proclaimed, not entirely accurately, in 1914, 'nowhere in the United Kingdom was the call of Empire more loyally, cheerfully and generously answered than in Ulster; nowhere throughout the far-flung dominions of the King did men rally to the colours with greater promptitude than in the Northern province'.[25] Redmond argued that 'The democracy of Great Britain listened to our appeal, and have kept faith with Ireland', and that, in return, 'It is now a duty of honour for Ireland to keep faith with them'.[26] For Ulster Unionists, on the other hand, betrayed, as they saw it, by those constitutional politics, the concern was not with Westminster but with the broader concepts of King and Empire, the same concepts that sustained unionism throughout the Home Rule crisis.

[23] 'When you see millions of the mouthless dead', in Jon Silkin (ed.), *The Penguin Book of First World War Poetry* (2nd edn., London: Penguin, 1981), 89. The united front abroad is itself partly myth: Jennifer Johnston's *How Many Miles to Babylon?* (1974; London: Penguin, 1988), shows two Irish soldiers of different classes and creeds unable to sustain in life a friendship that is under attack from the same bigotries in Flanders that existed in Ireland.
[24] 'The Great War in Modern Irish Memory', 153.
[25] 'Ulster Volunteers Review of the Year', *Belfast Newsletter*, 26 Dec. 1914, 7.
[26] 'Declaration issued by Mr Redmond on behalf of the Irish Party', 345.

The terms in which the Great War itself was fought, at least in its early months, are also terms for understanding the nature of the Irish conflict played out on the European stage. Britain fought the Great War in defence of the Pax Britannica, which despite, as she claimed, its virtue in having sustained peace in Europe for one hundred years, was under threat from German *Kultur*, Germany's growing military power, and Germany's potential economic supremacy. The war was therefore conceived, however inaccurately, as an imperial venture for the sake of 'liberty', order, and civilization (a broad claim that accounted, perhaps, for the absence of any more tangible, or at least consistent, war aims). Modris Eksteins suggests that in Germany the war was 'regarded ... as the supreme test of spirit, and, as such, a test of vitality, culture and life'. It was the outcome of a cultural concern with primitivism and spirituality: war was 'a life-giving principle', it was paradoxically suggested at the time, and a 'steppingstone to a higher plateau of creativity'.[27] The attitudes prevalent in 1914 could almost be seen as conducive to casting the conflict in terms of civility and barbarity: as the war progressed both sides cast the other in the role of barbarian and claimed the moral (spiritual) high ground for themselves alone. Events in Ireland followed, or perhaps foreshadowed, European developments: Ulster Unionism's perception of itself as the outpost of Empire with a civilizing mission and a duty to maintain order over troublesome 'natives' was counterbalanced by the rise of a cultural nationalism that sought to assert Irish independence through the distinctively 'Irish' virtue of spirituality, even irrationality, and was drawn towards violence as a means of making that cultural (national) claim. And Ireland shares in the inexplicable, virtually impossible to quantify, factors in the lead up to the Great War common to many European countries: bloodlust for its own sake, the idea that masculinity finds its true and necessary spiritual fulfilment in the shedding of blood, the desire to turn the principles of (romantic) nationalism developed through the nineteenth century from culture to action; affirmation of industrial prowess through warfare. In a way, Ireland's conflicting sympathies in the Great War give to the country the appearance of a microcosm of the wider European conflict.

It seemed likely, therefore, that two traditions, however stereotypical they may have been, would be validated through martyrdom on the

---

[27] *Rites of Spring: The Great War and the Birth of the Modern Age* (1989; New York: Anchor-Doubleday, 1990), 90.

Western Front, one centred on the 16th (Irish) Division, in which many
of the Irish National Volunteers enlisted; the other on the 36th (Ulster)
Division, which recruited largely from the UVF. The terms for remem-
bering the sacrifices made by Irish Great War soldiers seemed to be in
place by late 1914—for King and Empire, or, alternatively, for Ireland
and Freedom; distinctively 'Irish' versus distinctively 'Ulster' virtues. But
this, in the end, was not to be the case. In the aftermath of the Great
War, as Alvin Jackson writes, historians *did* supply 'two distinctive
devotional literatures to the two Irish states, and helped to fashion
two distinctive iconographical traditions'.[28] Those iconographical tradi-
tions, however, centre not on the wartime exploits of the Irish National
Volunteers, but on the Easter 1916 Rising in Dublin and the Ulster
Division's sacrifice on the Somme on 1 July 1916. As a result, the year
1916, rather than the Great War itself, is central in both unionist and
nationalist interpretations of history: 1916, Jackson writes, 'came to
represent a different sort of "magic number" to different types of Irish-
men', and it did so even as 'Protestants and Catholics were fighting and
dying together on the Western Front'.[29] The displacement of the aspira-
tions of the 16th (Irish) and 10th (Irish) Divisions onto the Easter Rising
is one reason why the Irish experience of the Great War itself has been
repressed in cultural memory. That repression takes the form either of
almost total neglect or of a historical rewriting, and reappraisal, to
bolster the competing mythologies which emerged as dominant in
Ireland from 1916 onwards.

To recognize the contradictions and complexities behind Ireland's
role in the Great War is to go some way towards explaining the
psychological incompatibility of, for example, Patrick MacGill and
Patrick Pearse, and to begin to understand some of the problems
encountered by Irish writers attempting to address the Great War,
problems symptomatic of the fact that the confusion which fed into
the eventual stalemate of Easter 1916 versus July 1916 was not allowed,
in either version of history, to survive it.[30] Irish memory of the Great

[28] 'Unionist History (I)', 63.
[29] Ibid. 62.
[30] As R. F. Foster argues, the 'ferment of ideas unleashed in the very early
1900s... might be as easily identified with reconciliation between cultural traditions as
with confrontation', yet the story has too often been read 'backwards—over the
shoulder, in a sense, across the gulf created by the events of 1914–18'. The 'idea of
inevitable confrontation' has been brokered through the century. In contrast, Foster, along
with other historians, has more recently 'queried... the view that cultural diversity is

War has been until recently a tale of two histories—not necessarily the two that might have been told from the perspective of 1914, but ones which prove equally reductive.

II

The 1916 Easter Rising exposed flaws in the Redmondite position as it simultaneously hardened the unionist one.[31] As such, it not only displaced memory of nationalist Ireland's participation in the war, in hardening the unionist line, it also helped to disallow internal recognition of complexities and contradictions in the unionist stance. And the Rising's cultural legacy has, it appears, almost completely sidelined the legacy left by the Great War in the Republic of Ireland. Ireland does not have an anthologized or canonized tradition of Great War literature; but it does have an anthologized canon of Easter Rising literature. The aesthetic canon is closely allied with the victorious political canon. It is difficult to imagine that 'the 1916 poets' could mean anyone other than the 1916 rebels, or that any Irish poet on the Western Front in 1916 could usurp the title. One perhaps slightly too easy view might be that the Easter Rising literature *is* Ireland's Great War literature. More accurately, one might say that it is part of Ireland's Great War legacy, but it is not the only part. As R. F. Foster points out, politically, 'the vital conditions of germination were provided by the First World War.... 1916 depended on the European War scenario'.[32] He rejects the post-1921 historiography which views the Great War merely as a British event. Likewise, 1916's cultural legacy requires consideration not in isolation from the Great War, but in the context of the Great War.

The Easter Rising in Dublin captured the imagination of what was to become the Irish Free State in the same way that patriotism captured English and German imaginations in and before 1914. It succeeded in doing so in spite of, or perhaps because of, its relatively small death toll

inevitably confrontational' by pointing to some of the more complex and contradictory elements in pre- and post-1916 developments. See Foster, *Paddy & Mr Punch: Connections in Irish and English History* (1993; London: Penguin, 1995), 22–4, 26.

[31] It should also be noted that, as Paul Bew has argued, the Sinn Féin position was no less flawed than the Irish Party one, even though Sinn Féin outmanoeuvred the Irish Party in elections after the Rising. Bew describes Sinn Féin's line on Ulster as 'wildly inconsistent'. See Bew, *Conflict and Conciliation in Ireland 1890–1910: Parnellites and Radical Agrarians* (Oxford: Clarendon, 1987), 219.

[32] *Paddy and Mr Punch*, 279.

in comparison with events at Verdun and the Somme in the same year.[33] The testimony of an Irish soldier serving in the British Army suggests the potentially enormous impact the Rising could have on perceptions of the Great War:

I went to the war for no other reason than I wanted to see what war was like, to get a gun, to see new countries, and to feel a grown man. Above all I went because I knew no Irish history and had no national consciousness.... Thus through the blood sacrifices of the men of 1916, had one Irish youth of eighteen been awakened to Irish Nationality. Let it also be recorded that those sacrifices were equally *necessary* to awaken the minds of ninety per cent of the Irish people.[34]

The desires which led to his enlistment in the British Army were, he implies, fundamentally natural desires, but in the end they found their outlet not just in any war, but in a battle (of sorts) which invoked nationalist rather than simply national feeling. The Rising, in this formula, puts the supposedly misguided spirit of Ireland back on track, and harnesses those impulses of romantic nationalism that could not find adequate fulfilment in the Great War. The sense that Redmond took the wrong road, failed in some way to understand Irish national identity and aspiration, received concrete expression after the Rising.[35] Roger Casement, in the dock, pointed out the 'irrationality' of the Redmondite position:

We have been told, have been asked to hope, that after this war Ireland will get Home Rule as a reward for the life-blood shed in a cause which, whoever else its success may benefit, can surely not benefit Ireland.... Home Rule, when it comes, if come it does, will find Ireland drained of all that is vital to its very

[33] The fatal casualties of the Rising in Dublin consist of 64 insurgents, 132 crown forces, and about 230 civilians.

[34] Tom Barry quoted in W. I. Thompson, *The Imagination of an Insurrection: Dublin, Easter 1916* (New York: OUP, 1967), 105.

[35] It is a view that became something of a commonplace, although it also depends on, in Foster's phrase, 'reading the story backwards' (*Paddy & Mr Punch*, 23). In contrast to this view, Paul Bew has persuasively argued that 'Far from being cut off from the people, the Irish party echoed their concerns all too accurately', that 'it seems more reasonable to see the party as shot through by the same ambiguities and complexities which afflicted the people'. Its electoral demise, he suggests, stems not from the fact that Redmond missed the point before 1916, but that the key issue *after* 1916 was seen to be that of Ireland's right to nationhood rather than agrarian radicalism, and that having outflanked the Irish Party on this issue, as the Easter Rising executions gave 'legitimacy to a new challenge to the Irish party', Sinn Féin was then able, even if without consistency in policy, or new objectives, to outflank it on the others. See Bew, *Conflict and Conciliation in Ireland*, 210–14.

existence, unless it be that unquenchable hope that we build on the graves of the dead. We are told that if Irishmen go by the thousands to die *not* for Ireland, but for Flanders, for Belgium...they were winning self-government for Ireland [*sic*]. But if they dare to lay down their lives on their native soil, if they dare to dream even that freedom can be won only at home by men resolved to fight for it there, then they are traitors to their country.

But history is not so recorded in other lands. In Ireland alone, in this twentieth century, is loyalty held to be a crime.[36]

Pearse, one of the perpetrators of that 'crime', shared in the 'terrible readiness, indeed a thirst, for what Yeats was to call "the blood-dimmed tide"' that characterized many in Europe in 1914.[37] '[B]loodshed', Pearse wrote, 'is a cleansing and satisfying thing, and the nation which regards it as the final horror has lost its manhood'.[38] And as Lyons points out, with the outbreak of war in Europe, 'whatever fires burned beneath the surface of his mind before 1914...erupted almost uncontrollably':

The last six months have been the most glorious in the history of Europe...It is good for the world that such things should be done. The old heart of the earth needed to be warmed with the red wine of the battlefields. Such august homage was never offered to God as this, the homage of millions of lives given gladly for love of country.[39]

That Pearse is often compared with Rupert Brooke, glorifying the pouring out of 'the red | Sweet wine of youth', indicates if nothing else a similarity of national impulses between Ireland, England, or Germany, where patriotism was seen to be vindicated through bloodshed, and when the enormous appeal of 'immortality' had not yet collapsed in the face of experience.

Pearse took the ideas of heroism and sacrifice out of the hands of Redmond's Irish Party, projected onto them a different meaning, and placed them firmly in Dublin, not on the Western Front. On Easter Monday, 24 April 1916, around 1,000 Irish Volunteers (the movement which had broken away from Redmond's National Volunteers in 1914) occupied key buildings in Dublin (and elsewhere) and proclaimed from the steps of the Post Office that Ireland was now a republic. After five days of fighting, the rebels surrendered to the British Army, and most of

---

[36] 'Speech from the Dock, 1916', in Deane (gen. ed.), *Field Day Anthology of Irish Writing*, ii. 299.

[37] George Steiner, quoted in Lyons, *Culture and Anarchy in Ireland*, 91.

[38] Quoted ibid., 90.

[39] Ibid. 91–2.

the leaders were subsequently executed by firing squad. As insurrections go, it was not a military success. Nevertheless, the execution of the rebels had a much greater imaginative impact in Ireland than the deaths of thousands in the Great War. The Rising, with its relatively few casualties and obvious failure of intent, acted as a catalyst for subsequent events in history that led to the marginalization of the Great War experience. At this point, 'military success' is evidently no longer a relevant criterion for measuring 'success'. While Pearse may have shared the impulses of sacrifice and heroism prevalent in Europe, the thirst for bloodshed, he also understood the sort of context in which those impulses could be given free rein. That context was not the battlefields of France, where heroism itself died a death, where the sheer scale of atrocity rendered individual sacrifice futile, and where the difficulty in enshrining in popular memory the 'ultimate sacrifice' lay in the fact that it was made, on average, by over twenty Irishmen every day for four and a half years. The 'imagination' behind Easter 1916 depends upon contrast with events on the Western Front for its effect.

W. I. Thompson, in *The Imagination of an Insurrection*, suggests that Pearse's self-image was Jesus Christ (crossed with Cuchullainn) and hence, 'The mythical image of Pearse as savior demanded the reality of crucifixion'.[40] He suggests that Pearse 'decided that his death was not the cost but the reward of sacrifice'.[41] F. S. L. Lyons writes: 'It is still disputed amongst historians as to whether the few hundred men who went out on Easter Monday, 1916, to wage war against the superior power of the British Empire did so in the expectation of victory or in the foreknowledge of defeat.'[42] Pearse's writings indicate a desire for martyrdom, and that desire is incompatible with the notion of military success. But whether or not Pearse rebelled in certain knowledge of military failure, he also did so with an understanding that from small-scale revolutionary action, in which the rebel's death can raise him to heroic stature if only because the odds are stacked against him, the imagination of the people can, after the event, be awakened to revolutionary fervour. In 'The Mother', written shortly before his execution, he anticipates the success through failure that will follow upon his death. Crucially, he also dictates the terms of remembrance:

---

[40]   *The Imagination of an Insurrection*, 118.
[41]   Ibid. 122. See also Lyons, *Culture and Anarchy in Ireland*, 87–92 for discussion of Pearse's Messianism.
[42]   *Culture and Anarchy in Ireland*, 92.

...I do not grudge
My two strong sons that I have seen go out
To break their strength and die, they and a few,
In bloody protest for a glorious thing,
They shall be spoken of among their people,
The generations shall remember them,
And call them blessed...[43]

The Rising was blood sacrifice, but it was a sacrifice which in acknow-ledging and accepting the futility of the gesture overcame futility in the very act of making the gesture. In doing so, the imagination had a role to play on a scale beyond that possible in, for example, the England of 1916, where the poet attempted to counterbalance somewhat imaginat-ive journalism and propaganda with a note of sanity. Notes of sanity do not resound very loudly in much of the Easter Rising literature con-temporaneous with the event. Thompson writes:

If one values life, the rebels with their Republic of Ireland were insane fanatics who had no understanding of reality; if one values death, then the realistic critics of the fanatics were men of limited vision: standing squarely upon reality they made sensible speeches without realizing that it was precisely reality that the revolutionaries had pulled out from under them.[44]

Effectively, so the story goes, Pearse, MacDonagh, and Plunkett ima-gined an event into existence. Eventually, history caught up with that imagined version of events: however indifferent the response to Pearse's Proclamation of the Irish Republic, the tide of public opinion turned in his favour during and after the executions.

Francis Ledwidge, Tom Kettle, and Monk Gibbon, all of whom served with the British Army in the Great War, illustrate the shift in consciousness, the 'awakening', that the Rising provokes. Alice Curtayne writes of Francis Ledwidge that 'he never saw anything in war but waste and futility' and 'tended to recoil from it even in his verse'.[45] In 1917, he still proposed the standard arguments to explain his enlistment in the British Army: 'is not every honour won by Irishmen on the battlefields of the world Ireland's honour, and does it not tend to the

[43] Pearse, *Selected Poems*, 28.
[44] *The Imagination of an Insurrection*, 117.
[45] *Francis Ledwidge: A Life of the Poet (1887–1917)* (London: Martin Brian & O'Keefe, 1972), 164.

glory and delight of her posterity?'[46] For Ledwidge the question is rhetorical, but with hindsight he was right to pose it as a question, since subsequent events in Ireland undermined the sentiment. In some ways, memory has followed the pattern James Connolly anticipated in 1915 (although the nationalist rather than the working-class struggle displaced the Great War): 'Some of our class have fought in Flanders and the Dardanelles; the greatest achievement of them all combined will weigh but a feather in the balance for good compared with the achievements of those who stayed at home and fought to secure the rights of the working class against invasion.'[47] The problems surrounding the Irish National War Memorial are a case in point. After considerable debate, the proposed location for the memorial was changed from central Dublin to Merrion Square, to Phoenix Park, and finally to Islandbridge, where it was, as Keith Jeffery points out, 'removed from the centre of attention'.[48] Jane Leonard described the memorial in 1986 as being in a 'sorry state' of 'neglect and desecration' which 'symbolizes the persistent indifference to the War' and indicates a desire on the part of successive administrations to 'guard the people from historical awareness lest they remember too much'.[49]

The contradiction Ledwidge, Kettle, and Gibbon sensed in their positions as soldiers in the British Army and Irish writers sympathetic to the nationalist cause, a contradiction created and exposed by the Easter Rising, is indicative of the problem of memory in Ireland, a problem which has persisted through the century. It was also a problem anticipated at the time. Tom Kettle, a former Home Rule MP killed on the Somme in 1916, remarked with some bitterness (and accuracy) after the Easter Rising: 'These men will go down in history as heroes and martyrs, and I will go down—if I go down at all—as a bloody British officer'.[50] Ledwidge joined the British Army, he said, 'because . . . I would not have her say that she defended us while we did nothing at home but pass resolutions'.[51] Yet he was obsessed not by the Great War, as were so many English soldier poets, but by Easter 1916, and recognized in 1916 a split in nationalist feeling caused by the Rising

---

[46] Francis Ledwidge, 'To Katherine Tynan', 19 June 1917, quoted ibid. 183.
[47] 'A War for Civilisation'.
[48] 'The Great War in Modern Irish Memory', 152.
[49] Jane Leonard, 'Lest We Forget: Irish War Memorials', in Fitzpatrick (ed.), *Ireland and the First World War*, 67.
[50] Quoted in J. B. Lyons, *The Enigma of Tom Kettle* (Dublin: Glendale Press, 1983), 293.
[51] Quoted in Curtayne, *Francis Ledwidge: A Life of the Poet*, 83.

which he hoped, for his own sake, would heal: 'I...am not without hope', he wrote in June 1917, 'that a new Ireland will rise from her ashes in the ruins of Dublin, like the Phoenix, with one purpose, one aim, and one ambition. I tell you this in order that you may know what it is to me to be called a British soldier while my country has no place amongst the nations but the place of Cinderella'.[52] He wrote over twenty poems on the subject of the insurrection, including the one for which he is best remembered, 'Thomas MacDonagh', a poem which Heaney calls the most 'perfect...realization of his gifts'.[53] (One can also argue that it is an elegy for the dead of the Great War, although that inference is based only on mood and tone.) Significantly, there are no poems by Ledwidge directly about the Great War to equal his Easter Rising poems in stature: if he links himself with the mood of the people, and the rebels, it seems he can do so only at the cost of denying the path he chose for himself.

For Monk Gibbon, one of the few Irish Great War memoirists, the case is even more extreme. His role in suppressing the Rising caused a change in sympathy that subsequently made his position as an officer on the Western Front untenable. Monk Gibbon, from an 'ardently unionist' family, on leave in Ireland when the Rising took place, served for Easter week in the barracks in Dublin and was commended by his superiors for his part in quelling the Rising. He served for eighteen months behind the lines in France, sent a letter of resignation to the British Army on the grounds that he objected to killing, later entered hospital with shell-shock, and was subsequently deemed fit only for home service. The Easter Rising was the point where Gibbon interrogated the rights and wrongs of war, and questioned his loyalties: in suppressing the Rising, he felt that 'the sympathies of all parts of Dublin...were on our side. There were too many Dubliners fighting with Irish Regiments...for the population to feel that this was the right moment to embarrass England.' His own sympathies, however, after the murder of Sheehy-Skeffington, were, ironically, probably 'amongst the very first to be transferred in some small measure to Sinn Féin'. The executions consolidated that sympathy, as they did also for the Dublin population.[54]

Irish republicanism has tended, understandably, to want to forget that Irish nationalists fought in the army which executed the 1916 rebels.

---

[52] Quoted ibid. 180.

[53] Seamus Heaney, introduction to *Francis Ledwidge: Selected Poems*, ed. Dermot Bolger (Dublin: New Island Books, 1992), 19.

[54] See Monk Gibbon, *Inglorious Soldier* (London: Hutchinson, 1968), 31–2.

Kettle's attitude, and, to a lesser extent, Ledwidge's, are characterized by bitterness, by a recognition that although they and the Easter 1916 insurgents might have been driven by similar motives, this does not heal a division—which also incorporates a judgement—between those who chose the 'right' action, and those who did not. For the soldiers who chose to enlist in the Great War under the impression that this was the best action to take on the road to Irish independence, the Easter Rising 'proved' what its protagonists had always believed: the fallaciousness of that choice. In the changes wrought in Ireland by the Rising, and the Civil War, Ireland's Great War soldiers became, at best, only the incidental casualties of history. That judgement has remained implicit even in some well-intentioned attempts at commemorative inclusiveness. A commemorative statue and plaque were erected in honour of Tom Kettle in St Stephen's Green, but the tribute was delayed for over twenty years, one of the reasons for the delay being an objection by the Commissioners of Public Works to the phrase 'Killed in France'. The objections, J. B. Lyons notes, 'astonished Kettle's friends, who never envisaged the occasion as a political one, and offended his relatives'.[55] In the end, the epitaph used was from one of Kettle's own poems, a sonnet written in 1916, and the choice brilliantly combines moral certainty with historical ambiguity: 'Died not for flag, nor King, nor Emperor, | But for a dream, born in a herdsman's shed | And for the secret scripture of the poor.'[56]

AE's poem, 'To the Memory of Some I Knew who are Dead and who Loved Ireland', laments the deaths of three casualties of the Easter Rising—Pearse, MacDonagh, and Connolly—and three Irishmen who died in the Great War—Alan Anderson, Tom Kettle, and William Redmond (John Redmond's brother). The poem appeared in the *Irish Times* in December 1917, and is, F. S. L. Lyons points out, 'the only major utterance of that time to mourn the death both of those who fell in the Rising and those who fell on the western front'.[57] Equally significant is its failure to do so successfully. While its final stanza seeks, optimistically, an ideal future unity, 'sees the confluence of dreams | That clashed

[55] See J. B. Lyons, *The Enigma of Tom Kettle*, 305–6.
[56] Quoted ibid. 300.
[57] *Culture and Anarchy in Ireland*, 107. Declan Kiberd, in *Inventing Ireland: The Literature of the Modern Nation* (London: Jonathan Cape, 1995), 240, reiterates Lyons's observations, describing the poem as the 'only significant poem of the time to lament the Irishmen who died in both conflicts'—Thomas MacDonagh and Tom Kettle. Terence Denman, citing the same two stanzas of the poem, is less positive about its sentiment. See *Ireland's Unknown Soldiers*, 176.

together in our night, | One river, born from many streams', the poem, in style, structure, even layout, inadvertently reinforces the distinction between the two forms of sacrifice. It recognizes the seductiveness of the Easter Rising myths of Messianic sacrifice; it cannot help but sound bewildered by the choice of the Great War soldiers:

> Their dream had left me numb and cold,
>   But yet my spirit rose in pride,
> Refashioning in burnished gold
>   The images of those who died,
> Or were shut in the penal cell.
>   Here's to you Pearse, your dream not mine,
> But yet the thought, for this you fell,
>   Has turned life's water into wine.

> *You who have died on Eastern Hills*
>   *Or fields of France as undismayed*
> *Who lit with interlinkèd wills*
>   *The long heroic barricade,*
> *You, too, in all the dreams you had,*
>   *Thought of some thing for Ireland done.*
> *Was it not so, O shining lad,*
>   *What lured you, Alan Anderson?*

> I listened to high talk from you,
>   Thomas MacDonagh, and it seemed
> The words were idle, but they grew
>   To nobleness by death redeemed.
> Life cannot utter words more great
>   Than life may meet by sacrifice,
> High words were equalled by high fate,
>   You paid the price, You paid the price.

> *You who have fought on fields afar,*
>   *That other Ireland did you wrong*
> *Who said you shadowed Ireland's star,*
>   *Nor gave you laurel wreath nor song.*
> *You proved by death as true as they,*
>   *In mightier conflicts played your part,*
> *Equal your sacrifice may weigh,*
>   *Dear Kettle, of the generous heart.*[58]

---

[58] 'AE', 'To the Memory of Some I Knew Who are Dead and Who Loved Ireland', repr. in Owen Dudley Edwards and Fergus Pyle (eds.), *1916: The Easter Rising* (London: MacGibbon and Kee, 1968), 220–1.

The poem fails, unlike Yeats's 'Easter 1916', to balance lament and judgement, 'High words' and a 'high fate' dwindling to the banal 'You paid the price, You paid the price', a cliché which falls flat the first time, and does not redeem itself by repetition. There are, however, any number of uninspired Easter Rising poems, and the interest lies primarily in what AE has to say about the Great War casualties. To attempt a commemoration of Kettle which locates his death on the battlefields of France is to run counter to the spirit of the times. AE's poem, though well-intentioned, does not rise to the challenge it sets itself, indulging in conventional euphemisms—'You proved by death as true as they, | In mightier conflicts played your part'—that are also historically ambiguous. Nowhere does he throw a spanner in the works equivalent to Yeats's 'For England may keep faith | For all that is done and said' in 'Easter 1916'. In a way, AE applies Easter 1916 myths of victory through death and defeat to the First World War. In attempting to write the Great War soldiers back in to nationalist Ireland, the poem also apologizes for them. It celebrates the Easter Rising martyrs—'hope lives on age after age' that their sacrifice might win 'Earth with its beauty'. Less evocatively, he also affirms that Redmond too *'had Ireland in [his] care'*. Italicized, indented, sidelined, an argument is made only in parentheses: the Great War soldiers are no more than the handmaids of the insurgents. And why must Kettle prove 'by death as true' as the 1916 insurgents? Had he not already proved it in life? Kettle's own war poems, though equally slight, do point the difference between the mentality of Irish soldiers in the British Army and the Easter 1916 rebels, that the former did not work on the assumption that wanton sacrifice meant future victory, rather it was simply a wasted expenditure of life: 'The trumpets summon death, and Ireland rallies— | Tool or free? We have paid, and over paid, the price.'[59]

This is not to break a butterfly on a wheel for no reason. AE's poem subscribes, implicitly, to an argument which even now informs reclamation of the Republic's Great War dead. They can be remembered, by AE, and can be remembered now, only in terms of their nationalist sacrifice. Even so, they are seen less as patriots than as victims, and as victims they become more explicable, and much more sympathetic characters. (Seamus Heaney's poem 'In Memoriam Francis Ledwidge' works

[59] Tom Kettle, 'A Nation's Freedom', *Poems and Parodies* (Dublin: The Talbot Press, 1916), 82.

precisely on those terms.)[60] Sean Lemass's tribute in 1966 to the Republic's Great War soldiers was both highly significant, a breakthrough speech, and also, unintentionally, not without a slight sting in the tail:

In later years it was common—and I also was guilty in this respect—to question the motives of those men who joined the new British armies at the outbreak of the War, but it must, in their honour, and in fairness to their memories, be said that they were motivated by the highest purpose, and died in their tens of thousands in Flanders and Gallipoli, believing that they were giving their lives in the cause of human liberty everywhere, not excluding Ireland.[61]

Their intentions were pure, even though they were wrong, not perhaps the greatest tribute. Henry Harris, in an essay on Ireland's Great War soldiers, 'The Other Half Million', included in a collection of essays designed to commemorate the fiftieth anniversary of the Easter Rising, quotes Lemass's speech and concludes: 'Erin has remembered them'.[62] But while the first question—whether or not they are remembered— may have been answered, the second, still under negotiation, must always be *how* they are remembered.

Despite the recent resurgence of interest in Irish involvement in the Great War (of which more anon), inclusiveness can still be an elusive goal. Declan Kiberd's recent *Inventing Ireland: the Literature of the Modern Nation* acknowledges the prevailing Zeitgeist by including a chapter on 'The Great War and Irish Memory', but then falls into, rather than challenges, the reductive mythologies that have dominated memory. 'For decades after independence', he writes, 'the 150,000 Irish who fought in the Great War...had been officially extirpated from the record'. 'Such amnesia', he suggests, 'was weird...considering the manifest links of mood and mentality between the Easter rebels and the battlers at the Somme'.[63] Two problems arise here: first, Kiberd considers only those who fought 'for the rights of small nations and for Home Rule'; second, he misses the point that the Irish Party's commitment to a democratic rather than insurrectionary path heightened rather than healed the sense of division after the Rising.[64] When Kiberd notes

---

[60] See also Ch. 5 Sect. IV below.
[61] Quoted in Edwards and Pyle (eds.), *1916: The Easter Rising*, 115.
[62] 'The Other Half Million', ibid.
[63] *Inventing Ireland*, 239.
[64] Tom Dooley discusses the ways in which the Great War actually 'crystallised differences between the two nationalist traditions' ('Southern Ireland, Historians and the First World War', *Irish Studies Review*, 4 (Autumn 1993), 5).

the sympathy many Irish soldiers in the British Army would have felt for the rebels, and then describes that feeling as causing 'confusion',[65] he confuses sympathy with overt support or involvement, and inadvertently finds the reasons for the 'amnesia' he describes as 'weird'. The sympathy, as Tom Kettle was aware, goes hand in hand with exclusion: one action validates itself by invalidating another. To link mood and mentality entails some impossible manipulation of time and space. Kiberd writes: 'The rebels emulated the demeanour of the British Army and proved that, in an issue which truly engaged their sympathies, they could be as brave as any. Accordingly, the soldier-poet Francis Ledwidge found no great difficulty in writing a lament for his friend Thomas MacDonagh'.[66] But he reverses and thereby ignores the true difficulty of memory in order to find it surmountable: one would look in vain, in other words, for a Sinn Féiner poem lauding the achievements of the British Army on the Western Front. Nor does he offer any explanation for the absence of the Great War in Ledwidge's own verse. (The real point of such remarks seems to be to rescue the rebels from any imputation of cowardice.) In effect, Kiberd, like others before him, tries to redress amnesia by suggesting that the Great War was rather like the Easter Rising: he is therefore able to argue that there is no real need to be amnesic about it. He recycles the English Great War myths critically explored in Fussell's *The Great War and Modern Memory*, and implies that these myths, suitably conflated with Easter Rising myths, offer an insight into Irish memory of the Great War.[67] In doing so, he not only elides the problem of memory by privileging the Easter 1916 origin myth he purports to confront, he fails to distinguish between Irish and English experiences of the war, and writes out of Irish history those soldiers—south as well as north—who fought in defence of, rather than in reaction against, imperial ideology.

III

Less than three months after the Easter Rising, the Ulster Division was decimated on the first day of the Battle of the Somme. The casualties at Thiepval numbered over 5,000, of whom over 2,000 were killed. The Somme was, and is, the single worst day in British military history, with 60,000 casualties, and 20,000 dead. Ulster, with 10 per cent of the entire

[65] *Inventing Ireland*, 239.   [66] Ibid.   [67] See ibid. 247.

British casualties, rated second only to Yorkshire as the region which suffered the most on that day. They were the only division at the Somme to reach the third German trench system, and this in spite of the fact that they were fighting their first battle. Of the nine VC's awarded on 1 July 1916, four were given to the 36th (Ulster) Division.

Understandably, for the Ulster Unionists, remembering the Great War means, in effect, remembering the Somme. Here, it seems, the numbers do speak loud and clear across the decades. Where nationalist, and also southern unionist, soldiers in the Great War have been forgotten, the northern unionist contribution is remembered—in Orange marches, in Remembrance ceremonies, through Northern Ireland's Somme Association, and more recently, with the opening of the Somme Heritage Centre in Newtownards.[68] The Remembrance rites may be high profile; the act of remembering has proved more difficult. Remembrance of the Ulster contribution is problematic precisely because it is prominent, because it has been so politically determined.

The 36th (Ulster) Division was, in many ways, unique within the British Army. It shared with many of Kitchener's new army divisions a localized recruitment pattern, one which was to prove catastrophic on the high casualty Western Front (the most notorious instance in England being that of the 'Accrington Pals'). As Tom Johnstone points out, 'Belfast streets, town districts or little villages provided whole platoons in a way which made them enlarged families.'[69] But the 36th Division also had a history and unity before 1914, one which reinforced those local alliances. Battalions from the UVF were transferred with little, if any, alteration, into the new 36th Division. It was given an unusual degree of independence, in, for example, the choosing of its own (unionist) leaders for the Division, and in its recruitment arrangements. The Division also had, as a result, a unique religious and political exclusivity: it was predominantly Protestant and unionist. Although it has been suggested that it contained no Catholics, the number, before 1916, would certainly have been negligible, probably less than twenty. Cyril Falls, in his history of the 36th Division, picks up on the religious

---

[68] The centre does, of course, cover both Catholic and Protestant contributions to the Great War. It devotes space to the histories of all three Irish divisions—the 16th (Irish), the 10th (Irish), and the 36th (Ulster). In the words of its promotional leaflet, it aims to provide 'a basis for the two traditions in Northern Ireland to come together to learn of their common heritage'.

[69] *Orange, Green and Khaki*, 220.

element as a major factor in the life of the Division: 'Religious feeling inspired the men of Ulster in those days of training, and remained with them in the days of war.'[70] The 36th Division was the pride of the 'Imperial Province' of Ulster—'Resolution, self-reliance, and the spirit that knows no surrender and no defeat are present in full measure in every unit of the Division'[71]— and it became the focus for the allegiance formerly given to the UVF. Its Protestant unionist nature meant that any feats performed by the Division were recognizably Ulster Protestant feats and could be claimed as such in unionist mythology. If Ulster Volunteers entered the war with the hope that recognition of their 'sacrifice' would give them political leverage, they appeared to start with an advantage over the Irish National Volunteers, who never shared that degree of political homogeneity—nationalism in the Irish Volunteers in 1914 ranged from constitutional nationalism to revolutionary politics—and who were never transferred wholesale into the 16th (Irish) Division, even if many of them did choose to enlist. But two things resisted easy incorporation into unionist mythology, and led to the wide gap which opened between experience and ideology. The first was the nature of the Great War itself; the second was the apparent advantage of the nature of the Division. As Tom Johnstone points out, there is one fairly obvious problem which results from the organization of a division like the 36th on local lines: 'When a unit recruited heavily from the same sparsely populated rural area suffers severe battle casualties, the instant effect on a small community is terrible. But in the heady atmosphere of 1914, this possibility was in the future and not then a consideration.'[72]

Martin Middlebrook suggests that the Battle of the Somme was lost 'by a matter of seconds—the interval between the lifting of the artillery barrage and the arrival of the first wave at the German trenches'—an interval which allowed time for the Germans to lift their guns from the deep dugouts in which they had been protected from the British artillery barrage, and simply fire into the waves of British troops advancing— slowly—across No Man's Land. It was an unimaginative plan, one which was to prove lethal for over 20,000 people, and it 'refused to credit [the] troops with having any skill and robbed them of all chance to

[70] Cyril Falls, *The History of the 36th (Ulster) Division* (1922; Belfast: The Somme Association, 1991), 16.
[71] 'Order of the Day' issued by General Nugent to the Ulster Division on 29 June 1916, quoted in the *Northern Whig*, 6 July 1916, 8.
[72] *Orange, Green and Khaki*, 220.

use their initiative'.[73] The Ulster Division's experience of the opening of battle differed only slightly from this plan, but, as events were to show, crucially. If the battle was lost in that interval Middlebrook describes, it was also the point for the 36th Division where it was won: they left the trenches a few moments before the time scheduled for the first wave of troops, they advanced at speed—often running rather than walking— over No Man's Land, in part under cover of Thiepval wood, and arrived at the first line of German trenches almost before the Germans had time to respond. Nor did they form the 'waves' used by other Divisions, heading en masse towards the German lines. The stereotype of the martial Irishman—valiant, aggressive, heroic, with a daredevil spirit— is seemingly remote from the stereotype of the Ulster Unionist—en- trenched, defensive, immovable. The first of July points up the inad- equacies of those stereotypes, as much as the Division's military action offered a vision of how the static war could be won. But the Division's success was not matched by comparable achievements on either flank: the Ulstermen therefore penetrated further and further into the German lines—a process which left them exposed on three sides to enemy fire— and failed to receive reinforcements in sufficient time to consolidate their gains. Many of the casualties were suffered on a slow and painful retreat at the end of the day back across the ground gained at such high cost in the morning. As Brian Gardner points out: 'They were confused. They thought they had won a costly victory. But it had turned out something like defeat.' Writing in 1968, he also suggested that 'There is bad feeling about this in Ulster to this day, many survivors believing they were let down by English divisions on their flanks'.[74] The Ulster Division showed initiative, skill, heroism, imagination, but it did so in a context which appeared not to value those qualities at all.

The Somme was in many ways the turning point for English culture and modern memory: the ideals of 1914, sustainable through the first two years of war, could not be sustained after 1916. Derek Mahon calls the English generation of 1916 'dumbfounded on the Somme'. In a way he is right: the 'old phrases' that, as Edward Thomas points out, 'come back alive in war-time',[75] no longer seemed adequate after 1916. A new

[73] Martin Middlebrook, *The First Day on the Somme: 1 July 1916* (London: Allen Lane, 1971), 280–1.

[74] *The Big Push: The Somme 1916* (London: Sphere Books, 1968), 90.

[75] *A Language Not to be Betrayed: Selected Prose of Edward Thomas*, ed. Edna Longley (Manchester: Carcanet New Press, 1981), 222.

voice appeared in post-1916 English war literature—not the voice of heroic sacrifice for a good cause, but one of irony, anger, and frustration. In Ulster, disillusionment with the war came, as it did for England, on the Somme in 1916, but, for various reasons, it was without a focus and even without a voice. There is no fiction from this time which deals with the unionist experience on the Somme; nor is there any poetry, with the exception of a small quantity of ephemeral verse.[76] In a way, this is astonishing: thousands dead, a culture in turmoil, anger, and bitterness against the war, widespread grief, political insecurity, and yet, on the whole, no cultural or even, one might say, unofficial record of this from the community concerned.

Understanding of the First World War in England depends a great deal on, or, from another perspective, is dictated by, the literary efforts both during and after the war of those who actually took part in it. The extent to which Paul Fussell relies on these sources as a means of understanding modern memory is indicative of the phenomenon of a 'literary war'. The official histories and pamphlets, the popular, pro-pagandist literature, and so forth, published under the restrictions of the Defence of the Realm Act, and guaranteed not to offend conservative sensibilities, are no longer held to tell the 'truth' about war: the crucial and canonical texts for understanding the English experience of the Great War have become war memoirs by Graves, Sassoon, Blunden, and others, or the trench lyrics of Owen, Rosenberg, or Sassoon. In Ulster, although a flood of books appeared in the war and immediate post-war years about the Ulster Division at the Somme, these were, on the whole, by unionist politicians and historians, often with an agenda that sought not to remember the Somme but to dictate the way in which the Somme should be remembered. The Somme was incorporated into a seamless thread of unionist history's military successes, a history of loyalty to the Crown and to Protestantism stretching from the Battle of

---

[76] Keith Jeffery, in his survey of Irish fiction of the First World War, notes that he 'found nothing in fiction about the response of loyalist Ulster to the conflict', although Ulster is 'well-served' in non-fiction ('Irish Prose Writers of the First World War', in Kathleen Devine (ed.), *Modern Irish Writers and the Wars* (Gerrards Cross: Colin Smythe, 1999), 17, 267 n. One soldier who served with the Division (not previously a UVF member), Harry Midgely, published a volume of poems, *Thoughts from Flanders*, in 1924. On the whole the verse reiterates 1914–style patriotic ideals of death and glory, and looks forward to a glorious future raised from the ashes of war. Several poems, some by those serving in the army, appeared in newspapers in Ulster in the weeks after 1 July.

the Boyne to 1916 (and beyond).[77] Cyril Falls strikes a remarkably positive note in his description of the men of the Ulster Division eleven days after the battle:

Sun was shining on the old Flemish village. Officers and men wore marigolds in caps to honour the day [12 July]; the bands played 'King William's March.' The least practised eye could tell that to these men confidence was returning; that the worst of the horror they had endured had been shaken from their shoulders. They marched like victors, as was their right.[78]

Positively unbelievable perhaps, only ten days after such losses. In *The Great War: A Tribute to Ulster's Heroes*, a commemorative book published by the Citizen's Committee in Belfast in 1919 (and impressively subtitled *Ulster Greets her Brave and Faithful Sons and Remembers her Glorious Dead*), comparatively little space is devoted to the Battle of the Somme, which is surprising when one considers that it is the only major battle in which the original division, with its overwhelmingly Protestant character, took part. (Many of the replacements for the Division after July 1916 were conscripted from elsewhere in the UK.) The emphasis, as with Falls's history, is laid on the fact that the Ulster Division fulfilled all its obligations in the battle, not on the heavy price it paid in doing so, or on the negligible effect this huge expenditure of human life actually had on the course of the war. Cyril Falls carefully refuses to apportion blame for the failure of 1 July, but he is at pains to point out that the Ulster Division, in implied contrast to others, did exactly what was required of it: 'These men...felt that in all that had happened there was no reproach for them. They, at least, had accomplished their task in the face of incredible difficulties.'[79] Other myths have been perpetuated to the extent that they now appear, in one form or another, in almost every history of the Battle of the Somme: the Ulstermen, aware that 1 July was the anniversary of the Battle of the Boyne, went into the attack wearing

---

[77] First and foremost amongst these texts is, of course, Falls's *History of the 36th (Ulster) Division* (1st pub. 1922.) Other examples are Ronald McNeill, *Ulster's Stand for Union* (London: John Murray, 1922), in which he affirms the reliability of Ulster, her willingness to make sacrifices on a huge scale for England (demonstrated at the Somme), as against the possibly well-intentioned, but fundamentally untrustworthy and unreliable Redmond-ites. Even less balanced is Ernest W. Hamilton's *The Soul of Ulster* (2nd edn., London: Hurst and Blackett Ltd., 1917), which describes the Ulster Protestants' 'resolution' and 'courage' as 'unshakeable'; the 'curse of [Catholic] Ireland', on the other hand, is 'lack of moral courage' (138, 149).

[78] *History of the 36th (Ulster) Division*, 63.

[79] Ibid.

Orange sashes and shouting 'No Surrender!', 'Remember the Boyne!'. Like most First World War myths, this one probably contains an element of truth, but has been grossly exaggerated by those seeking to incorporate the Somme into an unbroken thread of unionist history. Malcolm McKee, a veteran of the Great War, challenged those myths in an article for the *Belfast Telegraph* in 1966:

What nonsense is stuck onto the story... Certainly Major Gaffikin waved an Orange handkerchief, but orange was the colour of our battalion... If he had said (and if anybody could have heard him) 'Come on, boys, this is the First of July!'—how many would have known the Boyne was fought on the first of July? I don't know why they plaster such incidents on our battle. Nothing was further from my mind than the Boyne on the Somme.[80]

History, he complains, has denied the truth of his experience. To find that truth, it is necessary to shatter the 'memories' that have dominated in Ulster since the battle took place. It is not a task that could have been undertaken fifty years earlier. As Philip Orr points out, a 'kind of self-censorship' usually exists for some time after a war is over. But he also notes that 'in the case of the Ulster Division, the period of inhibition, before a proper confrontation with the realities of the Great War, seems to have been an especially long one, reflecting... the reluctance of some Ulster people to confront with honesty their own place in history and, in particular, to question the true nature of their link with Britain'.[81] The Somme symbolizes, for loyalists, the union sealed with blood. Michael MacDonagh noted in 1917 that 'By an astounding transformation of events', the Ulster Division 'were to bleed and give their lives for all they revere and cherish, not in Ulster but on the hills and in the woods of Picardy'.[82] 'The Battle for which the UVF so long and so diligently prepared was not denied them', A. T. Q. Stewart writes, arguing that 1 July 1916 was, for the Ulster Division, a battle in defence of the union, even though it 'is known to history as the Battle of the Somme'.[83] The 'old covenanting spirit, the old sense of the alliance of "Bible and Sword"' was, for Falls, 'reborn' in the men of the Ulster Division.[84]

[80] Quoted in Philip Orr, *The Road to the Somme: Men of the Ulster Division Tell Their Story* (Belfast: Blackstaff Press, 1987), 218.

[81] Ibid., 227.

[82] *The Irish on the Somme* (London: Hodder and Stoughton, 1917), 27.

[83] *The Ulster Crisis* (London: Faber, 1967), 237.

[84] *History of the 36th (Ulster) Division*, 16.

The link between 1912 and 1916 is now so well established, it no longer requires explication: Gordon Lucy's *The Ulster Covenant: A Pictorial History of the 1912 Home Rule Crisis* carries a photograph of Carson signing the Covenant on the front cover, and, without comment, a painting of the charge of the 36th Division on 1 July on the inside cover: one is seen as a consequence and vindication of the other.[85]

David Miller explains that Ulster's relationship with England has always been seen by Ulster in terms of a contractual bond: the Bill of Rights in 1688 'is understood as a once-for-all transaction—a contract undertaken with King William'. Hence, the times when Ulster resisted the British parliament were times when that contract was seen as broken or undermined by England.[86] Ulster Protestantism's commitment to the Great War was, likewise, based on the premiss that to give to England meant also to receive. (It is for this reason that unionist interpretations of the Great War have underplayed the contribution of nationalist Ireland and northern Catholics.)[87] F. S. Boas's 'The Men of Ulster', which first appeared in the *Newtownards Chronicle* in October 1914, expresses this sentiment:

So, forward the men of Ulster for the Empire and the King!
Though their own fate be in debate, no thought of wavering!
The sword half drawn in her own behoof, in Ulster's red right hand
Will leap from the scabbard and flash like fire, for the common Motherland.

What of the men of Ulster? Hark to their armèd tread,
As they turn their backs on the Province, and face to the front instead.
And wherever the fight is hottest, and the sorest task is set,
Ulster will strike for England—and England will not forget![88]

---

[85] *The Ulster Covenant: A Pictorial History of the 1912 Home Rule Crisis* (The Ulster Society: New Ulster (Publications) Ltd., 1989).

[86] Miller, *Queen's Rebels: Ulster Loyalism in Historical Perspective* (Dublin: Gill and Macmillan, 1975), 62–4.

[87] In 1932, C. J. O'Donnell published *Outraged Ulster: Why Ireland is Rebellious, by An Ulster Catholic* (London: Anglo-Eastern Publishing Co. Ltd.), a violent protest against the Ulster Protestant treatment of Catholics in the north of Ireland who had, he states, 'believed in the righteousness of the war … waged for the freedom of a small and wronged nation', had fought for England and thereby demonstrated their loyalty (he points out that five full regiments were raised from the Catholic population of Belfast), their only reward to be persecuted and, in some cases, driven out of Belfast by Protestant violence (53–4). It is not a perspective which has reverberated to any degree in Protestant-dominated commemoration of the war.

[88] Repr. in *Songs of Ulster and Balliol* (London: Constable and Company Ltd., 1917), 14.

Loyalty, although it proclaims itself as unconditional, an essential Ulster Protestant quality, is in fact something which is given under certain conditions.[89] Boas's 'England will not forget' works as aspiration, affirmation, and warning. In unionist interpretations of events in the Great War, emphasis was placed on the fact that Ulster fulfilled its part of the contract. The 'betrayal' of Ulster in 1916 thus came in two ways: first, the Ulster Division was, it seems, wantonly sacrificed on the banks of the Somme, and second, despite that sacrifice, the British government began negotiations with Irish republicans following the Easter Rising. (Yeats seems to have been the only person in Ireland at this time even to hint that England was capable of keeping faith with anybody.) Ulster Unionism was, in a way, in a catch-22 position after the Somme: it could not take action and rebel, or in fact do much more than shout betrayal at the government, when it was with the other hand pointing to Easter 1916 as proof of Ulster's loyalty and nationalist Ireland's traitorous perfidy. The Somme was caught in the middle of this confusion: it was projected as success in the loyalist myths of history, but it was also futile sacrifice because it did not yield the anticipated reward from England.

In this sense, some of the ways in which the Rising can be explained also apply to the Ulster Division on the Somme. For both events, attempts were made to dictate in advance the terms of remembrance. But the Rising has been amenable to imaginative expression in this respect in a way the Somme has not. In the Battle of the Somme, the reality was very different from the imagined event—the notorious battle plan. In the Easter Rising, an imagined event which had little basis in reality at the time—the foundation of an Irish Republic—subsequently altered the nature of that reality. Perhaps history is never so amenable to the workings of the imagination as before it actually happens, even if any amount of revision can be attempted afterwards. The Somme was beyond literal or imaginative control: if it had been incorporated into literature with any fidelity to the original experience, it would potentially have lost whatever value it might have had politically in Ulster, and if

---

[89] Edward Carson defined it in terms of essentialism in his maiden speech to the House of Lords in 1921: 'Loyalty is a strange thing. It is something which you cannot get by merely sitting round a table and trying to find a formula for an Oath of Allegiance which means nothing. It is something born and bred in you . . . inherited in you, and that is the safety of the State.' As a result, there is some irony in the fact that he also warned 'do not try us too high' (Deane (gen. ed.), *Field Day Anthology of Irish Writing*, iii. 362).

fidelity to the experience had been abandoned, literature would have dwindled to mere unionist propaganda. The political disillusionment characteristic of post-1916 English poetry, however much it may have been shared, hardly provides a workable example for an insecure domestic political situation in Ulster that could not afford artistic mutiny. In a peculiar way, therefore, the absence of a literature about the Great War in Ulster in the war and post-war years is the most accurate measure of history available: there does not appear to have been at the time any frame of reference in which both the Somme and Ulster unionism could be treated imaginatively in a way which would enable them both to receive their due. (From this point of view, it is not so much that Ulster's Great War soldiers have been forgotten; rather they have suffered from an overdose of ceremonial remembrance.)

The problem is compounded by that fact that Ulster loyalism is not, as has been pointed out, a tradition generally associated with imagination and poetry.[90] Miller suggests that the 'honest Ulsterman' motif emerged in 1885 partly because honesty was the virtue associated with the keeping of bargains. The Irish nationalist hero's 'prime virtue' on the other hand, is 'his willingness to die for his country'.[91] It is these 'honest Ulsterman' qualities which were praised during the war, and which did not allow for the imaginatively powerful image of the sacrificial victim that permeates much Easter Rising literature. Edward Carson defined the true quality of the Ulsterman in terms of manly inflexibility: 'if I know anything about Ulster I know this, that men like you, who have once made up your minds, will never be diverted from what you believe to be the right course until you have successfully reached the goal for which you set out.'[92] The poetry that appeared in Ulster newspapers following the Somme tried to pull together the ideals of Protestantism and the virtues of sacrifice. But the qualified success of the Ulster Division's exploits did not lend themselves to imaginative expression with the same ease as Easter 1916's 'failure'. Most of the popular poetry in Ulster avoided the reality of death, and if it followed the nationalist tradition of citing one's dead in order to validate one's political claims, it

[90] See Joe McMinn, 'Language, Literature and Cultural Identity', in Jean Lundy and Aodán MacPóilin (eds.), *Styles of Belonging: The Cultural Identities of Ulster* (Belfast: Lagan Press, 1992), 48.

[91] *Queen's Rebels*, 116.

[92] Sir Edward Carson speaking to men of the Antrim Regiment of the Ulster Volunteers, quoted in the *Belfast Newsletter*, 2 Oct. 1914, 7.

did so not with the rhetoric of martyrdom, but with a consciously optimistic, sometimes insensitive, and generally triumphant note:

> 'Dead,' do you call these heroes?
> Dead? who have given birth
> To all that makes life living—
> To all that is of worth;
> No, never, never write it—
> This 'death' is Freedom's girth!
>
> This wounding is for homeland—
> For Britain's winsome weal—
> Through all the years advancing,
> A theme for song, a peal
> That swings in jubilation—
> How Ulster met the steel![93]

F. S. Boas makes a similar case in 'Ulster on the Somme', a poem which attempts consolation, but with a rhetoric which is, unlike that of the earlier 'Men of Ulster', painfully inadequate, and which cannot do anything other than subscribe to the version of events laid down in 1914:

> Life?—'twas a little thing to give:
> Death?—'twas a toy to try.
> They knew that Ulster dared not live,
> Did they not dare to die.[94]

The Somme was, for the Ulster Division, a military success that turned to failure in the context of the whole battle; the Rising worked the other way around, as a military failure which, in the political situation pertaining in wartime, was turned to the insurgents' advantage. The irony is that the reversal of events—the gradual 'success' of Easter 1916 and the erosion of Ulster Protestant illusions regarding the Somme— did not bring about a corresponding reversal of the apparently inspirational or uninspirational nature of the subject matter. The question hovering behind both events is that of how far violence can be validated: in other words, are there forms which are 'right' (the Rising) and forms which are 'wrong' (the Great War, the Irish Civil War)? Certain forms of bloodshed in Ireland have attained, through the idea of sacrifice for a good cause, a tragic status in the imagination, and others have not.

[93] William J. Gallagher, 'The Red Hand of Ulster: Somme—July 1st, 1916', *Belfast Evening Telegraph*, 12 July 1916, 2.
[94] *Songs of Ulster and Balliol*, 15.

Since the same event is open to different interpretations in this way—the Great War in England has a tragic status and imaginative impact it has never attained in Ireland—the tragic quality of any response to history must be informed by the socio-political reality of the time. If violence in Ulster loyalism is perceived as legitimate on contractual and rational terms, and in Irish nationalism on sacrificial and irrational terms (terms which deny that it has to be 'legitimate' at all), the method of reading Irish history that leaves the republican in 1916 with everything to gain, if it is applied to the Somme, leaves the Ulster Protestant with everything to lose. In addition, Ulster Protestantism inevitably avoids the rhetoric associated with Irish republicanism. But the rhetoric which character-ized, and still characterizes, Ulster Protestantism was not adequate in the war and immediate post-war years to the task of presenting the Great War experience in terms other than those which were restrictive and, ultimately, damaging. The Somme in loyalist history might be the culmination of a process of self-defence that stretches back through history to the Battle of the Boyne, but the fundamental problem with the Somme is its innate irrationality as an event. As McIlwaine puts it in Frank McGuinness's *Observe the Sons of Ulster Marching Towards the Somme*, 'The whole of Ulster will be lost. We're not making a sacrifice ... you've seen this war. We are the sacrifice.'[95] The sheer scale and stupidity of the battle make it lie uneasily in the Ulster Protestant mythology designed to accommodate it. That unease is an indictment not only of the Great War, but also of an inadequate rhetoric and mythology which cannot tolerate what it cannot control.

IV

The Battle of the Somme and the Easter Rising functioned, in their different ways, as part of the origin myths of Northern Ireland and the Irish Free State respectively. They became events which were held to encapsulate the inherent qualities of the true Ulster Protestant (proud, reticent, unimaginative) or true Irish Catholic (spiritual, voluble, imagin-ative), oppositional stereotypes used and abused on both sides. But they have this in common: they simplify interpretations of history, and in doing so leave completely out of the equation those Irish soldiers who

[95] *Observe the Sons of Ulster Marching Towards the Somme* (London: Faber, 1986), 51. McIlwaine quotes here Kipling's 'Ulster 1912', the rhetoric of the Home Rule Crisis recontextualized on the Western Front.

fought in the Great War and yet were committed to an independent Ireland, or indeed those who fought for no complex political reason at all—those, in other words, whose actions cannot be easily explained in one or other version of events. One reason for the past neglect of Ireland's Great War literature by combatants, which, though not extensive, does exist, is perhaps that most of its writers fall into these categories: they speak from and for a history repressed both north and south of the border. 'The origin of states', said Marx, 'gets lost in a myth in which one may believe but one may not discuss'; to do so, in Ireland, is to uncover an infinitely more varied experience of, and response to, the Great War than has generally been acknowledged. (Terence Brown's exploration of Irish culture in the Great War simultaneously recognizes and breaks this prohibition in its title: 'Who Dares to Speak?'.)[96] In recent years, interest in the Irish experience of the Great War has been reawakened, in part through the pioneering work of Philip Orr, Terence Denman, Keith Jeffery, George Boyce, David Fitzpatrick, Thomas Dooley, and others.[97] The historical revisionism of the last fifteen years in relation to the domestic politics of this period—notably Paul Bew's work on Redmondism—coincides with, and has helped to inspire, the resurgence of interest in Ireland's role in the Great War. If historians earlier in the century neglected or oversimplified the Great War, that process has recently undergone a dramatic reversal.

One effect of this reversal has been the growing interest in, and search for, Ireland's Great War literature. The first studies of Irish culture and the Great War have, variously, brooded on both the absence of an Irish literary response to the war, and on the critical neglect of that re-

---

[96] 'Who Dares to Speak? Ireland and the Great War', in Robert Clark and Piero Boitani (eds.), *English Studies in Transition: Papers from the ESSE Inaugural Conference* (London: Routledge, 1993), 226–37.

[97] See Orr, *The Road to the Somme*; Denman, *Ireland's Unknown Soldiers*; Thomas P. Dooley, *Irishmen or English Soldiers?: The Times and World of a Southern Catholic Irish Man (1876–1916) Enlisting in the British Army during the First World War* (Liverpool: Liverpool UP, 1995); Fitzpatrick (ed.), *Ireland and the First World War*; D. George Boyce, *The Sure Confusing Drum: Ireland and the First World War* (Swansea: University College of Swansea, 1993); Myles Dungan, *Irish Voices from the Great War* (Dublin: Irish Academic Press, 1995); Jeffery, 'The Great War in Modern Irish Memory'; Thomas Dooley, 'Southern Ireland, Historians and the First World War', *Irish Studies Review*, 4 (Autumn 1993), 5–9; Timothy Bowman, 'The Irish at the Somme', *History Ireland*, 4/4 (Winter 1996), 48–52. Jane Leonard's work on First World War Remembrance in Ireland has exploded many of the myths surrounding the war—see Ch. 5 below—as has Gillian McIntosh's research into unionist interpretations of history in the 20th cent. See *The Force of Culture*.

sponse.[98] The First World War 'revival' in England pre-dates the Irish one by over thirty years: the lead up to the fiftieth anniversary of the Armistice helped to trigger new research and publication (as did the eightieth anniversary). A. J. P. Taylor's accessible *The First World War: An Illustrated History* appeared in 1966; interest in the war's literature was also reawakened by the publication of new and influential critical studies— Bergonzi's 1965 *Heroes' Twilight: A Study of the Literature of the Great War*, John H. Johnstone's 1964 *English Poetry of the First World War*. These consolidated the idea that Great War poetry was, on the whole, poetry by combatants. Brian Gardner's 1964 anthology, *Up the Line to Death*, implicitly endorsed that view. The book was designed to counterbalance previous (now little-known) war anthologies which had not devoted a great deal of space to soldier poets, and to thereby rescue some of those soldier poets from obscurity. The success of the endeavour may be measured by the fact that the anthology's original purpose exists now itself in the realm of obscurity. 'War poetry' has come to mean, specifically, the 'trench lyric' in popular perception, to the extent that it has recently become necessary to challenge the conjunction. War memoirs—including those by Sassoon, Blunden, Brittain, Campion Vaughan—have been reprinted as a consequence of the revival in interest. Anthologizing Great War poetry is still a thriving industry in England, more so than in relation to any other single event in English history.

In contrast to the over-anthologized English canon of Great War poetry, Ireland's Great War literature, if this is defined as work by those who participated in the war, is a diffuse set of writings. The origins of some works of art in the Great War have, as Jeffery notes, been forgotten;[99] Terence Brown, on the other hand, suggests that 'the silence of the country's writers speaks volumes', that it was 'as if the Irish had agreed collectively, if for widely differing reasons, to dismiss from consciousness their own involvement in the greatest cataclysm ever to have befallen European civilization'. He finds it 'extraordinary that there are no Irish war poets', with the exception of Francis Ledwidge.[100] Both arguments are valid. Ledwidge, perhaps because of the absence of any

[98] See Brown, 'Who Dares to Speak? Ireland and the Great War'; Keith Jeffery, 'Irish Culture and the Great War', *Bullán*, 1/2 (Autumn 1994), and 'Irish Prose Writers of the First World War'; Edna Longley, 'The Rising, the Somme and Irish Memory', *The Living Stream: Literature and Revisionism in Ireland* (Newcastle, Bloodaxe, 1994).

[99] 'Irish Culture and the Great War', 87–8.

[100] 'Who Dares to Speak? Ireland and the Great War', 229–30.

other obvious context in which to read him, is probably the only Irish writer whose work is considered primarily in relation to the Great War, however little he engaged with it. On the whole, the reputations of Ireland's 'soldier poets' are established in other areas. Tom Kettle is viewed primarily as essayist and politician. C. S. Lewis, in spite of the fact that his first collection of poems, *Spirits in Bondage*, consists mainly of poems about the war and about Ireland, is seen predominantly as an English academic and religious writer. Since his Great War service hardly helps the Ulster Unionist version of history, he has, until recently, been forgotten.[101] Monk Gibbon is a minor figure in the Irish canon in spite of, not because of, his war experience. Thomas MacGreevy fits into the 1930s Modernist tradition. Patrick MacGill is 'The Navvy Poet', not the war poet (the popularity of his war memoirs, notably amongst soldiers, during the war itself is now sometimes forgotten). As will be seen, notably in the case of W. B. Yeats, the principle also extends to those non-combatants writing in Ireland during the war.

The search for Ireland's war literature has begun to lead, in some cases, to a reconsideration of the Great War as a productive context in which to read work by those who served in the army. Poems by Kettle and Ledwidge were included in Anne Powell's 1993 *A Deep Cry*, along with introductory biographical essays. The publication of Ledwidge's *Selected Poems*, with the Heaney seal of approval in the form of an introduction and postscript, has raised his profile in Ireland, and also that of the work of his biographer, Alice Curtayne. Susan Schriebman's 1991 edition of Thomas MacGreevy's *Collected Poems* prioritizes MacGreevy's war experiences (unlike the earlier Redshaw edition introduced by Samuel Beckett). MacGreevy's poetry, she writes, 'stands as a testament' to 'two events which were to change the course of his life: the Great War and the Irish Civil War', and in the annotations she illuminates the texts with this principle in mind.[102]

Nevertheless, to attribute too much importance to these writers, as poets at any rate, by virtue of their combatant status, may be to offer

---

[101] *Spirits in Bondage* was first published in 1919, and has been out of print for several decades. It was reprinted in C. S. Lewis, *The Collected Poems*, ed. Walter Hooper (London: Fount Paperbacks, 1994), but the reprinting has not redressed the total neglect of these poems, none of which has been anthologized in connection with the Great War. Lewis gives a brief account of his wartime service, and reasons for enlistment in *Surprised by Joy* (1955; London: Fount, 1977).

[102] *Collected Poems of Thomas MacGreevy: An Annotated Edition*, ed. Susan Schriebman (Dublin: Anna Livia Press, 1991), p. xix.

a misleading, or at least a very limited, picture. As Keith Jeffery notes, 'The Irish cultural response to the Great War has not by any means been confined to the wartime period or the years immediately following. Indeed, over the years there has been a simmering of interest on the part of Irish writers with the First World War.'[103] The Great War is a productive context in which to read the work of those serving in the army, but this is not where Ireland's best war poetry is written. The example of England, with its powerful tradition of soldier poetry, has not always been helpful. The tendency to associate war poetry with soldier poetry in England is reductive, but that has not prevented its working prescriptively, to the detriment of understanding in relation to different cultural traditions. George Orwell's view of the Great War, that it 'was only a heightened moment in an almost continuous crisis',[104] reverberates in Irish history possibly to a greater degree than in England. The Great War in Ireland cannot be separated in memory from the violence that preceded and followed it, or from the sense, which in some ways persisted through the century, of what Ernest Gellner calls 'the condition of pervasive, latent war'.[105] Hugh Middleton writes that

Even without active war-fighting, the presence of an armed force ... uniforms, flags and other symbols, and an administrative and managerial structure that encourages the style of leadership most likely to succeed under conditions of intense intergroup conflict, all serve as a continuing reminder of the potential threat from outside, and function, therefore, as important psychological bastions of internal cohesion.[106]

The argument reverberates culturally as well as politically, and it does so in England and Ireland. But its applicability to the Irish case is more obvious. After the post-war partition of Ireland, the Irish Free State and the 'statelet' of Northern Ireland both worked, with differing degrees of success, towards internal cohesion under conditions, particularly in the North, similar to those Middleton describes. Both Paul Fussell and Jon Silkin quote, in their closing chapters, Francis Hope's judgement that 'In a not altogether rhetorical sense, all poetry written since 1918 is war

---

[103] 'Irish Culture and the Great War', 93.

[104] 'Inside the Whale', in *The Collected Essays, Journalism and Letters of George Orwell*, ed. Sonia Orwell and Ian Angus, i (London: Penguin, 1970), 575.

[105] 'An Anthropological View of War and Violence', in Robert A. Hinde (ed.), *The Institution of War* (New York: St Martin's Press, 1992), 78.

[106] 'Some Psychological Bases of the Institution of War', in Hinde (ed.), *The Institution of War*, 42.

poetry'.[107] Although memory of the Great War may have been officially repressed, or misrepresented, Irish poetry in the twentieth century presents a more complex picture, both during the war and, more usually, after it. It has done so notably in the last thirty years. '[W]ar', Orwell argued, 'is only "peace intensified"'.[108] The comment is in some ways peculiarly pertinent to the Irish experience of the Great War: it partially explains the absence of a cohesive, prominent response to the European conflict in Ireland between 1914–18 comparable to that which exists in England; it simultaneously accounts for the fact that war pervades and informs much of Ireland's twentieth-century literature, a literature that responds to (and reacts against) the reductive histories of internal 'intergroup conflict' consolidated in the First World War.

[107] Jon Silkin, *Out of Battle: The Poetry of the Great War* (1972; London: Ark, 1987), 347–8; Fussell, *The Great War and Modern Memory*, 325. Fussell quotes the comment with more approval than Silkin, who reads in it an attempt to sideline the achievement of the soldier poets themselves.

[108] 'Inside the Whale', 576.

CHAPTER TWO

W. B. Yeats: Creation from Conflict

...he seemed too odd a fish to adorn
A twentieth-century war.

Louis MacNeice[1]

I

'I find I can keep the thought of the war away from me and go on with my work', Yeats announced in September 1915.[2] Some weeks earlier, he outlined a more notorious plan for the war years: 'I shall keep the neighbourhood of the seven sleepers of Ephesus, hoping to catch their comfortable snores till bloody frivolity is over'.[3] It is not an ambition which has endeared him to many of his critics, and it seems to establish terms for understanding Yeats in the Great War. He has not been, and is still not, without his believers in relation to these comments. Arthur Lane, celebrating the responsible poetics of the English soldier poets, complains that Yeats issues a 'professional-poet disclaimer of responsibility'.[4] Jon Stallworthy, Owen's biographer, finds Yeats 'undistracted by compassion, unmoved by the prospect of suffering' in relation to the violence and bloodshed of Europe.[5] Declan Kiberd's only comment in relation to Yeats and the Great War is that Yeats 'denied a high degree of reality to the Great War, and...refused to write a poem about it on request'.[6] T. R. Henn expounds a view which has now become

---

[1] 'Autumn Sequel: Canto IV', in MacNeice *CP*, 347.

[2] Quoted in James Longenbach, *Stone Cottage: Pound, Yeats and Modernism* (New York & Oxford: OUP, 1988), 184.

[3] 'To Henry James', 20 Aug. [1915], *The Letters of W. B. Yeats*, ed. Allan Wade (London: Rupert Hart-Davis, 1954), 600.

[4] *An Adequate Response: The War Poetry of Wilfred Owen and Siegfried Sassoon* (Detroit: Wayne State UP, 1972), 51.

[5] 'W. B. Yeats and Wilfred Owen', *Critical Quarterly*, 11/3 (Autumn 1969), 214. Stallworthy makes these comments in relation to 'The Second Coming', written three months after Owen was killed.

[6] *Inventing Ireland: The Literature of the Modern Nation* (London: Jonathan Cape, 1995) 246.

something of a commonplace: that the Easter Rising and the Civil War were the crucial events in the formation of Yeats's aesthetic, and that 'the larger war in Europe had passed him by'.[7] His study of 'Yeats and the Poetry of War' concentrates exclusively on war in Ireland—the Easter Rising and the Troubles that followed it.[8]

To take Yeats at face value as one of the seven sleepers is to misrepresent the level of his engagement with the Great War. That misrepresentation stems from two related perspectives: the first is one of Anglocentricity, the assumption that the English literary response to the war is the correct response; the second has more to do with the reluctance, for whatever reason, to acknowledge the true extent of Irish involvement in the Great War, and its impact on Irish culture. Arthur Lane implies that Yeats fudges the issue, that he is in some way guilty for not facing the subject matter of the war with the sense of moral urgency that characterized Owen's or Sassoon's poetry: the only 'adequate response' here is, unquestionably, the English soldier-poet response. Denis Donoghue, on the other hand, sees Yeats's response, or rather non-response, to the war in political terms: 'Yeats', he writes, 'did not feel inclined to put his genius to work in England's cause', though he was ready enough to speak when the Easter Rising 'set his verses astir'.[9] In this formulation, the Great War has little, if anything, to do with Ireland and Irish causes. Kiberd's 'The Great War in Irish Memory' in *Inventing Ireland* throws English Great War myths in with Easter 1916 myths, and mixes them together in order to produce Irish Memory. Yeats is not in the final formula.

Yeats *is* culpable, not for ignoring the war, since he did not do so, but for helping, in his prose criticism, to consolidate the view that the tragedy of the Great War was primarily an English not an Irish tragedy, and, as such, that it was remote from Irish cultural life. As Peter McDonald points out, unlikely as it may seem, 'the most catastrophic

[7]   *The Lonely Tower* (2nd edn., London: Methuen, 1965), 20.
[8]   See *Last Essays* (Gerrards Cross: Colin Smythe, 1976), 81–97. More recently, Jacqueline Genet, in an essay on 'Yeats and War', also mentions the Great War only briefly on the grounds that 'Ireland was only marginally involved' in the conflict, and that 'There is not much commentary on the First World War in Yeats's works'. Her discussion, like Henn's, focuses on the Easter Rising, the War of Independence, the Civil War, and the rise of fascism up to the Second World War. See Genet, 'Yeats and War', in Kathleen Devine (ed). *Modern Irish Writers and the Wars* (Gerrards Cross: Colin Smythe, 1999), 36–7.
[9]   Donoghue, *We Irish: Essays on Irish Literature and Society* (Berkeley and Los Angeles: University of California Press, 1986), 185.

event in Irish history in the year 1916 [is] ignored by Yeats ... [T]he dead from the Irish and Ulster divisions at the Somme are silent in [his] writing'.[10] Yeats's self-presentation is in many respects deceptive; the war influences his thinking, and it is a presence, if a shadowy one, in the poetry. But Yeats himself denies its impact on Irish culture, and as part of a long-standing Irish nationalist agenda, he places the Great War on the English side of an English–Irish opposition.

That opposition works in terms of culture, politics, and literary traditions. Yeats, throughout his life, perceived the struggle between Ireland and England as a struggle between a spiritual nation on the one hand, and a materialist, capitalist, industrialized society with a tendency to admire what Yeats hated above all—'the literature of the point of view'[11]—on the other. Imperialism was the worst manifestation of such a society, and the Great War was undoubtedly the worst manifestation of imperialism. The Great War was the industrialists' war, a war fought by a people remote from Yeats's ideal society of artists, aristocrats, and peasants. J. B. Priestley describes the outbreak of war in 1914 as 'a challenge that was almost like a conscription of the spirit'.[12] For Yeats, that spiritual challenge is located elsewhere, in the attempt to restore to literature and society 'the ancient religion of the world'.[13] Patriotism may be an admirable quality, but as early as the Boer War, Yeats differentiates between 'patriotism of the fine sort—patriotism that lays burdens upon a man' and the 'patriotism that takes burdens off', and complains that the British Press in particular seemed only to understand 'the sort that makes a man say "I need not trouble to get wisdom for I am English, & my vices have made me great"'.[14] To accept, uncritically, the burden of Empire is to travel light; the burden of responsibility towards a country is a challenge of the 'fine sort'. 'Contemporary English literature', Yeats writes, 'takes delight in praising England and her Empire, the master-work and dream of the middle class'.[15] His own spiritual challenge is

---

[10] 'Yeats and Remorse', Chatterton Lecture on Poetry 1996, *Proceedings of the British Academy*, 94: 184.

[11] *E & I*, 511.

[12] Quoted in Peter Vansittart, *Voices from the Great War* (1981; London: Pimlico, 1998), 262.

[13] *E & I*, 176.

[14] 'To Henry Newbolt', *c.*25 Apr. 1901, in *The Collected Letters of W. B. Yeats 1901–1904*, ed. John Kelly and Ronald Schuchard, iii (Oxford: Clarendon, 1994) 63.

[15] 'The Literary Movement in Ireland', in Lady Augusta Gregory (ed.), *Ideals in Ireland* (1901; New York: Lemma, 1973), 90.

thus, almost as if by default, fundamentally nationalist, antagonistic both to the fruits and demands of imperialism.

Politically, the Great War places Yeats, shuttling back and forth between Dublin and London, in a complex position. When the Great War began, as Elizabeth Cullingford explains, 'The protector of "little Belgium" was oppressor of little Ireland, and Home Rule still hung in the balance'.[16] The idealism that sent men to the recruiting offices in 1914, the faith in England and English virtues, would hardly find sympathy with any Irishman who resisted English imperialism in Ireland. Yeats, in addition, was habitually patronized by English critics: 'he is . . . so Irish', an article in *Poetry Review* claimed in 1914, 'that it requires an Englishman to criticise him'.[17] While he is not unsympathetic to the huge losses of the war, he is inevitably less sympathetic to the cause, describing it in 1915 as an 'inexplicable war . . . a sacrifice of the best for the worst'.[18] At no time does Yeats advocate a pro-German stance—to do so may well have been personally catastrophic: 'I have friends fighting in Flanders. . . . How can I help but feeling [*sic*] as they feel and desiring a German defeat'.[19] But he does not suggest at any point that it is Ireland's moral duty to assist England in securing that defeat. In other words, he treads carefully, never committing himself in public either to wholehearted support or condemnation. That ambiguity finds perfect expression in the debate over Joyce's Civil List pension, secured partly through Yeats's endeavours in 1917. Yeats writes to Gosse: 'it never occurred to me that it was necessary to express sympathy "frank" or otherwise with the "cause of the Allies". . . . I certainly wish them victory, and as I have never known Joyce to agree with his neighbours I [*a line missing where the paper has been torn and mended*] in Austria has probably made his sympathy as frank as you could wish'.[20] The Allies, noticeably, are 'them' not us; 'Frank' sympathies, openly acknowledged, might have secured something more ominous than a pension.

While Yeats might be prepared to split hairs on a personal level, in broader terms, he tends to view the Great War as the inevitable result of a system and culture from which he consistently tried to protect the Irish people. In 1902 he argues passionately that the Irish must not let 'the

---

[16] *Yeats, Ireland and Fascism* (London: Macmillan, 1981), 87.
[17] Eric Chilman, 'W. B. Yeats', *Poetry Review* (Jan.–June 1914), 70.
[18] Letter to Lady Gregory, 18 Feb. 1915, quoted in Longenbach, *Stone Cottage*, 117.
[19] Quoted in Cullingford, *Yeats, Ireland and Fascism*, 87.
[20] 'To Edmund Gosse', 28 Aug. [1915], *The Letters of W. B. Yeats*, ed. Wade, 600–1.

enemy root up our rose-garden and plant a cabbage garden instead'.[21] The enemy is the utilitarian, Empire-building middle class. And the Irish people need to be protected from the Great War since it was, from the outset, a middle-class war. Eksteins describes it as

the first middle class war in history. If previous wars were wars of dynasticism, of feudal and aristocratic interests, of princely rivalries, then the First World War was the first great war of the bourgeoisie. It is therefore hardly surprising that the values of this middle class should have become the dominant values of the war, determining not only the behavior of individual soldiers but the whole organization and even strategy and tactics of the war.[22]

That it is a middle-class war is, for Yeats, both its failing and, paradoxically, its virtue, since this is the very quality which enables him to simultaneously dissociate the war from an ideal Ireland, and utilize it as a form of opposition to the values he propounds. The opposition between two different ways—English and Irish—of responding to the subject of the Great War, is one which in its essentials is not new in his thinking, but its terms are reinforced by the events of 1914–18. Brooding in 1928 on the ways in which the Great War can be incorporated into literature, he writes that

The English critics feel differently. To them a theme that 'bulks largely in the news' gives dignity to human nature, even raises it to international importance. We on the other hand are certain that nothing can give dignity to human nature but the character and energy of its expression.[23]

This is the Boer War stance revisited, combined with Yeatsian resistance to the notion that history makes the poet. By the time he compiles the 1936 *Oxford Book of Modern Verse*, and delivers, in the same year, the radio broadcast on 'Modern Poetry', the distinctions he draws between English and Irish literary traditions seem to be set in concrete, at least in terms of his critical prose. The 'Modern Poetry' broadcast is an implicit defence of Yeats's Great War stance; a recycling of English Great War myths; an assertion of the heroic in Irish poetry; and a denial of modernism in Ireland.

The negation by the Great War of heroic ideals is now itself almost legendary. The myth of 1914, with its cloudless sky and idealism—

---

[21] *E & I*, 174.
[22] *Rites of Spring: The Great War and the Birth of the Modern Age* (1989; New York: Anchor-Doubleday, 1990), 177.
[23] Quoted in Joseph Hone, *W. B. Yeats 1865–1939* (London: Macmillan, 1942), 389.

'Never such innocence again', as Philip Larkin phrased it—gives way to what Louis Mairet describes as 'the spectacle of a civilization turning against itself to destroy itself' in the face of which 'reason', or the social and cultural myths underwriting pre-war experience, 'cannot cope'.[24] Bergonzi suggests that in Shakespeare's *Henry IV Part 1*, Hotspur 'exemplifies the moral virtues of heroism' but Falstaff 'evacuates the word "honour" of all the densities of meaning that it held for Hotspur', and that 'one or other of these attitudes…will certainly be present when war is talked about'. Characteristic of those who fought in the Great War is the fact that 'the Hotspurian mode in time gave place to the Falstaffian'.[25] The change, broadly speaking, is from the sentiment of Rupert Brooke's 'Honour has come back, as a king, to earth', to that of Wilfred Owen's 'old Lie: Dulce et decorum est | Pro patria mori'. Even the war's own title of 'Great' has a suitably anachronistic ring to it, which perhaps accounted for an increasing desire to change it after the event.

Yeats, attuned to the myth of 1914, suggests that until the war, poets 'wrote as men had always written', but that

established things were shaken by the Great War. All civilised men had believed in progress, in a warless future, in always-increasing wealth, but now influential young men began to wonder if anything could last or if anything were worth fighting for.[26]

He recognizes the loss of established tradition in England, but he also implies that such a loss can be dissociated from the Irish tradition since it was preoccupied with increasing wealth (cabbage gardens). 'Irish poetry', he claims, 'moves in a different direction and belongs to a different story'. He notes that the war engenders the 'new poetry' of T. S. Eliot, with its 'satiric intensity', but while the English movement was 'checked by the realism of Eliot' and 'gave way to an impersonal philosophical poetry', he claims exemption for Ireland on the grounds that it 'still has a living folk tradition'. Irish poets have 'restored the emotion of heroism to lyric poetry'.[27]

Where English poets sense disruption, Yeats affirms tradition and continuity, and in doing so appears to write the war out of Irish literary

[24] Quoted in Eksteins, *Rites of Spring*, 215–16.

[25] *Heroes' Twilight: A Study of the Literature of the Great War* (London: Constable, 1965), 11–12, 17.

[26] *E & I*, 499.

[27] *E & I*, 506–7.

history. But his own work tells a different story again, a rather more complex story about the accommodation of the Great War within the Irish tradition, and within the continuities of Yeats's aesthetic. Yeats's response to the war is, at first sight, very different from that of the English soldier poets, but the level of his poetic engagement with the war can hardly be determined by questionable expectations about poetic content. Irish memory of the Great War is not the same as English memory, and to assume that eradication of any war repression in Irish memory will reveal something rather similar to English memory is hardly reasonable. Thus far Yeats's distinction between the two traditions holds good. Nevertheless, and almost in spite of those issues, even if the war appears to be on the margins of Irish history, something which its casualty rate belies, it is the catalyst or framework for other events— the Easter Rising, the Civil War—that, continuing as they do a line of violence originating before 1914, radically alter both Ireland and Yeats. The events of the Great War might be remote from his society of artists, aristocrats, and peasants, but they are not remote from contemporary Ireland. The way in which Yeats negotiates with the Great War provides a context for and a contrast to his approach to the Rising and the Civil War: the responses to all three events in his poetry may be seen as inextricably linked. The complexity and often the elusiveness characterizing his treatment of the Great War indicate not that it 'passed him by', but that the war's place in Irish memory, and in Yeats's aesthetic, is considerably more ambiguous than is generally acknowledged.

In claiming to close his eyes to 'bloody frivolity', Yeats is publicly disingenuous in a manner belied by his work. He is disingenuous, not because he is disinterested, but because the Great War triggers a disruption in his thinking which takes some years to resolve. He is clear before the war on what he sees as the results of conflict:

I think that all noble things are the result of warfare; great nations and classes, of warfare in the visible world, great poetry and philosophy, of invisible warfare, the division of a mind within itself, a victory, the sacrifice of a man to himself.[28]

By 1915 he is less clear, or at least less explicit, about ways in which modern warfare can be accommodated in this theory. '[G]reat... classes' suggests the aristocratic, chivalrous warfare of a bygone age that bears no resemblance to the carnage of the Western Front. Yeats's

[28] *E & I*, 321.

warfare in the invisible world becomes problematical not simply because it has to internalize a warfare in the visible world, but because that 'visible warfare' consists of unprecedented, impersonal, mechanized slaughter. Judged according to the standards of pre-1914 battle, the conduct of the Great War can only be seen as ignoble. Nor does it result in any 'noble things'; on the contrary, it became, for many, 'absurd...because of the failure of the postwar experience to justify the war'.[29] As Edmund Blunden put it, 'Neither race had won, nor could win, the War. The War had won, and would go on winning.'[30] As with Wilfred Owen and the other Great War soldier poets, if war is to be the subject matter of poetry, it is also, in the Great War, the enemy of poetry.

II

Yeats is neither immune to nor indifferent to this Great War dilemma, although it is certainly the case that the wars in Ireland intensified (and helped to resolve) the issues raised in 1914–15. In his reactions to other contemporary responses to the war, notably Sean O'Casey's *The Silver Tassie* and Wilfred Owen's poetry, Yeats can be seen as testing the capabilities of his own aesthetic in relation to that subject matter, divining the possibilities for poetry in a process of elimination. Throughout the war, he consistently confronted the question of his responsibility as a poet in wartime, even if his answers were not always to everyone's taste. As James Longenbach has shown, Yeats, wintering at Stone Cottage in the war years, was repelled by the war-poetry fever that gripped the British newspapers, and sought to distance himself from it as far as possible.[31] His opinion of Wilfred Owen, expressed forcefully almost twenty years after the war, is the most extreme manifestation of his 'distaste for certain poems written in the midst of the great war'.[32] Famously, he excluded Owen's work from *The Oxford Book of Modern Verse* in 1936, complaining that Owen 'is all blood, dirt and sucked sugar-stick.... There is every excuse for him, but none for those

[29] Eksteins, *Rites of Spring*, 297.
[30] Quoted in Paul Fussell (ed.), *The Bloody Game: An Anthology of Modern War* (London: Scribners, 1991), 34.
[31] See Longenbach, *Stone Cottage*, 112.
[32] W. B. Yeats (ed.), *The Oxford Book of Modern Verse* (Oxford: Clarendon, 1936), p. xxxiv.

who like him.'[33] Bernard Bergonzi attributes the tone of the remarks partly to 'senile rancour' and 'jealousy',[34] and the anthology is, unquestionably, idiosyncratic. But once again, Yeats may be misrepresented in the controversy. His very famous letter about Owen was written in the midst of what was, for Yeats, an unexpected furore about *The Oxford Book of Modern Verse*, and the note of impatience possibly has more to do with the critics' reaction to the anthology than with any particularly vindictive feeling towards Owen. It is also worth emphasizing the extent to which Yeats, in his correspondence, appears to have been, initially, bewildered by that reaction, though he rapidly joins battle once he has grasped how the lines are drawn. The initial bewilderment may serve to illustrate the different place the Great War holds in English and Irish cultural memories, exemplified by the extraordinarily privileged place combatant poetry holds in the former. Yeats writes: 'When I excluded Wilfred Owen, whom I consider unworthy of the poets' corner of a country newspaper, I did not know I was excluding a revered sandwich-board Man of the revolution, and that somebody has put his worst and most famous poem in a glass-case in the British Museum— however, if I had known it, I would have excluded him just the same.'[35] With such remarks, Yeats challenges both the thirties generation's socialist affiliations, and, connected to this, its celebration of Great War poetry. More broadly, his refusal to privilege such poetry strikes at the heart of English cultural memory of the 'literary' Great War. Whether Yeats's judgements of the poetry are right or wrong, the terms of his argument still prove unacceptable in a culture that faithfully collects and anthologizes every scrap of Great War soldier poetry it can find, that still commemorates the Great War through its verse.[36]

The complaint against blood and dirt is simply another way of saying that Owen was 'too near [his] subject matter to do ... work of permanent importance'.[37] But in Yeats's terms, Owen is not necessarily disadvantaged by the actual experience of fighting in the war; rather, he disadvantages himself by deliberately narrowing his range in order to communicate his point of view. The soldier poets, he writes, 'felt bound,

[33] 'To Dorothy Wellesley', 21 Dec. [1936], *The Letters of W. B. Yeats*, ed. Wade, 874.
[34] *Heroes' Twilight*, 125.
[35] 'To Dorothy Wellesley', 21 Dec. [1936], *The Letters of W. B. Yeats*, ed. Wade, 874.
[36] The 80th anniversary of the Armistice was marked for example by the publication of a new anthology of *Poems of the Great War* (London: Penguin, 1998), which largely contains work by the soldier poets.
[37] *E & I*, 500.

in the words of the best known, to plead the suffering of their men';
Yeats rejects those poems on the grounds that, in Matthew Arnold's
phrase, 'passive suffering is not a theme for poetry'.[38] In other words, in
the face of extreme external pressure, they chose to work within certain
limitations. Stallworthy suggests that Owen's draft preface, which ap-
parently articulates those limitations, would have seemed to Yeats 'the
most pernicious heresy':[39]

This book is not about heroes. English poetry is not yet fit to speak of them.
    Nor is it about deeds, or lands, nor anything about glory, honour, might,
majesty, dominion, or power, except War.
    Above all I am not concerned with Poetry.
My subject is War, and the pity of War.
The Poetry is in the pity.[40]

One way of reading Owen's preface is to assume that he views poetry as
a product of history in that contemporary events dictate the poet's
themes and role: the poet cannot alter the course of history, or shape
future consciousness. The 'heresy' for Yeats, if one accepts this reading
of the preface, lies in Owen's readiness to make a moral and temporal
choice at the expense of aesthetic freedom, to allow the war as subject
matter to take precedence over the luxury of imaginative autonomy.
Such a compromise is inconceivable in Yeats: 'To speak of one's
emotions without fear or moral ambition, to come out from under the
shadow of other men's minds, to forget their needs, to be utterly
oneself' is, he claims, 'all the Muses care for'.[41] Embedded in Yeats's
criticism of Owen is the English–Irish cultural opposition that is re-
inforced by the experience of the war. His sense that the English rather
than the Irish admire 'passive suffering' in art pre-dates the well-known
introduction to the *Oxford Book of Modern Verse* by more than twenty-five
years, and the terms of the critique of Great War literature are already in
place. In 1910, Yeats writes:

I liked *The Shadow of the Glen* better than *Riders to the Sea*, that seemed for all the
nobility of its end, its mood of Greek tragedy, too passive in suffering... Synge
answered: 'It is a curious thing that *Riders to the Sea* succeeds with an English but

---

[38]   *Oxford Book of Modern Verse*, p. xxxiv.
[39]   'W. B. Yeats and Wilfred Owen', 214.
[40]   *The Poems of Wilfred Owen*, ed. Jon Stallworthy (London: Chatto & Windus, 1990),
192.
[41]   *E & I*, 339.

not an Irish audience, and *The Shadow of the Glen*, which is not liked by an English audience, always succeeds in Ireland...'.[42]

He reiterates this view, and the English–Irish opposition within it, in the polemical *On the Boiler*: 'The English are an objective people; they have no longer a sense of tragedy in their theatre; pity... has taken its place.'[43]

Nevertheless, the non-combatant Irish playwright Sean O'Casey, praised by Yeats for his Civil War plays, fares little better in relation to the Great War. He, like Owen, is castigated for a betrayal of the imagination. Yeats rejects his First World War play, *The Silver Tassie* (a play which draws its theme from Owen's 'The Disabled'), for the Abbey Theatre. O'Casey's recognition that the Great War is a subject which needs to be addressed does not itself solve the problem of how to address the subject. Yeats writes to O'Casey: 'you are not interested in the great war; you never stood on its battlefields or walked its hospitals, and so write out of your opinions' (a reference back to 'literature of the point of view'). He describes O'Casey's 'great power of the past' as being 'the creation of some unique character who dominated all about him'. This is the stage character's role, but it is also the poet's role, and in the same letter, Yeats goes on to outline what might be seen as an agenda for addressing the war in literature:

The mere greatness of the world war has thwarted you; it has refused to become mere background, and obtrudes itself upon the stage as so much dead wood that will not burn with the dramatic fire. Dramatic action is a fire that must burn up everything but itself... the whole history of the world must be reduced to wallpaper in front of which the characters must pose and speak.
Among the things that dramatic action must burn up are the author's opinions; while he is writing he has no business to know anything that is not a portion of that action.[44]

The standards here apply also to poetry since poetry is, as he perceives it, inherently dramatic: the poet is, he writes, 'more type than man, more passion than type. He is Lear, Romeo, Oedipus, Tiresias; he has stepped out of a play'.[45] To write about the war means, equally, to resist the war and all it represents by fighting and defeating the greatness of the

[42] *E & I*, 336.
[43] W. B. Yeats, *Explorations* (London: Macmillan, 1962), 428.
[44] 'To Sean O'Casey', 20 Apr. 1928, *The Letters of W. B. Yeats*, ed. Wade, 741.
[45] *E & I*, 509.

war itself. At first sight, Yeats's criticisms seem contradictory: Owen fails to write successfully about the Great War because he stood on its battlefields; O'Casey fails because he did not. But the only 'war' of note is the war between poet and history, between visible and invisible warfare. The battle to reduce momentous historical events to 'wallpaper' is the one which, in Yeats's terms, Owen and O'Casey intentionally set out to lose.

Yeats's 'On being asked for a War Poem', often quoted as his manifesto for a correct, *non serviam* response to the war, seems to suggest that the problem later identified in relation to Owen and O'Casey is insoluble. It also suggests Yeats is indifferent to that problem:

> I think it better that in times like these
> A poet's mouth be silent, for in truth
> We have no gift to set a statesman right;
> He has had enough of meddling who can please
> A young girl in the indolence of her youth,
> Or an old man upon a winter's night.[46]

'It is', he claims in 1915, 'the only thing I have written of the war or will write'.[47] The poem is disingenuous in several respects; the gloss even more so. As Cullingford points out, 'setting the statesman right had always been, and would continue to be, one of Yeats's favourite pastimes in Ireland'. He is, she argues, deliberately evading political alignment either with Pearse or with Redmond, and by doing so eliminates the possibility that his art could be perceived as journalistic or propagandist.[48] Like the later 'Politics', it apparently places the poet in the ivory tower, but in doing so serves a political purpose. The poem is also disingenuous because it implies that a level of experience exists to which poetry cannot provide an adequate response: the only way of coping with what he later describes as the 'filthy modern tide' is to ignore it. His own judgement on the poem is equally deceptive. It is not the only thing he writes of the war; rather it is very obviously a poem not about the war. Peter McDonald traces the unusual history of the poem—its various title changes, the way in which it is recycled by Yeats for different literary enterprises—suggesting that 'far from setting itself to be worthy of its occasion, the poem in question had always adapted occasions to suit

---

[46] *CP*, 175.
[47] 'To Henry James', 20 Aug. 1915, *The Letters of W. B. Yeats*, ed. Wade, 600.
[48] *Yeats, Ireland and Fascism*, 86.

itself'.[49] One of those occasions may be the need to resist the war-poetry fever sweeping through Britain during the Great War. The title is altered, in 1917, from 'A Reason for Keeping Silent' to 'On being asked for a War Poem'. This is not an attempt to cash in; the alteration indicates a desire to opt out, to distance himself from what is rapidly becoming a stereotypical sub-genre. In following the revised title with something that is so obviously not a 'war poem' in the sense in which the category is commonly understood, he dissociates himself from the popular perception of the 'true' war poets, and frees himself from the expectations that perception generates.

Yeats misjudges Owen, not only by using him as a whipping boy for the expression of ideas that pre-date the publication of Owen's work by several years, but also because 'war poetry' is a category both poets try to negotiate, if not to avoid. 'Above all I am not concerned with Poetry', proclaims Owen; but as his work and his correspondence indicate, he is concerned primarily with poetry, with seizing every experience he can that might enable his poetry. In an earlier draft of his preface, he writes that the 'true war poets must be truthful'; the definition is altered simply to 'true poets'. Owen's preface is less a statement of his (heretical) aesthetic beliefs than it is a quarrel with an imagined readership, an attempt to dictate reception. 'English poetry is not yet fit to speak of [heroes]', might be understood rather as 'English society is not yet fit to read about them': the poems themselves—notably 'Apologia Pro Poemata Meo'— support that reading. The concern dominating the preface is the possibility that he may be misunderstood—that his poems may console, that they may even, inadvertently, glorify war. Poetry may be compromised, but by its audience not its author. Yeats too can 'scorn' his audience, even more passionately, and certainly more arrogantly, than Owen. But as the mutations of 'On being asked for a War Poem' indicate, he will also elevate or adapt the society and the situation to suit the art. 'Truth' means something different for each poet. If Owen's concern is to be truthful, to present events as they are, then Yeats's is to transform events into what they should be—grist to his poetic mill.

The Great War's 'mere greatness' proves less malleable for Yeats in that respect than the Easter 1916 Rising, where the lower middle-class Catholics 'Coming...From counter or desk' can be transformed into tragic heroes partly by virtue of being written out in a verse.[50] In the

---

[49] 'Yeats and Remorse', 179.   [50] *CP*, 202.

handful of poems Yeats writes between 1914 and 1918 which are directly inspired by events in the Great War, if not necessarily war poems, he experiments with different forms and themes in an attempt to resolve the question of poetic responsibility in wartime. The fact that Robert Gregory is elegized four times in the space of a few months indicates not so much intense poetic engagement with the Great War as Yeats's profound difficulties in commemorating an Irishman who gave his life in that war. In the first three elegies—'An Irish Airman Foresees his Death', 'In Memory of Major Robert Gregory', and 'Shepherd and Goatherd'—the war is mentioned, at best, obliquely. Only in 'Reprisals' can Yeats be tied down to the Great War (although the poem's more immediate trigger is the Anglo-Irish War), and 'Reprisals' does not find a place in his *Collected Poems*.[51] In 'An Irish Airman Foresees his Death', nothing in the poem necessarily locates Gregory's death in the First World War; similarly, in 'Shepherd and Goatherd', the man who 'died in the great war beyond the sea' could be almost any man (everyman) in any age.[52] 'Shepherd and Goatherd', seldom identified as a 'war poem', has, in effect, no more or less claim to this title than 'An Irish Airman', although the artificial, timeless quality of its pastoral elegizing distances the mourning from contemporary history. The war does not impose itself on these two poems either with a greatness that thwarts the poet, or, as might be expected, as the most culturally significant war in Western Europe.

All these poems share a view of Robert Gregory as individualist artist, a 'subjective' man. Gregory is not Yeats's solution to the problem of writing about the Great War, he is a cause of the problem because the individual death demanded an instant response where mass carnage did not. In addition, commemoration of Gregory was, for Yeats, a political minefield. Robert Gregory's pro-Empire political stance was hardly in tune with an Ireland whose support for Sinn Féin was increasing in the later years of the war.[53] Phase 12 of *A Vision*, for which Nietzsche is cited as the example, is 'the phase of the hero, of the man who overcomes himself, and so no longer needs...the submission of others, or...conviction of others to prove his victory. Solitude has been born at

---

[51] 'In Memory of Major Robert Gregory' appeared in the *English Review* in Aug. 1918. All three Gregory poems appeared in *The Wild Swans at Coole* in 1919. 'Reprisals', written in 1919, was not published until 1948.

[52] *CP*, 160.

[53] See R. F. Foster, *W. B. Yeats: A Life*, i. *The Apprentice Mage* (Oxford: OUP, 1997), 363.

last'. It is also the 'phase of immense energy because the *Four Faculties* are equidistant. The *oppositions...* are balanced by the *discords*'.[54] It is in these Nietzschean terms that Gregory's sacrifice is explained in 'An Irish Airman Foresees his Death':

> Nor law, nor duty bade me fight,
> Nor public men, nor cheering crowds,
> A lonely impulse of delight
> Drove to this tumult in the clouds;
> I balanced all, brought all to mind,
> The years to come seemed waste of breath,
> A waste of breath the years behind
> In balance with this life, this death.[55]

Yeats, like others, envisaged the Great War, in its early days, as full of the potential to rejuvenate a jaded Europe: 'Nietzsche', he writes in August 1914, the day after Britain declared war on Germany, 'was fond of foretelling wars for the possession of the earth that were to restore the tragic mind, & banish the mass mind which he hated.'[56] Like others who idealized the war's potential, he was quickly disillusioned. But by 1918, in 'An Irish Airman', that disillusionment appears to have been reversed. Elegizing Gregory, he is able to recapture the Nietzschean tragic mind, in terms which cast Gregory, like Yeats's later Protestant Ascendancy, as one 'Bound neither to cause nor to state',[57] whose country is only 'Kiltartan Cross'. The poem represses any sense that Protestant patriotism towards Ireland could also be, in Gregory, patriotism towards Empire.

The war, it would seem, is not so much reduced to wallpaper as stripped off altogether. But while the motivation behind Gregory's involvement in the war might prove problematical, the manner of it is not. The Great War has an unexpectedly inspirational role to play in 'An Irish Airman', to the extent that Yeats is able to reassert qualities the war had apparently negated—individual heroism, the sense of tragedy, the prophetic capabilities of art. Individual skill, strength, and purpose were useless in the mass slaughter of a dawn 'push', and the subject Yeats does not touch upon, either in his poetry or his prose criticism, is trench warfare—'dead wood that will not burn with the dramatic fire'. But

---

[54] *AV*, 127.   [55] *CP*, 152.
[56] Yeats to Lennox Robinson, 5 Aug. 1914, quoted in Longenbach, *Stone Cottage*, 108.
[57] 'The Tower', *CP*, 223.

Robert Gregory, in serving with the Royal Flying Corps, can represent the survival of the heroic at a time when heroism was debased by mechanized slaughter. As Eksteins points out:

The air ace was the object of limitless envy among infantry, mired in mud and seeming helplessness. Soldiers looked up from their trenches and saw in the air a purity of combat that the ground war had lost. The 'knights of the sky' were engaged in a conflict in which individual heroism still counted, romantic notions of honor, glory, heroism, and chivalry were still intact. In the air, war still had meaning. Flyers were the 'aristocracy of war'—'the resurrection of our personality,' as one writer put it.[58]

'An Irish Airman' is unusual in Yeats's oeuvre, with its futuristic elements, its implicit celebration of new technology, but the new technology is the vehicle for an old theme. The war exists merely as a backdrop for heroic action, for the Irish airman's 'lonely impulse of delight'. The 'century of middle-class love'[59] expended on the ground lacks the dramatic potential that Yeats finds in the aristocracy of the air. In the end, 'An Irish Airman' transforms war into aesthetics: the aristocrat, artist, air ace creates, in death, a perfect moment, an individual work of art.

Where the war retains the characteristics of glorious warfare, heroism can be celebrated; when it cannot receive Yeatsian approval, it becomes internalized and subsumed by an idiosyncratic vision of history. 'In Memory of Major Robert Gregory' seems to explore a more conventional view of the war: the pre-war deaths that can be made to make sense; the wartime senseless slaughter. '[T]hought | Of that late death', he writes, 'took all my heart for speech'.[60] In 1910 after the death of J. M. Synge, Yeats writes:

There is in the creative joy an acceptance of what life brings, because we have understood the beauty of what it brings, or a hatred of death for what it takes away, which arouses within us, through some sympathy perhaps with all other men, an energy so noble, so powerful, that we laugh aloud and mock, in the terror or the sweetness of our exaltation, at death and oblivion.[61]

The death of Robert Gregory seems not to allow that 'sweetness of . . . exaltation'. Assembling imaginatively 'the friends that cannot sup

[58] *Rites of Spring*, 264–5.
[59] F. Scott Fitzgerald, *Tender is the Night* (1934; London: Penguin, 1986), 68.
[60] *CP*, 152.
[61] *E & I*, 322.

with us', the poet cannot accustom himself to the loss of the 'perfect man'. But this is partly because Gregory is, in the poem, larger than life, certainly larger than the war which took his life. Foreshadowing the later comments to O'Casey, Yeats writes of Gregory: 'Some burn damp faggots, others may consume|The entire combustible world in one small room|As though dried straw'. After his death, both Yeats and Bernard Shaw pay tribute to Robert Gregory. Shaw writes: 'To a man with his power of standing up to danger . . . war must have intensified his life as nothing else could; he got a grip of it that he could not through art or love. I suppose that is what makes the soldier'[62] Yeats, in 'A Note of Appreciation', published in the *Observer* in 1918, suggests that men, like Gregory, 'whose lives are to be an ever-growing absorption in subjective beauty . . . seek through some lesser gift, or through mere excitement, to strengthen that self which unites them to ordinary men'.[63] In Shaw's formulation, Robert Gregory, like other brave and adventurous men, found ultimate fulfilment in war. Yeats offers an extraordinarily convoluted explanation for enlistment which suggests that Gregory merely used the war to resolve certain aesthetic dilemmas. 'Objective', Yeats's description of the English, means, in the context of *A Vision*, primary, reasonable and moral; the 'subjective' is emotional, aesthetic, antithetical. Robert Gregory might have died fighting for the Empire, but as a 'subjective' fly in the ointment, he may also be seen as travelling on the contrary gyre which brings about a new antithetical age.

III

Seeds of the 1922 *A Vision* are scattered across the Gregory elegies, and with good reason. Gregory as one of the 'aristocracy of war', as 'the resurrection of our personality', seems tailor-made for *A Vision*, and vice versa. The Great War is not merely accommodated into the philosophies of *A Vision*; it is a major force behind the formulation of that vision in the war years and after. The automatic writing which inspires *A Vision* begins in 1917, hard on the heels of Yeats's other crucial wartime prose work, *Per Amica Silentia Lunae*. *Per Amica* is preoccupied with the dead. *A Vision* takes that preoccupation and tries to make historical and poetic sense of a Europe where destruction occurs on a

---

[62] Letter to Lady Gregory, 1918, quoted in Colin Smythe (ed.), *Robert Gregory 1881–1918: A Centenary Tribute* (Gerrards Cross: Colin Smythe, 1981), 27–8.
[63] Quoted ibid. 16.

scale never before seen. James Longenbach argues that the 'intricate world of *A Vision*... was built as a conscious alternative to the world shaken by the Great War': it is, in Yeats's terms, the sacred book that the world needs from the seven sleepers (or Yeats) after the war.[64]

A Vision's purpose is twofold: it engages with and critiques contemporary history and politics; it also enables the poet to dissociate himself from contemporary history. That dual and contradictory purpose is achieved through multi-layered conflicts in the book. 'The whole system' of *A Vision*, Yeats writes in the second version, 'is founded upon the belief that the ultimate reality, symbolized as the Sphere, falls in human consciousness . . . into a series of antinomies.'[65] *A Vision* is, in a way, Yeats's response to the problem of reconciling internal and external, or visible and invisible warfare: it places one historical age in conflict with another, and the poet in conflict with history. The antithesis underpinning *A Vision* is that of primary and antithetical: '*Primary* means democratic. *Antithetical* means aristocratic'.[66] Furthermore, 'The *primary* is that which serves, the *antithetical* is that which creates'.[67] Its fundamental argument, central to Yeats's poetry from the Great War onwards, is that 'An age is the reversal of an age'.[68] A primary age in history is in conflict with an antithetical age: one or the other may be uppermost depending on the point reached in the historical cycle, but the age which is uppermost always contains within it its opposite and therefore the seeds of its own destruction. In addition, an individual's place in the cycle does not necessarily synchronize with contemporary history. In other words, it is perfectly possible to be an antithetical (creative) man in a primary (servile) age or vice versa. For Yeats, this is a win-win situation: the world, and contemporary history, in conflicting with the poet, are thereby made subservient to him on two counts: first, they will, eventually, give way to the next aristocratic age of which the poet is the forerunner; second, in situating himself in opposition to his world he privileges his poetry on the Blakean premiss that 'Contraries are positive'.[69] If the primary phase is the enemy of poetry, it brings about the antithetical age where poetry can 'Climb to [its] proper dark'.[70]

A Vision accommodates the Great War in such a way that its 'greatness' can be refuted. For Yeats, the Great War, traditionally seen in

---

[64] See Longenbach, *Stone Cottage*, 132–3.   [65] *AV*, 187.
[66] *AV*, 104.   [67] *AV*, 85.   [68] 'Parnell's Funeral', *CP*, 319.
[69] *AV*, 72.   [70] 'The Statues', *CP*, 376.

England as the breaking point with the past, and as disrupting a linear historical progression, is part of a cyclical narrative of history. It may seem apocalyptic, but it is as much a beginning as it is a middle and an end. (In that sense, he is attuned to the different historical resonances of the war in an Irish context—that it cannot be separated from preceding and subsequent violence.) The Great War, and the Civil War, as the culmination of the trends of a primary age, will in fact bring about the antithetical qualities they appear to have destroyed. In the introduction to *A Vision*, in the 'Stories of Michael Robartes and his Friends', Robartes proclaims:

'After an age of necessity, truth, goodness, mechanism, science, democracy, abstraction, peace, comes an age of freedom, fiction, evil, kindred, art, aristocracy, particularity, war.... [P]repare for war, prepare your children and all that you can reach, for how can a nation or a kindred without war become that "bright particular star" of Shakespeare, that lit the roads in boyhood?...Love war because of its horror, that belief may be changed, civilisation renewed.'[71]

This is not far from Mairet's view, quoted above, of the Great War as 'a civilization turning against itself to destroy itself', but it suggests something alien to English attitudes towards the war—that the spectacle is ultimately, if inadvertently, productive. The Great War is an obvious force behind such remarks, with its mechanism, science, and abstraction—all the characteristics of modern mass warfare. But 'peace'? As with Yeats's pre-war attitudes, two different understandings of 'war' are apparent: the noble warfare that renews civilization is not the abstract, mechanized, impersonal struggle that took place on the Western Front. But that mechanized struggle serves its purpose in helping to engender a new age where the war to be loved lies in the future.

Implicitly, then, the whole structure of *A Vision* offers a sweeping indictment of contemporary history. That indictment is made more explicitly in Yeats's studies of the individual phases of history. The Great War falls in Phase 22, one of the two phases of 'struggle and tragedy'.[72] History, entering the last quarter of the Great Wheel, moves towards the completely objective Phase 1, after which the antithetical tincture will be reborn. And in Phases 22 to 25, some of Yeats's intense dislikes in relation to the Great War era are in evidence: realism, pity, propaganda, stupidity, socialism. In Phase 22, in the 'world of action', 'men will die and murder for an abstract synthesis...It is a phase as

[71] *AV*, 52–3.   [72] *AV*, 83.

tragic as its opposite, and more terrible, for the man of this phase may, before the point of balance has been reached, become a destroyer and persecutor, a figure of tumult and of violence'. If this in itself is not antipathetic to Yeats's thinking, the problem with this phase, he continues, is that man's system 'will become an instrument of destruction and of persecution in the hands of others'.[73] The self and anti-self, poet and daimon opposition is explored in *Per Amica Silentia Lunae*; in *A Vision* it is refined into a highly complex system. It is also, as Yeats implicitly recognizes in this particular instance, a characteristic of the Great War era: the persecutor is also the persecuted; the individual is, often involuntarily, in the service of the collective; mutually exclusive claims are made to fight for the abstractions of King and Country. Yeats, always aware of the seductiveness of action in wartime, disallows, in this phase, pure, individualist devotion to a military cause. The Great War is not to be celebrated: 'In the man of action, in a Napoleon, let us say, the stupidities lie hidden, for action is a form of abstraction that crushes everything it cannot express. At Phase 22 stupidity is obvious'.[74] (Gregory's devotion is, of course, out-of-Phase, aesthetic, and therefore exceptional.) The effect, in artistic terms, is that by the time Phases 23 and 24 are reached, 'Men and women ... create an art where individuals only exist to express some historical code, or some historical tradition of action and of feeling'.[75] Owen may be a case in point, since according to Yeats he denies conflict in order to plead the suffering of his men. Yeats himself, needless to say, belongs not in any of the subservient primary phases, but in the antithetical Phase 17 where a 'poet ... of the greatest kind' can 'conceive of the world as a continual conflict'.[76]

A Vision works, through such indictments, to validate Yeatsian poetics at a crisis point in history. Rewritten over a period of seven years— from 1917 to 1925—it affirms, in its final version, the political and artistic stance Yeats consolidates from the Great War to the late 1920s. The transition from his Great War poems to the Civil War poems illustrates a growing confidence in this stance. Elizabeth Cullingford discusses 'An Irish Airman Foresees his Death', 'Reprisals', and 'Meditations in Time of Civil War' in terms of the ways in which they reflect Yeats's changing political sympathies: 'An Irish Airman', as Yeats argued, 'was written to express Protestant patriotism towards Ireland', though it ends by praising the 'lonely impulse of delight'; 'Reprisals' is a

---

[73] *AV*, 161.   [74] *AV*, 162.   [75] *AV*, 170.   [76] *AV*, 144.

poem written with a political purpose, and indicates Yeats's 'loathing of the Tans and Auxies'; 'Meditations', on the other hand, 'reflects his lack of partisanship' on the Treaty issue. Thus, she describes 'Reprisals' as 'a complement and answer to "An Irish Airman Foresees his Death"' in that 'The behaviour of the Black and Tans invalidates even the "lonely impulse of delight"'.[77] Yeats is, in effect, claiming disillusionment:

> Yet rise from your Italian tomb,
> Flit to Kiltartan cross and stay
> Till certain second thoughts have come
> Upon the cause you served, that we
> Imagined such a fine affair:
> Half-drunk or whole-mad soldiery
> Are murdering your tenants there.[78]

The phrase 'we | Imagined such a fine affair' is, however, ambiguous. If Yeats is disillusioned, it is because he succumbed to pre-conscription idealism about the nature of the Great War, and the nature of England and English promises. But he loses any such illusions within weeks: by 1915 he describes the war as 'bloody frivolity' rather than a fine affair; and he leaves the question of whether 'England may keep faith' unanswered even in 1916. That the 'fine affair' was 'imagined' suggests a poetic role in shaping consciousness: by implication, Yeats could be the creative deceiver as well as the victim of deceit. If 'In dreams begins responsibilities', Gregory's 'good death' has been undermined because, in 'Reprisals', in holding to his dreams he abandons his responsibilities: 'battle joy may be so dear | A memory, even to the dead, | It chases other thoughts away.' There is inevitably a contradiction here. Yeats's tragic hero is also a man who neglects his own kind, yet in 'An Irish Airman' it would be irresponsible of him, in artistic terms, to do otherwise. 'Reprisals' does not rewrite 'An Irish Airman'. There is, Cullingford writes, at times a dichotomy between Yeats's 'private and his prophetic stance'.[79] If both these poems are, in a sense, self-indulgent, 'Reprisals' indulges the 'private' rather than the 'prophetic' Yeats.

These poems reveal Yeats's shifting political sympathies in response to certain historical events; more generally they are also illustrative of

---

[77] See *Yeats, Ireland and Fascism*, 107–8, 112.
[78] *The Variorum Edition of the Poems of W. B. Yeats*, ed. Peter Allt and Russell K. Alspach (New York: Macmillan, 1957), 791.
[79] *Yeats, Ireland and Fascism*, 161.

changes in his approach to the subject of war in poetry. Shortly after Robert Gregory's death, J. B. Yeats writes to his son:

The way to be happy is to forget yourself. That is why Robert Gregory was happy.... Yet there are two ways of forgetting yourself and two ways of being happy. To forget yourself as in the war, seeing nothing but its vastness.... Or to forget yourself in some movement for reform... Yet there is another way of self-forgetting which does not require any enormous machinery such as sanguinary war. It is of course that of art and Beauty....

Now you see the antagonism between a state of war and the practice of art and literature. (War) offers an easier way of forgetting yourself and willing to be happy we grasp at it with eagerness, and all the poets desert the difficult paths they have been climbing; it is so much easier to carry a rifle and a knapsack than to try to write poetry.[80]

If 'An Irish Airman' glorifies the first of these 'ways of forgetting', and 'Reprisals' subsequently questions it, 'Meditations in Time of Civil War', fulfilling the promise of *A Vision*, takes the conflict between prophetic and private stance, poet and man of action, and transforms it into the subject of the poem. It celebrates, implicitly, the difficult path of art not war, or, more accurately, the eternal war of art. A universally held belief of those who fought in the Great War was that their experience could not be understood by anyone who had not 'been through hell'. Edmund Blunden, in the 'Preliminary' to *Undertones of War*, spoke for many when he claimed 'no one will read it who is not already aware of all the intimations and discoveries in it... by reason of having gone the same journey. No one? Some, I am sure; but not many. *Neither will they understand*—that will not be all my fault.'[81] Yeats grasps in the Civil War what his English counterparts do not always understand in the Great War—the unbridgeable gap between the soldiers' experience and his own. As a result, the distance has to be turned into a dialectical strength. Yeats's own 'great war' is, he says, 'a war of the past and the future, of a noble past that tries to keep itself unchanged, hoping, perhaps vainly, the deluge will begin some day to fall, that the dove will some day return bringing with it a green bough'.[82] If the anti-heroic has reached its zenith in the primary age, then to resist anti-heroism becomes a heroic gesture in itself, indicating a fidelity to the concepts of

[80] 'To W. B. Yeats', 10 June 1918, *Letters to his Son W. B. Yeats and Others 1869–1922*, ed. Joseph Hone (London: Secker & Warburg, 1983), 247–8.
[81] (1928; London: Penguin, 1982), 7.
[82] Quoted in Cullingford, *Yeats, Ireland and Fascism*, 10–11.

the aristocratic era that conflict will bring about. In 'Meditations in Time of Civil War', the soldier at Yeats's door is 'An affable Irregular, | A heavily-built Falstaffian man'.[83] While the issues at stake are of Shakespearean magnitude, the heroic and the tragic ground has been reserved not for the soldier but for the poet. If it appears initially that war has written Yeats out of history—'I complain | Of the foul weather, hail and rain, | A pear-tree broken by the storm'—it is detachment from contemporary violence that makes his final gesture of the poem, to 'turn away and shut the door', a heroic action, a 'lonely impulse of delight'. Bergonzi suggests that after the Great War, particularly in English writing, 'heroism, as a kind of behaviour, might still be possible, but not the rhetoric and gestures of heroism'.[84] Yeats circumvents this judgement: 'Meditations' asserts heroic attitude over heroic action, and refuses to admit the impossibility of either.

Wallace Stevens, also a great apologist for the heroic imagination in time of war, writes in 1942:

For the sensitive poet, conscious of negations, nothing is more difficult than the affirmations of nobility and yet there is nothing that he requires of himself more persistently, since in them and their kind, alone, are to be found those sanctions that are the reason for his being and for that occasional ecstasy, or ecstatic freedom of mind, which is his special privilege.

It is hard to think of a thing more out of time than nobility. Looked at plainly it seems false and dead and ugly. . . . [W]e turn away from it as from something repulsive and particularly from the characteristic that it has a way of assuming: something that was noble in its day, grandeur that was, the rhetorical once. But as a wave is a force and not the water of which it is composed, which is never the same, so nobility is a force and not the manifestations of which it is composed, which are never the same. . . . It is a violence from within that protects us from a violence without. It is the imagination pressing back against the pressure of reality.[85]

A Vision is a poetics of war, one which applauds noble warfare and aristocratic virtues and opposes them to an age of democracy and ignoble warfare. Its 'violence . . . within', the doctrine of conflict at its centre, liberates Yeats's poetic response to the 'violence without'—the Great War, the Anglo-Irish War, the Civil War. At the end of the first version of the book, as if to reinforce the view that the vision is forged in

---

[83] *CP*, 229–30.   [84] *Heroes' Twilight*, 222.
[85] *The Necessary Angel: Essays on Reality and the Imagination* (London: Faber, 1960), 35–6.

response, and as a counter to, war, he writes: 'Finished at Thoor Ballylee, 1922, in a time of Civil War'.[86] The phrase also conjures up an image, however inaccurate, of the poet in his tower, stylistically arranging experience into a Yeatsian *Weltanschauung*, while battle rages around (beneath) him. There are poems in Yeats's oeuvre which are, as he points out, 'unintelligible' without certain elements of the original version of *A Vision*,[87] but underneath its sometimes incomprehensible 'harsh geometry'[88] is an aesthetic vision crucial to *The Tower*, the poetry which it made possible. In 1922, Yeats speculates: 'I wonder will literature be much changed by that most momentous of events, the return of evil.' In the same letter, he says that he himself 'write[s] better for all the uncertainty'.[89] If *A Vision* is a poetics of war, *The Tower* contains the poetry which has the greatest claim to be called war poetry.

Paul Fussell explains the problem confronting the poets who fought in the First World War as one of language:

finding the war 'indescribable' in any but the available language of traditional literature, those who recalled it had to do so in known literary terms. Joyce, Eliot, Lawrence, Pound, Yeats were not present at the front to induct them into new idioms which might have done the job better.[90]

In 'The Tower', 'Meditations in Time of Civil War', and 'Nineteen Hundred and Nineteen' the possibilities of language and rhetoric are stretched to the limit in order to confront, but not compromise with, the present reality. The 'war' in and of these poems works, as with *A Vision*'s historically mutating gyres and individual reincarnations, on at least two levels: visible versus invisible warfare, and the division of a mind within itself. At times, all three poems begin to sound like a perpetual rehearsal for a voice that cannot appear. Any conclusion reached is destabilized: 'But I have found an answer' followed by a further question. The only guiding principle is that of 'The Tower'—'As I would question all, come all who can'.[91] Stan Smith describes the discourse 'repressed in every poem and philosophical vision' as 'the discourse of history itself', a history which, in spite of this repression, 'emerges as a vision of

---

[86] *AV*, 184.

[87] See *AV*, 19.

[88] *E & I*, 518. The geometry offers, Yeats notes, only 'an incomplete interpretation' of the vision to which it aspires.

[89] 'To Olivia Shakespear' [? Apr. 1922], *The Letters of W. B. Yeats*, ed. Wade, 680.

[90] *The Great War and Modern Memory* (London: OUP, 1975), 174.

[91] *CP*, 221–2.

terror'.[92] The relationship between history, which is changeable, and the work of art, imaged in 'Meditations in Time of Civil War' as Sato's sword (or, put another way, between the pressures of visible and invisible warfare), is an ambivalent one, but in the end there is no real question as to the mutual dependence of the two: 'only an aching heart | Conceives a changeless work of art'.[93] If history is 'this filthy modern tide',[94] it is, in this image, not so much repressed as it is a naturally irrepressible force, variable in its impact, which demands constant attention and/or resistance. It is resisted, in 'Meditations in Time of Civil War', to mark the limits in language of a moral and political, as well as an aesthetic world beyond those imposed by an empty and ultimately self-defeating rhetoric. The First World War poets, surely confronting the filthy modern tide at its filthiest, lack, as Yeats sees it, psychological distance, which is not necessarily repression; they do not challenge history effectively because they are swamped by it. However disturbing Yeats's response to war proves for his critics, the strength of his example is evident in the frequent echoes of Section II of 'Meditations' in contemporary Northern Irish poetry:

> An acre of stony ground,
> Where the symbolic rose can break in flower,
> Old ragged elms, old thorns innumerable,
> The sound of the rain or sound
> Of every wind that blows.[95]

Poetry can only flourish in the space Yeats has cleared for it; in doing so he does not deny the reality of the time, or the difficulty involved ('stony ground'), but he does suggest that the difficulty is an essential part of the flowering as well as an endangerment of it. Adversity, by implication, inspires 'Befitting emblems of adversity'.

The individualist stance, the constant reassertion of the 'I' in this sequence of poems, is illustrative of both the virtue and the problem of the Yeatsian inheritance. At a traumatic time in history, politicians generally accepted the premiss that it was better to be wrong with the people than right against them: this ultimate compromise of principle was, for example, made by liberals in England at the outbreak of war as

---

[92] *The Origins of Modernism: Eliot, Pound, Yeats and the Rhetorics of Renewal* (London: Harvester Wheatsheaf, 1994), 205.

[93] *CP*, 228.

[94] 'The Statues', *CP*, 376.

[95] *CP*, 226.

a means of retaining power. Yeats, in contrast, opts for being 'right' in the solitary role, and assumes in that role, against the odds, a great deal of power. In 'The Tower' and 'Meditations', the poet is preoccupied with that which he will leave behind; in both poems, any foreseeable problems with the inheritance are projected on to the inheritors. In Section IV of 'Meditations', poetry itself is under threat: 'And what if my descendents lose the flower...'; but Yeats pre-empts a possible decline and turns it on its head: 'whatever flourish and decline | These stones remain their monument and mine'.[96] The poetry will be a testament to history whether it (history) is good (flourishes) or bad (declines). The 'curse'—'May...this stark tower | Become a roofless ruin'—ensures that even decline, over which the poet can have no control, is turned in appearance into combative action, power beyond the grave. The tower stands or falls with the age, but it is less a barometer than a judgement: if it is perceived as a 'roofless ruin', the last gasp of the Ascendancy, then the strength of the indictment is in its absence rather than its presence. It is a view which is highly dependent upon the philosophy of A Vision, on the assumption that what goes around comes around: 'The Primum Mobile that fashioned us | Has made the very owls in circles move'. That philosophy cannot easily be condemned as a transcendental search for an ultimate truth; Plato himself is in Yeats's terms something of a failure because 'to die into the truth is still to die'.[97] The Yeats of 'He Tells of the Perfect Beauty' is deconstructed in 'Meditations in Time of Civil War' in a retrospect on his own naivety: the perfect beauty is that which cannot be told, unless the world is shrouded from view by a dense Celtic fog. In the war years, as Longenbach discusses, Yeats was preoccupied with writing his memoirs, with telling the story of one tragic generation of the 1890s as another tragic or lost generation was being created on the Western Front. In 'Nineteen Hundred and Nineteen', 1890s decadence—'Loie Fuller's Chinese dancers'—gives way to something more reminiscent of the 1914–18 dance of death:

> So the Platonic Year
> Whirls out new right and wrong,
> Whirls in the old instead;
> All men are dancers and their tread
> Goes to the barbarous clangour of a gong.[98]

---

[96] CP, 229.   [97] AV, 271.   [98] CP, 234.

These are the men manipulated throughout time by the merciless gyres of history; on another level they represent, in 1919, the dead of a Europe that 'hurried them off on its own furious path'.

Passive suffering is not a theme for poetry; but neither any more is passive beauty. In 'Nineteen Hundred and Nineteen', Yeats's self-imposed and unresolved angst as the antithetical poet in the primary age, is imaged in the swan:

> Some moralist or mythological poet
> Compares the solitary soul to a swan;
> I am satisfied with that,
> Satisfied if a troubled mirror show it,
> Before that brief gleam of its life be gone,
> An image of its state;
> The wings half spread for flight,
> The breast thrust out in pride
> Whether to play, or to ride
> Those winds that clamour of approaching night.[99]

The swan may be the 'I' in conflict with society, but it is also in conflict with itself. Even a portrait as ambiguous as this one finds itself in an implied question ('whether' is ambiguous) born of a struggle in the verse: 'I am satisfied', qualified with 'Satisfied if', qualified again with an image formed only through another image, the mirror, to establish nothing more unifying than the dilemma at the heart of all three poems, 'Whether to play, or to ride . . .'. If the lines imply a choice, the choice is apparently never made, leaving 'play' as permanently transitional. In *A Vision*, Yeats writes, 'The cones of the *tinctures* mirror reality but are in themselves pursuit and illusion . . . the Sphere is reality'.[100] The end of pursuit and illusion may be the final image of the swan, but 'reality' is then the end of art:

> The swan has leaped into the desolate heaven:
> That image can bring wildness, bring a rage
> To end all things, to end
> What my laborious life imagined, even
> The half-imagined, the half-written page.

Seamus Heaney's reading of 'Meditations in Time of Civil War' suggests that Yeats's inheritors are dominated by a liberal conscience seeking

---

[99] *CP*, 234–5.   [100] *AV*, 73.

resolution. He sees 'The Stare's Nest by My Window' as an affirmation of the truth that 'The end of art is peace'. In this poem, he writes,

[Yeats's] great fur coat of attitude is laid aside, the domineering intellect and the equestrian profile, all of which gain him a power elsewhere, all laid aside. What we have is a deeply instinctive yet intellectually assented-to idea of nature in her benign and nurturant aspect as the proper first principle of life and living. The maternal is apprehended, intimated and warmly cherished[101]

Heaney works hard here for a humanitarian reading Yeats is always reluctant to offer: the decline in values is more likely to be his subject matter than the incubation of the values themselves in, for example, a stare's nest. The invocation to nature is made first and foremost to strengthen the poet whose 'wall is loosening'.[102] 'The Stare's Nest' is the only section in the poem where the poet is 'closed in'—an echo is Owen's 'on us the doors are closed'.[103] It is also the only section where he claims to be writing in the midst of, rather than simply in time of, civil war. The obvious conclusion is that poetry struggles in such a position, dominated by the limitations imposed on its own possibilities, and leaves the poet clutching at straws (or at least at honey bees). But since for Yeats, 'the end of art is peace' means, among other things, the end of art, nature is invoked less as a proper first principle than as a means of sustaining the first principle of poetic strength. The honey bee, in mythology, nourished Jupiter and Pindar—the god, the ageing lyric poet. The refrain—'O honey-bees, | Come build in the empty house of the stare'—calls for a form of nourishment for the poet, and does so because this section is the only one in which destruction is concrete: 'Last night they trundled down the road | That dead young soldier in his blood'. It is a moment where heightened consciousness of memory dominates, belying the poem's title 'Meditations'. It is also a moment which finds a parallel in 'Nineteen Hundred and Nineteen' where 'There lurches past...That insolent fiend Robert Artisson'.[104] The poet's reaction to both images is one of fascination and recoil. But since the three poems appear in reverse order of composition, the insolent fiend engendered by art, the imaginative creation, rather than the passive dead soldier, is the final legacy of the sequence.[105] The reordering of the

---

[101]   Preoccupations: Selected Prose 1968–1978 (London: Faber, 1980), 112.
[102]   CP, 230.   [103]   'Exposure', The Poems of Wilfred Owen, 162.   [104]   CP, 237.
[105]   The poems are dated as follows: 'Nineteen Hundred and Nineteen', 1919; 'Meditations', 1923; 'The Tower', 1926, and were first published in 1919, 1921, and 1927 respectively (see Variorum Edition of the Poems of W. B. Yeats, 407–28).

sequence also implies that 'The Stare's Nest' has enabled a vision of reality in 'Nineteen Hundred and Nineteen', not that it is the vision itself. In 'Meditations in Time of Civil War', it is followed by 'I see Phantoms of Hatred . . .'. The lines open up again as the poet climbs to the tower top, and sweep with the length and range of the poet's own vision of contemporary realities. 'The Stare's Nest' 's 'We had fed the heart on fantasies, | The heart's grown brutal from the fare', echoes, rather more negatively, 'Easter 1916' 's 'Too long a sacrifice | Can make a stone of the heart'. But the close of 'Meditations in Time of Civil War' seems to find an answer to 'Easter 1916' 's 'O when may it suffice?':

> I turn away and shut the door, and on the stair
> Wonder how many times I could have proved my worth
> In something that all others understand or share;
> But O! ambitious heart, had such a proof drawn forth
> A company of friends, a conscience set at ease,
> It had but made us pine the more. The abstract joy,
> The half-read wisdom of daemonic images,
> Suffice the ageing man as once the growing boy.

'[H]eaven's part' in 'Easter 1916', and Wordsworth's childhood vision, can be the ageing man's part as well but only through the introduction of another category: to accept that resolution involves a greater degree of compromise, and to remain 'resolutely irresolute'—to 'turn away and shut the door'. Whatever choice is made, the requirement for making it is acceptance of the fact that there is no such thing as a conscience set at ease.

The assertion of heroism, the conflict set up between noble poet and ignoble war (or world), also resonates in the last poems. In 'A Crazed Girl', the girl 'Hiding amid the cargo of a steamship, | Her knee-cap broken' makes 'No common intelligible sound' but is 'A beautiful lofty thing, or a thing | Heroically lost, heroically found'.[106] In 1918, Wilfred Owen affirmed his poetry was 'not about heroes'. In the late 1930s, when heroism is, in some senses, a post-Owen debased literary currency, Yeats mints both word and concept afresh. He oscillates between finding and losing themes, between pity and prophecy. But the theme, or image, he elects to keep is not a denial of aesthetic confidence, it is that confidence reaffirmed in the guise of insanity or humility. The

[106] *CP*, 349.

desire to reaffirm traditional values is not uncharacteristic of the post-war years; it is the joy of affirmation, the symbiotic relation of violence to greatness and to creativity, that has proved for some critics the disturbing element in Yeats's poetry. Resistant to the implications of this vision, Seamus Heaney singles out those poems in which, he argues, Yeats's 'tenderness towards life and its uncompletedness is at odds with and tending to gain sway over the consolations of the artificial work'. As with his reading of 'Meditations', he attempts to tip the scales towards the humanist Yeats in the last poems, suggesting that in 'The Man and the Echo', 'the voice of conscience and remorse opposes itself to the artistic choice that the old man has lived out all his life'. The final 'anguished cry of a rabbit' symbolizes this voice:[107]

> But hush, for I have lost the theme,
> Its joy or night seem but a dream;
> Up there some hawk or owl has struck,
> Dropping out of sky or rock,
> A stricken rabbit is crying out,
> And its cry distracts my thought.[108]

But this reading is, implicitly, to unbalance that which is always held in creative tension. Peter McDonald writes that 'Yeats's imagination settles on remorse, and is able to act upon it, as part of the attempt to "hold in a single thought reality and justice"', that his 'dealings with remorse ... do not allow emotion—whether it is regret, pain, humiliation, grief, or simple frustration—to overcome the proper freedom of poetic action'.[109] The cry of the stricken rabbit might be the cry of humanity, of the frightened victim, and the voice of conscience, but since it distracts 'thought'—the holding together of reality and justice—it is also the point where the poem ends and the poet has lost his theme. If he is to respond to contemporary events with pity, it might be at the expense of the hard-won position as prophet of tragic joy whose 'last kiss is given to the void'.[110] Ultimately, the theme, like the girl, is 'Heroically lost, heroically found'.

---

[107] Heaney, *Preoccupations*, 111.
[108] *CP*, 395.
[109] 'Yeats and Remorse', 206.
[110] 'To T. Sturge Moore', 17 Apr. [1929], in *W. B. Yeats and T. Sturge Moore: Their Correspondence*, ed. Ursula Bridge (Westport, Conn.: Greenwood Press, 1978), 154.

IV

For Yeats, the poetry is in the conflict, never in the pity. That position is
one learned, or constructed, partly in response to the Great War. It is
also, paradoxically, a position which has encouraged the view that
Yeats's work can be dissociated from the Great War. In *A Vision*,
'pity' dominates Phase 23 (the post-war years);[111] Yeats, however, is
safely ensconced in Phase 17. As Eksteins points out, 'The bourgeois
literature of disenchantment with the war wallowed in pity' and Yeats,
like Pound, had 'no tolerance for so ignoble a sentiment'.[112] Poems such
as 'The Gyres' or 'The Statues' would bear this out: 'Irrational streams
of blood are staining earth . . . We that look on but laugh in tragic joy.'[113]
The poet exists here in contradistinction to the 'filthy modern tide' of
humanity. Even Pound is moved from Phase 12 to join the humanitar-
ians of the later phases because he feeds the starving cats in Rapallo.[114]
It is also an act which, for Yeats, casts not entirely favourable new light
on Pound's 'praise of writers pursued by ill-luck, left maimed or bed-
ridden by the War'.[115] But the context of Eksteins's remarks in relation
to Pound and Yeats is problematical:

> The Nietzschean invocation to 'live dangerously' became the sole command-
> ment of Nazism. . . . To live dangerously means never to accept the status
> quo; it means to act the adversary constantly; it means to exaggerate, to
> provoke. It means permanent conflict. 'Nazism is,' said Hitler, 'a doctrine of
> conflict.'
>
> In this *Weltanschauung*, pity, compassion, the Sermon on the Mount, all
> become relics. Pity was nothing but bourgeois sentimentality, said Goebbels.
> . . . If this kind of memory of the war and if bourgeois decadence in general were
> to be overcome, there could be no room for pity.[116]

Michael North describes the perceived challenge facing the post-war
poets as the demand for 'aesthetic modernism' to 'effect the liberation
that liberal democracy had promised but failed to deliver'.[117] Yeats's
sympathies with fascism are understandable in the climate of the 1920s:
fascism proposed a political as well as an aesthetic resolution to that
challenge, saw the two, in fact, as mutually dependent. '[A] doctrine of
conflict' is central to Yeats's aesthetic, and central to *A Vision*. Where

---

[111] *AV*, 166.   [112] *Rites of Spring*, 314.   [113] *CP*, 337.
[114] See Richard Ellmann, *Yeats: The Man and the Masks* (London: Penguin, 1987), 240.
[115] See *AV*, 5–6.   [116] *Rites of Spring*, 313–14.
[117] *The Political Aesthetic of Yeats, Eliot, and Pound* (Cambridge: Cambridge UP, 1991), 2.

liberalism fails to reconcile its principles to a state of war, fascism circumvents the difficulty through its supreme indifference to the moral dilemmas of liberalism. As Howard explains, 'The slogan "Fascism means War" was almost tautological: Fascist ideologies never pretended anything else'.[118] Vincent writes of fascism:

politically orchestrated violence was given the intellectual gloss of social poetry. Violence had an almost aesthetic appeal. . . . [V]italism could be allied, by almost imperceptible shifts of logic, to all artistic creative experience, via the all-inclusiveness of concepts like intuition and instinct. In the same way that it is difficult to unpack the emotional experience of artistic creation into abstract theory, so equally with heroic, crusading political violence. Violence becomes alchemically transmuted into an aesthetic mystery.[119]

But while aesthetic mystery may be positive, a doctrine of conflict allied with a militaristic, hegemonic state, is far from the Yeatsian ideal. *A Vision*'s translation of subjective experience into symbol is, in a way, hijacked and transformed through developments in Italy and Germany in the 1920s and 1930s into a political philosophy that Yeats, on a personal level, could not condone, a political philosophy which, while it might rest upon a doctrine of conflict, simultaneously disallows the protesting individual voice. Yeats travels the authoritative road towards aesthetic freedom, but, as Cullingford shows in *Yeats, Ireland and Fascism*, even if his politics and aesthetic are inseparable, they are not synonymous with his political activity, which, he claimed, was geared towards the creation of 'a modern, tolerant, liberal nation'.[120] If poetry is exempt from social obligation, which is not the same as social function, Yeats as senator and national cultural figure is not. R. F. Foster points out that while Yeats 'condemned "democracy" in artistic terms, as encouraging shoddiness and sentimentality, he clearly saw it as a political good'.[121] In effect, he risks being caught between a poetry of which he does not entirely approve, wallowing in 'pity', and an aesthetic principle that might ultimately bind him to cause and state, an aesthetic principle of invisible warfare that becomes visible experience.

But, as Stan Smith points out, the 'central contradiction of Yeats's poetry in the 1920s' is that '*The Tower*, which Yeats spoke of as "evidence

---

[118]   *War and the Liberal Conscience* (London: OUP, 1981), 101.
[119]   *Modern Political Ideologies* (Oxford: Blackwell, 1992), 154.
[120]   W. B. Yeats, quoted in Cullingford, *Yeats, Ireland and Fascism*, 165.
[121]   *W. B. Yeats: A Life*, i. (Oxford: OUP, 1997), 513.

to show that my poetry has gained in self-possession and power",
nevertheless carries with it...a message of failure and defeat'.[122]
Throughout the 1920s and 1930s, Yeats holds to the principle of conflict
in aesthetic terms, but separates himself from its political con-
sequences—in terms of fascism or liberalism—by irrevocably linking
conflict to defeat. Conflict is the only constant in *A Vision*, but he also
writes:

> Without...continual Discord through Deception there would be no con-
> science, no activity; Deception is a technical term of my teachers and may be
> substituted for 'desire'. Life is an endeavour, made vain by the four sails of its
> mill, to come to a double contemplation, that of the chosen Image, that of the
> fated Image.[123]

Desire (as opposed to 'pity') is deception: in other words, it only exists
while it remains thwarted. The organizational principle here is that of
discord, but also that of defeat. The poet always wins, only because, as in
'Meditations in Time of Civil War', he is always on the losing side. In
April 1929, Yeats wrote that Ezra Pound 'confirmed a conception I have
had for many years, a conception that has freed me from British liberal-
ism and all its dreams. The one heroic sanction is that of the last battle of
the Norse Gods, of a gay struggle without hope. Long ago I used to
puzzle Maud Gonne by always avowing ultimate defeat as a test.'[124] The
conception is a way in which Yeats can separate himself from a failed
philosophy (and political system) without resorting, like so many poets
in the inter-war years, to extreme ideologies as the only viable altern-
atives; and with 'long ago' he claims implicitly to have pre-empted the
failure of British liberalism at the end of the Great War—events be-
tween 1914 and 1922 serve not to change his opinion but only to prove
his instinct right.

The claim is much more significant when one considers that Yeats
finds British liberalism to be a failure at the same time as do many British
liberals. The experience of warfare between 1914 and 1918, and the
unjustifiably harsh imperialist demands of the Versailles Treaty placed
an intolerable strain on British liberalism. Warfare, when it came in 1914,
highlighted the central contradiction in liberal ideology—its refusal to

---

[122] *The Origins of Modernism*, 163.
[123] *AV*, 94.
[124] 'To T. Sturge Moore', 17 Apr. [1929], *W. B. Yeats and T. Sturge Moore: Their
Correspondence*, 154.

pursue the theory of individualism to its logical conclusion—and in doing so served to reveal the extent to which liberalism was obliged to compromise that ideology to retain political power. As a result of compromise and confusion, the Liberal Party suffered a loss of credibility from which it never recovered. The liberalism which dominated British 'democracy' from the mid-nineteenth century to the outbreak of the Great War disappeared, in name at any rate, from the political scene in 1923 with a move towards socialism. Yeats's 'freedom' from the liberal dilemma is also a claimed freedom from the moral questions engendered by war. It accepts that ideas of progress have been destroyed in the Great War, and proposes instead a progress in reverse, one that works on the premiss that to lose is to gain: 'Our literary movement would be worthless but for its defeat.'[125] '[O]ptimistic perfectibilism', which characterized the nineteenth- and early twentieth-century liberal mind was, as Andrew Vincent points out, 'dashed on the fields of the Somme', leading to a loss of hope about the future of mankind.'[126] Loss of hope for Yeats on the other hand is transformed into an element in the dialectical strength of his aesthetic. He engages, then, as completely, if more obliquely, than others, with the unresolved issues raised by the Great War as they affect the western world.

Such engagement has too often been seen as the preserve of the 'war poets' (by which is meant the soldier poets of the First World War), where the mere fact that a response to war exists can be seen as sufficient in itself, and therefore exempt from ordinary critical judgement. ('There is', Yeats writes, 'every excuse' for Owen's supposed poetic inadequacies.) In contrast, the fact that Yeats responds to the war takes second place behind the disputes concerning the politics implicit in the response. From both perspectives, a certain amount of reductive misinterpretation takes place. Yeats is highly critical of what he himself terms the 'war poets'; he makes concessions in view of the extremity of their situation (concessions which do not, however, extend to their advocates); and he attempts to dissociate himself from their 'tradition'. Nevertheless, the poetry of Yeats, perhaps more than that of any of his contemporaries in the 1920s and 1930s, goes some way to prove the unhelpfulness of the term 'war poetry', and to indicate that war poetry, like war, probably needs rescuing from its friends as well as its enemies.

---

[125]   *W. B. Yeats and T. Sturge Moore*, 154.   [126]   *Modern Political Ideologies*, 53.

In a way, the fate of the 'war poets' is paradigmatic of the fate of war in twentieth-century history. Von Strandmann argues that from the Second World War onwards, the character of warfare has changed to the extent that Clausewitz's theory of the nexus between war and politics is no longer applicable: nuclear potential deprives war of any rational or justifiable basis.[127] But as regards the First World War, the justification and strategy of war remained fatally unchanged from the nineteenth century. Clausewitz argues, famously, that

War is only a part of political intercourse, therefore by no means an independent thing in itself.
We know, certainly, that War is only called forth through the political intercourse of Governments and Nations; but in general it is supposed that such intercourse is broken off by War, and that a totally different state of things ensues, subject to no laws but its own.

We maintain, on the contrary, that War is nothing but a continuation of political intercourse, with a mixture of other means ...

War is an instrument of policy; it must necessarily bear its character, it must measure with its scale: the conduct of War, in its great features, is therefore policy itself, which takes up the sword in place of the pen, but does not on that account cease to think according to its own laws.[128]

The tendency with the Great War has been to grant it an exceptional status and a life of its own quite separate from the policy actually controlling events—'the War had won and would go on winning'. It may appear utterly irrational, but it was not, and a plea of irrationality might be in some way a denial of culpability. Whether rightly or wrongly, the number of casualties was deemed acceptable in view of the advantages to be gained by continuing the war, even though the apocalyptic imagery deployed by those who encouraged enlistment attempted an elevation of the war from natural (political) to supernatural status: 'We are fighting ... for Christ against anti-Christ. And so the battle is not ours, it is indeed Armageddon.'[129] In a way, then, the emphasis placed on the uniquely devastating character of the Great War, its profound and unprecedented impact on culture, can obscure the contextual reality of the war. It becomes marginalized because, as an event, it attains a unique status within history. War qua war may deceptively be seen as

[127] Hartmut Pogge von Strandmann, 'History and War', in Robert A. Hinde (ed.), *The Institution of War* (New York: St Martin's Press, 1992), 50–5.
[128] Carl von Clausewitz, *On War* (1832), trans. J. J. Graham and ed. Anatol Rapoport (London: Penguin, 1982), 402, 410.
[129] An Anglican Dean, quoted in Hinde (ed.), *The Institution of War*, 90.

an end in itself. To confront the reality of the Great War, not just the brutality and the death toll with which everyone is so familiar, but the political and cultural reality which inspired and informed those events, is to interrogate the condition of humankind in the twentieth century in a way that encompasses other battlegrounds beyond those which can tie down the 'war poet' in mud, trenches, and helplessness. Ironically, the event which stands out in twentieth-century history is also the event whose literature is perceived as being in some way alien to the twentieth-century literary tradition. Robert Graves, for example, felt that his war experience left him marginalized, that while he was playing a part in momentous historical change, T. S. Eliot, in his London cafés, was poised to project great literary change on the world. The Great War is not a temporary aberration in the normal progression of civilization, it is part of that progression. But as liberal confusion indicates, it necessitates (as Yeats recognized) a redefinition of ideas of progress.

Whatever the implications for liberal thought post-1918, to consider the Great War in isolation from its political context is to reconstruct history in a way which makes it a potentially safer arena for and from poetry. To demand a different court of appeal for the soldier poets may be to do them an injustice in the act of appearing to do the opposite. Thus, 'war poetry' which refers primarily to the Great War, can be hermetically sealed off (in various anthologies) in spite of the amount of attention paid to it. Like war, it is sanitized if it is perceived in isolation: whatever its social and political criticisms, 'war poetry' will not bring about change if these criticisms can be confined to an emergency situation. As Simon Featherstone points out, 'The very term "war poetry" risks the isolation of the work within the artificial enclosure of the war years, and suggests a kind of writing relevant only to the extraordinary circumstance of war'. It risks perpetuating the notion that 'the politics of war are fundamentally different to the politics of peace'. Instead, Featherstone argues convincingly that it is, primarily, political poetry, that Owen's and Sassoon's poetry should be read as criticism of 'the betrayal of the individual by the state'.[130]

To consider Yeats's poetry as war poetry is to redefine, or rather to extend the idea of war to the idea of conflict, of which actual warfare is, as it was for the soldier poets, only one manifestation. John Mueller, considering the institution of war, argues that

[130]   *War Poetry: An Introductory Reader* (London: Routledge, 1995), 53, 58.

Conflict, like war, is natural. But unlike war, conflict is natural and inevitable because it is impossible for everyone to have exactly the same interests.... But peace...is quite compatible with conflict, contentiousness, hostility, racism, inequality, hatred, avarice, calumny, injustice[131]

As Michael Howard points out, 'war is simply a generic term for the use of armed force by states or aspirants to statehood'.[132] A consistently anti-war stance has often proved a difficult, if not contradictory, position to maintain, particularly since one cannot, in this formulation, oppose war and simultaneously support a struggle for national liberation. The only thing the poets who fought in the Great War really declare is opposition to a particular war fought in a particular way. Sassoon's 1917 Declaration against the war is often read as a pacifist statement, but it is in reality an objection to the reasoning behind the Great War, not war per se: 'I believe that this war, upon which I entered as a war of defence and liberation, has now become a war of aggression and conquest...I am not protesting against the conduct of the war, but against the political errors and insincerities for which the fighting men are being sacrificed.'[133] Clausewitz suggests that war is 'merely another kind of writing and language for political thoughts', that although it has 'a grammar of its own...its logic is not peculiar to itself'.[134] As a result, the soldier poets, like Yeats, put conflict of interests—between soldier and politician, war and Christianity, front and home, just and unjust war—at the heart of the aesthetic. Under the enormous external pressure of their situation, that conflict of interests is too often perceived simply as resistance to the war.

'[W]ar', Wallace Stevens writes, 'is only a part of a war-like whole'.[135] It is primarily in this sense that it appears in Yeats's poetry, all the more obviously since the poetry is free from the imbalance in reception, and at times intention, found in the work of the soldier poets. Conflict is defined by Yeats as the source of poetry, in a formula that also reverberates in perceptions of the Great War: 'All creation is from conflict, whether with our own mind or with that of others, and the historian who dreams of bloodless victory wrongs the wounded veterans'.[136] As

[131] 'War: Natural, But Not Necessary', in Hinde (ed.), *The Institution of War*, 24–5.
[132] *War and the Liberal Conscience*, 134.
[133] Sassoon, *The Complete Memoirs of George Sherston* (1937; London: Faber, 1972), 496.
[134] *On War*, 402.
[135] *The Necessary Angel*, 21.
[136] *Autobiographies* (London: Macmillan, 1955), 576.

Martin Stephen points out, while the protest poetry of Owen and
Sassoon has become, in popular perception, the proper way to remem-
ber the Great War, other veterans may be saying something different.[137]
Yeats forges, as much as finds, opposition in his world, and claims
openly that he would do so to enable his work: 'If I found myself
a director of men's consciences, or becoming any kind of idealized
figure in their minds, I would, or I fancy that I would, display or even
exaggerate my frailties.'[138]

  Related to a doctrine of conflict, and perceived as problematizing it,
are, inevitably, the comments he makes concerning 'real' warfare: 'De-
sire some just war, that big house and hovel, college and public-
house...may know that they belong to one nation.'[139] Even in the
late 1930s, Yeats is contradictory on the subject of war, veering from
sympathy with the bloodthirsty policy of Mitchel—' "Send war in our
time, O Lord!" '[140]—to the more dismissive comment, 'If war is neces-
sary...it is best to forget its suffering as we do the discomfort of
fever.'[141] The distance between his views always comes at the point
when the poet's ideas and his context overlap in a way which could
potentially put poetry at risk. The different attitudes to war are, in fact,
expressions of fundamentally different conceptions of war and, by
extension, of poetry: the Mitchel invocation is a plea for dignity and
energy, creative conflict; the dismissiveness a rejection of propagandist
literature. Yeats's only comments on military developments in the Great
War are characteristically perverse, suggesting the 'victory of the skilful,
riding their machines as did the feudal knights their armoured horses'
rather than of the 'drilled and docile masses': 'During the Great War
Germany had four hundred submarine commanders, and sixty per cent
of the damage done was the work of twenty-four men'.[142] It is a reading
of the Great War which has if nothing else the virtue of originality,
a reading which rewrites history in terms of Yeatsian (via Robert

[137] See Martin Stephen, *Poems of the First World War: 'Never Such Innocence'* (London: J. M.
Dent, 1993), p. xi. He points out that veterans remember the war with sadness and
repulsion, but predominantly with pride. A recent documentary interviewed survivors of
Passchendaele. One veteran argued that it *had* been worth the sacrifice, since 'the Ger-
mans were bent on world domination'. Another affirmed with pride that 'we held our
own'. (*The Soldier's Pilgrimage*, BBC2, 11 Nov. 1998).
[138] *Autobiographies*, 576.
[139] *Explorations*, 441.
[140] 'Under Ben Bulben', *CP*, 398.
[141] *Oxford Book of Modern Verse*, p. xxxv.
[142] *Explorations*, 425.

Gregory) heroics. But 'some just war' is characteristically vague. Actual war, when it does appear, always fails, like the actual Ireland, to live up to Yeats's expectations of it. The poet who labours in the service of an 'imaginary Ireland'[143] also labours in the service of an imaginary war. As Roy Foster has noted, 'only partly joking': 'for Yeats's life, the only analyst you need is Clausewitz. And Yeats certainly lived as if following the maxims of the great theorist of war.'[144] Glorification of war, in imaginary if not real terms, may be inherent in this, but in the context of Yeats's thinking, the only just war is the one which is lost. '[V]ictory', in the post-war world is, as it was pre-war, 'the sacrifice of a man to himself'. Clausewitz argues that

War is ... chameleon-like in character, because it changes its colour in some degree in each particular case, but it is also ... a wonderful trinity, composed of the original violence of its elements, hatred and animosity, which may be looked upon as blind instinct; of the play of probabilities and chance, which make it a free activity of the soul; and of the subordinate nature of a political instrument, by which it belongs purely to the reason.

The first of these three phases concerns more the people; the second, more the General and his Army; the third, more the Government. ... A theory which would leave any one of [these three tendencies] out of account, or set up any arbitrary relation between them, would immediately become involved in such a contradiction with the reality, that it might be regarded as destroyed at once by that alone.[145]

Clausewitz may be a helpful figure for understanding Yeats up to a point, but Yeats, like war, is chameleon-like in character with an underlying consistency. He is prone to imaginative identification, as he sees fit, with up to all three tendencies, or, in the case of real warfare, with none of them. And he celebrates, or exaggerates, the arbitrariness of the relation between them, supremely indifferent to, more probably delighting in, the ensuing contradiction with reality. One is tempted to speculate that if the prevailing trend in the 1920s had been belief in a heroic 'gay struggle without hope', Yeats might have advocated in his poetry the dreams and aspirations of liberalism. While the link between war and politics is indisputable in Yeats, the nature of it never belongs 'purely to the reason'.

---

[143] *E & I*, 246.
[144] 'Writing a Life of W. B. Yeats', *Irish Review*, 21 (Autumn/Winter 1997), 96.
[145] *On War*, 121–2.

To castigate Yeats for illiberal views may be to miss some of the difficulties that he constantly struggled to accommodate and/or negotiate in the relation between visible and invisible warfare. It can also be a way of denying the history and responsibility of liberal ideology on the grounds of apparently non-totalitarian, non-ideological, (non-existent) consensual politics. Equally, to work, as Heaney does, for a humanizing of Yeats, is also to do him less than justice. One reason why Yeats is not considered as a 'war poet', at least in relation to the Great War, may be because the tendency has been, deceptively, to equate 'war poet' with 'anti-war poet', and to judge Great War poetry according to the preoccupations of the famous Great War soldier poets. It is a tendency, in other words, which has sometimes assumed that a form of conscientious objection to war must be inherent in war writing. That Yeats's work does not receive attention in relation to the Great War, in comparison with its perceived response to other historical events, notably the Easter Rising and the Civil War, indicates that the Great War tends to fall between two versions of literary history: in England, the view that the soldier-poet response to the war is a norm by which other responses can be judged; in Ireland, the assumption that the Great War has a minimal impact on indigenous literary development. Yeats's role in propounding the latter view, and his high-profile criticism of the soldier-poet response, should not obscure recognition of the influence of the Great War in the formation of his aesthetic, notably in the 1920s, or the fact that such influence disrupts the categories he himself endorses.

CHAPTER THREE

Robert Graves: Resisting the Canon

> I feel Somme trenches give me the right even to
> blasphemy of the Holy Spirit if I feel so inclined.
>
> Robert Graves[1]

> It was a virtue not to stay,
> To go our headstrong and heroic way
>
> Robert Graves[2]

I

Derek Mahon suggested in 1974 that

The time is coming fast, if it isn't already here, when the question, 'Is So-and-so really an *Irish* writer?' will clear a room in seconds. Was Kafka a Czech writer or a German one? Picasso a Spanish painter or a French one? These questions are interesting up to a point, but there is no need to find answers to them. Was Yeats, after all, an Irish poet or an English one? The answer is, both.... The question is semantic, and not important except in so far as the writer himself makes it so.[3]

The comments are made in relation to Louis MacNeice; they serve also as a useful starting point for an understanding of Robert Graves. Mahon's combination of disingenuousness and perceptiveness characterizes critical views of Graves's position in Irish and English literary traditions, as much as Mahon's own comments about Graves give the lie to his conclusion above. The question, in other words, is also important insofar as other writers make it so: hence, as will be seen,

---

[1] 'To Robert Nichols', 2 Feb. 1917, *In Broken Images: Selected Letters of Robert Graves 1914–1946*, ed. Paul O'Prey (London: Hutchinson, 1982), 66.

[2] 'The White Goddess', *Complete Poems*, ii, ed. Beryl Graves and Dunstan Ward (Manchester: Carcanet Press, 1997), 179.

[3] 'MacNeice in Ireland and England', in Terence Brown and Alec Reid (eds.) *Time Was Away: The World of Louis MacNeice* (Dublin: Dolmen Press, 1974), 113.

the reconsideration of MacNeice in the light of his influence on contemporary Irish poets. Graves's anthology history is complex; his self-definitions even more so. For Mahon, Graves is 'an honorary Irishman at best', an 'odd inclusion[s]' in *The Faber Book of Irish Verse*.[4] In contrast, John Montague not only includes him in that anthology, but he gives him more space than he gives to either F. R. Higgins or John Hewitt, and uses him as a constant reference point in the introduction.[5] Graves himself claims in 1959 that his poems 'have never adopted a foreign accent or colouring; they remain true to the Anglo-Irish poetic tradition into which I was born'.[6] In the English tradition, Graves is seen as a canonical figure because of *Goodbye to All That* and *I, Claudius*; in recent years he has been excluded altogether from (versions of) the Irish canon. None of Graves's work is included in the 1986 *New Oxford Book of Irish Verse*, or in the 1991 *Field Day Anthology of Irish Writing*. Nor is there an entry for Graves in the 1996 *Oxford Companion to Irish Literature*. But although the War is the event which apparently locates him within English history and the English class system (via *Goodbye to All That*), it is also the event which directs him poetically in a way which has been seen as tangential to the twentieth-century tradition of English poetry. Hence, the first full-length study of Graves's poetry, published in 1960, states, rather confusingly, that 'Robert Graves's place in English poetry is an isolated one', but that 'Though partly Anglo-Irish and partly German by descent, Graves is essentially an English poet'.[7] And 'Anglo-Irish', Graves's own perspective, is equally problematical: while it might designate any or all Irish writing in English, it has also been associated more specifically with the Irish Literary Revival and/or the Ascendancy and, as a result, the term does not sit comfortably on any writer after 1922. In one sense, then, if Graves is born into an 'Anglo-Irish poetic tradition', the tradition, unlike the poet, does not survive the Anglo-Irish War.

The question is on one level, as Mahon rightly points out, 'semantic'. But the semantic quibble is also in this case, as with MacNeice, indicative of the more complex issue of how the poet locates himself, and is located within, history. Graves is, from a critical point of view, relatively

---

[4]   'Mother Tongue', review of John Montague (ed.), *The Faber Book of Irish Verse, New Statesman*, 29 (Mar. 1974), 452.
[5]   See Montague (ed.), *The Faber Book of Irish Verse* (London: Faber, 1974), 24, 29, 34–5.
[6]   Foreword to *Collected Poems 1959* (London: Cassell, 1959).
[7]   J. M. Cohen, *Robert Graves* (London and Edinburgh: Oliver and Boyd Ltd., 1960), 3.

neglected on both sides of the Irish Sea, in spite of his popularity. He receives attention in most (though not all) studies of First World War poetry, though as a secondary figure in relation to Owen, Rosenberg, or Sassoon. Full-length studies of his poetry and prose have appeared in the last thirty years, and journals were and are published devoted solely to Graves criticism. But the neglect is of a slightly different kind. He is too often perceived as a transcendental eccentric whose White Goddess thinking seduces a few disciples, but whose influence for most contemporary poets is stylistic only after the 1920s: it is primarily in these terms that his influence on the Movement is acknowledged. The form of neglect is symptomatic of the canonical confusion surrounding his work. The confusion itself is in part a result of the turbulent history of the war years in Ireland and England and the quest in both countries for a kind of national self-definition. It is also a result of Graves's own self-understanding acquired in response to that past. In other words, perceptions, and self-perceptions, of Graves's place in Irish, English, and Anglo-Irish traditions have been distorted, sometimes deliberately, by and in his response to the Great War. That response dominates Graves's work from the First World War years to the 1940s *The White Goddess* and, implicitly, beyond. In a sense, Graves's aesthetic can be seen as committed solely to the attempt to deal with the effect of the war. The attempt has potentially interesting implications for English and Irish literary traditions, if only because, in the process, anything and everything becomes expendable. His 1916 claim, quoted above, that 'Somme trenches give me the right even to blasphemy of the Holy Spirit' is never made so explicitly again, but it hovers behind his entire poetic career. The war, one might say, allows Graves to break all the rules. But a contrary impulse also holds sway: while the Great War permits, even forces, Graves to challenge political and literary canons, he retains, from 1914 throughout his career, a belief in the 'virtue' of the 'headstrong and heroic' gesture in the chivalrous war.

As with Yeats, actual warfare not only fails to live up to the heroism enshrined in the aesthetic, it also necessitates a re-evaluation of the poet's place in English and Irish literary traditions. In 1938, Graves, in 'Recalling War', gives what is perhaps his most accessible explanation of what war, more specifically the Great War, symbolized for him in terms of English literature, culture, and society. The poem is later excluded from his *Collected Poems*, as are the majority of what might be categorized his 'war poems':

War was foundering of sublimities,
Extinction of each happy art and faith
By which the world had still kept head in air,
Protesting logic or protesting love,
Until the unendurable moment struck—
The inward scream, the duty to run mad.[8]

Where the exclusion of the 'war poems' might be seen as Graves's exercising of quality control, the suppression of 'Recalling War' is more complex. The poem is a bitter denunciation of the First World War and of the post-war politics which ultimately bring about the Second. It mocks the 'old importances'—'Wine, meat, log-fires... A weapon at the thigh...Even...a use again for God', all of which are 'tasteless honey oozing from the heart' because they are in the service of a bankrupt mythology.[9] Graves identifies both the tragedy of failed idealism and the need for idealism. 'Recalling War' is a crucial transitional poem, one which articulates the problem that dogged his poetry from 1916 onwards, but also one which recognizes that to 'run mad' may be an inescapable 'duty'. The poem articulates a dilemma; it does not suggest a solution. In a sense, the remainder of Graves's career, from 1938 onwards, is devoted to 'recalling war', to upholding that duty, but doing so in a context where 'art', 'faith', and 'protesting love' are central to, rather than sidelined by, the conflict. Once that context has been established the earlier poem is, in effect, redundant.

Michael Kirkham, in a 1969 study of Graves's poetry, identified four distinct stages in Graves's career: the first, up to 1926, was, he writes, 'one of confusion', of neurasthenia, of 'restless experiment' with minimal success. The years 1926–38 were 'the period of Laura Riding's influence'. From 1938 to 1959 Graves's work was 'dominated by the mythology of the White Goddess'; and from 1959 onwards, Graves begins another phase, celebrating the Black Goddess, drawing on the teachings of Sufism.[10] The distinctions drawn between these phases are useful, but as Kirkham also notes, there are underlying consistencies in spite of several false starts. The war neurosis of the early period has, he argues, 'made a permanent impression on [Graves's] personality and

---

[8] *Complete Poems*, ii. 92.
[9] The later version, in the *Complete Poems*, reads 'tasty honey'. The earlier version is repr. in Robert Graves, *Selected Poems*, ed. Paul O'Prey (London: Penguin, 1986), 98.
[10] *The Poetry of Robert Graves* (London: Athlone Press, 1969), 4–7.

therefore on the nature of his love poetry ever since'.[11] All these periods in Graves's work are dominated by two main concerns, both of which stem from the war and immediate post-war years: first, the search for a framework in which to write about, or perhaps more importantly, not write about the war itself; second, the need to situate his work in a context where he is freed from literary and political allegiances. Graves is preoccupied throughout his career with the same questions: how to understand, and write, history; how to write his personal and literary history; how to cope with the Great War. Those questions converge on and in *The White Goddess*: the book does not resolve conflict, but, as with Yeats's *A Vision*, it does, in both senses of the word, contain it. The framework Graves finds, one which works on the Yeatsian assumption that 'All creation is from conflict', proves as liberating for Graves's 1940s poetry as *A Vision* proved for Yeats's wartime 'Tower' sequence.

That poetic liberation comes slowly. During the Great War itself, Graves writes nothing to compare with the best of Owen's or Sassoon's work. In 'Strange Meeting', Owen outlines a potential aesthetic: 'I would go up and wash them from sweet wells, | Even with truths that lie too deep for taint'. But he also acknowledges that his responsibility to communicate the experience and horror of war denies him this path: a different kind of 'truth' is required. In contrast, Yeats condemns the soldier poets for precisely that attitude, for, in his view, sacrificing aesthetic principles in order to articulate suffering. Graves is incapable at this stage of wholehearted commitment to either approach, sharing neither Yeats's imaginative confidence, nor Owen's (and Sassoon's) single-mindedness about the role of the war poet. Twenty years after the war, he claims, in effect, that his only concern is with the 'truths that lie too deep for taint'. In the early 1920s he argues that poetry can only aspire to such truths: he acknowledges poetry as 'the dominating ideal', but an ideal which is 'remote and unrealizable'.[12] As one might expect, Graves's criticism serves primarily to illuminate the nature of his own poetry. In the early 1920s, caught between two states of mind, he treats neither the truth of war, nor truth, with the skill of his contemporaries. And at no point in this period does he come close to Owen's achievement, an achievement unrecognized by Yeats, which is to combine these two things.

[11] Ibid. 7.
[12] *The Common Asphodel: Collected Essays on Poetry 1922–1949* (London: Hamish Hamilton, 1949), p. viii.

Ironically, one of the reasons for imaginative paralysis may be the fact that Graves is never able to betray his commitment to a cause—in this instance the Great War—in a way which might have enabled his poetry in the war years. His early responses to the war are, unsurprisingly, stereotypical (although, as with all letters home from the trenches, to be treated with caution): 'I always enjoy trenches in a way, I must confess: I like feeling really frightened and if happiness consists in being miser-able in a good cause, why then I'm doubly happy. England's is good cause enough and the trenches are splendidly miserable.'[13] But however suspect this attitude may be, in late 1917, while he does not put it in quite the same terms, he does argue that one should be 'ready for pride's sake to finish your contract whatever it costs you', and that he 'believe[s] ... in keeping to agreements when everybody else keeps them'.[14] In 1927, in *A Survey of Modernist Poetry*, Graves dissociates himself from the characteristics of the war generation of Modernists. Nevertheless, his comments do shed light on the difficulties he himself experienced some years earlier. The 'lost generation' is, he writes, a generation which 'has tried everything and like Ecclesiastes found it vanity'. It is

a generation that the War came upon at its most impressionable stage and taught the necessity for a self-protective scepticism of the stability of all human relationships, particularly of all national and religious institutions, of all existing moral codes, of all sentimental formulas for future harmony. From the War it also learned a scale of emotional excitement and depression with which no subsequent variations can compete; yet the scale was too nervously destructive to be wished for again.[15]

In this analysis, it is not simply the experience of war that invalidates institutions, but the soldier poet's ultimate commitment to his role within the Great War. If the war taught scepticism about almost every-thing that had previously been taken for granted, then paradoxically it demanded, and received, an unparalleled commitment to the war itself as an aberrant substitute for all other institutions, to 'the duty to run mad'. There is, in these terms, no adequate response to the experience of war, at least in any conventional way, since the experience itself invalidates any frame of reference in which the response can be made.

---

[13] 'To Edward Marsh', 15 Mar. 1916, *In Broken Images*, 43.
[14] 'To Siegfried Sassoon', 27 Oct. 1917, ibid. 85.
[15] Robert Graves and Laura Riding, *A Survey of Modernist Poetry* (London: Heinemann, 1927), 226.

J. B. Priestley describes the outbreak of war as 'a conscription of the spirit . . . a challenge to what we felt was our untested manhood'.[16] But the spirit is then betrayed by the nature of the Great War itself. Since, in Graves's view, 'The disillusion of the War has been completed by the Peace, by the continuation of the old régime patched up with political Fascism',[17] all institutions and moral certainties—literary, political, re-ligious—remain open to reconstitution or outright rejection even after commitment to the war has ended. Far from being liberating, that situation is paralysing: the spirit conscripted, with no worthy cause. Hence, the early poem 'Peace', written in 1918 before the Armistice, imagines two directions in which the peaceful world can go, both equally reductive—repetition of the state of war, or a faked, ignorant, and therefore illusory happiness. Effectively trapped, and unable to propose an alternative, the poet concludes: 'Better we had all died at first'.[18] Anticipating 'Peace' differs little from 'Recalling War' since in both 'the future we devote | To yet more boastful visions of despair'.[19]

In Graves's literary criticism in the early 1920s he develops a theory of poetry in response to the effect of the Great War. *Poetic Unreason*, published in 1925 after being, as he describes in the Author's Note, 'cast and re-cast nine times', attempts an analysis of his own situation as a poet, but like the later 'Recalling War' it does not find a satisfactory solution. The book is significant in two ways: its methodology and approach pre-empt the later *The White Goddess*; but it is differentiated from the later period by an attitude which is fundamentally historicist. In *Poetic Unreason* he argues that

Literary history if it can be written at all had best be written in this style, a study of mutations with an account of their necessity according to the religious, political, economic and other interests of the environment which produced them.[20]

It is precisely this historical approach which he later goes to some lengths to deny, but it is central to *Poetic Unreason*, to the extent that the poet, and the poems, are little more than the tools of society. It is, he writes, the poet's duty to 'stand in the middle of the larger society to

[16] Quoted in Peter Vansittart, *Voices from the Great War* (1981; London: Pimlico, 1998), 262.

[17] Graves and Riding, *A Survey of Modernist Poetry*, 226.

[18] *Poems about War*, ed. William Graves (London: Cassell, 1988), 67.

[19] 'Recalling War', *Complete Poems*, ii. 92.

[20] *Poetic Unreason and Other Studies* (London: Cecil Palmer, 1925), 251–2.

which he belongs and reconcile in his poetry the conflicting views of every group, trade, class and interest in that society; he must be before he is a poet in any full sense, scientist, philosopher, mechanic, clerk, bagman, journalist'.[21] 'Every poem', he asserts, 'can only be fairly judged in its own context'.[22] Barely recognizable here is the author of *The White Goddess*, where the poet has only one responsibility—devotion to the Muse.

Graves's conception of the aesthetic in *Poetic Unreason* works on the Yeatsian principle that 'All creation is from conflict'. 'Poetry', he argues, 'presupposes a conflict in the poet's mind of which [the] poem is the expression or the expression of its solution'.[23] The book is designed to

show Poetry as a record of the conflicts between various pairs of Jekyll and Hyde, or as a record of the solution of these conflicts. In the period of conflict, poetry may be either a partisan statement in the emotional or in the intellectual mode of thought of one side of the conflict; or else a double statement of both sides of the conflict, one side appearing in the manifest statement, that is, in the intellectual mode, the other in the latent content, that is, in the emotional mode, with neither side intelligible to the other.[24]

The Jekyll and Hyde theory stems, obviously, from Graves's neurasthenia, and, through the influence of W. H. R. Rivers, his interest in Freudian theory. The early poems explore the split personality, the 'witting' waking self, and the 'unwitting' nightmare self. In 'The Pier-Glass' the cracked mirror gives back a reflection of the schizophrenic nature of experience. The 'dishevelled' self with 'Sleep-staring eyes' hovers between life and death, is forced once again to confront the question 'Kill or forgive?', and answers in a way which foreshadows the later sacrificial violence in *The White Goddess*: 'Kill, strike the blow again, spite what shall come.' 'Reproach' challenges the poet's alter ego: 'I know not even your name … Speak, speak, or how may a child know | His ancestral sin?'[25] The Great War soldier poet always worked as two different people. Sassoon writes that 'One cannot be a good soldier and a good poet at the same time', yet fills both roles;[26] Owen, in

---

[21] *Poetic Unreason and Other Studies* (London: Cecil Palmer, 1925), 82.
[22] Ibid. 29.   [23] Ibid. 124.   [24] Ibid. 52–3.
[25] 'The Pier-Glass', *Poems 1914–1926* (London: Heinemann, 1927), 72–3. The second half of the poem was subsequently cut, and the revised version appears in *Complete Poems*, i, ed. Beryl Graves and Dunstan Ward (Manchester: Carcanet Press, 1995), 118–19. 'Reproach', *Complete Poems*, i. 120.
[26] *Siegfried Sassoon's Diaries 1915–1918*, ed. Rupert Hart-Davis (London: Faber, 1983), 271.

'Strange Meeting' confronts the anomaly of the enemy as friend, agon-
izes over his role as Christian and killer. For Graves, who reads about his
own death in the newspapers, a 'death' reported to his family on his
twenty-first birthday, that sense of the dual self is even more exaggerated.
As a result, although there are several obviously neurasthenic poems in
the 1921 *The Pier-Glass*, a collection which is both 'a reaction against
shell-shock' and 'an attempt to stand up to the damned disease',[27] more
often than not, the latent subject of war is suppressed in the early poems
under a 'manifest', often light-hearted and trivial content. The 1920
collection *Country Sentiment* is, Graves writes, a collection of 'nursery
toys' with some 'occasional corpses that blunder up' among them.[28]

The terms of the Jekyll and Hyde theory are expanded in *Poetic
Unreason* in response to social and political circumstances to encompass
debates about Romanticism and Classicism, and relative and absolute
truth. The Great War demonstrates to Graves that poetry can only be
judged relatively:

The recent War with its immediate sequel of peace and depression provides an
easy example of unusually violent flow and ebb in the sea of literary criticism; it
is now possible to read that history without much prejudice and to see how the
national aesthetic canons of good and bad, corresponded closely with, and were
no more stationary than national political sentiment.[29]

It is this reading of literary history that he spends his career from 1927
onwards undermining. But in *Poetic Unreason*, he accepts the correspond-
ence between 'national political sentiment' and 'national aesthetic
canons' as inevitable, concerned primarily that poetry and politics
should be as sensitive as possible to each other's mutations. Thus, his
criticism of Sassoon in 1918—'you seem to think there are more people
who love War than there really are in this fifth year of war with our $3\frac{1}{2}$
million casualty list. And poetry shouldn't be all propaganda because
a war is on'[30]—is not an indictment of Sassoon for dancing attendance
on public opinion in his poems. It is rather the opposite: Sassoon is at
fault because he lacks sensitivity to public requirements of poetry.
Graves, on the other hand, with a detachment from the act of writing
that the later White Goddess muse poet would never condone, is quick

---

[27] Robert Graves, 'To Edmund Blunden', 10 Mar. 1921, *In Broken Images*, 124.
[28] 'To Siegfried Sassoon', 9 July 1918, ibid. 95.
[29] *Poetic Unreason*, 18–19.
[30] 'To Siegfried Sassoon', 26 Aug. 1918, *In Broken Images*, 101.

to recognize in 1919 that 'war poetry is played out . . . commercially, for another five or ten years' and that 'Country Sentiment is the most acceptable dope now . . . the name I've given my new poems'.[31]

Throughout *Poetic Unreason*, Graves defends those aspects of poetry misunderstood, or misrepresented, in their historical context. In other words, he defends the 'illogical element' on the grounds that good and bad in poetry are only relative terms, and open to negotiation. (By 1948, the 'illogical element' is defended in absolute terms.) '[N]ational aesthetic canons of good and bad' mutate in response to historical events; similarly, he argues that Classicism and Romanticism have been judged, or misjudged, throughout literary history in terms of political debates. In *A Survey of Modernist Poetry*, Graves and Riding argue the necessity for distinguishing 'false modernism, or faith in history, from genuine modernism, or faith in the immediate, the *new* doings of poems (or poets or poetry) as not necessarily derived from history' or 'from conscientious imitation of the time-spirit'.[32] In *Poetic Unreason*, while Graves might be fully aware of the ways in which political sentiment can misrepresent artistic achievement, he is concerned not to transcend history, but to negotiate passage for his own poetry by working through, not above, a political quagmire. The arguments, he later points out, are 'not confidently drawn'.[33] They *are* confidently drawn in *The White Goddess* when he no longer reveals an insecurity about his own status and role as poet. 'The Illogical Element in Poetry', in *Poetic Unreason*, defends the idea that later becomes central to *The White Goddess*: 'associative thought is as modern and reputable a mode as intellectual thought'.[34] He argues that 'though Romantic thought cannot be exactly foreseen, neither any more can intellectual thought'.[35] The difference in the earlier book is that the arguments of *Poetic Unreason* are very obviously formulated in response to canonical and political judgements:

It will be found I believe that wherever the Greek tradition survives strongly and there is a recrudescence of this conflict between Classically and Romantically inclined poets it will always be contemporary with a political conflict between Order and Liberty.

---

[31] 'To Edmund Blunden', 12 July 1919, ibid. 113.
[32] Graves and Riding, *A Survey of Modernist Poetry*, 158.
[33] *The Common Asphodel*, p. ix.
[34] *Poetic Unreason*, 127. The idea resurfaces in the discussion of analeptic or proleptic thought in ch. 19 of *The White Goddess*.
[35] *Poetic Unreason*, 133.

Order is so strongly upheld nowadays that Romanticism, except where it is deified in Poetry or mysticism, has long been banished to the nursery of the 'primitive' community.[36]

Graves describes his own attitude in the early 1920s as 'increasingly historical', that he tended to view modern poets as 'writing behaviour-istically according to the political camps into which they were divided'.[37] *Poetic Unreason*, however much it foreshadows aspects of *The White Goddess*, does not prove liberating for Graves because it has its sights too firmly fixed on those political camps, particularly the ones which might exert the strongest claims on him, or misrepresent his work.

II

By the late 1940s, his public stance has altered considerably. The first edition of *The White Goddess* was published in 1948, and while it might share some of the concerns of *Poetic Unreason*, these have now become latent content. In 1949 Graves writes:

for the last twenty-two years [I] have abandoned the view that the poet is a public servant ministering to the caprices of a world in perpetual flux. I now regard him as independent of fashion and public service, a servant only of the true Muse, committed on her behalf to continuous personal variations on a single pre-historic or post-historic poetic theme; and have thus ceased to feel the frantic strain of swimming against the stream of time.[38]

The introduction to *The Common Asphodel* is Graves's overview of his criticism from the early 1920s to the White Goddess era. He discards the 'historical' approach taken in *Poetic Unreason* and in his other works from the early to mid-1920s. He does not reject the stance taken with Laura Riding in *A Survey of Modernist Poetry*, since this book marks the beginning of a progressive de-historicizing. In 1927 he and Riding write:

True modernist poetry can appear equally at all stages of historical development from Wordsworth to Miss Moore. And it does appear when the poet forgets what is the correct literary conduct demanded of him in relation to contemporary institutions (with civilization speaking through criticism) and can write a poem having the power of survival in spite of its disregarding these demands.[39]

---

[36] Ibid. 126.   [37] *The Common Asphodel*, p. ix.   [38] Ibid. p. x.
[39] Graves and Riding, *A Survey of Modernist Poetry*, 186–7.

In 1949, he takes this a stage further, in claiming freedom from all spatial and temporal ties, except where they are essentials of the Muse herself. In such a context, the scepticism the war engendered can be ignored, and the notion of the adequacy or inadequacy of a poem's response to events within history is effectively defunct. The criteria by which 'national aesthetic canons' make value judgements are, it might appear, once again called into question. But in effect, Graves is not demanding a different court of appeal; rather he is invalidating any such judgements, regardless of the 'national political sentiment' from which they arise, by virtue of the imaginative autonomy bestowed on him by his Muse.

It is at this point that one is in danger of accepting Graves's criteria as sufficient explanation of and justification for his role as a poet, of accepting that 'divine' inspiration is autonomous and the poet's apparent freedom from the stream of time not a construct but a 'gift'. It is to credit Graves with an objectivity towards politics, history, and what might be termed 'geography' that he does not have; to accept 'the White Goddess' in a way which one would not accept, nor would be required to accept, Yeats's 'Vision'. In 1927, Graves misleadingly conflates 'history' and 'the time-spirit'. '[I]mitation of the time-spirit' means, in effect, either succumbing to, or challenging, the sentimental formulas and moral codes of the era. To claim that poems should not necessarily be derived from history is, for Graves, a way of saying that poetry should not be propagandist, either in the style of Jessie Pope, *or* of Siegfried Sassoon. Graves and Riding draw a distinction in *A Survey of Modernist Poetry* between 'poetry as something developing through civilization and as something developing organically by itself'. They argue that 'poetry does develop in the sense that it is contemporaneous with civilization; but for this reason it has even to protect itself from civilization, to resist, to a certain extent, contemporaneous influences'.[40] But to criticize poetry derived from history in this sense is not to say that a poem does not derive from within history. By 1949 that distinction, always blurred, seems to have disappeared, and with good reason. To set, as Graves does, 'fashion and public service' against a 'pre-historic' or 'post-historic' theme is to reduce engagement with history to nothing more than time-serving propaganda, and thus claim the impossible—the ability to disengage. Poetry no longer needs to 'protect itself from . . . contemporaneous influences' since it is, in this formula, unthreatened.

---

[40] Graves and Riding, *A Survey of Modernist Poetry*, 163.

Both Graves and Yeats are highly eclectic, constructing belief systems that will enable the poetry. But Yeats explicitly attempts to construct a tradition and define a taste by which he should be both judged and enjoyed; Graves treats the enabling of poetry as an arbitrary consequence of the system. The central figure of *A Vision* is Yeats himself; the whole system was revealed to him in order that he might have 'metaphors for poetry'.[41] In *The White Goddess*, while Graves is undoubtedly central to what is an intensely personal and autobiographical book, he still claims that the poet acts as servant of an objective reality not creator of a subjective system. Graves purports to project himself outside history, tradition, or moral judgement, under the guise not of escapism but of newly discovered mythological truth. Where Yeats constructs, in *A Vision*, a 'philosophy of history', Graves writes in *The White Goddess* a 'historical grammar to the language of poetic myth'[42] which is offered as a key to understanding his autonomy as poet outside (above) the constraints of history (in the 'time-spirit' sense) and community. As one might expect, it is a key that proves somewhat elusive, the problem being as elusive as the key itself: 'how to forge a pair of tongs with which to hold the red-hot metal while one is forging a pair of tongs'.[43]

Cryptic parts of it may be, but on the whole, *The White Goddess* is less esoteric than 'Graves-speak' implies. The contradiction at the heart of the book is that as it attempts to liberate the poetic imagination from the stream of time, it is fundamentally concerned with history, and not merely the recovered history of a mythological past. Like Yeats's *A Vision*, *The White Goddess* is first and foremost a war book: it enshrines conflict at the heart of creativity, applauds aristocratic warfare, and revalidates the 1914 'conscription of the spirit' in new terms. 'Desire some just war'; 'Love war because of its horror, that belief may be changed, civilisation renewed', was Yeats's notorious attitude in the 1920s and 1930s, formulated in response to the carnage of the Great War and the Irish Civil War. In the Second World War, Graves writes:

the Cypriots understood the mystery of the God of the Year by describing him as *amphidexios*... and putting a weapon in each of his hands. He is himself and his other self at the same time, king and supplanter, victim and murderer, poet and satirist... [P]oets are aware that each twin must conquer in turn, in an

---

[41] *AV*, 8.

[42] Robert Graves, 'To Derek Savage', 16 Dec. 1946, *Between Moon and Moon: Selected Letters of Robert Graves 1946–1972*, ed. Paul O'Prey (London: Hutchinson, 1984), 38.

[43] Ibid.

agelong and chivalrous war fought for the favours of the White Goddess . . . The war between Good and Evil has been waged in indecent and painful way during the past two millennia because the theologians, not being poets, have forbidden the Goddess to umpire it, and made God impose on the Devil impossible terms of unconditional surrender.[44]

The trigger for such remarks is less the whole past two millennia than it is the identity crisis experienced by the Great War soldier—victim and murderer—and the impossible terms of unconditional surrender imposed at Versailles, terms which, in part, engendered the Second World War. The book engages, if obliquely, with the politics of the 1940s and thus, over its shoulder, with the politics of the Great War and inter-war period, and it does so through a demythologizing that works within the tradition of Vico and Herder. The ' "master-key" of Vico's science' is, as Paul Hamilton writes, 'the discovery of the mythological or *poetic* sources of civilization', and the 'exercise in poetic interpretation' is required in order to comprehend the present position and evolution of modern society.[45] For Graves, the language of poetic myth and the fruits of poetical inspiration are essential components in the process of historical analysis. To understand myths not as 'absurd fiction[s]',[46] but as the proper descriptions of truth in a particular historical period is also, in a sense, to demythologize. In consequence, *The White Goddess* is far from apolitical in its implications; one might go so far as to claim that it borrows the methodology, and the tradition, which underpin not only turn-of-the-century cultural nationalism but also 1940s Nazism. In doing so the book attempts to challenge nationalist or fascist ideologies on their own terms.[47] It has, therefore, a seriousness, and a contemporary resonance, that too often lurk unseen behind the layers of moon goddesses, magic mushrooms, and analeptic visions.

The White Goddess is the culmination of a process which seeks, not so much to sanitize violence, as to legitimize some forms of violence, and not others, within a revised historical framework. In doing so, the poet is also able to reassert the value of poetry in an ironic and largely unsym-

---

[44] *The White Goddess*, ed. Grevel Lindop (4th edn., London: Faber and Faber, 1999), 437.
[45] *Historicism* (London: Routledge, 1996), 35.
[46] Graves writes: 'I use the word "myth" in its strict sense of "verbal iconograph" without the derogatory sense of "absurd fiction" that it has acquired' (*The White Goddess*, 17).
[47] See e.g. *The White Goddess*, ch. 26, 'Return of the Goddess' (pp. 465 ff.), which challenges Hitler's reading of history.

pathetic age, to resolve, or hold together, contrary thoughts. The violence that paralysed the poet, as a poet, in the Great War is transformed in *The White Goddess* into an enabling and essential aspect of the poetic imagination and poetic truth:

Cerridwen abides. Poetry began in the matriarchal age and derives its magic from the moon, not from the sun. No poet can hope to understand the nature of poetry unless he has had a vision of the Naked King crucified to the lopped oak, and watched the dancers, red-eyed from the acrid smoke of the sacrificial fires, stamping out the measure of the dance, their bodies bent uncouthly forward, with a monotonous chant of: 'Kill! kill! kill!' and 'Blood! blood! blood!'[48]

Graves's constant reorganization of his *Collected Poems*—the exclusion of early work and the inclusion of, and emphasis on, most of the poetry written after a complex mythology has evolved as an explanation of his verse—suggests that he, as much as, or even more than, Yeats, faces experiential problems that demand the appearance of resolution before poetry is possible. That he resorts, unlike Yeats, to what looks, initially, to be a purely transcendental 'solution' indicates a depth of conflict within the poet that must be in part attributable to his experience of war and his consequent neurasthenia. Miranda Seymour also argues, persuasively, that the death of Robert's son, David, in the Second World War, while serving with Graves's former regiment, the Royal Welch, 'acted as a catalyst' for the White Goddess mythology.[49] The divided self is no longer the problem in *The White Goddess*, it is the central feature, and strength, of the poet/lover. The 'God of the Year' is in many respects an autobiographical figure, one who encapsulates Graves's conflicts as dutiful soldier and dedicated poet: he is 'victim and murderer, poet and satirist'. The poet's task is creative; the satirist's destructive.[50] The inherent contradiction in the soldier poet's position—creator and destroyer—is the catalyst for the Jekyll and Hyde theory of poetry Graves expounds in *Poetic Unreason*. But in *The White Goddess*, the 'God of the Year' also appeases guilt: the poet/soldier is no longer paralysed by a contradictory role, since 'his right hand does not know what his left hand does'.[51] The split personality becomes central to an aesthetic that seeks rather than evades violence.

[48] Ibid. 439.
[49] See, *Robert Graves: Life on the Edge* (London and New York: Doubleday, 1995), 305, 308–9.
[50] *The White Goddess*, 435.   [51] Ibid. 437.

The '*amphidexious*' self in *The White Goddess* reworks the soldier-poet dilemma; it also serves its purpose in relation to 'national aesthetic canons' and 'national political sentiment'. If Graves is caught in a conflict between the roles of poet and soldier, he is also caught between English and Irish traditions. From this point of view, his early views on Romanticism and Classicism might be seen as preparing the way for use of mythology, more importantly Celtic mythology, without the nationalist connotations inevitably attendant upon Celticism at the time of the Irish Literary Revival (and after), and without being condemned by the English Establishment as a frivolous member of that 'profoundly irresponsible, and profoundly lovable race that fight like fiends, argue like children, reason like women',[52] which his parentage renders possible. Half-German, half-Irish, he represents division between Celt and Teuton united within the English tradition, and it is in these terms that the problem of the divided self is later transformed into a symbolic dialogue between the Muse and history. As Fussell puts it:

Being a 'Graves'... is a way—perhaps the only way left—of rebelling against the positivistic pretensions of non-Celts and satirizing the preposterous scientism of the twentieth century. His enemies are always the same: solemnity, certainty, complacency, pomposity, cruelty. And it was the Great War that brought them to his attention.[53]

Bergonzi describes Graves, in his early work, as 'a quintessential Georgian', but one whose Irish background 'separated him from the more conventional love of rural England of the other Georgians', his 'attachment to myth' a 'constant element in his poetry'.[54] In a way, this is to take Graves's explanations of self too literally. 'Irishness' is not an innate quality, nor is 'myth' specifically Irish. For Graves, a poet born and reared in England, it is the Great War which necessitates a revaluation of his 'soul-landscape', a process which his Irish descent complicates as much as it assists. What would be true to say, however, is that Graves seizes upon the 'Celtic element', as others have done before him, because it represents symbolic separation from the England he comes to know and not to love in the Great War. Ireland is conventionally a means of interrogating, perhaps reforming, but certainly contrasting

---

[52] Rudyard Kipling quoted in Graves, *The Common Asphodel*, 223.

[53] *The Great War and Modern Memory* (London: OUP, 1975), 206.

[54] *Heroes' Twilight: A Study of the Literature of the Great War* (London: Constable, 1965), 65.

English imperialism. His precursor in this is Matthew Arnold, who, in his *Study of Celtic Literature*, takes the Celticism of Wales and Ireland as a possible means of overcoming the tendencies of Victorian England which he dislikes: the Celts, Arnold claims, are 'inextricably bound up with us, and ... we English ... have ... a thousand latent springs of possible sympathy with them'.[55] He seeks to cancel out what he perceives as the faults of English and Irish character by combining the best of both; to restrain the Celtic temperament and soften the English one. His ideal is the 'fusion of all the inhabitants of these islands into one, homogeneous, English-speaking whole, the breaking down of barriers between us'.[56] That ideal is created by combining 'the good of our German part, the good of our Latin part, the good of our Celtic part'.[57] In 1925, Graves's views, expressed in relation to the English ballad, and an implicit defence of his own ancestry, are not dissimilar:

> where the air and fire of the Gael, the sea and fire of the Norse, the earth and fire of the Saxons can be reconciled in amity with other lesser contributions, that fifth essence or quintessence of poetry appears, which is variously known as the spirit of wonder, as genius, as divine inspiration. . . . The prominent poets of a relatively unmixed race usually have in them very few contradictions with which their poetry can make play and enlarge itself[58]

Arnold's Celt–Teuton theories have become, in the context of Irish politics, notorious. He is perceived as setting up a masculine–feminine, England–Ireland opposition which is then subverted by Irish nationalism in order to inspire loyalty to the (female) Irish nation persecuted by the aggressive English (male). Seamus Deane suggests that Arnold provided Ireland (inadvertently perhaps) with a cultural myth, that his version of 'killing Home Rule by kindness', because it came too late, accidentally colluded in the Irish nationalist campaign and was responsible, in part, for its eventual sectarian character.[59] If Arnold's theory was designed primarily to address the problems of England, Ireland functioning only as a means of illustrating those problems—'No service England can render the Celts by giving ... a share in her many good qualities, can', he writes, 'surpass that which the Celts can at this moment render England, by communicating to us some of theirs'[60]—

[55] *On the Study of Celtic Literature* (London: Macmillan, 1903), p. xx.
[56] Ibid. 10.   [57] Ibid. 145.
[58] *The English Ballad: A Short Critical Survey* (London: Ernest Benn Ltd., 1927), 36.
[59] 'Arnold, Burke and the Celts', *Celtic Revivals* (London: Faber, 1985), 17–27.
[60] *On the Study of Celtic Literature*, p. xii.

most interpretations have, for their own agendas, dragged him into a sphere he was not particularly concerned to address, that of Irish politics. Graves begins with an Arnoldian Celtic–Saxon fusion, for which he later substitutes his White Goddess: only in the goddess is the quintessence of poetry found. But there is not necessarily any alteration in his views; like Arnold he is concerned to address both art and England. They are, however, recast in non-geographical, apolitical, and impersonal terms in order to free him, unlike Arnold, from aesthetic or political canons.

'Ireland' functions in his aesthetic as the symbolic realm associated with eroticism, fear, the unknown, that which cannot be controlled, the romantic and the divine. What is remarkable, and for Graves, essential, is how little any of his perceptions of Ireland and 'Irishness' relate to Ireland itself. He admits to being Irish (wholly or half as the context demands) only when it is advantageous to do so, in other words when admission takes on symbolic resonance in the all-encompassing mythology surrounding his poetry. In *Goodbye to All That*, his early erotic experiences, and the mingled terror and pleasure they evoke in him, are forerunners of the goddess-love of his later years, and it is notable that these symbolic encounters, or 'memories', are associated with the Irish or 'Irish' characteristics.[61] One might wonder, therefore, why Graves does not evoke the Irish connection more often and more explicitly. His view of the Anglo-Irish War gives a clue to the problem of inheritance. Graves, reading an ancient Irish poem, feels 'an extreme conflict between the Gospel doctrine of forgiveness and the natural warlike spirit of the Irish'. The poem, he says,

had a particular appeal to me who am at one moment a sentimentalist of extreme republican sympathy and at another convinced by what amounts to a religious axiom that both sides in the Anglo-Irish quarrel have been equally in the wrong. My appreciation of the satire amounted to a recrudescence of the sentimental spirit more than usually repressed of late[62]

Irish republicanism can be a 'conscription of the spirit' in the way English patriotism was perceived in 1914. But Graves's experience of war makes problematical any sentimental devotion to a political or worldly struggle. Freedom from history may be the concern of many poets; for Graves, with the knowledge that land is bought with blood, it

---

[61] *Goodbye to All That* (1929, 2nd edn., 1957; London: Penguin, 1960), 20–3, 39.
[62] *Poetic Unreason*, 167.

is freedom from geography that is of equal importance. Celticism, as it relates to Ireland, is highly politicized; the 'romanticism' of the ancient legends which his father, Alfred Perceval Graves, celebrates in his introduction to *The Book of Irish Poetry* is intimately bound up with the Irish Literary Revival, and with romantic nationalism:

> These sprays of Druid oak and yew,
> And Red Branch rowans hoar with dew,
> And sedges sighing from the strand
> Whence Oiseen rode to Fairy Land [63]

Hence, for Robert Graves, the idea of Ireland is relevant, or those elements he chooses to emphasize from ancient Ireland, but only when divorced from the context of the real Ireland. Celtic myth might be redemptive for Graves, the 'Celtic Twilight' is less so. 'Celtic' is, or seems to be for Graves, not only an appropriate substitute for 'Ireland', but equally interchangeable with 'Wales'. In this context, his comment that 'My father...broke the geographical connexion with Ireland, for which I cannot be too grateful to him',[64] becomes less flippant and more comprehensible. One might think that if England, with all its ideas, is to be so completely abandoned, as it is at the end of *Goodbye to All That*, Ireland could offer an alternative focus for loyalty. But geographical connection with Ireland might have stultified the growth of a complex and, for the poet, redemptive mythology, a mythology which can uphold the notion of loyalty, but never of loyalty to place. A 'lost land' can lose its romantic appeal in the midst of civil war, and Kathleen ni Houlihan become, as AE described her, 'a vituperative old hag'.[65] Graves, sent to Ireland in 1918, paints a stereotypical picture—'a nearly naked girl-child, who sat down in the gutter and rummaged in a heap of refuse for filthy pieces of bread...a donkey, which began to bray'—and says 'I had pictured Ireland exactly so, and felt its charm as dangerous'.[66] Dangerous because it could demand of him involvement on a less than transcendental level, he avoids that involvement on the somewhat spurious grounds that 'as an Irishman [he] did not care to be mixed up in Irish politics'.[67]

---

[63] *The Book of Irish Poetry* (Dublin: Talbot Press; London: T. Fisher Unwin, n.d.), p. xliii.
[64] *Goodbye to All That*, 15–16.
[65] Quoted in F. S. L. Lyons, *Culture and Anarchy in Ireland 1890–1939* (Oxford: OUP, 1982), 108.
[66] *Goodbye to All That*, 229.   [67] Ibid.

Daniel Hoffman suggests that Graves, in the search for a tradition, 'at first spurned these materials so close at hand', his Celtic heritage, 'because of his father's professional identification with Irish letters'.[68] The father 'motif' is, Edna Longley points out, immensely popular in contemporary Northern Irish writing. It 'suggests one means of getting at the various configurations the past assumes in [the poet's] imagination[s]'; it is 'through parents that the individual locates himself or herself in history, and Irish history remains in many respects a family affair'.[69] The Graves family, on a more literal level, illustrates both these preoccupations, and the canonical chaos that can ensue. If there is little consensus about Graves's 'identification with Irish letters', the same is true, though for different reasons, of his father, Alfred Perceval Graves. John Montague appropriates Robert Graves as an Irish poet, but dismisses Alfred Graves as a 'minor Victorian' revivalist.[70] On the other hand, Alfred Perceval Graves, unlike Robert, is included in the *Oxford Companion to Irish Literature*, perhaps by virtue of being born and brought up in Ireland (although, as the cases of John Montague and Tom Paulin suggest, this has never been a criterion for Irish canonization). The post-First World War relationship between Graves and his father is indicative of Gravesian anxieties about the past and location of the self in relation to that past. *Goodbye to All That* and Alfred Perceval Graves's autobiography *To Return to All That* are, on one level, texts engaged in a family squabble (about historical accuracy and the depiction of various members of the Graves tribe) which is also a squabble about the impact of the Great War and 'Irishness'. Alfred Perceval Graves writes: 'there is much in his [Robert Graves's] autobiography that I do not accept as accurate. For the change in his outlook I hold the war and recent experiences responsible.'[71] Having acknowledged this, he remains critical of those who 'encourage youngsters to write off their lives at thirty-three'.[72] In a way, this is symptomatic of the failure in understanding between generations that the war brought about. Where his father suggests a continuum, Robert Graves works

[68]   *Barbarous Knowledge: Myth in the Poetry of Yeats, Graves and Muir* (New York: OUP, 1967), 13.
[69]   ' "When Did You Last See Your Father?": Perceptions of the Past in Northern Irish Writing 1965–1985', *The Living Stream: Literature and Revisionism in Ireland* (Newcastle: Bloodaxe, 1994), 152.
[70]   *Faber Book of Irish Verse*, 34.
[71]   *To Return to All That* (London: Jonathan Cape, 1930), 318.
[72]   Ibid. 343.

on the assumption that the past, to borrow a phrase from another Great
War survivor, is 'a foreign country: they do things differently there'.[73]
Robert Graves adopts this principle literally: 'I went abroad, resolved
never to make England my home again; which explains the "Goodbye
to All That" of this title.'[74] The same feeling is articulated by many other
Great War survivors, notably Vera Brittain, who writes: 'I have had—
like many, I suspect, of my War generation contemporaries—two quite
separate lives ... Between the first life that ended ... in 1918, and the
second that began ... in 1920, no links remain.'[75] Alfred Perceval Graves
has other grumbles. He implies that Robert Graves evades proper
acknowledgement of his Irish cultural inheritance, and complains that
his own role in Robert's career goes unrecorded: 'He gives me no credit
for the interest I always felt and showed in his poetry. During the War
I offered poems of his to editor after editor, and ... arranged ... for the
publication of *Over the Brazier*.'[76] Graves, in other words, whatever the
connotations of 'Anglo-Irish' later in life, chooses not to remember
a poetic debut made under the auspices of a leading light of the
Irish Literary Society. To deny the father is to deny a cultural tradition,
a stable past, and to attempt to redefine the self as ahistorical and
wandering free.

   In an early poem, 'The Poetic State', Graves resists the Irish past; in a
way it is a poem which attempts denial of the Muse. 'Poetry is', he writes
'my father's trade', and the poem attempts to 'annul the curse' of the
ancient Irish triad 'Which holds it death to mock and leave a poet ...
death likewise to love a poet' and 'death above all deaths to live a poet'.
The poem is later excluded from his *Collected Poems*: resistance to the
triad—the refusal to see himself as 'the desolate bard'—and the avowal
of self-determination in the face of tradition, implies resistance to the
goddess.

> But mocked, I see my weakness in that mocking,
> And loved, I charge myself with that love-making,
> Nor am I marked with beast's or angel's marking.[77]

---

[73] See L. P. Hartley, *The Go-Between* (1953; London: Penguin, 1958), 1.
[74] *Goodbye to All That*, 279.
[75] *Testament to Youth* (1933; London: Fontana, 1979), 495.
[76] See *To Return to All That*, 324, 333. Robert Graves does, however, dedicate *The English Ballad* (1927) to his father.
[77] *Complete Poems*, i. 274–5.

The emphasis on self is fallible; devotion, on the other hand, has connotations of infallibility. When the triad, 'It is death to mock a poet, to love a poet, to be a poet' reappears some years later in *The White Goddess*, it has been 'justified' and accepted in the context of his 'historical grammar of poetic myth' and freed from the personal associations that inspire 'The Poetic State'.[78] He makes use, then, of the mythology popularized by the Irish Literary Revival, but does not follow a conventional Revivalist path. (In view of the fact that Alfred Perceval Graves comes under fire from Seamus Deane as one who, in his song-writing, aided a 'sentimental and bowdlerizing process' in Ireland, it seems Graves was wise beyond his years not to get involved.)[79] *The White Goddess* draws on the conventional resources of the Revival, and Lindop goes so far as to suggest it might be the last product *of* the Irish Revival.[80] But its concern, politically speaking, lies more with Hitler, the Versailles Treaty, and the onset of the Cold War—'Mercury and Pluto black-guarding each other, while Apollo wields the atomic bomb as if it were a thunderbolt'[81]—than with turn-of-the-century cultural national-ism or the love of the land Daniel Corkery, in the 1930s, finds essential for the Irishman. The poetic landscape Graves constructs is beyond familial and temporal ties, and cannot be Ireland or England, in any realistic way, for that reason. Of the time spent in Wales in his childhood he writes:

Having no Welsh blood in us, we felt little temptation to learn Welsh, still less to pretend ourselves Welsh, but knew that country as a quite ungeographical region. . . . Had this been Ireland, we should have self-consciously learned Irish and local legends; but we did not go to Ireland, except once when I was an infant in arms. Instead we came to know Wales more purely, as a place with a history too old for local legends; while walking there we made up our own. . . . On our visits to Germany I had felt a sense of home in a natural human way, but above Harlech I found a personal peace independent of history or geography. The first poem I wrote as myself concerned those hills.[82]

The inference, as regards Ireland, is fairly obvious: his Irish blood will demand collusion in a nation's history and culture; whereas to know

[78]   *The White Goddess*, 441.

[79]   Deane, 'Popular Songs', in Deane (gen. ed.), *The Field Day Anthology of Irish Writing* (Derry: Field Day, 1991), ii. 76.

[80]   Grevel Lindop, introduction to *The White Goddess*, p. xii.

[81]   *The White Goddess*, 467.

[82]   *Goodbye to All That*, 34–5.

a place 'purely' is not to know it in any empirical sense at all. The self, as Graves constructs it, only comes into existence with the illusion of temporal and spatial independence. Wales is available to Graves as a kind of Ireland with the politics taken out. For MacNeice, it is a place where 'Celtic myth and Roman leadmine spill', which seems, in consequence, 'half way home, | One half of me approved and one half contraband'.[83] For Graves, it is not freighted with any of the burdens that the concept of 'home' brings with it. It is the landscape of 'Lost Acres', a place with no obligations, and no past—'we have no need | To plot these acres of the mind | With prehistoric fern and reed'—and, in a sense, no present: 'To walk there would be loss of sense.'[84]

Earlier than MacNeice, Graves sets up what can be conveniently termed an England–Ireland opposition, but unlike MacNeice (or, for that matter, Arnold), he restates that opposition in transcendental terms: 'None greater in the universe than the Triple Goddess!'[85] Celticism role-plays in an aesthetic based on conflict, but what Graves is denying Ireland (had he given it any thought) is the truth of Irish existence—its materialism, industrialization, its fairly large-scale participation in the event, the war, which causes the division in Graves's psyche that the mythology is designed to heal. Perhaps there is no greater myth than the one which leads him to assert his Irish identity in 1970; that Ireland is one of the few countries left 'where the name of Poet is everywhere honoured'.[86]

III

In some ways, considering his use and abuse of the Celtic element, it is surprising to find that Graves's closest poetic 'descendants' are, like his ancestors, Irish. Graves's own problematical constructions of Ireland and Irishness may account for the fact that Derek Mahon both denies him a place in the Irish tradition, yet, paradoxically, in claiming him as a poetic father figure, also locates him within his own tribe. (Mahon responds in the same convoluted way to MacNeice in that his critical perceptions of MacNeice, inevitably perhaps, do not account for the effect of his own poetry in altering those perceptions.) Graves's

[83] 'Autumn Sequel', canto v, in MacNeice, *CP*, 350.
[84] *Complete Poems*, ii. 6.   [85] *The White Goddess*, 492.
[86] 'Address to the Poets', in *Between Moon and Moon*, 279.

influence on Irish poetry works in two contradictory ways: he appears, in contrast to Yeats, to offer imaginative freedom with no political or moral obligations as a possibility; the space for poetry does not, as it does with Yeats, appear to have been cleared only after enormous struggle with the 'filthy modern tide'. But insofar as his influence is limited, he simultaneously forces recognition that there is no such freedom: for Graves, as for anyone else, it is an illusory sense of liberty, one which is obtainable only at enormous cost. He negotiates his way through the tangle of Anglo-Irish literary and political relations without explicitly acknowledging that he is doing so. In this sense, the implications, possibly even deceptions, of his aesthetic have been more profoundly understood and recognized by his poet descendants than by those who construct or deconstruct 'national aesthetic canons of good and bad', and find Graves relatively easy to ignore. Derek Mahon rightly condemns those 'who still dismiss him as an ivory-tower poet' as failing to understand 'the implications of his work'.[87]

The debt to Graves is, on one level, as it is for the Movement, stylistic. But Graves's location of the self in relation to history, the way in which he has dealt with a violent past and asserted a poetic role, is also an influence. Graves is reinterpreted in Derek Mahon's and Seamus Heaney's writings as a more effectively subversive figure than criticism of Graves's poetry has generally acknowledged him to be. The 'banished gods' in hiding in Mahon's poetry from a desecrated world and waiting for the right time to reassert their role owe something to Graves's mythology, as does Heaney's explication of violence as 'a struggle between the cults and devotees of a god and a goddess'.[88] While Mahon accepts that 'the shadow of Yeats has to be there somewhere; it's like being influenced by Shakespeare', Graves is listed (along with MacNeice and Beckett) as a literary enthusiasm, one of the true poets Plato would have banished.[89] Michael Longley cites Graves (along with MacNeice) as a 'still potent influence[s]'[90] and a 'much-loved poet';[91] for John

[87] 'Womanly Times', review of *Between Moon and Moon*, ed. Paul O'Prey, *Literary Review*, 75 (Sept. 1984), 8.

[88] *Preoccupations: Selected Prose 1968–1978* (London: Faber, 1980), 57.

[89] 'Derek Mahon Interviewed', by William Scammell, *Poetry Review*, 81/2 (Summer 1991), 5.

[90] 'The Longley Tapes', interview by Robert Johnstone, *Honest Ulsterman*, 78 (Summer 1985), 20.

[91] 'Q & A with Michael Longley', interview by Dillon Johnston, *Irish Literary Supplement*, 5:2 (Fall 1986), 22.

Montague, Graves is 'one of my heroes'.[92] The Gravesian inheritance, though, like the Yeatsian one, is not without its problems. Heaney relates goddess devotion directly to the 'stream of time', to 'fashion and public service', tangling himself up in the gendering of politics (and, consequently, the politics of gender). Mahon can never entirely lose the ironic sensibility that his experience of the twentieth century has engendered, however much he might be driven by a similar impulse to articulate values propounded by Graves: a sense of the numinous in everyday life, a confident assertion of divine power.

One can see the extent and the limitations of Graves's influence in comparing his poems 'An English Wood' and 'Rocky Acres' with Derek Mahon's 'The Return', or Louis MacNeice's 'Woods'. In 'An English Wood', 'nothing is that harms'. But even if it is offered as a moment of 'quietude', it is not the place of inspiration: 'No bardic tongues unfold | Satires or charms.'[93] This is similar to what MacNeice calls 'this other, this English choice', which is less of a choice than it might appear because, he goes on to say, 'in using the word tame my father was maybe right'.[94] Graves's 'Small pathways' which 'idly tend | Towards no fearful end'[95] find their echo in MacNeice's parody of English pastoral: 'windows browed with thatch, | And cow pats—and inconsequent wild roses'.[96] The lines also owe something to, and mock, Rupert Brooke's 'The Old Vicarage: Grantchester', with its 'Unkempt... English unofficial rose'.[97] So MacNeice is parodying, more specifically, a certain type of English pastoral, that associated with an insular, pre-war, patriotic idyll. Echoes of Graves and MacNeice also make up the elements of Mahon's 'mild woods' in the 'English' setting in which 'The Return' opens. It is not 'An English Wood' but a 'wild land' which Graves chooses in 'Rocky Acres' as 'beloved by me best':

> The first land that rose from Chaos and the Flood,
> Nursing no valleys for comfort or rest,
> Trampled by no shod hooves, bought with no blood.[98]

[92] *The Figure in the Cave and Other Essays* (New York: Syracuse University Press, 1989), 54.
[93] *Complete Poems*, i. 158.
[94] MacNeice, *CP*, 231.
[95] *Complete Poems*, i. 159.
[96] MacNeice, *CP*, 231.
[97] *The Poetical Works*, ed. Geoffrey Keynes (London: Faber, 1970), 68.
[98] *Complete Poems*, i. 83–4.

It is a landscape defined largely in terms of what it is not: it is not Christian, nor England, nor populated, nor does it exist within the confines of history, even geography: 'Time has never journeyed to this lost land'. It also bears some resemblance to the landscape to which Mahon returns, but the point Mahon is making in 'The Return' is that the geographical and emotional connection is not a matter of choice, and can never be severed, however much it might be challenged: the 'last stubborn growth' has 'nothing to recommend it | But its harsh tenacity'.[99]

Mahon, as with any other poet writing during the Northern Ireland Troubles, could not be described as a 'war poet' in the restricted sense in which the term is often used. But if the basis for comparison is the work of Owen, Sassoon, or Rosenberg, Graves himself is not a 'war poet'. What would perhaps be true to say is that Mahon is responding to the Great War insofar as his response to Northern Ireland in the 1970s is both indebted to Graves's trench experience and to the aesthetic developed in consequence of that experience. Mahon evades the role of poet of the 'Troubles' in the same way that Graves rejects the harsh realism of the war poets: echoing Graves's 1918 judgement, Mahon suggests that Sassoon 'was artistically naïve', as a consequence of which 'his satirical war sketches, forceful as they were then, have dated badly'.[100] Nor can he propose moments of pastoral to counter violence in the way Heaney finds possible in, for example, 'The Harvest Bow'. It is not a solution that works for Graves either. Bergonzi attributes this distance from English pastoral to his Irish background, but 'Irishness' is not the common denominator in Graves and Mahon. What is common to both of them is the need for certainty, a value system, a faith that their own religious and geographical contexts cannot give to them in any organized or conventional form. Where they differ is in the degree to which the poet can be committed to any such value system. In Mahon's view, the trauma of the Great War prevented Graves from remaining 'a Georgian nature poet with a touch of the Celt about him', urging him instead into the writing of 'a modern poetry'. But it is also a modern poetry 'based on the conviction "that society was once matriarchal"'.[101]

---

[99]   *Poems 1962–1978* (Oxford: OUP, 1979), 99.
[100]   'Break of Day in the Trenches', review of *Out of Battle* by Jon Silkin, *Irish Times*, 20 Feb. 1988, Weekend 9.
[101]   Mahon, 'Uncle Robert', review of *The Assault Heroic* by Richard Perceval Graves, *Irish Times*, 20 Sept. 1986, 4.

So Graves, with this conviction, sees irony, the 'keynote to modernism' as 'a passing historical phenomenon'.[102] Fussell, on the other hand, suggests that 'there seems to be one dominating form of modern under-standing; that it is essentially ironic; and that it originates largely in the application of mind and memory to the events of the Great War'.[103] If Graves has overcome irony, then, ironically enough, it is Mahon who, two generations later, suffers the profoundly ironic sensibility which is his inheritance from the Great War. Graves can at least assume belief in the goddess; Mahon cannot. The final irony is that if the impact of the Great War on modern society is such that 'religious' certainty is an impossibility, it is Graves, the war veteran, who has reinvented a certainty, and Mahon, as inheritor of the post-war 'modern age' who has lost it. As a result, when Graves is 'thronged by angels',[104] Mahon tends to be surrounded by Milton's angels barring the way to Paradise with 'dreadful faces thronged and fiery arms'.[105] Mahon, like Graves, might seek to reinstate the female principle: in 'Rage for Order', the poet's 'talk of justice and his mother' is 'the rhetorical device | of an etiolated emperor', which places him, like other potentially redemptive symbols, 'gasp[ing] for light and life', and, as with Graves's goddess, marginalized by history when the female principle is denied— 'Nero if you prefer, no mother there'.[106] But he does so from a position which is felt to be considerably more embattled than Graves's, and, possibly, more honest, if one acknowledges that Graves's celebration of the matriarchal provides a framework for affirming a heroic masculinity. If one takes two love poems—Mahon's 'Preface to a Love Poem',[107] and Graves's 'The Word'[108] published a year later—one is written before and the other after the authors' first-hand experiences of viol-ence. The similarities are obvious. Both acknowledge the existence of an absolute value beyond language: Graves's 'Word is unspoken' and Mahon's love poem remains unwritten; Graves's lovers 'substitute

---

[102] *The Common Asphodel*, p. ix.
[103] *The Great War and Modern Memory*, 35.
[104] 'The Word', *Collected Poems* (London: Cassell, 1975), 342.
[105] Mahon, 'Craigvara House', *Selected Poems* (London: Viking; Oldcastle: Gallery Press, 1991), 157.
[106] *Poems 1962–1978*, 44. The original version, in *Lives* (London: OUP, 1972), 22, reads 'The rhetorical | Device of a Claudian emperor—'.
[107] *Night-Crossing* (London: OUP, 1968), 13. The poem first appeared in *Dublin Magazine* in 1966.
[108] *Collected Poems* (1975), 342 (1st collected 1967).

a silence' and Mahon offers 'a substitute | For final answers'. But iron-
ically, the criticism that has been made of Mahon, that he 'approaches
reality "at one remove"', using literariness as 'a recurrent technique for
putting a distance between the middle-class self and its panic',[109] is one
that, as Longley points out, 'fakes the evidence' by presenting Mahon's
poem as being written with knowledge of a violent past and present.[110]
It is rather Graves who, writing with that knowledge, is, in his later
poetry, 'Driving two hearts improbably together | Against all faults of
history',[111] and yet escapes whipping.

At this point, Graves's (and Riding's) criticisms of Yeats, made from
1927 to the end of his career, begin to appear rather disingenuous. Yeats,
Graves claims,

observing that his old poetical robes have worn rather shabby, acquires a new
outfit. But the old romantic weaknesses are not so easily discarded: even when
he writes of 'Lois Fuller's Chinese Dancers'—a high-brow Vaudeville turn—
instead of Eire and the ancient ways... Such are the shifts to which poets have
been driven in trying to cope with civilization and in rejecting or keeping up
with, from an imagined necessity of action, the social requirements that seem to
be laid upon poetry.[112]

Yeats begins with an apparently stable symbolism, which he then re-
writes and disrupts as he sees fit throughout his career. Graves starts
from conclusions which he admits were 'not confidently drawn'[113] and
gradually strengthens a position in which he can affirm that 'the good-
ness of poetry is not moral goodness, the goodness of temporal action,
but the goodness of thought, the loving exercise of the will in the pursuit
of truth'. 'Moral definitions', he argues, 'may be invented for historical
emergencies' but 'moral, or local, truth is finally unreal'.[114] Con-
sequently, he condemns Yeats for adapting his thought to 'historical
emergencies' and thus compromising truth, writing in 1960 that 'Yeats
developed a brilliant verse technique but found nothing worth saying of
his own; so he went out like an indigent countryman with no sheep to
shear, and collected strands of wool from the hedges and brambles of

---

[109] Stan Smith, *Inviolable Voice: History and Twentieth Century Poetry* (Dublin: Gill and
Macmillan, 1982), 189.
[110] Edna Longley, *Poetry in the Wars* (Newcastle: Bloodaxe, 1986), 173.
[111] 'Timeless Meeting', *Collected Poems* (1975), 519.
[112] Graves and Riding, *A Survey of Modernist Poetry*, 178.
[113] *The Common Asphodel*, p. ix.
[114] Riding and Graves, 'Poetry and Politics', ibid. 283.

other men's fields.' Since Yeats 'prefers the violent expression of error to reasonable expression of truth', Graves dismisses him as guilty of 'worse than fraud'.[115] In so doing, he misjudges him on two counts. First, however many new outfits Yeats acquires, he appears throughout as the poetic sorcerer never the historical apprentice: the 'violent expression of error' consistently protects that position. Second, Yeats's career conforms to the view of poetic genius espoused by Graves before he adapted (by apparently de-historicizing) his own thought in response to changing historical circumstances from the late 1920s onwards. The lives of poetic geniuses, Graves writes, 'symbolise and include the principal conflicts of the period in which they lived, and the solution or most favourable attitude towards these conflicts which has been found hitherto, occurs in the work of these individuals'.[116] Yeats, too, could lay claim to Graves's opening stance in *The White Goddess*: 'I have never intentionally undertaken any task or formed any relationship that seemed inconsistent with poetic principles; which has sometimes won me the reputation of an eccentric.'[117]

Graves refuses to compromise aesthetic principles in the face of historical emergencies: in this he stands, with Yeats, and in spite of his misreading of Yeats, as an example to a later generation of poets also confronted by such emergencies. But, going a step further than Yeats, he also denies or suppresses throughout his career the process of artifice and construction which has given him the illusion of freedom from place and from history. 'The Vow' laments

> ...an uninstructible world of men
> Who dare not listen or watch, but challenge proof
> That a leap of a thousand miles is nothing
> And to walk invisibly needs no artifice.[118]

In *The White Goddess*, the author presents himself as no more than a historical interpreter who puts the facts together to form a narrative. In its own way, Yeats's claim that *A Vision* was dictated to his wife by Spirits was no less deceptive, but while Yeats at one point took his system literally, his 'reason', he writes, 'soon recovered': the system 'stands out clearly' as an imaginative one.[119] 'The White Goddess' owes a debt to Yeats which suggests that Graves's disapproval of the

---

[115] 'To the *Observer*', 5 Mar. 1960, *Between Moon and Moon*, 194–5.
[116] *Poetic Unreason*, 243.   [117] *The White Goddess*, 13.
[118] *Collected Poems* (1975), 310.   [119] *AV*, 25.

means by which Yeats maintains aesthetic freedom, and holds contrary thoughts in balance, need not necessarily devalue the end. In 'Sailing to Byzantium', Yeats wishes for the 'artifice of eternity', and, in 'The Fisherman', turns to the imagination 'In scorn' of his audience.[120] Echoing Yeats, Graves writes in 'The White Goddess',

> All saints revile her, and all sober men
> Ruled by the God Apollo's golden mean—
> In scorn of which we sailed to find her
> In distant regions likeliest to hold her
> Whom we desired above all things to know,
> Sister of the mirage and echo.[121]

But Yeats's acknowledgement of an 'artifice of eternity' implies a self-consciousness about the poet's 'constructive' role that Graves refuses to acknowledge. 'Byzantium' is a complex symbol for art itself; and although one might describe the White Goddess in the same terms, it is equally true that Graves projects her onto his audience as more than a symbol, as a deity who is unknowable and inexplicable. For Graves there are certain emotional conflicts engendered by his experience of war which can never be rendered admissible to the poet's aesthetic in terms other than those laid down by his White (or Black) Goddess, where pain is not eliminated, but in the act of 'worship' the poet can 'forget cruelty and past betrayal | Heedless of where the next bright bolt may fall'.[122] The Great War destroys any conventional notion of a system; and to give that horror shape in a conventional way would be to compromise the experience of it. The 'religious' certainty which Graves constructs as a focus for poetry is, therefore, one which exists as a certainty for him only because the operation of 'divine grace' is arbitrary in the extreme: 'Exchange of love looks' can come 'unsought | And inexpressible' (or presumably not come at all) to which the poet must 'stand resigned'.[123] Governments, and people, may betray; but one can never be betrayed by the woman whose duty it is to betray. As he writes in 'Beware Madam', 'The muse alone is licensed to do murder'.[124]

'To Juan at the Winter Solstice' and 'The White Goddess' might stand, then, as amongst the most perfect 'war poems' Graves ever wrote. In 'The White Goddess', conventional religion is spurned—the 'saints

[120] Yeats, *CP*, 218, 167.   [121] *Complete Poems*, ii. 179.   [122] Ibid.
[123] 'Timeless Meeting', *Collected Poems* (1975), 519.   [124] Ibid. 243.

revile her'—as are the profiteers, the 'sober men | Ruled by the God Apollo', whose willingness to give is in direct proportion to what they will receive. The Great War soldier, or the Muse poet, gives unstintingly without hope of reward. The goddess is sought 'In distant regions', away from the despised home front, where nobody understands. 'It was a virtue not to stay, | To go our headstrong and heroic way' is a reminiscence of 1914, which brings back in 1944 a mindset apparently destroyed for ever by the disillusioning nature of the Great War. Spring, in the poem, is the time of renewal and regeneration—'Green sap of Spring in the young wood a-stir | Will celebrate the Mountain Mother'—but it is also the time of offensives and destruction: renewal is always renewal through death. This is no longer the 'tasteless honey' of the bankrupt mythology of 'Recalling War', but an equally destructive delight in the woman with 'hair curled honey-coloured to white hips'. If 'Recalling War' identified the problem in relation to the First World War—'Extinction of each happy art and faith...'—'To Juan at the Winter Solstice' and 'The White Goddess' find a way of resolving it in the Second. In 'To Juan at the Winter Solstice' there is 'one story and one story only':

> Water to water, ark again to ark,
> From woman back to woman:
> So each new victim treads unfalteringly
> The never altered circuit of his fate[125]

These are Sassoon's men, wearied and numbed after battle, 'with an almost spectral appearance';[126] they are Eliot's crowd flowing over London Bridge; they are the endless stream of new recruits sent to the Front. Most noticeably, they are Yeats's dancers in another war poem, 'Nineteen Hundred and Nineteen', whose 'tread | Goes to the barbarous clangour of a gong'. But there are differences. Where Kitchener pointed a finger with 'Your Country Needs You', the Virgin 'crooks a finger, smiling', and the suitor is seduced into battle. It is devotion to woman not country, even though she is also demanding the ultimate sacrifice. The madness of the duty to the goddess, critiqued in the patriarchal context of 'Recalling War' as anathema to art, is an inevitable consequence of Graves's post-First World War trauma, and what looks at

---

[125] *Complete Poems*, ii. 150–1.
[126] Siegfried Sassoon, *The Complete Memoirs of George Sherston* (1937; London: Faber, 1972), 362.

times like transcendental insanity is actually closer to poetic and military integrity. As with 'The White Goddess', in 'To Juan at the Winter Solstice', 'Her sea-grey eyes were wild | But nothing promised that is not performed'. This is the crucial difference from service to King and Country: the Great War soldiers were let down during and after the war, but service to the goddess is military service where trust is absolute and suffering a small price to pay.

The lack of critical attention to Graves's poetry in England and Ireland might suggest that his denials of artifice and his lamentations for 'an uninstructible world of men' are made from an 'untouchable' position. Graves, an influential figure for some contemporary Irish poets, and therefore, one might assume, a prime candidate for inter- rogation on the grounds of moral responsibility, has been largely ignored in recent years. But Graves does not transcend the social and political reality of his time, he only appears to transcend it, and his exclusion from critical debate points to the inadequacy of the debate not the poet. This is not to historicize his aesthetic into nothing more than ideologically-determined strategy. Rather it is to point out that leaving his work unchallenged, outside time and space, allows, paradoxically, perpetuation of the connection he himself perceived between 'national political sentiment' and 'national aesthetic canons' in its most reductive form. Donald Davie's dismissal of Graves's later career as irresponsible and apolitical is symptomatic of misreading based on an assumed connection between aesthetic value and explicitly political verse (Yeats's 'literature of the point of view'):

Graves, once the social historian of *The Long Week-End*, withdrew forty years ago to Majorca and has since found a retreat even more securely insulated from British social and political realities—the mythological Never-Never Lands ruled over by goddesses, white and black, where lately he seems to have been joined in mumbo-jumbo by Ted Hughes. Amis is too responsible to take that way out.[127]

The only person insulating Graves from social and political realities here is Davie. '[M]umbo-jumbo' hardly accords with Mahon's more sensitive view of Graves's later work as 'traumatised' and 'exorcising'.[128] Graves is neglected not because he is harmless, a love poet or muse poet in his ivory tower, but because the opposite is true. Ironically, it may be the case that if critics have found it difficult to accept *The White Goddess* as

[127] *Thomas Hardy and British Poetry* (London: Routledge, 1973), 102.
[128] 'Break of Day in the Trenches', review of *Out of Battle*, 9.

a war book, it is not because of its avoidance of social and political realities, but because the realities, the values associated with war, that it embodies and upholds, are ones that do not sit comfortably with a post-1918 (insulated?) society. That he has not been co-opted for various literary canons should not be read simply as rejection, but as a perfected resistance to them which their limitations allow. And because he is neither under fire nor without influence, one might draw the conclusion that his existence, as it was meant to, complicates and thereby to some extent invalidates the 'national aesthetic canons' he went to some trouble to avoid.

CHAPTER FOUR

Louis MacNeice: Between Two Wars

'The war which broke us? Which war? Or which peace?'

Louis MacNeice[1]

I

Samuel Hynes, in *A War Imagined: The First World War and English Culture*, outlines the ways in which the Great War has been remembered in English literature, and suggests that it is that kind of remembrance, consolidated in the late 1920s into what he calls a 'Myth of the War', which informs attitudes towards the Great War in England up to the present day. The 'Myth' has several elements which can be summarized as follows: innocent young men went to war for democracy and were slaughtered needlessly in battles planned by stupid generals; the soldiers' real enemies therefore became the 'old men' at home, and as a result they rejected the values of the society that had sent them to war, separating the younger generation from the past and from its cultural inheritance.[2] For the most part, in post-war literature which deals with the subject of the Great War, some or all of these principles of under-standing the war are present. It is, in effect, a war remembered through the way in which it has been imagined. Paul Fussell, in *The Great War and Modern Memory*, traces the peculiarly literary nature of the war through to the present: now even his own commentary on the war has, as Geoff Dyer points out, become 'part of the testimony it comments upon'.[3] England, it might be said, has absorbed the Great War, or more accurately, what Hynes finds to be the 'Myth of the War', to the extent that writers now treat the subject imaginatively almost as if by right of experience. The effect of the Myth is one that will run and run: the break

---

[1] 'Autumn Sequel', canto XIX, *CP*, 409.
[2] *A War Imagined: The First World War and English Culture* (New York: Atheneum, 1991), p. xii.
[3] *The Missing of the Somme* (London: Penguin, 1995), 84.

with the past can never be healed, the 'old guard' can never be trusted again, and the old values hold no meaning for contemporary society. As George Orwell writes, 'By 1918 everyone under forty was in a bad temper with his elders . . . The dominance of "old men" was held to be responsible for every evil known to humanity, and every accepted institution from Scott's novels to the House of Lords was derided merely because "old men" were in favour of it.'[4]

Hynes reduces the 'Myth of the War' to two propositions: 'the old betray the young; the past is remote and useless',[5] and accepts these as informing principles behind the work of Modernist and thirties generation writers. If there is something which can be called a 'Myth of the War' in Ulster, it bears little resemblance to this. It is, rather, the understanding of events which is to be found in Frank McGuinness's *Observe the Sons of Ulster Marching Towards the Somme*. Its basic themes are: Ulster Protestants, unlike Catholics, rallied to the Imperial flag without hesitation, believing that to fight for the Empire was to fight for Ulster; they made a blood sacrifice on the Somme in protest against Home Rule; they were betrayed by the Empire, and thus by the imperial principles they believed themselves to be fighting for. All those elements are in McGuinness's play: they prompt the 'No Surrender' attitude at its close, leaving that mentality as the final word and the ongoing position. (The play is not so much a commentary on that myth, but a first imaginative articulation of it.)

The 'Myth of the War' in England differs in fundamental ways from the myth in Ulster Protestant memory: the former perceives all pre-1914 values, not entirely accurately, as shattered; the latter reaffirms them without equivocation, because they *have* been shattered, and because the political situation demands, for reasons of internal security, that reaffirmation. Certain attitudes are characteristic of both places: the sense of betrayal, the mistrust of the British government. But if the myth in Ulster were to be reduced to two propositions, they would probably go something like this: the English betray the loyalists; the past is present and consistently utilized. Hynes stresses the 'irreversible pastness of the past' felt in English culture.[6] Geoff Dyer, following on from this, sees

---

[4] *The Road to Wigan Pier* (London: Penguin, 1979), 121.

[5] *A War Imagined*, p. xii.

[6] Quoted in Edna Longley, *The Living Stream: Literature and Revisionism in Ireland* (Newcastle: Bloodaxe, 1994), 150.

that the war has led to a peculiar kind of preservation of the past, 'as past', simply because it has been destroyed.[7] It is sealed off from the present in a way which makes it, as a rule, only a subject for nostalgia. In Ireland, on the other hand, what is stressed is the 'irreversible present-ness' of the past.[8] As MacNeice points out in 'Valediction': 'history never dies, | At any rate in Ireland',[9] a comment relevant to both loyalist and republican memory, north or south of the border. 'Irish Catholics and Ulster Protestants', Edna Longley writes, 'not only tend to remem-ber different things, but remember them in different ways'.[10] But for both, the issue is one of how past events validate present action, how a continuity can be found that justifies as well as inspires the present—hence the incantation of dates: 1690, 1798, 1912, 1916. The importance of the past lies in the way it provides parallels for the present, not, as in England, in the provision of a yardstick for measuring social and political change.

The Ulster 'Myth of the War', as with the English one, is only part of the story, and remembrance in both Ireland and England is informed in part by social and political expediency. In England the perceived break in history characteristic of Modernist writing is not a wholly accurate reading of the war—as Hynes points out, the old did not die in the First World War, they lived on into the post-war world and provided a continuity of sorts; in Ulster the emphasis placed on continuity, on a unbroken thread of unionist history stretching back from the Somme to the Boyne, neglects the disruptions and discontinuities felt outside the purely political (propagandist) sphere. How the Great War is re-membered has been the subject of many studies of English culture. In Ireland it has always been as much a question of whether one remem-bers it at all, or, in Ulster, whether a certain type of remembrance beyond a politically motivated stereotyping is even possible. Conse-quently, for any post-war Irish writer who is also closely associated with the English literary tradition, there are at least two, probably three, different contexts to be negotiated in relation to the Great War.

MacNeice both exemplifies and revises aspects of war mythologies on either side of the Irish sea. The main perceptions of MacNeice's position in Irish and/or English literary canons in themselves echo differing cultural attitudes towards the First World War: it is either the

---

[7] *The Missing of the Somme*, 5.   [8] Edna Longley, *The Living Stream*, 150.
[9] *CP*, 52.   [10] *The Living Stream*, 69.

most significant historical event in terms of cultural influence in the twentieth century; or it is unimportant in comparison with domestic events in Ireland at the same time, except as a historical backdrop—a classic example might be Brendan Clifford's *Ireland in the Great War*, the subtitle and focus of which is *The Irish Insurrection of 1916 set in its Context of The World War*; or, finally, its complexity as a cultural influence in Ireland is properly revealed and understood only in a context where different attitudes and interests uniquely intersect. So MacNeice has generally appeared either on the margins of an English tradition, part of the 'Auden Generation', but a minor poet in comparison with Auden, or has been rejected by the 'Irish' tradition because of his Ulster, Church of Ireland background and English education, as a result of which he apparently fails to express in his poetry what Mahon (with irony) calls the 'National Aspirations'.[11] Alternatively, and more recently, his reputation has, Mahon suggests, 'come to rest' in the North of Ireland, where he is the claimed or attributed ancestor of contemporary Northern Irish poets Longley, Mahon, Muldoon, and Carson.[12] In such a context, his failure to express fully either English national sentiments or Irish national aspirations (both of which tend towards sentimentality) becomes a creative strength and a political virtue.

II

Samuel Hynes towers over the thirties generation as does Paul Fussell over the Great War. He does so not only because of *The Auden Generation: Literature and Politics in England in the 1930s*, but also because, in *A War Imagined*, he has consolidated the ground rules for understanding the thirties writers in relation to Edwardianism and the Great War. A fascination running through *The Auden Generation* is the long-term effect of the First World War, and the subtext of *The Auden Generation* forms the basis for his later study of the Great War in English culture: the First World War, he claims, 'dominated the lives of those who were children then as much as it did the lives of their elders'.[13]

---

[11] Mahon, 'MacNeice in England and Ireland', in Terence Brown and Alec Reid (eds.), *Time Was Away: The World of Louis MacNeice* (Dublin: Dolmen Press, 1974), 117.

[12] Introduction to Derek Mahon (ed.), *The Sphere Book of Modern Irish Poetry* (London: Sphere Books, 1972), 14.

[13] *The Auden Generation: Literature and Politics in England in the 1930s* (London: Bodley Head, 1976), 17.

In both studies, his observations regarding the effect of the Great War on English culture are subtle, perhaps even definitive. But Hynes passes judgement on Yeats, MacNeice, Stephen MacKenna, Bernard Shaw, and others, as if such observations are equally appropriate to Ireland. One might not wish to draw the lines as decisively as Yeats, with his claim that Irish poetry 'moves in a different direction and belongs to a different story', particularly since Yeats's own work sometimes gives the lie to that statement. Nevertheless, for MacNeice, however 'Anglicized' he might seem, English cultural history is always qualified by the experience of Ireland. Inclusion of his work in a study of 'literature and politics in England' is, as a consequence, both productive and problematical.

In the final chapters of *A War Imagined* and the opening of *The Auden Generation*, Hynes illustrates how the First World War was 'the peculiar shaping force' of the thirties generation, the event which at least partially gave the thirties poets a sense of being a 'generation', as it had also previously defined the war poets as a distinct group. For the thirties generation, Hynes writes, 'awareness of the world and awareness of the war came at the same time'. In that world they were 'isolated . . . like the survivors of some primal disaster, cut off from the traditional supports of the past'.[14] The feelings of the next generation towards the war, Hynes describes as 'deeply ambivalent', encompassing 'revulsion at the brutality and waste of it', guilt at not having fought, and envy of those who had. Isherwood, Orwell, and Philip Toynbee all articulate those feelings. Isherwood wrote that the 'young writers of the middle 'twenties were all suffering, more or less subconsciously, from a feeling of shame that we hadn't been old enough to take part in the European war'. For Orwell, the 'idea "War"' aroused 'a complex of terrors and longings'. Toynbee, as a boy, 'remember[s] murmuring the name "*Passchendaele*" in an ecstasy of excitement and regret'.[15] 'My particular generation', Orwell writes, 'became conscious of the vastness of the experience they had missed. You felt yourself a little less than a man, because you had missed it.'[16]

The anxieties and aspirations of the thirties generation find expression in Auden's exhortation to Isherwood to 'Make action urgent and its

[14] *The Auden Generation: Literature and Politics in England in the 1930s* (London: Bodley Head, 1976), 17, 20.
[15] Quoted ibid. 21.
[16] 'My Country Right or Left', in *The Collected Essays, Journalism and Letters of George Orwell*, ed. Sonia Orwell and Ian Angus, i (London: Penguin, 1970), 589.

nature clear'.[17] With the end of the Great War and the end of conscription came the resurfacing in a particularly acute form of the age-old problem of one's responsibility as artist and man. The overriding imperatives of a state of emergency, it seemed, had temporarily resolved that dilemma. The soldier poets, who appeared to have known how to act and had acted, were envied (and admired) for the possession of moral and artistic certainties that arose, paradoxically, out of the very event that destroyed such certainties for future generations. For Stephen Spender, in the 1920s 'Shadow of War', the question is 'What can I do that matters?',[18] a line that actually carries more than one question—in other words 'what can *I* do', in comparison perhaps with what they did, or what actually matters in a world where it is felt that no value systems have been carried over from the pre-war society. The years 1914–18 are a watershed: the world before the war is a mystery, the fascination with the past a fascination with something that, because it has so completely disappeared and no longer gives any clues as to how one might expect the future to be, cannot be understood.

MacNeice's responses to the Great War, while they do have something in common with those of his English friends, are sufficiently complicated by his nationality to make him an uneasy bedfellow of Auden, Spender, and Day Lewis, particularly if they are understood as a generation defined by the English post-war world in which they come to maturity. The inclusion of MacNeice in Hynes's study of the thirties generation is not in question, since his work is not separable from English literary or political history in the 1930s. But neither is it safely or unequivocally ensconced within it. Obliquely, if never openly, recognizing this, Hynes attempts to have his cake and eat it, on the one hand to praise MacNeice as an English poet when, in *Modern Poetry* and *Autumn Journal*, MacNeice offers definitive studies of a generation from within, and on the other to attribute those characteristics of MacNeice's poetry that distinguish him from his contemporaries—his 'melancholy', his apparently 'apolitical' position during the 1930s—to the fact that he is Irish.[19]

---

[17] 'To a Writer on His Birthday', in Robin Skelton (ed.), *Poetry of the Thirties* (London: Penguin, 1964), 169.

[18] *Collected Poems 1928–1985* (London: Faber, 1985), 34. The poem was written in the 1920s and included in *Poems* (London: Faber, 1933) as 'Who live under the shadow of a war'.

[19] *The Auden Generation*, 295.

The tendency to judge Irish poetry by reference to English history is implicit in *A War Imagined*. Few of the 'great Edwardians', Hynes claims, found 'an adequate wartime voice' in the Great War, in evidence of which he cites the literary silences of Arnold Bennett, Bridges, Kipling, and Galsworthy, but also that of Yeats, who published no poems in 1916.[20] By implication, Yeats should have responded to the profoundly felt change which 1916, with the Somme, the introduction of conscription, and the growing recognition of the horrors of trench warfare, brought about in English society. But Yeats, of course, did respond to the Great War, as he also responded to 1916 in writing about the Easter Rising, although he delayed publication of those poems for some time since the audience, rather than the voice, proved inadequate. And 'The Second Coming', written in January 1919, finds its voice and vision in the traumatic upheaval of the war years. As MacNeice points out, 'There have been many such poems since the Great War'. But, significantly, he is also sensitive to the different historical resonances of such poems in Yeats's oeuvre: 'Yeats differs from the others in that he implies that even the coming anarchy has its place in a pattern'. Yeats's vision is tragic, but it is also heroic, and as such it contrasts with the 'sheer dissolution' of *The Waste Land*.[21] Only if the context is Anglocentric, if he is expected to respond with certain modes of thinking characteristic of 1920s England, is Yeats 'silent'. The same problem reappears in relation to Yeats and Owen. Hynes writes:

Nearly two decades after the war had ended, W. B. Yeats refused to include poems by Owen in his *Oxford Book of Modern Verse* because, he said, 'passive suffering is not a theme for poetry'. Historically speaking, he was wrong of course; the First World War had changed all that.... Once the soldier was seen as a victim, the idea of a hero became unimaginable: there would be no more heroic actions in the art of this war.[22]

There are two fallacies here. First, and particularly prevalent in the response to Yeats's comments, is the view that Yeats's evaluation of Owen's poetry as passive suffering is sound even though his judgement of the aesthetic principle behind it is misguided—Hynes like others defends Owen from Yeats according to Yeats's reading of Owen's poetry. Second, and more important, is the assumption hovering behind these lines that any aesthetic can be somehow proved or disproved in

---

[20] *A War Imagined*, 103.
[21] MacNeice, *PWBY*, 119–20.   [22] *A War Imagined*, 215.

terms of its relation to an abstract idea of English history. Heroism may vanish from English Great War literature; it is under no obligation to do so from Irish literature.

Although MacNeice's reaction to the Great War is not Yeats's, it is equally instructive to note that difference in perspective which separates him from his English contemporaries. In *The Poetry of W. B. Yeats* he writes:

Even now many Englishmen are unaware of the Irishman's contempt for England. Although brought up in the Unionist North, I found myself saturated in the belief that the English are an inferior race. Soft, heavy, gullible, and without any sense of humour. They had an ugly way of speaking and they had covered the world with machines. They were extraordinarily slow in the uptake. In my eyes they were so much foreigners that when the Great War broke out in 1914 (I was then nearly seven) it was some time before I could make out whether it was the English or the Germans who were the enemy.

Yeats was always conscious that the English were foreigners or, to put the emphasis more correctly, that he was a foreigner among the English.[23]

The comments offer a corrective about MacNeice as much as Yeats. Even the ' "dour" Ulsterman and the free-and-easy Southerner (both epithets need qualification) have much more in common with each other', he suggests, 'than either has with the Englishman'.[24] Nothing in MacNeice's critical writings suggests a feeling of guilt because he 'missed out' on the war. Since he would never have been conscripted, the imperatives would not have been his. And since he gave qualified support to the cause of Irish independence from Britain, the cultural pressures brought to bear on volunteers, and idealized by the post-war generation in England—'action urgent and its nature clear'—would hardly apply in the same way. The ideals of the Englishmen who enlisted are themselves part of the 'Myth of the War'. However little the post-war world celebrates those particular ideals, it does still celebrate the notion of service to a cause. C. S. Lewis, on the other hand, writes:

I was compelled to make a decision which the law had taken out of the hands of English boys of my own age; for in Ireland we had no conscription. I did not much plume myself even then for deciding to serve, but I did feel that the decision absolved me from taking any further notice of the war. . . . I put the war on one side to a degree which some people will think shameful and some incredible.[25]

The above passage is preceded by a lyrical description of his home in the North of Ireland, a place which is seen as a world apart: 'a different world . . . the thing itself, utterly irresistible, the way to the world's end, the land of longing'. He makes, in effect, concessions to a dual inheritance: to England in the decision to serve, and to his Ulster background in the reluctance to submerge himself in the English patriotic fervour of the war years. Since, therefore, his work does not help to consolidate the war myths that appeared in England or Ulster he receives little attention in studies of the First World War.

Lewis, on the whole, exempts himself from the Irish–English political debate; MacNeice's response is more evidently complex. His 'Irishness' is called into question by one school of thought as much as it is forgotten by another, but the difficulties of the Irish context are also compounded by the post-war xenophobia of the English context. Hynes traces in popular fiction of the 1920s a tendency to defend an idealized England, quoting among other examples John Buchan's 1924 novel, *The Three Hostages*:

The moral imbecile . . . had been more or less a sport before the war; now he was a terribly common product, and throve in batches and battalions. Cruel, humourless, hard, utterly wanting in sense of proportion, but often full of perverted poetry and drunk with rhetoric—a hideous, untamable breed had been engendered. You found it . . . very notably among the sullen murderous hobbledehoys in Ireland.[26]

Ironically, in describing MacNeice, in *The Auden Generation*, as a 'professional lachrymose Irishman',[27] Hynes falls into a stereotyping as unhelpful as the very stereotyping of Ireland and Irishmen he picks up on in *A War Imagined*. And MacNeice himself evades the whole truth somewhat when he writes that 'Many English people cannot see [Ireland] clearly because she gives them a tear in the eye'.[28] Contempt, hatred, even fear, are also apparent in England in the post-war years: the Great War is succeeded, after all, by a war between England and Ireland. The 'idealized England' establishes itself, in part, in contradistinction to Ireland. Buchan's *The Three Hostages* attributes the increasing madness of

[25] *Surprised by Joy* (1955; London: Fount Paperbacks, 1977), 128.
[26] Quoted in *A War Imagined*, 357.
[27] *The Auden Generation*, 334.   [28] *PWBY*, 46.

society, the decline from civility into barbarity, to the Great War, but not primarily to those who fought: 'The classes who shirked the War are the worst—you see it in Ireland'.[29] A conflict of interests and a self-preservatory role-playing are evident in MacNeice's first years in England: he plays the Irish buffoon to gain popularity, describes Carson as 'a pity' out of loyalty to his father and Home Rule, but feels instantly disloyal to a unionist, burns an effigy of the Kaiser in a spirit of patriotic fervour on Armistice Day but knows it to be a cheap gesture, and, in a well-known passage in his autobiography, reveals the contradictory pull on his loyalties of two attitudes neither of which can be reasonably said to reflect fully his own opinions:

On the Twelfth of July Powys came into my dormitory and said: 'What is all this they do in your country today? Isn't it all mumbo-jumbo?' Remembering my father and Home Rule...I said Yes it was. And I felt uplifted. To be speaking man to man to Powys and giving the lie to the Red Hand of Ulster was power, was freedom, meant I was nearly grown up. King William is dead and his white horse with him...But Powys went out of the dormitory and Mr. Cameron came in, his underlip jutting and his eyes enraged. 'What were you saying to Mr. Powys?' Oh this division of allegiance! That the Twelfth of July was mumbo-jumbo was true, and my father thought so too, but the moment Mr. Cameron appeared I felt rather guilty and cheap. Because I had been showing off to Powys and because Mr. Cameron being after all Irish I felt I had betrayed him.[30]

While the demands made on loyalty by the Red Hand of Ulster should not be underestimated, neither should the demands for conformity made by an England that was at that time particularly intolerant and insular. Not surprisingly, the confusion of MacNeice's childhood develops into a resistance to all failed or failing historical myths: 'I will not give you any idol or idea, creed or king'.[31] For MacNeice, no identity myths are absolute, and if they are projected as such they play personal experience false.

In 'Carrickfergus', MacNeice explores his relations to Ulster, England, and, through them, the Great War. The social and historical location of the poem epitomizes a felt disunity that continues into the poet's adult life and leads him to eschew any simple loyalties. As with other thirties poets, awareness of the world and the war come together,

[29] *The Three Hostages* (1924; London: Penguin, 1953), 13.

[30] MacNeice, *The Strings are False* (London: Faber, 1965), 78–9.

[31] 'Train to Dublin', *CP*, 28.

but MacNeice grows into an awareness of a very different culture, and suggests that the experience of England restricts rather than encourages that growth. Michael Roberts wrote in the 1930s that 'we can no more forget the world of politics than the soldier-poets could forget the wounded and the dead'.[32] Explicitly, the dilemmas facing 1930s writers are linked to the First World War poets; it is a way of suggesting that the next generation did not, after all, miss out on the 'war'. For the thirties generation, the Communist Party was, Orwell suggests, 'simply something to believe in...a church, an army, an orthodoxy, a discipline'.[33] Though a different context applies, theoretically at least one could feel action to be urgent and its nature clear.

When Hynes calls MacNeice 'at best a reluctantly political man', or 'apolitical with a good heart',[34] he narrows the scope of 'politics', and assumes that the kind of commitment which was 'urgent' and 'clear' to some of MacNeice's contemporaries was the only political stance available. Those comments also suggest that the question of political involvement, in other words involvement with everyday politics, can be raised to a moral issue. Roberts certainly validates it in those terms by emotive reference to the experience of a previous generation, and unless that frame of reference is accepted, one might wonder why the fact that MacNeice is 'apolitical' necessitates a defence of his moral character ('with a good heart'). Mahon straightens out various misconceptions about MacNeice by pointing out that his writing is *profoundly* superficial', that 'the surface *was* the core';[35] in the same way, one might say that he is profoundly political. Orwell argues that many 'middle class' 1930s writers 'too young to have effective memories of the Great War...can swallow totalitarianism *because* they have no experience of anything except liberalism'.[36] This does not hold true for MacNeice, however, with a background where political disputes, antagonisms, and mutually exclusive political claims force themselves on consciousness fairly early. Hynes writes that 'if the time allowed, [MacNeice] would have been content to go on as he was, a charming Irish classicist with upper-class tastes and a gift for making melancholy poems',[37] but he thereby misses the way in which the public sphere, from the very beginning of his career, interweaves with MacNeice's personal

---

[32] Quoted in Hynes, *The Auden Generation*, 161.
[33] 'Inside the Whale', in *The Collected Essays*, i, 565.
[34] *The Auden Generation*, 295, 299.   [35] 'MacNeice in England and Ireland', 115.
[36] 'Inside the Whale', 565.   [37] *The Auden Generation*, 370.

experience. MacNeice is never without the sense of crisis and doom that reverberates in the political as well as personal sphere: 'When I was five the black dreams came; | Nothing after was quite the same'.[38] Melancholia is neither a harmless aesthetic tool nor a soulful evasion of the real world.

'Carrickfergus' exemplifies the complexity (rather than the charm and melancholy) of MacNeice's position, dealing simultaneously with private and what might be called collective memories, each of which imposes different responsibilities on the poet. It is a 'collective' memory which dominates the first four stanzas of the poem. Past invasions are responsible for the divisions and inequalities of the present: 'The Scotch Quarter was a line of residential houses | But the Irish Quarter was a slum for the blind and halt'. Guilt runs through the poem: the 'Norman walled this town against the country | To stop his ears to the yelping of his slave', an attitude which contrasts sharply with the sensory alertness of the poem's speaker. But the difference in attitude does not, he recognizes, necessarily narrow the distance between 'invader' and 'slave'. MacNeice is still 'born to the anglican order, | Banned forever from the candles of the Irish poor', and the move to England in the 'camouflaged' steamer at the end of the poem puts the blinkers on him, although against his will, as surely as the Norman once voluntarily 'Stopped his ears'.

From the sixth stanza to the end of the poem, the Great War emerges as the dominating feature: 'The war came and a huge camp of soldiers | Grew from the ground in sight of our house . . .'. The tone and perspective of the verse is kept for the most part on a kind of nursery footing: the child who observes has the dominant voice rather than the adult who interprets. The result, in 'Marching at ease and singing "Who Killed Cock Robin?" | The troops went out by the lodge and off to the Front', is that the lines are overlaid with an ironic awareness all the more potent because the irony lies in what was outside the child's perspective, in what has been left out of the story. The child might remember 'Who Killed Cock Robin?', popular as a nursery rhyme, but what stands out in that stanza is simply 'Killed'; and the troops singing it are marching to the Front, in all innocence one assumes, to die. Syntactically, the poem begins to run away with itself when he envisages the war, in the tone and with the concerns of a child, lasting for ever:

[38] 'Autobiography', *CP*, 183.

> I thought that the war would last for ever and sugar
>> Be always rationed and that never again
>
> Would the weekly papers not have photos of sandbags
>> And my governess not make bandages from moss
> And people not have maps above the fireplace
>> With flags on pins moving across and across—[39]

As with other things, the war impacts on MacNeice in the public and the private sphere. The years 1914–18 are crucial formative years for him: the death of his mother, the Ulster crisis, the move to England, are all encompassed in the sense of loss that pervades 'Carrickfergus', and find expression in the images he retains from the Great War and from Ireland's past. The way in which MacNeice identifies with the war cannot be separated from the way he identifies with England and Ireland. And it is the Great War which reaches into a never-ending future in the child's imagination, as do the problems of identifying completely with either country, in a perfect expression of movement and stasis combined. The line 'moving across and across' stylistically imitates attitudes characteristic of the war—that despite constant activity, in real terms in a war of attrition no movement was taking place—with a line end that neither ends nor goes anywhere. In the final stanza of the poem, the poet finds himself relocated in a context which, while it suggests unity, simplicity, and an escape from the dark, potentially violent world of Ulster, also dulls the sensory alertness that informed his understanding of the past and grasp of the realities present:

> I went to school in Dorset, the world of parents
>> Contracted into a puppet world of sons
> Far from the mill girls, the smell of porter, the salt-mines
>> And the soldiers with their guns.[40]

By implication, things are simpler in England: it is Ireland that brings the war into focus for the poet, or rather brings the past into focus in relation to the present war. In a sense, of course, there could be no escape from the war in an English public school at that time, but the cultural pressures of wartime England, while they might have been greater, did not allow for the disunity that gives 'Carrickfergus' its energy as a poem.

[39] *CP*, 69–70.   [40] *CP*, 70.

III

Even as it serves to illustrate MacNeice's difference from his English contemporaries, 'Carrickfergus' also contains the elements which lead to his marginalization in the 'Irish' tradition. One might say that MacNeice himself has unwittingly provided the ammunition for the ranged guns of Irish Irelanders, defending an indigenous Irish canonical purity, and Ulster regionalists, extolling the virtues of the 'rooted' man. Prone to a humility and regret inconceivable in Yeats, MacNeice appears to outlaw himself from Irish Ireland ('Banned forever...') almost before anyone else has the chance to do it for him. His memories of Ireland in 'Carrickfergus' are not its National Aspirations, but its imperial war involvement, the Norman conquest, its industrial north, in other words, the 'Anglican' order of things. It is one thing to have this background; it is quite another to find acceptance within a certain tradition of Irish poetry if one does not seek redemption from it (in the style of George Russell) by at least attempting to express Irish National Aspirations, which include, Mahon suggests, 'patriotic graft and pious baloney', and without the inclusion of which one cannot really write Irish poetry. MacNeice's view of 'Official Ireland', was, as Mahon points out, increasingly 'one of positive distaste, which is alright coming from Austin Clarke but bad manners from a Northern Protestant'.[41]

In 1931, Daniel Corkery published the polemical and nationalist study *Synge and Anglo-Irish Literature*, in which he claimed that 'the three forces which, working for long in the Irish national being, have made it so different from the English national being, are (1) The Religious Consciousness of the People; (2) Irish Nationalism; and (3) The Land'.[42] MacNeice, by this token, is not an Irish being. In addition, Corkery's view of England and Ireland in the Great War, while it had its precursors in the 1916 insurrectionaries, and still has its descendants among northern nationalists, excludes aspects of Ulster's history as much as it elides the question of Irish involvement in the war:

Not Ireland itself, under its alien ascendancy, has been more war-ravaged than parts of Europe: indeed there is hardly a spot of European ground that has not in this regard more resemblance to Ireland than to England—England fattening and refattening its haunts of ancient peace, century after century, while its soldiers campaigned abroad. We recollect that in the early stages of the Great

---

[41] 'MacNeice in England and Ireland', 117.
[42] *Synge and Anglo-Irish Literature* (1931; Dublin: Mercier Press, 1966), 19.

War a writer in an English review mentioned how struck he was with the resemblance he noted between the small towns and villages of Poland and those of Ireland: he did not, however, bethink himself of the untoward circumstances that had brought the similarity about.[43]

MacNeice's view of history is not Anglocentric, but neither is it 'Corkerian', and in the Ireland of the 1930s, his status as an Irish writer was negligible. To some extent, Yeats's national broadcast on 'Modern Poetry' in 1936 confirms, if not intentionally, MacNeice's exclusion from what Mahon calls the 'charmed circle, known and feared the world over, of Irish poets'.[44] Yeats writes:

It was in Eliot that certain revolutionary War poets, young men who felt they had been dragged away from their studies, from their pleasant life, by the blundering frenzy of old men, found the greater part of their style... [T]heir social passion, their sense of tragedy, their modernity, have passed into young influential poets of today: Auden, Spender, MacNeice, Day Lewis, and others.[45]

To some extent, this is the familiar war myth again. The real point of his remarks here, however, is to acknowledge the influence of the war poets on the thirties generation: MacNeice, unlike Yeats, does see Owen, along with Eliot, Graves, and Lawrence, as one of the 'finest poets in England'.[46] Yeats does not explicitly handcuff 'social passion' here to communism and open fire on them both (even if he might like to) and so does not on those grounds misjudge MacNeice. But he does the younger poet a disservice in 'Modern Poetry'. He argues that the Great War radically altered the writing of the post-war generation in England—and MacNeice is counted as one of that generation—but it left Irish poetry untainted:

The English movement, checked by the realism of Eliot, the social passion of the War poets, gave way to an impersonal philosophical poetry. Because Ireland has a still living folk tradition, her poets cannot get it out of their heads that they themselves, good-tempered or bad-tempered, tall or short, will be remembered by the common people.[47]

In evidence, Yeats proceeds to quote St John Gogarty's work as 'among the greatest lyric poetry of our time'.

The position MacNeice seems obliged to defend, according to Yeats's view of Irish and English traditions, is that he is both Irish and in-

---

[43] *Synge and Anglo-Irish Literature*, 37.   [44] 'MacNeice in England and Ireland', 117.
[45] *E & I*, 499–500.   [46] *PWBY*, 178.   [47] *E & I*, 506.

fluenced by the changes wrought by the First World War. (Or, to put it another way, that English and Irish literary traditions are not mutually exclusive but intimately and productively related.) The apparent incompatibility of those two things reveals more about the Great War and Irish memory than it could ever reveal about MacNeice. Ironically, the case Yeats makes for the influence of English Great War poets on MacNeice's work serves ultimately only to disprove the terms of his own argument. In a broadcast debate between F. R. Higgins and MacNeice in 1939 on the subject of modern poetry, the arguments of Yeats's 'Modern Poetry' broadcast are revisited, this time with an opposition. Higgins, like Yeats, claims that when one considers 'the spirit informing poetry written in English since the European War' and 'the inner features most evident in the poetry of today', one finds that 'the abundance of such verse is, of course, written in England'. '[P]ure poetry', he goes on to say, 'comes from Ireland'. For MacNeice, his own experience of history negates such an argument: it is, he says, an 'impure age, so it follows that much of its poetry, if it is honest... must be impure'.[48] He is, implicitly, accused by Higgins in the debate of trying to escape from his own Irishness; what he defends is an understanding of an impure age dependent in part on that Irishness. One wonders at times if MacNeice is to be criticized more by the Irish for not being Irish, or for being Irish but without due appreciation of the spiritual gifts with which he is thus endowed.

Such views on Irish poetry, current in the 1930s, have been substantially revised in the last thirty years, and this particular critical debate is now reasonably well-trodden ground. But the still occasionally evident reluctance on both sides of the border to address the issue of how far the First World War impinged on Irish as well as English poetic practice puts MacNeice in the position of pathfinder between traditions, and, for those seeking canonical stability, permanent problem (witness Higgins's chaotically argued attack which has little to do with modern poetry and everything to do with persuading MacNeice to come into the fold). The easiest label to attach to MacNeice is always 'exile': his differences are thereby accounted for and condoned. It is also the label he was inclined at times to attach to himself. One might think, in fact, that having said goodbye to his country so often—'Farewell, my country, and in

---

[48] Quoted in the Prologue to Paul Muldoon (ed.), *The Faber Book of Contemporary Irish Poetry* (London: Faber, 1986), 17.

perpetuum'; 'From all which I am an exile'; 'she will not | Have me alive or dead'—there is little need for anyone else to speed his departure. But MacNeice exiles himself from a type of Irishness rather than the country itself, claiming instead a multiplicity of cultural influences: England, the West of Ireland, the North of Ireland, as in 'Carrick Revisited'—'Torn before birth from where my fathers dwelt, | Schooled from the age of ten to a foreign voice'. Like Michael Longley after him, he exists, there-fore, betwixt and between, in 'this interlude' which is not an absolute.[49] Since he refuses to invalidate any part of his experience, the act of rejection is always compromised by the possessive pronoun: 'Ireland, my Ireland', 'Farewell my country'. That refusal also in part accounts for the proliferation of oxymorons, parentheses, and central caesuras in his poetry explored by Terence Brown.[50] A 'duality of cultural reference' does not necessitate reconciliation, only acceptance of diversity. When MacNeice describes himself in 'Western Landscape' as 'neither Bran-don | Free of all roots nor yet a rooted peasant', but still claims his right to 'add one stone to the indifferent cairn', he undermines De Valera's Ireland of rural peasants and John Hewitt's dictum, written in the same year as 'Western Landscape', that the Ulster writer 'must be a *rooted* man'.[51] If the experience of Ireland qualifies that of England, the same principle applies the other way around. The First World War permeates MacNeice's imagination as much as the dream of the 'Land of the Ever Young'; neither country retains exclusive rights over aspects of his imagination.

The tradition that sidelines MacNeice in Ireland is also the tradition that sidelines the Irish experience of the Great War. Seamus Deane, in *A Short History of Irish Literature*, writes about O'Casey's *The Silver Tassie* and Yeats's rejection of the play, but avoids discussion of the First World War in Irish literature: the pertinent issues in the controversy are 'realism' versus the need for a main protagonist. He points out that the First World War, the Russian Revolution, and the Irish 'Troubles' contribute to Yeats's 'charged vision', but omits discussion of any Irish soldier poets—Ledwidge, MacGill, Kettle. Similarly, Jennifer Johnston's *How Many Miles to Babylon?*, one of the outstanding fictional accounts of

---

[49] *CP*, 225.

[50] See Brown, *Louis MacNeice: Sceptical Vision* (Dublin: Gill and Macmillan, 1975), chs. 6–7.

[51] Hewitt, 'The Bitter Gourd: Some Problems of the Ulster Writer', in *Ancestral Voices: The Selected Prose of John Hewitt*, ed. Tom Clyde (Belfast: Blackstaff Press, 1987), 115.

Irish enlistment in the First World War, is contextualized in a tradition of fiction dealing with the decay of the Big House.[52] While not disputing any of these readings as far as they go, and without wanting to attribute to Ledwidge or MacGill an importance in Irish literary history that, on one level, they do not have, it is worth noting that in a history of English literature, to omit discussion of the Great War's impact on twentieth-century writing would be almost impossible. It is perhaps ironic that Deane finds it possible only because *A Short History of Irish Literature* implicitly subscribes to a typically English view of Great War literature—one which is inappropriate to the Irish tradition—that it is predominantly by combatants. Since Ireland's Great War soldier poets are hardly the big players in literary terms, the war is largely unmentioned. Declan Kiberd's inclusion of a chapter entitled 'The Great War and Irish Memory', in *Inventing Ireland: The Literature of the Modern Nation*, is symptomatic of a growing recognition that this aspect of Irish history has been repressed. But the book noticeably fails to include any sustained consideration of MacNeice's work, or of the work of Michael Longley and Derek Mahon, both of whom share many of MacNeice's themes and concerns.

Traces of the First World War—its imagery, its myths—are littered throughout MacNeice's poetry, and cannot be explained merely as a manifestation of his 'English' side, since he draws as much on Yeats, notably Yeats in wartime, as on the English Great War and post-war poets. He finds initially, as do other thirties poets, that *The Waste Land* is the text that defines a generation: Fussell argues that part of its appeal was that it was 'more profoundly a "memory of the war" than one had thought ... [with] its archduke, its rats and canals and dead men, its focus on fear, its dusty trees ... and not least its settings of blasted landscapes and ruins'.[53] It is, in that sense, the perfect expression of the post-war human condition, and MacNeice, in considering it, extends its scope outside England to emphasize its universality. He writes:

However deep one's ignorance, historically, of the Decline of the West, it has been since World War I something that must hit one in the marrow at adolescence; anyhow Waste Lands are not only community phenomena, there must be one somewhere in each individual[54]

[52] See Deane, *A Short History of Irish Literature* (London: Hutchinson, 1986), 159, 164–5, 225.
[53] Paul Fussell, *The Great War and Modern Memory* (London: OUP, 1975), 326.
[54] 'When I was Twenty-One', in *Selected Prose of Louis MacNeice*, 232.

The Waste Land is a way of understanding the western world in the 1920s, but also, more fundamentally, of understanding the self that comes to maturity in that world. Whatever the appeal of 'self-deception', which tantalizes in *Autumn Journal*, XVI, there is 'no immunity' either for Ireland from that world or in Ireland for the self.[55] An early poem, 'River in Spate', is obviously indebted to Eliot, and to the First World War poets, with its 'assault and battery' of words: 'helter-skelter the coffins come and the drums beat . . . The corpses blink in the rush of the river . . .'.[56] The imagery reappears, refined and more effective, throughout *Autumn Journal*, where the First World War is a touchstone for understanding the present and the future—the Second World War.

   Autumn Journal's significance lies partly in the fact that it is an epitaph for a generation, partly in the fact that in the process of writing it it becomes apparent that there can be no such thing signed, sealed, and delivered, in response to contemporary crisis. The fault-lines exposed in the late 1930s existed also in the earlier part of the century. Hence, Section I is as much an ironic farewell to August 1914 as it is to the Long Weekend between the wars: the two become almost indistinguishable, and the mythic status in memory of both is apparent. In approaching the subject of war in the 1930s, the First World War has to be elegized all over again, a resurrectional act that denies, even as it writes, epitaphs. MacNeice, less susceptible than others of the thirties generation to English political enthusiasms, has less backtracking to undertake and is quick to detect, because he never believed in, failing myths. August 1938 is primarily evocative of August 1914, but with the advantage of a hindsight that learned not to trust illusions in the last war and recognizes them again:

Close and slow, summer is ending in Hampshire,
   Ebbing away down ramps of shaven lawns where close-clipped yew
Insulates the lives of retired generals and admirals
   And the spy-glasses hung in the hall and the prayer-books ready in the pew
And August going out to the tin trumpets of nasturtiums . . .[57]

That 'the home is still a sanctum under the pelmets, | All quiet on the Family Front', is one such illusion. If the lights can apparently go out all over Europe for a second time, it does suggest that they were never really turned back on again after the First World War. 'Parapet' hovers

[55] *CP*, 133.   [56] *CP*, 6.   [57] *CP*, 101.

behind 'pelmet': by implication there is no 'sanctum' anywhere for anyone. The division in England between war zone and home, a division which was never as clear-cut in Ireland, is, the inter-war years have shown, a fallacy. Gareth Reeves detects 'Home Front' as the military metaphor behind 'Family Front' in these lines.[58] The phrase's more obvious debt is 'All quiet on the Western Front', which, while it still locates blame for the present crisis in the Versailles Treaty, the 'Peace' of the last war, also reminds of the reaction against war in the 1930s and the obvious dangers of a contradictory attempt to fight for peace. Remarque's phenomenally best-selling *All Quiet on the Western Front*, which was first published in 1929, and which had sold over a quarter of a million copies by September of that year, consolidated certain views about war: that it was pointless, nihilistic, and exploitative. It inspired anti-war attitudes, but the attitude itself is not preventative. 'All quiet on the Family Front' not only takes on the Myth of the War (the old men are to blame), it takes on the consequences of belief in that myth, and explores what 'we learn after so many failures, | The building of castles in sand, of queens in snow'. 'Insulate[d] . . . lives' come in many shapes and forms. He writes 'summer is going | South as I go north', and one senses that a past is being left behind for good, that there is no common ground between the retired generals and 'the rebels and the young'.[59] But in effect, one can no more break with the past than with the present. In Section XXII he attempts that break—'I have taken my ticket south, I will not look back . . . Let us flee this country and leave its complications'—but finds that 'There is nothing new to learn'.[60] MacNeice, like Yeats, stresses continuity: past feeds into future and vice versa. The 'Myth of the War' is utilized by Yeats in the mid-1930s to 'protect' the Irish tradition; MacNeice, on the other hand, affirms continuity by exposing its fallacies in relation to the next war. The flow of MacNeice's river in the poem is not disrupted by history; rather it is history, and to recognize that it cannot be disrupted—'no river is a river which does not flow'[61]—is to suggest that there are only variant readings of it at any given time, all of which may be inadequate. Throughout *Autumn Journal*, the world comes back on the poet; and it is ignorance of that world's

[58] Michael O'Neill and Gareth Reeves, *Auden, MacNeice, Spender: The Thirties Poetry* (London: Macmillan, 1992), 194.

[59] *CP*, 102.

[60] *CP*, 146.

[61] *CP*, 102.

plurality, an ignorance which resists historical imagination, that receives his strongest criticism. 'The bloody frontier | Converges on our beds', and cannot be refuted or ignored: 'it is no good saying | "Take away this cup".[62]

Because the Great War is implicitly to blame for the state of the world, it is the war to which MacNeice instinctively turns when addressing the issue of conflict. Part of its appeal, in the *Autumn Journal* sections on Spain and the imminent Second World War, is that its ready-made images can both evoke and simultaneously deconstruct idealism, probably a fairly accurate measure of the confused ideology leading up to the Second World War. Spain is to the thirties poets what Flanders was to the Georgians:

> . . . Spain would soon denote
> Our grief, our aspirations;
> . . . our blunt
> Ideals would find their whetstone . . . our spirit
> Would find its frontier on the Spanish front,
> Its body in a rag-tag army.[63]

The 'rag-tag army' instantly evokes a memory of what Robert Graves describes as 'the amateur, desperate, happy-go-lucky, ragtime, lousy army of World War I'.[64] There is, MacNeice is acutely aware, some 1914–style idealism on the Spanish issue, an idealism which, because of the events of 1914–18, needs only to be hinted at to raise awareness of tragedy. George Orwell writes:

The thing that, to me, was truly frightening about the war in Spain was not such violence as I witnessed . . . but the immediate reappearance in left-wing circles of the mental atmosphere of the Great War. The very people who for twenty years had sniggered over their own superiority to war hysteria were the ones who rushed straight back into the mental slum of 1915.[65]

That same problem is apparent in *Autumn Journal* in relation to the forthcoming Second World War. In Section VII, with the lines 'They want the crest of the hill . . .' and 'searchlights probe the heavens . . .', MacNeice inclines towards, and parodies, the 'high' diction character-

---

[62] *CP*, 109.

[63] *CP*, 112.

[64] 'The Poets of World War II', in *The Common Asphodel: Collected Essays on Poetry 1922–1949* (London: Hamish Hamilton, 1949), 310.

[65] 'Inside the Whale', 567.

istically associated with, and a casualty of, the Great War.[66] The rhetoric
is in ironic contrast to the events it describes—no steeds or warriors
here, but 'anti-aircraft guns' and 'bacilli'. But the differences may be little
more than superficial. The 'soldiers in lorries' are in 'tumbrils'—sacrifi-
cial lambs to the slaughter whose only advantage over their predecessors
in the Great War is that they are forewarned of their fate. 'I feel
astounded', he continues, 'That things have gone so far'. Yet the irony
of these lines is that deep down things have gone nowhere. The political
outlook of his generation, defined in relation to one war, is bound to
compromise in the face of another, and to replay what was once resisted:

> ... the issue
>   Involving principle but bound in fact
> To squander principle in panic and self-deception—
>   Accessories after the act,
> So that all we foresee is rivers in spate sprouting
>   With drowning hands
> And men like dead frogs floating till the rivers
>   Lose themselves in the sands.
> And we who have been brought up to think of 'Gallant Belgium'
>   As so much blague
> Are now preparing again to essay good through evil
>   For the sake of Prague ...[67]

The difference between fighting for Prague or for Belgium is primarily
one of tone and attitude: it does not involve a change in action. The
vision of horror in *Autumn Journal*—'men like dead frogs'—is not, as in
the early 'River in Spate' a vision of a post-war world based on a war
remembered, it is remembrance in advance of the fact using the imagery
available from the previous war. (Oddly, the Second World War itself
does not spawn such images, probably because they *were* so readily
available in advance.)

  Despite all the efforts of the thirties generation to understand their
role in relation to the war, MacNeice suggests that the contradiction
inherent in an attempt to 'essay good through evil' confounds them as it
confounded the liberal generation of 1914. (The problem is one to
which he returns again and again, in *The Poetry of W. B. Yeats* and, after
the Second World War, in *Autumn Sequel*: 'Did we know | That when that
came which we had said would come, | We still should be proved

---

[66] See Fussell, *The Great War and Modern Memory*, 21–2.   [67] *CP*, 113–14.

wrong?'[68]) In Section VII of *Autumn Journal*, the attempt to avoid such dilemmas—'Glory to God for Munich'—an attempt which, in presuming to learn from the First World War, does the opposite, is itself critiqued by MacNeice. The escape 'into the green | Fields in the past of English history' is an attempt to recapture innocence after experience, a refusal to 'look back to the burning city'. But 'The Czechs | Go down and without fighting', the phrase hinting back to the down-and-out sufferers of the Depression years, and if he was oblivious before he cannot be oblivious now: 'I no longer | Docket a place in the sun'. By implication, the politicians involved in Munich are accused of a childlike innocence that is dangerous. MacNeice on the other hand has 'no ivory tower, no funk-hole'.[69] There is no escape, either in pure aestheticism, or, as Yeats also concluded, in pure action. As with the First World War poets, the demands of the time place demands on poetry which, even if they are impossible, are preferable to a poetry which exempts itself from responsibility. Even failure, with appropriate Yeatsian gestures, can be heroic: 'That Rome was not built in a day is no excuse | For *laissez-faire*, for bowing to the odds against us . . .'.[70]

The 'irreversible presentness' of the past is a constant theme in *Autumn Journal*. The stylized form of remembrance of war, which is still current in England, takes on the quality of nightmare in Section XV. Remembering victims of the Great War, in England and Ulster, can be a way of assuaging guilt, a way of not remembering: in *Autumn Sequel* war remembrance in London dwindles to ahistorical ritual: 'London now prepares | Old guys to burn and poppies to remember | Dead soldiers with and soup for the Lord Mayor's | Banquet, all items proper to November'.[71] (Those tokens are in ironic contrast to the painful remembering in the powerful and elegiac Lament for the Maker, Dylan Thomas, in the same poem.) In *Autumn Journal*, the war victims provoke feelings of guilt; they are both victims and killers. The sentiment is hardly the well-known 'Age shall not weary them | Nor the years condemn', from a poem which anticipates in advance of the fact the way in which the fallen will be remembered, and which obliquely suggests soldiers were privileged to die;[72] rather it presents a nightmare scenario in which they are both wearied and condemned:

---

[68] *CP*, 334.   [69] *CP*, 116–17.   [70] *CP*, 128.   [71] *CP*, 400–1.

[72] Laurence Binyon, 'For the Fallen', in David Roberts (ed.), *Minds at War: Essential Poetry of the First World War in Context* (Burgess Hill: Saxon Books, 1996), 56–7. The poem first appeared in *The Times* in Sept. 1914.

> . . . I cannot see their faces
> Walking in file, slowly in file;
>
> .　　.　　.　　.　　.
>
> 　　Where have we seen them before?
> 　Was it the murderer on the nursery ceiling
> 　　Or Judas Iscariot in the Field of Blood
> 　Or someone at Gallipoli or in Flanders
> 　　Caught in the end-all mud?[73]

The lines are reminiscent of Eliot's description of the crowd flowing over London bridge (or Yeats's men treading the ever-turning gyres of history); they are reminiscent also of descriptions of the file of men marching past the Cenotaph on Remembrance Day, men who represent not the living but the dead, though their 'guilt' lies in being amongst the former. MacNeice's ghosts include those who betray as well as those who are betrayed: the complexities of memory conflict with remembrance, denial of the past with a sensed responsibility to the past.

The nightmare of *Autumn Journal*, XV fuels the indictment of Ireland in Section XVI. 'Nightmare leaves fatigue: We envy men of action', he begins, revisiting Yeats's debate in 'Meditations in Time of Civil War'. But as Yeats also concludes, the desire to be the man of action in wartime is the desire for an uncomplicated role, a way of viewing the world in simple binary oppositions, and a self-indulgence:

> . . . I envy the intransigence of my own
> 　Countrymen who shoot to kill and never
> See the victim's face become their own
> 　Or find his motives sabotage their motives.[74]

The consequence of such a liberating intransigence is in fact political and imaginative sterility. Thus, Maud Gonne, with all the potential to view Irish history in its full complexity—an English mother, a soldier father, and nationalist sympathies—opts instead for a myth of history to validate present action that binds people to 'continuance of hatred'. Paul Fussell suggests that the atmosphere of 'simple antithesis' dominated the Great War, encouraging a 'modern *versus* habit: one thing opposed to another not with some Hegelian hope of synthesis involving a dissolution of both extremes . . . but with a sense that one of the poles embodies so wicked a deficiency or flaw or perversion that its total submission is

---

[73] *CP*, 130.　　[74] *CP*, 131.

called for'. This is 'the atmosphere in which most poems of the Great
War take place, and that is the reason for the failure of most of them as
durable art'.[75] MacNeice applies to Ireland artistic lessons learned partly
from the Great War, and discovers a failure of rhetoric north and south:

> And one read black where the other read white, his hope
>   The other man's damnation:
> Up the Rebels, To Hell with the Pope,
> And God save—as you prefer—the King or Ireland.[76]

This is the world in black and white, politics as a zero-sum game, and is,
he suggests, due to man's 'basic illogicality; he just cannot cope with the
world in colour'.[77]

IV

If the Second World War forces into perspective the First World War,
and vice versa, for MacNeice it also forces into perspective Ireland,
Yeats's Ireland, and the relationship between war and poetry. It is
significant that the onset of war is the time when MacNeice's need to
evaluate his own relationship with Yeats finds its most detailed expres-
sion. Yeats, in wartime, forges a poetics of war in *A Vision*. MacNeice, in
The Poetry of W. B. Yeats, attempts to come to terms with that Yeatsian
vision, to take and discard from it as he sees necessary, in the context of
a different war. And it is in defining his relationship with Yeats that he
comprehensively addresses the issues of art, Ireland, and war, which
preoccupied both poets throughout their careers. As with Yeats, the
primary concern is to defend the role of poetry in wartime, but to do so
against any populist expectations about that role.

In *The Poetry of W. B. Yeats*, MacNeice emphasizes two main themes
that affect any understanding of the impact of the Great War on his
work, and, revealed through this, his understanding of his place in
English and Irish traditions: first, that 'the Auden school' is in some
ways closer to Yeats than to Eliot; second, that Eliot was misunderstood
by Yeats, the two poets having more in common than either ever
acknowledged. Edna Longley suggests that 'MacNeice's consciousness

[75]   *The Great War and Modern Memory*, 79, 82.
[76]   *CP*, 132.
[77]   *Selected Literary Criticism of Louis MacNeice*, ed. Alan Heuser (Oxford: Clarendon,
1987), 112.

of Yeats . . . bridges his own double context'.[78] It is, more specifically, his consciousness of the relation between Eliot and Yeats, or, to narrow it further, between two different ways of imagining war, which bridges that context. Yeats's reading of modern poetry—Irish poetry's living folk tradition; its rejection of modernism—acquired a status among his disciples that Yeats never fully accords it in his own poetry. On the contrary, his instinct as an artist is towards what Seamus Deane dismissively describes as 'literary unionism'.[79] The phrase requires rehabilitation in relation to both poets. MacNeice, a poetic descendant but not an acolyte, is at pains to point out that an Irish separatist approach to poetry does not yield the results Yeats would have wanted:

> Most of his Irish successors followed him in eschewing the industrial world and in writing their verses carefully, but they followed him in little else. There is rarely much meat on their poems. Yeats himself seems at times to have felt impatient with them, to have turned away towards English poets who were breaking his own rules.[80]

MacNeice's own impatience with the sub-Yeatsian approach, in the sphere of literature and politics, is evident in his attitude towards Ireland in the Second World War. In *Autumn Journal*, Ireland appears at times as representative of an illusory escapist zone—'the linen which I lie on came from Ireland | In the easy days | When all I thought of was affection and comfort'; 'Ireland is small enough | To be still thought of with a family feeling'—although that feeling is exposed as a myth: 'It is self-deception of course . . .'.[81] In 'The Closing Album' (originally titled 'The Coming of War') Ireland is used, on one level, as a focal point for contrast with the rest of Europe: 'a hundred swans | Dreaming on the harbour . . .'; 'distant hills | Made as it were out of clouds and sea'. The image of a Celtic Twilight Ireland, a dream of pastoral, is one so far removed from the commercial culture across the water that he marvels 'What a place to talk of War'.[82] The reason why one must talk of war comes in the first section, 'Dublin'. The 'mist on the Wicklow hills | Is close', true, but only as close (or far) as 'the Irish to the Anglo-Irish | As the killer is close one moment | To the man he kills . . .'. Dublin is not an

---

[78] *Louis MacNeice: A Study* (London: Faber, 1988), 27–8.
[79] *Heroic Styles: The Tradition of an Idea* (Field Day Pamphlet No. 4; Derry: Field Day, 1984), repr. in *Ireland's Field Day* (Notre Dame, Ind.: University of Notre Dame Press, 1986), 50.
[80] *PWBY*, 179–80.
[81] *CP*, 110, 133.   [82] *CP*, 165–6.

escape from the world; at best it provides a vantage point for the poet who, like 'Nelson on his pillar', is 'Watching his world collapse'.[83] Stylistically, the example behind this poem is Yeats's 'Easter 1916'; like 'Easter 1916' it searches for perspective in a context where everything familiar has been overturned. When war finally and inescapably invades 'The Closing Album', in the 'nameless' Section V, the sense of place is destabilized. If Ireland appeared as the war-free zone, the place of stability, two things become apparent by the end of the poem: that there is no escape in Ireland any more than anywhere else, and that in realizing that fact, the poet still discovers in the self the qualities which counterbalance war. Because they are not explicable, they cannot be legislated into existence any more than out of it. The poem's final question, like many of MacNeice's questions, is not really a question at all, since it remembers in the act of querying why one should remember:

> And why, now it has happened
> And doom all night is lapping at the door,
> Should I remember that I ever met you—
> Once in another world?[84]

Through the way he approaches Ireland in the Second World War, MacNeice negotiates with a Yeatsian Ireland. The 'hundred swans' in 'Galway' look back to Yeats, as does the third stanza of 'Neutrality' with its 'ducats of dream and great doubloons of ceremony'.[85] He critiques Irish neutrality in the Second World War partly through a critique of Yeats's 'A Prayer for my Daughter', where to counteract the 'great gloom' in his mind, Yeats turns to 'custom and ceremony' as the begetters of 'innocence and beauty'. That kind of activity has become for MacNeice, when it extends outside the scope of Yeats's poetry, dangerously introspective:

> But then look eastward from your heart, there bulks
> A continent close, dark, as archetypal sin,
> While to the west off your own shores the mackerel
> Are fat—on the flesh of your kin.[86]

Yeats, one might say, formulates a system which, while it might enable his own poetry, is not of itself workable for later poets. In content at least, he 'is not a poet to imitate'.[87] MacNeice writes that

---

[83] *CP*, 163–4.   [84] *CP*, 167.   [85] *CP*, 202.
[86] *CP*, 203.   [87] *Selected Literary Criticism of Louis MacNeice*, 64.

The modern poet is very conscious that he is writing in and of an industrial epoch and that what expresses itself visibly in pylons and gasometers is the same force that causes the discontent and discomfort of the modern individual, the class-warfare of modern society, and wars between nations in the modern world.[88]

In Yeats's poetry, where aeroplanes, Zeppelins, and trains have at best only a walk-on part, a way is found of dealing with that modern world. The strength of his example, however, lies in the fact that he demonstrated the possibility of uncompromising survival as a poet in the modern world, rather than in the method used to do so. For the thirties generation 'play[ing] Hamlet in the shadow of the gas-works', T. S. Eliot seems to be the true precursor.[89] But this view is one which MacNeice substantially revises in the 1930s. The essay in which it is explained is, significantly, entitled 'Eliot and the Adolescent'. That *The Waste Land* was a profoundly influential poem for the post-war generation is not disputed. But influence is not static, nor is it always conscious, and, as with poetry itself, is not something which exists in a vacuum. MacNeice compares *The Waste Land* with 'The Second Coming', and finds that

The mere difference in versification between Eliot and Yeats represents here an essential difference in attitude; for Eliot both hope and heroism have vanished with regular metric, with punctuation. When the Auden school appeared, who were nominally affiliated to Communism, they showed much superficial resemblance to Eliot but, below the surface, they were actually nearer to Yeats . . . Like Yeats they opposed to the contemporary chaos a code of values, a belief in system, and—behind their utterances of warning—a belief in life, in the dignity, courage and stamina of the human animal.[90]

This view is elaborated upon throughout *The Poetry of W. B. Yeats*. But side by side with the exploration of the differences between Yeats and Eliot, and therefore the different levels of influence they have on the 'Auden school', is a recognition of similarities. MacNeice does not simply reverse the roles of the two main protagonists; rather, in revising the conventional view of Eliot in relation to the thirties, he also interrogates Yeats's critical reading of Eliot's poetry, and reinterprets the thirties poets in the light of a cross-cultural, English–Irish scenario. Yeats, he suggests, since he 'failed to see the peculiar virtues of Eliot, must almost certainly have failed to see his own affinities with him'. And for MacNeice they overlap on fairly crucial points:

[88] Ibid. 72.   [89] Ibid. 149.   [90] *PWBY*, 120–1.

They both hanker for a hierarchic social system. They both combine speculative and sceptical habits with a somewhat frustrated urge to religion. They both dislike the liberal conceptions of progress and democracy; Eliot described the modern world as 'worm-eaten with liberalism'.[91]

Eliot's work is not simply 'a reaction against Yeats and Yeats's poetry'; rather, MacNeice argues that 'Yeats's account of Eliot's poetry is inadequate and incorrect'.[92] More accurately, he points out that his own generation react against, and respond to, both of them. MacNeice himself hankers after a very different social system from the hierarchical. Yeats's rejection of liberalism, his refusal to recognize the industrial revolution, on one level limit his influence as much as Eliot's abandonment of 'hope and heroism'.

But if both Yeats and Eliot offer a world-view which is alien to the next generation, in MacNeice's scheme of things, Yeats still comes out on top as the poet whose work is, regardless of his politics, relevant to the dilemmas of the late 1930s in a way Eliot's is not. He does so because war, and its relation to poetry, is the overriding concern of *The Poetry of W. B. Yeats*, as it is also the overriding concern of Yeats's post-1916 writing. Poetry still seeks answers to the questions raised by the Great War, and is under pressure to validate and revalidate its function in response to subsequent crises—the Second World War, Auschwitz, the Cold War, the Northern Irish Troubles. In this context, the motivation behind MacNeice's study of Yeats is instantly understandable: *The Poetry of W. B. Yeats* affirms, above all else, the value of poetry on its own terms at a time when historical crisis threatens its validity. Yeats stands as MacNeice's precursor in this: *A Vision*, (like *The White Goddess*), is amongst other things a work of literary criticism which defends poetry in time of war.

The consequences of MacNeice's study—not least of which is that Yeats's poetry and politics became separable for MacNeice in a way they would not be without a war-dominated context—are, for the thirties generation and for war poetry in general, far-reaching. In the introduction to *The Poetry of W. B. Yeats*, MacNeice writes:

If the war made nonsense of Yeats's poetry and of all works that are called 'escapist', it also made nonsense of the poetry that professes to be 'realist'. My friends had been writing for years about guns and frontiers and factories, about the 'facts' of psychology, politics, science, economics, but the fact of war made

[91] *PWBY*, 188.   [92] *PWBY*, 189.

their writing seem as remote as the pleasure dome in Xanadu. For war spares neither the poetry of Xanadu nor the poetry of pylons. I gradually inferred, as I recovered from the shock of war, that both these kinds of poetry stand or fall together. War does not prove that one is better or worse than the other; it attempts to disprove both. But poetry must not be disproved. If war is the test of reality, then all poetry is unreal; but in that case unreality is a virtue. If, on the other hand, war is a great enemy of reality, although an incontestable fact, then reality is something which is not exactly commensurable with facts. Yeats all his life was a professed enemy of facts[93]

Yeats, rather than Eliot, indulges what Mahon, after Wallace Stevens, describes as the poet's 'rage for order'. He does so, in MacNeice's view, not by falsifying experience, but by keeping 'his questions comparatively simple' and thus avoiding 'hopelessly inadequate answers'. Rupert Brooke, on the other hand, makes the mistake of trying to 'hitch his [romantic individualism] to the cause of the Allies in the Great War', an attempt which, because the Great War was 'a mere negation of ideals', was 'doomed to complete failure'.[94] MacNeice does not suggest that poets should avoid the Great War, but he implicitly endorses what Yeats once pointed out to others—that the Great War can never be a suitable subject for poetry if it is simultaneously allowed to disprove that poetry: as Yeats put it, 'The mere greatness of the world war has thwarted you'. One cannot blame a specific war—and one war may, after all, stand for any war—since it is also evident that if the Great War disproved Brooke's poetry, it did not disprove Owen's or Yeats's. MacNeice objects to the same thing in Rupert Brooke's poetry that he objects to in Irish or Ulster historical myths—'sentimental falsification'. That falsification is not vindicated by popular support, since the support merely 'widens the basis of the lie'. He argues instead for a transposition into poetry of 'personal values'. Revisiting ground trodden by Graves as critic in the 1920s, MacNeice writes that a poem

derives from and has to be referred back to life, which means, in the first instance, the life of the poet. In the same way the life of the poet, though also an individual thing, derives from and has to be referred back to the life outside him. Now a poem is ill-balanced either if it is too far removed from life or if it is too slavishly subordinate to it.[95]

Up to a point, Yeats and Eliot can represent these two poles: if, as with *The Waste Land*, the poet consciously adapts himself and his style to his

[93] *PWBY*, 17–18.   [94] *PWBY*, 30.   [95] *PWBY*, 29.

world, then he diminishes the proactive role of poetry; Yeats, on the other hand, 'repudiated realism' and 'at times... misrepresented the world in which he was living'.[96] The thirties poets, seeking a balance between these two things, argue for a system diametrically opposed to Yeats's own, but they still adopt a Yeatsian approach by asserting a viewpoint against the odds. MacNeice writes:

> Eliot... maintained that... if [the poet's] world is difficult and complex, his poetry must be difficult and complex (a theory exemplified by *The Waste Land*). Poets like Auden and Spender... returned to the old arrogant principle—which was Yeats's too—that it is the poet's job to make sense of the world, to simplify it, to put shape on it.

The problems of the Yeatsian inheritance—the fascist tendencies, the aristocratic elitism—are in some ways overcome without much difficulty in the next sentences:

> The fact that these younger poets proposed to stylize their world in accordance with communist doctrine or psychological theory (both things repugnant to Yeats) is comparatively irrelevant. Whatever their system was, they stood with Yeats for system against chaos, for a positive art against a passive impressionism.[97]

Liberalism, Hynes suggests, at the end of the 1930s, when it appeared to be dead and buried, seemed to 'rise from its grave like Banquo and demand new sympathy'.[98] To assert liberal values when they appear to have failed, is, then, a heroic gesture comparable with Yeats's rejection of them. (MacNeice's own 'Epitaph for Liberal Poets' takes a Yeatsian, if more light-heartedly expressed, view of the age as engendering its opposite: 'The Individual has died before'.)[99]

Because the strength of Yeats's example is dissociated from his politics, he and his Ireland are 'democratized' for subsequent generations: as mediated through MacNeice, Yeats becomes a usable influence for a new generation of poets in wartime. The fundamental problem with Yeats's war poetry as a model is his corresponding attitude towards war. Yeats, MacNeice is aware, 'began to conceive of life as a developing whole, a whole which depends upon the conflict of the parts'. That he began, therefore, 'to write in praise of war', is for MacNeice 'a false inference from a premiss which is essentially valid'.[100] In other words, Yeats's 'All creation is from conflict' is accepted; 'Love war because of

[96] *PWBY*, 30.   [97] *PWBY*, 191.   [98] *The Auden Generation*, 301.
[99] *CP*, 210.   [100] *Selected Literary Criticism of Louis MacNeice*, 118.

its horror' is rejected. Where Heaney tries to re-evaluate Yeats in humanitarian terms, probably an impossibility, MacNeice works on the assumption that Yeats's politics and aesthetic are separable, not in the light of his poetry, but in the light of his influence: 'The spiritual lesson that my generation ... can learn from Yeats is to write according to our lights. His lights are not ours. *Go thou and do otherwise*. He can serve us also, perhaps, as an example of zest ... there is nearly always a leaping vitality—the vitality of Cleopatra waiting for the asp.'[101] This is a rejection of the Yeatsian aesthetic—a call to do otherwise—which is also, paradoxically, an endorsement of it, since to 'do otherwise' is central to Yeats's poetic principles.

V

That Northern Irish poets have brought MacNeice's reputation to rest in Ireland is now a commonplace. MacNeice lingered for years on the margins of the English tradition, one of the 'Auden School', but more recently, contemporary Northern Irish poets, writing in another war, have become the lens through which he is viewed. Most studies of the poet acknowledge, if they do not always accept, the line endorsed, implicitly or explicitly, by Derek Mahon, Michael Longley, Edna Longley, and Paul Muldoon. Peter McDonald, in his detailed study of MacNeice in his contexts, points out perceptively that 'canons in relation to which his work is often read are all liable to be *changed* by his writing, that the "1930s myth", as much as Irish "identity", becomes something different once it accommodates his poetry in full'.[102] MacNeice, he writes, 'has always sent the canonical compass bearings haywire'.[103] Contemporary Northern Irish poetry has done the same. The persistent MacNeicean echoes in Northern Irish writing indicate that a poet who remained in his lifetime 'homeless everywhere' has found, posthumously, a tribal homeland. MacNeice's endeavour to point to the limitations of the English and Irish literary canons, canons which were, in part, constructed in response to the traumatic upheaval of the Great War, remains pertinent to his 'descendants'. Longley,

---

[101] *PWBY*, 197.
[102] *Louis MacNeice: The Poet in his Contexts* (Oxford: Clarendon, 1991), 9. McDonald's introd., 'Canons and Contexts', provides an acute and concise overview of MacNeice's problematic position in the thirties generation, and the canon of Irish literature.
[103] Ibid. 5.

Mahon, and Heaney, working with the 'duality of cultural reference' that also characterizes MacNeice, have all in different ways suffered misrepresentation in English and/or Irish literary traditions.

Michael Allen describes a poetry reading which took place in Northern Ireland in 1966 involving Longley, Heaney, and Mahon, to celebrate the publication of the new edition of MacNeice's *Collected Poems*. The reading, Allen suggests, provides one of the first articulations of 'a revised selective canon of MacNeice to be established collaboratively by [Michael Longley] and his wife Edna (among others) between 1966 and 1988'.[104] The elements which make up that canon include articles by Michael Longley—'A Misrepresented Poet' (1967), 'A Note on the Irishness of Louis MacNeice' (1975); a series of publications on MacNeice by Edna Longley from 1983 onwards, culminating in a full-length study of his poetry in 1988; and also Michael Longley's editorship of the new MacNeice *Selected Poems* (in which role he replaces, appropriately enough, W. H. Auden). It was also suggested in the late 1970s that Michael Longley and Edna Longley would write the official biography of MacNeice.

Michael Longley writes in 1975 that since 'Ulster is a limbo between two (three?) cultures', judgements on MacNeice's poetry 'would be more precise if the Northern Irish context were taken into account'.[105] Earlier than this, Mahon applies MacNeice's philosophy to Northern Irish poetry when he claims that the Northern poet, 'surrounded as he is by the Greek gifts of modern industry...must, to be true to his imagination, insist upon a different court of appeal from that which sits in the South' and suggests that 'a war remains to be won...between...the fluidity of a possible life...and the *rigor mortis* of archaic postures, political and cultural'.[106] This may be a (self-) defence of a vulnerable position; but it has wider resonances. Michael Allen discusses ways in which the 'ideological tensions' involved in reclaiming MacNeice were apparent in the 1966 poetry reading.[107] MacNeice may be described as an Irish poet, an Anglo-Irish poet, or as an Ulster poet, with significantly different implications in each case. The neglect of

---

[104] Allen, 'Louis MacNeice and Michael Longley: Some Examples of Affinity and Influence', in Kathleen Devine and Alan J. Peacock (eds.), *Louis MacNeice and his Influence* (Gerrards Cross: Colin Smythe, 1998), 102, 104–5.

[105] 'The Neolithic Night: A Note on the Irishness of Louis MacNeice', in Douglas Dunn (ed.), *Two Decades of Irish Writing* (Cheadle: Carcanet Press, 1975), 99, 104.

[106] 'Poetry in Northern Ireland', *Twentieth Century Studies*, 4 (Nov. 1970), 93.

[107] See 'Louis MacNeice and Michael Longley', 104.

MacNeice outside a Northern-based context may be seen to affirm his influence as one of the elements which distinguishes Northern Irish from Southern Irish writing (although Derek Mahon, who implicitly makes this distinction, later rejects it).[108] For Edna Longley, MacNeice's view of the thirties generation as a generation which tried to put shape on the world serves as an implicit defence of the traditionalist, formalist nature of much contemporary Northern Irish poetry—itself trying to make sense of historical confusion. The question of responsibility as a poet in wartime inevitably resurfaces in Northern Ireland in 1968, and MacNeice, who engaged with that question in the Second World War, simultaneously emerges as a major figure in Northern Irish writing.

In much influential Northern criticism, notably Edna Longley's work in the 1980s, MacNeice enters the debate about 'the use or function of poetry' on his own terms. To project forwards, to bring MacNeice's reputation to rest in Northern Ireland is the key to relocating his writing in the context of two world wars. In the introduction to *Poetry in the Wars* Edna Longley writes: 'Perhaps "war", not "history" or "politics", covers the broadest imaginative contingencies; indicating that poetry engages—*as poetry*—on many battlegrounds.'[109] This statement should probably be considered in the light of the more controversial, and frequently criticized, 'Poetry and politics, like church and state, should be separated.'[110] Both comments appear to be validated in and by *The Poetry of W. B. Yeats*. To take 'war' as an inclusive category is to reiterate, through MacNeice's interpretation, Yeats's 'All creation is from conflict'. Poetry engages 'as poetry', not as propaganda or manifesto: it can therefore be in conflict with the 'facts' if not with 'reality'; and in engaging as poetry, it presumably stands on ground where it cannot be 'disproved'. And it is poetry's separation from 'politics'—which is not to say it is apolitical, merely that it is resistant to 'sentimental falsification'—that saves it, or should save it, from the disastrous misrepresentation of which MacNeice finds Rupert Brooke to be guilty. Ulster poets are, Edna Longley writes, 'sometimes the victims of improper expectations. Whatever causes they may support as citizens, their imaginations cannot be asked to settle for less than full human truth'.[111]

[108] See 'An Interview with Derek Mahon', by Terence Brown, *Poetry Ireland Review*, 14 (Autumn 1985), 11–19.
[109] *Poetry in the Wars* (Newcastle: Bloodaxe, 1986), 10.
[110] Ibid., 185.
[111] Ibid. Cf. MacNeice: 'a poem is vitiated if it relies upon a falsehood to life'. *PWBY*, 29.

Edna Longley's preoccupations, in *Poetry in the Wars*, are, like Mac-
Neice's, engendered by a world where the 'shockwaves' of the First
World War are still 'rippling through'. Northern Irish writers, as with
MacNeice earlier, look to the First World War poets to understand their
own crises. Problems of remembrance in relation to that war are still, in
Northern Ireland, sensitive and unapproachable ones. To understand
how the Great War can be approached imaginatively is also, then, in
Poetry in the Wars, to understand the role of poetry in the Northern
Ireland Troubles: the 'redefinition' of the Great War's 'literary and social
languages' is, Longley suggests, a 'continuing dynamic'. Northern Ire-
land's poetry is offered as a 'corollary' of Great War poetry, in its
'searching for balance—on a shifting front line—between close-up
and perspective, documentation and symbol, presumption and respons-
ibility'.[112] Because MacNeice's poetry has 'been there before',[113] he is
'canonized' as someone who is forced to disrupt canonical stability to
make sense of his own context. Longley plays out a situation in her
criticism which is played out by Northern poets themselves: the poetic
response to the First World War becomes a yardstick for both measur-
ing the Northern Irish poetic response to the Troubles, and challenging
expectations about that response. Samuel Hynes, as McDonald points
out, has more recently modified the views on MacNeice expressed in the
1976 *The Auden Generation*.[114] It is the 'renascence' in Northern Irish
poetry which has caused this change in perspective. Northern Ireland
provides a context for MacNeice, but, more significantly, it reworks
other contexts for him. The belated recognition of the importance of
the First World War in Irish history has been brought about in part
because of the unresolved questions that resurfaced in the Northern
Ireland Troubles. To evaluate MacNeice from the perspective of the
later conflict is also to force his re-evaluation in terms of the earlier one.
And, conversely, if the First World War moves to centre stage, Mac-
Neice, with a way of remembering history and revising literary history
that certain forms of remembrance in both Ireland and England have
often obscured, moves with it.

[112] *Poetry in the Wars*, 12.
[113] Edna Longley, 'Louis MacNeice: "The Walls Are Flowing"', in Longley and
Gerald Dawe (eds.), *Across a Roaring Hill: The Protestant Imagination in Modern Ireland*
(Belfast: Blackstaff Press, 1985), 99.
[114] See *Louis MacNeice: The Poet in his Contexts*, 4.

Part II

The Northern Renascence

CHAPTER FIVE

Northern Ireland and the Politics of Remembrance

'At the beginning I was taken aback by the scale and ferocity of the violence. I continue to be dumbfounded by the awfulness of our situation. All my political prognostications have been wrong. I have written a few inadequate elegies out of my bewilderment and despair. I offer them as wreaths. That is all.'

Michael Longley[1]

I

Fifty years after the Armistice that ended the war to end all wars, Northern Ireland erupted into a violent conflict which, rather like the Great War, took many by surprise, in spite of the retrospectively knowledgeable readings of signposts to the conflict. 'A kind of double-think operates', Heaney noted in 1966: 'something is rotten, but maybe if we wait it will fester to death'.[2] Instead, the Civil Rights movement protests, which tried to redress that rottenness, mutated into a conflict organized on largely sectarian lines, whose unresolved difficulties lay in the founding and existence of the Northern Irish 'state' itself. The *Sunday Times* insight team noted in April 1969 that

The monster of sectarian violence is well out of its cage. The issue now is no longer Civil Rights or even houses and jobs. The issue is now whether the state should exist and who should have the power, and how it should be defended; and this is an issue on which the wild men on both sides have sworn for 40 years, frequently in blood, that they will never back down.[3]

---

[1] 'An Interview with Michael Longley' by Dermot Healy, *Southern Review*, 31/3 (July 1995), 560.
[2] Quoted in R. F. Foster, *Modern Ireland 1600–1972* (London: Allen Lane, 1988), 585–6.
[3] Quoted in Jonathan Bardon, *A History of Ulster* (Belfast: Blackstaff Press, 1992), 664.

Since the Troubles in Northern Ireland over the last thirty years have been caused in part by the far-reaching implications of an earlier period of conflict—1912 to 1922—the temptation to view contemporary Northern Ireland in terms of the First World War era appears to have been almost irresistible. In 1938, it was argued that 'the present system' in north-east Ulster 'forces all concerned to hostility, as it is a product of war machinery'.[4] And as such, in other words, how could Northern Ireland be anything other than a state *at* war. Significantly, the post-1968 Troubles are, or have been perceived as, a 'war'—Gerry Adams, at the 1987 Sinn Féin Ard Fheis, described the armed conflict as a 'war of attrition'.[5] Maurice Goldring, speculating on the reasons for such a perception, which is not necessarily applied to violent events elsewhere in the world, concludes:

War is not defined by the numbers of bombs and casualties. War is a state of mind as much as the use of military strength. It is obvious, dramatically clear, over here [Northern Ireland] that people have a war in their minds even if it is not on their doorsteps. Everybody knows that any move by any paramilitary group is politically as important as a political statement or agreement—often more so. War is the great simplifier. It is simple, clear. A barricade has only two sides. There are allies and enemies, victors and vanquished. You win or you lose. War excludes anything that is not related to the supreme aim of victory. Society in Northern Ireland seems to an outsider an oasis of certainties in a troubled world.[6]

In the British media, the conflict is often represented, or rather misrepresented, as stagnant and endlessly repetitive in its form: the ground(s) on or over which the conflict takes place have been popularly perceived as unchanging (witness the confusion caused to the media position by the 1994 ceasefire). As Jon Snow writes:

The record of the media in reporting Northern Ireland has, at best, been patchy. . . . For the bulk of the 'troubles', British-based TV's commitment to reporting the region was low. By . . . the mid-70s, the job had become a 'bomb watch'. Neither BBC nor ITV had much interest in any other way of approaching what was happening. . . . We had one rule throughout the 'troubles' at ITN. No death

---

[4] W. S. Armour, *Ulster, Ireland, Britain: A Forgotten Trust* (London: Duckworth, 1938), 16.

[5] Quoted in the *Irish News*, 9 Nov. 1987, 6. It is more likely that Sinn Féin would choose to use the word 'war', since it implies legitimate resistance rather than the civil disobedience unionism might claim IRA activity to be.

[6] 'On Top of That', *Fortnight*, 259 (Feb. 1988), 25.

from the violence was to go unreported. And so, for 25 years, we chronicled the killing. The viewer was as bored as the vast majority of politicians.[7]

At best, the situation appears to move one step forward only to take two steps back. The *Sunday Times* comments, quoted above, set the tone for the perceptions of the next three decades: a blood feud originating, at least in its present form, in the earlier part of the century, demanding blood sacrifices, and appearing to hold some essential quality which makes it unresolvable.

These perceptions of the Troubles find their parallel in the First World War, in the stagnant position of troops in the trenches, where one officer calculated that at their current rate of progress it would take 180 years to reach the Rhine,[8] who fought and advanced only to find themselves, a year later, back in the same trenches they started from, who believed that the war would last for ever, and who thus accepted that trench warfare had, in effect, become a permanent way of life. The Great War is the first 'war of attrition', the war which puts the phrase itself, without the quotation marks first tentatively applied to it, into common use. It is the ultimate manifestation of the cost, in human terms, of zero-sum political thinking, a war whose tale is too often told through its casualty figures rather than its political rationale. It is also the war in which the enemy shares one's own characteristics, suffers in the same situation. (It is partly this recognition that prompted the enormous success of Remarque's *All Quiet on the Western Front* in England.)

Viewing Northern Ireland through the lens of 1914–18 is a tendency reinforced by the rhetoric still current in the articulation of various political positions in the province. Echoing those who argued the inconsistency of Ulster Unionist behaviour in 1912–14 (the protestation of loyalty; the preparation for armed resistance; a seat in the War Cabinet for the man who approved and inspired that resistance), Seamus Mallon, discussing the unionist objections to the British Government's 1995 framework document, queried: 'Are the unionists now questioning the right of that sovereign British government', to which they declare loyalty? They have been accused, by Adams, of 'playing the Orange card' (again). John Hume noted the apparent contradiction in the unionist position if unionists were to reject proposals put forward by Westminster, since they accept British sovereignty, and therefore the British

---

[7] 'End of an Unseemly Era', *Fortnight*, 332 (Oct. 1994), 25.
[8] See Paul Fussell, *The Great War and Modern Memory* (London: OUP, 1975), 72.

Parliament.[9] With a return of the passive optimism enclosing divisive language characteristic of attitudes earlier in the century, a spokesperson from the Republic suggested that 'Hopefully we [the Republic] will persuade them [the unionists] one day to join us'.[10] At the other end of the spectrum, some of the loyalist rhetoric of recent years would not look out of place if it were called upon to deal with the 1912–14 Home Rule crisis again. Ian Paisley's and Robert McCartney's recent exhortations to unionists to refuse participation in all-party talks compared Trimble to Lundy, and invoked Edward Carson, who, the article points out, 'in the same hall in 1912 declared the Protestants of Ulster ready to use "all means which may be found necessary" to oppose a united Ireland'.[11] The article, ostensibly about Paisley, carried a photograph of Carson addressing Ulstermen in 1912. The 1914–18 connection is encouraged by other events—the IRA attack on Thiepval barracks; the Remembrance Sunday bombings. In view of the terms in which the conflict has been presented, by the media, by politicians, it is perhaps unsurprising to find a breakdown in the ceasefire discussed under the headline 'Ulster's return to trench war politics'.[12]

The grounding of the Northern Ireland conflict in the First World War colours the politics of remembrance of that war (or, as is also the case, vice versa). 'Here we go again', Kevin Myers remarked with resignation as Remembrance Sunday approached, 'the incorrigible failure to understand other people's passionately-held beliefs seasonally asserts itself'.[13] Edna Longley, in her illuminating essay, 'The Rising, the Somme, and Irish Memory', points out that 'Commemorations are as selective as sympathies' since 'They honour *our* dead, not your dead', and argues that in Ireland, 'when the Rising and the Somme came to be processed by state ideologies, the manner of their commemoration was shaped by sectarian idioms'. Commemoration does not transcend the contemporary scene; rather, it 'reinvents and reconstitutes according to present needs'.[14] Hence, the more recent, inclusive Remembrance cere-

---

[9] *Newsnight*, BBC2, 1 Feb. 1995. As discussed previously, unionism proclaims loyalty to the Queen and the Union over and above any Parliament which might undermine that Sovereign and Union.

[10] *A Question of Union*, Channel 4, 1 Feb. 1995.

[11] *Independent*, 1 Oct. 1997, 9.

[12] *Guardian*, 9 Dec. 1995, 4.

[13] 'An Irishman's Diary', *Irish Times*, 2 Nov. 1996, 13.

[14] *The Living Stream: Literature and Revisionism in Ireland* (Newcastle: Bloodaxe, 1994), 69–70.

monies are a consequence, not a cause, of political developments. The condition is not peculiar to Ireland—in England and elsewhere, the form of remembering the dead has always been determined, or predetermined, by considerations other than the purely altruistic or consolatory—but, as Longley's essay explores, the Irish context opens up 'further theological, as well as historical, contexts'.[15] The Republic of Ireland's attitude towards the Great War has, as previously noted, been characterized by a form of cultural amnesia only recently beginning to dissipate. In the North, the problem is double-edged, consisting both of amnesia *and* zealous, if not wholly accurate, forms of remembrance, with these two attitudes operating, broadly speaking, on either side of a sectarian divide.

The Great War's association with the Northern Irish conflict, both political and metaphorical, and the implications of the way in which the earlier war has been remembered in the North, converged and were sealed in memory on Remembrance Day in Enniskillen in 1987. An IRA bomb exploded as marchers assembled for the annual Remembrance Day ceremony at the war memorial, killing eleven people and injuring over sixty others. The bombing received more than usually widespread condemnation, and caused an almost unprecedented degree of shock, only equalled in recent years by the bombing at Omagh in 1998.[16] An emotive and emotional article by Frank McGuinness, in the *Irish Times*, was titled 'We are all children of Enniskillen now'. Echoing Yeats's 'Easter 1916', he averred that 'All is changed after Enniskillen'.[17] One reason why 'Catholic Ireland was especially shocked' was, Longley suggests, 'because a commemorative rite had been violated and the broken taboo, the *nefas*, was understood at a deep cultural level'. 'Did even the murders at the church in Darkley', she queries, 'cause as much revulsion?'[18] The visual impact of the aftermath of the bombing was

[15] Ibid. 69.
[16] The Soviet Union was 'unusually outspoken' about the Enniskillen massacre, its news agency, Tass, describing it as a 'barbaric act'. Ronald Reagan described the choice of time and place as a 'cruel irony' (*Belfast Telegraph*, 10 Nov. 1987, 4). The bombing was described as 'the most expensive Provo own goal since "the troubles" began', and it was speculated that '[coming back from Enniskillen' would be 'a more arduous and difficult task than even [the IRA's] most optimistic supporters imagine' (Ed Moloney, 'The Most Expensive Own Goal', *Fortnight* (Dec. 1987), 6). The IRA later attempted to distance themselves from the bombing, claiming the British Army had triggered the explosion by using a scanning device (Paul Bew and Gordon Gillespie, *Northern Ireland: A Chronology of the Troubles* (Dublin: Gill and Macmillan, 1993), 208).
[17] *Irish Times*, 13 Nov. 1987, 8.
[18] *The Living Stream*, 70.

profoundly felt. The war memorial at Enniskillen consists of a bronze statue of a soldier, standing with head bowed, on a stone plinth; the inscription reads 'Our Glorious Dead'. After the bomb, the memorial towered intact over a scene not unlike a battlefield. It was possible for even the least fanciful observers to feel that the Great War soldier was mourning the Enniskillen dead around him: past and present telescoped and reversed. 'At eleven o'clock today', someone observed, 'we should have been remembering the dead. Instead, we were digging them out.'[19]

Enniskillen reverberated through both North and South as a tragedy which also focused attention on the politics of remembrance, and on the division in Irish society over the events of the Great War. All the victims of the Enniskillen bombing were Protestant. At a Remembrance Day service in Northern Ireland, it was, and is, extremely improbable that they would be anything else: Enniskillen only underlined how much of a Protestant business remembering the Great War is. 'Our Glorious Dead' from the two world wars, the Poppy, Remembrance Day, and so on, are sentiments and symbols abjured by the nationalist community. The IRA's awareness of that fact made a town-centre bombing attack, theoretically a potentially random undertaking, in Seamus Mallon's phrase, 'totally sectarian'.[20] But, equally, the very fact that this state of affairs was underlined by the attack has caused more complex sentiments to surface in the last ten years. Jane Leonard points out that 'One of the ironies of Enniskillen has been that the bombing which aimed to obliterate those remembering in a northern Irish town subsequently propelled some southern towns into a cultural and practical reclamation of their own forgotten communities'.[21] Newspapers noted the fact that names on the Enniskillen memorial included Catholics as well as Protestants; a Franciscan monk from the Republic walked in the parade at the service in Enniskillen held on 22 November, wearing his British Army ex-service medals on his cassock. The argument over the rights or wrongs of poppy-wearing resurfaced with a new vehemence, and with new perspectives, in the Irish press.[22] (The arguments still continue: Kevin Myers heralded the onset of the annual debate in 1996 with the

[19] Quoted in the *Belfast Telegraph*, 9 Nov. 1987, 3.
[20] Quoted in the *Irish News*, 9 Nov. 1987, 5.
[21] 'The Twinge of Memory: Armistice Day and Remembrance Sunday in Dublin since 1919', in Richard English and Graham Walker (eds.), *Unionism in Modern Ireland*, (Dublin: Gill and Macmillan, 1996), 110.
[22] See *Irish Times* and *Irish Independent*, 14 and 23 Nov. , 1987.

rather world-weary comment, 'the poppy is upon us again'.)[23] And a letter to the *Belfast Telegraph* by a Belfast Catholic on 11 November 1987 broke Northern taboos by pointing out that 'the perpetrators selected a ceremony that affects all within our community. My own family lost members in two world wars, as did many Catholic families throughout this island.'

Remembrance, in some situations, relies on, and therefore creates, simplified versions of history. Thus, nationalists in Northern Ireland have distanced themselves from a record of involvement in a war which has been taken by unionists to symbolize loyalty to Britain; conversely, unionists choose to forget that northern Catholics enlisted in large numbers in the 16th (Irish) Division, as they also elide the fact that the 36th (Ulster) Division, contained some Catholics. Hence the anomalous situations which can bewilder those accustomed to a less rigidly divisive set of cultural codes: Remembrance ceremonies at, for example, the war memorial in Newry, the building of which was opposed by nationalists, are seen as a largely Protestant phenomenon; yet if the memorial were to record the names of the 'fallen', they might prove predominantly Catholic.[24] The sense of irreconcilable histories is inherent in Brian Moore's description of the cenotaph in Belfast as 'a white respectable phallus' (masculine, British) 'planted in sinking Irish bog' (feminine, Irish), his sense of, as Anthony Bradley describes it, a 'psychic landscape' which contains a 'legacy of antagonism'.[25]

In some ways, the complex, often contradictory, responses to Enniskillen revealed reductive versions of history to be precisely that. They also illustrated the fact that, even as late as 1987, the Irish response to the Great War, North and South, was still a largely unopened can of worms, and that the psychic landscape of the North, for all its outward certainties and simplicities consequent upon a state of war, was inwardly one of confusion and complexity. It is that complexity which is sensed

[23] 'An Irishman's Diary', *Irish Times*, 2 Nov. 1996, 13.
[24] For a detailed analysis of the problems and inconsistencies surrounding construction of war memorials in Ireland, see Jane Leonard, ' "Lest We Forget": Irish War Memorials', in David Fitzpatrick (ed.), *Ireland and the First World War* (Dublin: Trinity History Workshop, 1986). Leonard also explores and explodes certain fallacies concerning Irish involvement in, and remembrance of, the Great War, in 'The Twinge of Memory: Armistice Day and Remembrance Sunday in Dublin since 1919', 99–114.
[25] See 'Literature and Culture in the North of Ireland', in Michael Kenneally (ed.), *Cultural Contexts and Literary Idioms in Contemporary Irish Literature*, (Gerrards Cross: Colin Smythe, 1988), 45.

in much of Northern Ireland's literature, and which thus prevents the
'Ulster Renaissance' from falling into the trap of simple antagonisms
and inadequate language—both of which have characterized the polit-
ical scene—that poets and critics feared in the early 1970s. The best
poems of the Great War, as with the 'durable art' of contemporary
Northern Ireland, transcend simple antithesis, articulating instead Mac-
Neice's 'world in colour'. It is ironic that Bill Clinton, lauding as an
example to the Northern Irish people the 'melting pot' of American
society, chose to quote in illustration Louis MacNeice's 'Snow' with its
'drunkenness of things being various', a poem which arises from the
culture it was then held up to as focus for aspiration.[26] Such a tangled
state of affairs arises partly from the fact that, as Edna Longley writes,
'we are witnessing the last spasms of Green and Orange state-ideologies
which literature long ago found unworkable'.[27] Perceptions of the
poetic response in Northern Ireland have not always kept pace with
the poetry; the poetry is often several steps ahead of political rhetoric;
forms of remembrance have been interrogated and rehabilitated in
literature (most notably in Michael Longley's recent poetry), even as
the existent forms still resonate politically in ways which the poetry
undermines. In some ways, the art of war stands in opposition to
Goldring's description, quoted earlier, of war itself: if war is the 'great
simplifier', art, in contrast, complicates; it does not stand for one of two
sides, or exclude anything unrelated to a particular political position; it
does not win or lose, or even concede validity to that terminology; it
manifests, at times, an oasis of uncertainties. Cultural development, in
other words, has not toed the commemorative line in Northern Ireland,
even though poetry itself, in a different way, in Michael Longley's words
'commemorates . . . remembers and honours'.[28]

Edna Longley argues forcefully in her criticism for recognition of the
diversity of the Irish experience, rather than adherence to 'unworkable'
ideologies, and for the role played by literature, particularly Northern
Irish literature, in enabling that recognition: 'poetic diversity' is, she
argues, 'a frail silver lining of communal division'.[29] She is also acutely
sensitive to the fact that the Troubles can lead to 'improper expecta-

---

[26] *Guardian*, 1 Dec. 1995, 4.
[27] 'Opening Up: A New Pluralism', *Fortnight* (Nov. 1987), 25.
[28] Interview with the author, 11 July 1996.
[29] *Poetry in the Wars* (Newcastle: Bloodaxe, 1986), 16.

tions' of Northern poets through the exertion of pressure to subscribe in poetry to a particular political cause, as they can also inadvertently encourage reductive misreadings of the poetry, or of the nature of poetry, itself. In this sense, the connection she formulates in *Poetry in the Wars* between the First World War poets and Northern Irish poets is especially pertinent: Wilfred Owen's poetry, for example, honours and remembers the dead of the Great War with fidelity to the imagination rather than to popular expectation. It is also, as John Montague's speculations in the early 1970s illustrate—'the final judgement on the new Ulster Renaissance may well depend on their ability to learn a style from despair: it is the last quarter of the twentieth century we are entering, not the Georgian first'[30]—a connection sensed by Northern Irish poets themselves. Longley, Heaney, and Mahon all explore, in different ways, their relationship to Great War precursors. One reason may be the sense articulated by Mahon that, as with the Great War, 'The poetry and the "troubles" had a common source; the same energy gave rise to both'.[31] To acknowledge the link between art and violence means also to experience the temptation and pressure to compromise the former in the face of the overwhelming immediacy of the latter, a pressure which the best of the Great War soldier poets resisted. Another may be the unusually long 'period of inhibition' in the North 'before proper confrontation with the realities of the Great War':[32] Northern poets deconsecrate rhetoric in a way which apparently could not have been undertaken fifty years earlier, and to some extent find a model for that process in English poetry of the First World War.

II

But comparisons between contemporary Northern Irish poetry and First World War poetry can, misinterpreted, be as damaging as revealing. Perceptions of Northern Irish poets as 'neo-Georgians' may be problematical depending on whether 'Georgian' is seen as a derogatory or complimentary term. Wilfred Owen's association with Georgianism,

[30] Quoted in Robert Buttel, *Seamus Heaney* (Lewisburg: Bucknell University Press; London: Associated University Presses, 1975), 69.

[31] 'Derek Mahon Interviewed', by William Scammell, *Poetry Review*, 81/2 (Summer 1991), 5.

[32] Philip Orr, *The Road to the Somme: Men of the Ulster Division Tell Their Story* (Belfast: Blackstaff Press, 1987), 227.

his sense that 'Fame is the recognition of one's peers',[33] by whom he meant those included in Marsh's Georgian poetry anthologies, should rehabilitate it, as should the work of, amongst others, Edward Thomas, Robert Graves, and Edmund Blunden. The prominence of Rupert Brooke among the pre-war Georgians, and his notoriously idealistic response to war in the 1914 sonnets, undermines that rehabilitation, as does the complacent Anglo-centricity and 'pedestrian tendency' in 'run-of-the-mill Georgian poetry'.[34] Montague's sense of a link between the first and last quarters of the century verges on the critical-prescriptive: to survive, Northern Irish poets will have to come up with something 'new'. In contrast, Mahon more perceptively notes that the Northern 'renascence' is inherently something new which, far from floundering in a time warp, is in some ways moving the rest of Ireland forwards:

Not having been in the [Second World] war shunted Ireland to the sidelines, and I think she's been forced back into the twentieth century by events in the North, by the forgotten North. The nastiness reared its head as it had to sooner or later; the poet from the North had a new thing to say, a new kind of sound to make, a new texture to create. Looking back on it, there's a sort of inevitability that the new energy should have come from the North.[35]

In spite of this assertion, the attribution of 'neo-Georgianism' to Mahon, Longley, and Heaney has, on the whole, carried a negative charge because it takes Edna Longley's 'improper expectations' as acceptable criteria from which to pass judgement.[36] Equally, the state ideologies which persist North and South have influenced, or damaged, recognition of a process of rhetorical subversion if not the process itself.

Hence, the extent to which Heaney engages with the poetry of the Great War, and with the politics of remembrance in Northern Ireland, is underestimated because of his place in an imaginative tradition, closely allied to a political tradition, that sometimes eschews association with English history and culture. Conversely, for Mahon and Longley, if remembrance of the Great War, notably the Battle of the Somme, has

---

[33] 'To Susan Owen', 25 May 1918, *Collected Letters*, ed. Harold Owen and John Bell (London: OUP, 1967), 553.

[34] See James Reeves, introduction, to Reeves (ed.), *Georgian Poetry* (London: Penguin, 1962), p. xvii. His introduction provides a useful overview of the chequered history of the term 'Georgianism'.

[35] 'An Interview with Derek Mahon', by Terence Brown, *Poetry Ireland Review*, 14 (Autumn 1985), 12–13.

[36] *Poetry in the Wars*, 185. See also Ch. 4, Sect. V, above.

been dominated by Protestant, or unionist, culture in Northern Ireland, that dominance has had a longer-term, primarily negative effect on perceptions of Protestantism's cultural development. The Battle of the Somme has been widely perceived as the result of a failure in imagination: it was, unlike other disasters, unforeseen, unimaginative in tactics, and retrospectively unimaginable in its horror. Its military leader, Douglas Haig, has also become, in some respects, a symbol of that imaginative failure: 'there was', Paul Fussell suggests, 'a hopeless absence of cleverness about the whole thing, entirely characteristic of its author'. Of relevance to the battle's disastrous outcome were, he also hints, Haig's 'want of imagination and innocence of artistic culture'.[37] For Modris Eksteins, as for others, Haig is a man 'whose entire life and demeanor were the epitome of middle-class values and ambitions. Dour, religious, dedicated, hard-working, emotionally repressed, and yet a model of honor, achievement, and respectability, he is a symbol of an age . . . And yet he also represents the tragedy of an age.'[38] The epithets which crop up time and time again in relation to Haig—usually with wholly negative connotations—leave the impression of a fiercely Protestant, unimaginative, incompetent, rather bovine, and, from a post-war perspective at least, anachronistic leader: Fussell describes him as, 'stubborn, self-righteous, inflexible, intolerant . . . humorless'.[39]

In both Eksteins's and Fussell's critiques of the way in which Haig fought the Great War, a connection is implied between his faith and his failures. His Church of Scotland background, by implication, was not conducive to the imaginative forethought that could, hypothetically, have saved lives on 1 July 1916. Haig himself, in 1919, described the driving force behind his own activities as chief of the British general staff in the Great War, and behind the 'courage' and 'resolve' of all those involved, as 'the conviction that we were fighting, not only for ourselves and for our own Empire, but for a world ideal in which God was with us'.[40] The evangelical impulse behind involvement in the Great War is perhaps as obvious as it is now often unspoken: the King, as Defender of the Faith, in fighting an imperial war, must also be fighting a religious war. The war, Eksteins suggests, was a war of righteousness: 'To kill

---

[37] *The Great War and Modern Memory*, 12–13.
[38] *Rites of Spring: The Great War and the Birth of the Modern Age* (1989; New York: Anchor-Doubleday, 1990), 187.
[39] *The Great War and Modern Memory*, 12.
[40] Quoted in Eksteins, *Rites of Spring*, 191.

Germans was to purge the world of the Antichrist, the great beast from the abyss, and to herald the New Jerusalem. . . . Not since the wars of religion of the seventeenth century, and perhaps even the crusades, had men of the cloth encouraged killing for the greater glory of God with such enthusiasm.'[41] And the Great War was also, evidence from both England and Germany suggests, a war which initially appealed to Protestants rather more than to Catholics, because of their closer identification with the national cause (without any distraction from Rome), and the perception that the Protestant Church was ultimately the handmaiden of the State.

That evangelical impulse was subjected very quickly to ironic mockery: the trench newspaper, *The Wipers Times*, was renamed in April 1916 *The 'New Church' Times*, and with subversive humour proclaimed in its editorial:

> Oh! Ye of little faith, wake up and smile for the summer is upon ye. Let your step be brisk and your hearts light for 'even as ye have sown so shall ye not reap', and for that thank your lucky stars, for though ye have tried for eighteen months to lose the war yet have ye not succeeded and victory is at hand. So go ye unto the uttermost ends of darkness, yea, even unto Piccadilly and Westminster, and preach the gospel of cheeriness and hope.[42]

The soldier in the trenches identified with the crucified Christ, rather than with the crusader killing on behalf of that Christ, as much of the disturbing religious imagery in Owen's poetry, and some of the popular war myths—the crucified Canadian, the angels at Mons—suggest. The identification, however, served to weaken rather than strengthen ties with the Church (and through the Church, the State). The soldier was perhaps Christian with his burden, reaching no Celestial City but a landscape of horror and desolation. Fussell, in arguing that the movement in the Great War was towards, rather than away from, myth, points out that *The Pilgrim's Progress* is a frequent imaginative touchstone for the soldier. 'Protestant England' looks not to Dante for 'images of waste and horror' but to Bunyan.[43] But the fundamental difference between the soldier and Christian was the latter's purposeful movement through time and space, and the former's stagnation in hostile country. *The*

[41]   *Rites of Spring*, 236.
[42]   Repr. in Patrick Beaver (ed.), *The Wipers Times* (London: Peter Davis, 1973), 51–2 (1st pub. on the Western Front in newspaper form 1916–18).
[43]   *The Great War and Modern Memory*, 139–40.

Pilgrim's Progress, it seems, provided the metaphors of darkness, but not of light, the trials of the pilgrim without any of the progress, and no Celestial City awaiting at the end, not even the homes for heroes that had been promised. So to many of the combatants at least, the blaze of glory experienced by the warmongering religious maniac burnt itself out in the face of a barbaric conflict that appeared to be a denial of God's existence, as much as it was a denial of history, progress, and Western Christianity. Haig, and the religious views which sustained him, were, one might infer, anachronistic even before the war was over. As Fussell puts it, after the events of 1916, 'What could remain of confidence in Divine assistance...?'[44]

Anachronistic, intolerant, unimaginative, stubborn, repressed—these adjectives are also prevalent in descriptions of the Ulster Protestant community. Haig is sometimes used as the whipping boy for the sins of an imperial age forced to reinterpret aspects of its cultural identity in the trenches. He seems at times almost like the archetypal honest Ulsterman, whose 1912 Covenant was signed 'In sure confidence that God will defend the right', but who found in the post-war years that the tide of sympathy had turned against him. But Fussell's question 'What could remain of confidence...?' does still find an answer of sorts (though not the one he would anticipate) in Ulster. Haig's 1919 speech is, one might think, the kind of speech which could never be made again with conviction or without irony: English militant Protestantism was probably in its death throes even before that speech was delivered. But, on the other hand, Ian Paisley can still proclaim that the 'spirit' of 1688 'rested on a religious faith which eschews priestcraft and is begotten by faith in "the perfect law of liberty" the Holy Bible' and hope that 'that spirit will be re-born in the hearts of Ulster Loyalists today' who will not only 'commemorate that faith but participate therein' and hurl 'defiance at the enemies'.[45] If the war ironized the militant streak in English Protestantism, for various reasons it did not do so in Ulster Protestantism.[46]

---

[44] Ibid. 29.

[45] Foreword to Peter Robinson, *Their Cry was 'No Surrender'* (Belfast: Crown Publications, 1988), 14. The book is dedicated 'to all those whose answer to Ulster's enemies is still "No Surrender"' (3).

[46] Tom Paulin points out that *The Pilgrim's Progress* 'remains a powerful influence within Protestant populism in the north of Ireland' (introduction, to Paulin (ed.), *The Faber Book of Political Verse* (London: Faber, 1986), 37).

Perceptions of the role of the imagination in the Great War have helped to form negative perceptions of the Ulster Protestant imagination (or rather a perceived absence of any such thing) in the twentieth century. To oppose the unimaginative, representative imperial figure of Haig is to make a (metaphorical) stand for fluidity, tolerance, imaginative power, and modernity. The Ulster Protestant community's 'failure' to do so implies that it is also, like Haig, representative of the tragedy of an age. There is unquestionably a response to the Great War which is, according to unwritten rules of the modern age, perceived to be correct, a response based on an ironic self-awareness and a cultural reflexiveness inconceivable before 1914. The absence of such a response in Ulster still invites the criticism of which the following by Geoffrey Bell is characteristic:

Right they [the Protestant workers] are to remind the English ruling class that over 5,000 Ulster working-class Protestants died [*sic*47] in the Battle of the Somme so that Britain could gain a few more inches of land. The anniversary of that battle is another occasion when Orangemen march through the towns of Northern Ireland, quoting the words of Sir William Spencer [*sic*]: 'I am not an Ulsterman but yesterday the 1st of July as I followed their amazing attack on the Somme I felt I would rather be an Ulsterman than anything else in the world.'... They quote the words not with anger at the senseless carnage, at the way they were sacrificed so that well-fed, high-living Englishmen could enjoy themselves for a few more years. They are not bitter at the slaughter of their own people in one of the most pointless military battles the world has ever seen, a battle judged necessary at the time by those not of their class, not of their country. They are not angry, they are not bitter, they do not protest; they are proud.
That is their tragedy.[48]

Ulster Protestant pride, in this context, is symptomatic of a failure in understanding, of imprisonment within a mindset that the war itself should, theoretically, have invalidated. And in failing to recognize, in Bell's terms, the real source of their 'tragedy', then by implication Ulster Protestants have (typically) failed to recognize the imaginative potential of their own situation.

The 1920s in England were characterized by an apparent reaction against what can be loosely defined as 'repression'. One could go further

---

[47] Although the Ulster Division casualties on 1 July 1916 numbered in excess of 5,000, the number killed on that day was approximately 2,000.
[48] *The Protestants of Ulster* (London: Pluto Press, 1976), 144.

and claim that such a reaction has remained characteristic of twentieth-century culture. But for Eksteins, the desire not to think about the war was itself an 'act of repression... of one of the most consequential events of the age' which 'called forth the very opposite: the denial of repression',[49] the results of which were hedonism, narcissism, materialism, extravagance, the frenetic dance of the decade, and no mention of the fact that society was still rather short of men. That counter-act of repression, living for the moment, is apparently broken in England with the flood of war books, films, memoirs, and poems at the end of the decade, from which time the war is, theoretically, not only commemorated but remembered.

While the 1920s reaction against traditional values and authority was taking place (or at least appeared to be taking place) in England, Ulster Protestants were enshrining those values in a Protestant 'statelet' of Northern Ireland, re-establishing rather than subverting authority. The extent to which the two cultures developed differently, while retaining strong links, is painfully apparent today: in 1912, many Englishmen, sharing the Ulster Protestant value system, were outraged by the possibility that Ulster Protestantism could be betrayed by the Liberal government of the time, prompting, for example, the passionate response of Rudyard Kipling in 'Ulster 1912'. By 1996, Ulster Protestants were perceived by many simply as bigoted and intransigent,[50] a view consolidated by the Unionist Party's refusal to participate in the opening of the Northern Ireland Assembly in 1999. The Great War might be, as Eksteins claims, 'the axis on which the modern world turned',[51] but not everyone turned the same way. The notion of Protestantism as some kind of essential and self-defining feature, partially outweighing class differences and replacing national loyalties, survives in Ulster in a way it does not in England. As David Miller points out, although Belfast and the north-east corner of Ireland modernized simultaneously with mainland Britain, 'Orangeism sustained within

---

[49] *Rites of Spring*, 256.

[50] See e.g. popular opinion expressed in letters to the *Guardian* on 12 Feb. 1996 after the Canary Wharf bombing: 'The people of London are not prepared to carry the burden of unionist intransigence any longer... We owe the bigots of Northern Ireland nothing'; 'Is not the existence of Northern Ireland a denial of democracy?'; 'the loyalist community... must either integrate with a united Ireland, or leave'; 'Like Hong Kong, the province cannot remain a crown colony forever'.

[51] *Rites of Spring*, 237.

this modernizing society...the core of a community which cut across social classes, in which all were in some sense equal in their common Protestantism'.[52]

From one point of view, partly arising from the Great War, the link between Ulster's evangelical Protestantism and modernization becomes paradoxical if not untenable. George Bernard Shaw claimed, during the Home Rule debate, that Ireland had been 'kept out of the mighty stream of modern Protestantism by her preoccupation with her unnatural political condition'.[53] The Ulster Protestant community is, from such a perspective, a community which turns inwards upon itself, embodying all the more repressive aspects of Calvinist culture. In a sense, the Ulster Protestant reaction to the Great War was to affirm those aspects in spite of (because of?) the disintegration of founding principles outside the community—the idea of empire, the union, the Protestant ethic itself. So if Calvinist cultures have always had a problematic relation to the arts, that problem was compounded in Ulster with a war that appeared to make a mockery of the 'Haig-like' qualities which formed the basis of the Protestant ethic. The 'non-Protestant' imagination is, in a way, vindicated by the Battle of the Somme, because of the battle's disastrous outcome. Meticulously timed, planned, and executed, it still led to unimaginable horror. Yet, paradoxically, the ability to see the Great War's horror as unimaginable, is also to move beyond the narrow perspective of method and system to a point where imaginative paralysis begins to be defeated.

Terence Brown writes that the modern Ulster Unionist identity, forged between 1886 and the Great War, was 'an identity which subsumed manifold differences within northern protestant society in a fundamental, all-embracing opposition to the proposed constitutional change'.[54] Contempt from other (most notably Irish Literary Revival) quarters for the Ulster Protestant imagination does not pre-date this identity. Ulster Protestantism has always been able to mock its own stereotype: George Birmingham writes that 'Belfast...has not given to the world many eminent poets, philosophers or scholars...But it has

---

[52] *Queen's Rebels: Ulster Loyalism in Historical Perspective* (Dublin: Gill and Macmillan, 1975), 64.

[53] Quoted in Edna Longley and Gerald Dawe (eds.), *Across a Roaring Hill: The Protestant Imagination in Modern Ireland* (Belfast: Blackstaff Press, 1985), 61.

[54] *The Whole Protestant Community: The Making of a Historical Myth* (Field Day Pamphlet No. 7; Derry: Field Day, 1985), 10.

given birth to several mathematicians of quite respectable standing.'[55] But the most famous critique, and one which lacks the affectionate humour in Birmingham's indictment, is AE's: 'Ulster will not be able to express its soul or its Irish character so long as it looks to Great Britain for its cultural ideals. Unionism in Ireland has produced no literature.'[56] The unionism referred to here is the imperial unionist consciousness developed around the time of the first Home Rule crisis, a unionism characterized by excessive propaganda and chronic Anglophilia. By 1914, the popular images of Ulster Protestantism, as they still appear, and which are not characterized by Anglophilia, were consolidated. As Alvin Jackson explains, at the time of the Third Home Rule Bill, 'unionist imagery was ... both more influential than at any time in the past, as well as being further removed from the British patriotic imagery which had been an early inspiration within the movement'.[57] It is also, at least from an external viewpoint, an identity which fits rather too well with the Weberian view of Protestantism,[58] but to which the substantially revised version of Weber's thesis, emphasizing Protestantism's transformative capacity and revolutionary potential in relation to the modern world, rather than its (dubious) connection with capitalism, is seldom applied.

Unionism is, as O'Halloran explores in *Partition and the Limits of Irish Nationalism*, often stereotyped by an Irish nationalist viewpoint, but equally importantly it is also a self-stereotype, and one that appears to have cornered itself, artistically speaking, after the First World War. Weber's conception of the Protestant ethic features in both negative perceptions and positive self-perceptions of Ulster Protestantism. From either limited point of view, the imagination may be a casualty of political expediency. Traditionally, the relation of Protestantism, more specifically Calvinism, to the arts has been seen as one of (mutual) suspicion. Weber suggests that the 'entirely negative attitude of Puritanism to all

---

[55] *The Red Hand of Ulster* (London: Smith, Elder & Co., 1912), 14.

[56] Quoted in Longley and Dawe (eds.), *Across a Roaring Hill*, p. iii.

[57] 'Irish Unionist Imagery 1850–1920', in Eve Patten (ed.), *Returning to Ourselves: Second Volume of Papers from the John Hewitt International Summer School*, (Belfast: Lagan Press, 1995), 354.

[58] As expressed in Max Weber, *The Protestant Ethic and the Spirit of Capitalism* (1930) with introduction by Anthony Giddens (London: George Allen & Unwin Ltd., 1976). Cf. Sean O'Faolain's comment that 'Orangeism has never yet been associated with anything that did not pay' quoted in Clare O'Halloran, *Partition and the Limits of Irish Nationalism: An Ideology under Stress* (Dublin: Gill and Macmillan, 1987), 47.

the sensuous and emotional elements in culture' stems from the fact that these elements are 'of no use toward salvation and promote sentimental illusions and idolatrous superstitions'.[59] More recent viewpoints are that 'Protestantism, as a religion of the word, has had a "mixed" record when it comes to the arts', and that it has been 'uneasy about objectification of the divine drama in images which might themselves draw the devotion of the supplicant from the invisible God beyond the gods. It has often and maybe even usually been uneasy about unrestricted bodily attention, and has rather consistently feared the ecstasy of the dance through most of the years of its history.'[60]

The common denominator in the various views of Protestantism is the sense that it is driven by fear, and it is the idea of Protestantism as a religion of fear which survives to an unusual degree in Ulster. Vaslav Nijinsky's famous response to the Great War—his announcement at a private performance in 1919, 'Now I will dance you the war, with its suffering, with its destruction, with its death'[61]—is a gesture towards the arrival of a modern age made on the edge of insanity. The gesture stands in opposition to the stereotypical unionist sensibility: both might be informed by apocalypse, but seek relief in fundamentally different ways. Michael Walzer writes of the early Puritans:

Like Hobbes, they saw disorder and war as the natural state of fallen men, out of which they had been drawn by God's command and by the painful efforts of their own regenerate wills. But they lived always on the very brink of chaos, maintaining their position only through a constant vigilance and, indeed, a constant warfare against their own natural inclination and against the devil and his worldlings. The goal of this warfare was repression, and its apparent cause was an extraordinary anxiety.... In Puritan literature this same fearfulness is made specific in social terms. Once again, it is a fear which Hobbes would understand: the fear of disorder in society. It is apparent in the nervous hostility with which Puritan writers regarded carousal, vagabondage, idleness, all forms of individualistic extravagance ... country dances and urban crowds, the theater with its gay (undisciplined) audiences, gossip, witty talk... the list could be extended.[62]

---

[59]   *The Protestant Ethic and the Spirit of Capitalism*, 105.

[60]   See Richard McBrien, *Catholicism* (3rd edn., London: Geoffrey Chapman, 1994), 1198.

[61]   Quoted in Romola Nijinsky, *Nijinsky* (1933; London: Sphere Books, 1970), 337.

[62]   'Puritanism as a Revolutionary Ideology', in S. N. Eisenstadt (ed.), *The Protestant Ethic and Modernization: A Comparative View* (New York and London: Basic Books Inc., 1968), 120–2.

Ulster Protestantism, rather than embracing chaos in the spirit of the 1920s, dealt with it by a resistance which translated as repression. Walzer's description of the early Puritans still echoes in some aspects of Ulster Presbyterianism: the loyalist slogan 'The price of liberty is eternal vigilance' is symptomatic of this mentality. The fear, in 1918, was still the fear of the 'wild Irish' at the gates, threatening the union, threatening stability, a danger which became all the more immediate as Ireland dissolved into civil war in the early 1920s. The oft-cited 'siege mentality' of Ulster Unionists could be said to have its roots in Calvinism—'whithersoever you turn, all the objects around you are not only unworthy of your confidence, but almost openly menace you, and seem to threaten immediate death'[63]—and characterized their reaction at the end of the Great War, as it also, to some extent, characterized the reaction to the 1994 ceasefire, and characterizes reactions towards the issue of decommissioning. If political necessity dictated, and dictates, remembrance of history in one way as opposed to another, as it does also in England, art could be feared because of what Longley and Dawe describe as its 'power to penetrate communal neurosis',[64] the existence of which, in the interests of security, has not been openly acknowledged. From this angle, perhaps the Ulster and English ways of coming to terms with the Great War stem from the same source, one resulting in an explosion of art, decadence, uninhibited behaviour, and the other in an implosive rejection of instability, emotion, and generational conflict.

In neither case, of course, is this the whole story, but it is the latter perception of Ulster Protestant ideology which provides the basis for Frank McGuinness's influential 1986 play, *Observe the Sons of Ulster Marching Towards the Somme*; and it is the supposed moral high ground which comes with a conscious awareness of the possibility of reading history in an infinite number of ways that enables certain critiques of Ulster Protestant bigotry (although the sense of moral high ground undermines any such awareness). *Observe the Sons of Ulster* is a play more than usually bound up with the question of reception. It attempts to contextualize the artistic silence characteristic of Ulster Protestantism in the war and post-war period by focusing on unionist culture in a way which is both sympathetic and transgressive. It also records, on another level, the death of the artist (Kenneth Pyper), even though the 'artist' in

---

[63] John Calvin, quoted ibid. 121.
[64] Introduction to Longley and Dawe (eds.), *Across a Roaring Hill*, p. ix.

the play is the only survivor. The play does not, despite its reception, break the apparent silence of Ulster Protestantism on the subject of the Great War: on the contrary, its effect depends upon that silence's continuance, or at least on a belief in its continuance. Perhaps, therefore, one should be wary of claiming, as has often been the case, that McGuinness has given a voice to the voiceless in his dramatization of what John Wilson Foster calls an 'archetypal event in loyalist psycho-history'.[65] The play offers a version of events, a way of understanding, that both conforms with and subverts some of the stereotypes of the Ulster Protestant, turning the silence into an imaginary event by working in the space between loyalist rhetoric and the actuality of human suffering. The dance metaphor which opens and closes the play works on several obvious fronts—war, love, politics (Carson's dance)—but there is also some irony in the choice of metaphor to give shape to past and present because of Protestantism's suspicion of the dance: the elder Pyper invites his younger self into the dance unto death reminiscent of Nijinsky more than of post-war Ulster:

Ulster lies in rubble at our feet. Save it. Save me. Take me out of this war alive. Evil is come upon us. The temple of the Lord is darkness. He has ransacked his dwelling. The Protestant gods die. . . . Dance in the deserted temple of the Lord. Dance unto death before the Lord.[66]

The problematic of the Protestant imagination is as much one of perception as it is anything else. *Observe the Sons of Ulster*, it appears, was something which many people felt *should* exist in the Irish canon: the play was greeted, Joe McMinn suggests, with 'delight and relief—as if, finally, a tradition not associated with imagination or poetry was getting a chance to be heard with respect'.[67] Behind this reaction, there is a sense that the following assumption still holds: McGuinness has done for the Ulster Protestants what they could not (cannot) do for themselves—critique their own historical myths. Such an assumption is misleading—unless MacNeice, Mahon, Rodgers, Longley, and others are seen as self-expelled from their Protestant background, entailing a view of 'Protestant' culture as less than the sum of its parts—and

[65] 'Imagining the Titanic', in Patten (ed.), *Returning to Ourselves*, 334.
[66] Frank McGuinness, *Observe the Sons of Ulster Marching Towards the Somme* (London: Faber, 1986), 12.
[67] 'Language, Literature and Cultural Identity: Irish and Anglo-Irish', in Jean Lundy and Aodán MacPóilin (eds.), *Styles of Belonging: The Cultural Identities of Ulster*, (Belfast: Lagan Press, 1992), 48.

might explain why the *Irish Times*'s reviewer of the play called it 'one of the most comprehensive attacks ever made in the theatre on Ulster Protestantism'.[68]

It is rather, as Michael Longley describes it, a 'humane study of cultural confusion and military heroism'.[69] But one of the problems with the play is the temptation to read it as more than it can possibly be: it invites its audience, even in its title, to stand back and watch history, in contrast to Derek Mahon's 'watch me as I make history' ('Rage for Order'). To be able to 'Observe the Sons of Ulster Marching' implies a revelation of what is already there, the unfolding of the destiny of a community, when in fact the play also meditates as much on its own 'community' as on the one whose history it is apparently retelling. The 'Somme' in the title can symbolize more than the battle itself: the sons of Ulster are marching towards doom, sterility, political stagnation, attrition, the deserted temple (of Ulster) at the play's close. One can, it might be inferred, watch them marching towards a metaphorical Somme even now.

III

If the Somme can be appropriated as a symbol of the Ulster Protestant 'fate', so too can that other 'archetypal event in loyalist psycho-history', the sinking of RMS *Titanic* on 15 April 1912. Both events hold a more complex place in memory than remembrance might suggest. A recent documentary on the *Titanic*'s sister ship, the *Britannic*, showed footage of Belfast's Harland and Wolff shipyard at the height of its success, building the White Star liners *Olympic, Titanic, Britannic*, and so on. The footage was contrasted with pictures of the shipyard today, a forlorn sight of vast empty space, bleak and abandoned, with grass growing through the concrete.[70] The contrast has, if one chooses to interpret it that way, enormous symbolic potential: nature beginning to dominate a once industrial, man-controlled environment; the fate of the yard uncannily paralleling the fate of the ships it built; the end of the Victorian and pre-dating that, Enlightenment, dream; the decline of Ulster Protestant political and economic power; the disappearance, literally, of large

[68] *Irish Times*, 19 Feb. 1985, 10.
[69] Letter to the *Irish Times*, 2 Mar. 1985, 23.
[70] *Encounters*, Channel 4, 5 May 1996.

numbers of people from the face of the earth—the workers from the yard, the passengers from the ships, the soldiers in the Great War.

The temptation to read such symbolism into Belfast's association with the *Titanic*, and all the ship has come to represent in the modern imagination, is, because of the peculiar political position of Ulster Protestants, almost irresistible. The purpose here is not to challenge the *Titanic* myth itself as it is known throughout the western world. Unlike other more serious disasters, which capture public interest only briefly, the obsession with the *Titanic*'s disastrous maiden voyage has persisted throughout the century, suggesting that in the popular imagination, more than a ship was sunk in April 1912. It has acquired a significance out of all proportion either to the scale of the disaster, or to its economic and political effect on the British Empire. '[N]othing in the whole war moved me so deeply as the loss of the *Titanic* had done a few years earlier', George Orwell wrote. 'This comparatively petty disaster shocked the whole world, and the shock has not quite died away even yet.'[71] The loss of the *Titanic*, Jeremy Hawthorn writes, 'offered itself as a perfect symbol for a variety of things: over-confidence and complacency, the end of an era, a presage for the collapse of British invincibility and of the changes that would be wrought by the First World War'.[72]

The existence of such a belief in the *Titanic*'s significance on a broad cultural scale has to be considered as a backdrop to its more specific place in Ulster's historical myths. But in Belfast, the *Titanic* is a crucial symbol *for* and *of* the loyalist community: it is also, therefore, in view of the worldwide symbolic value it carries, a problematizing force in various perceptions of Ulster Protestantism's character and history. Three days before the *Titanic* sank, the Third Home Rule Bill was introduced into the House of Commons for a first reading. Against all the odds, the Bill never became law in the north-east of Ireland. Had it done so in the late nineteenth century, Harland and Wolff intended withdrawing the shipbuilding works from Belfast to mainland Britain, because there could be no 'security' or 'commercial confidence' under an Irish parliament.[73] The shipbuilding itself, then, may be more than a symbol: it is, or was (for the Protestant worker employed there),

---

[71] 'My Country Right or Left' (1940), in *The Collected Essays, Journalism and Letters of George Orwell*, ed. Sonia Orwell and Ian Angus, i (London: Penguin, 1970), 587.

[72] *Cunning Passages: New Historicism, Cultural Materialism and Marxism in the Contemporary Literary Debate* (London: Arnold, 1996), 88.

[73] Bardon, *A History of Ulster*, 404–5.

a tangible manifestation of the virtues of the union. But while unionism might identify itself, and be identified with, the *Titanic*, to state the obvious, the *Titanic* foundered in 1912 and Ulster Unionism did not. If one can connect the *Titanic*, the Somme, and Northern Ireland, the ways in which such associations are made are symptomatic of ideological positions that conflict with, or create an idea of, the past and present condition of Ulster Protestantism. Thus, if the sinking of the ship represents the end of Victorian complacency, and the Great War merely puts the rubber stamp on that end, Ulster Unionism, by implication, should have foundered with the ship, but instead survives as an ana-chronistic symbol of a sunken culture. On the other hand, if the loss of the *Titanic* was an enormous blow to Ulster Protestant pride—particu-larly to Belfast pride[74]—it is also true that a number of Irish Catholics went down with the ship, and that Irish Catholic suffering at Protestant hands extended beyond the Government of Ireland Act. The *Titanic* and the Somme are, in many ways, devastating events in loyalist history, but one could also argue that they were events which saved Ulster from Home Rule by what John Wilson Foster terms 'historical default': the apocalyptic sensibility characteristic of Presbyterianism lives in anticipa-tion of such disasters, even finds its approach to everyday life vindicated by them. Alternatively, the loss of the *Titanic* could be seen as retribution for the appalling anti-Catholic sectarianism of the shipyard: Protestant supremacy goes down with its ship.

Stephen Kern connects the outbreak of war with the sinking of the *Titanic*, and attributes both to the failure of the old order:

The arrogance, the lack of safety precautions, the reliance on technology, the simultaneity of events, the worldwide attention, the loss of life, all evoke the sinking of the *Titanic* as a simile for the outbreak of the war. The lookouts on the *Titanic* were blinded by fog, as the political leaders and diplomats and military men were blinded by historical shortsightedness, convinced that even

---

[74] St John G. Ervine, in *Changing Winds* (1917; London: George Allen & Unwin Ltd., 1930), explores the reasons why the loss of the *Titanic* had such an enormous impact: 'The sinking of the great ship had stunned men's minds and humiliated their pride.... "It isn't true," he kept on saying to himself... "She's a Belfast boat and Belfast boats don't go down..." He felt it oddly this loss.... It was not the drowning of a crowd of people or the drowning of Tom Arthurs that most affected Henry. It was the fact that a boat built by Belfast men had foundered on her maiden trip, on a clear cold night of stars, reeling from the iceberg's blow like a flimsy yacht. He had the Ulsterman's pride in the Ulsterman's power... "By God," he said to himself, "this'll break their hearts in Bel-fast!"' (337–8).

if war came it would not last long. On the eve of the disaster they shared a confidence that the basic structure of European states was sound, able to weather any storm. Europe, they were certain, was unsinkable. The concentration of wireless messages from the sinking ship...suggests the flurry of telegraph messages and telephone conversations exchanged during the July Crisis. Even the icebergs floating in the path of the liner had an analog in the eight assassins who lay in wait for Francis Ferdinand at various points on his parade route the day he was murdered.[75]

John Wilson Foster proposes instead that,

like the Somme, the loss of the *Titanic* has come to symbolize unconsciously the thwarted nationhood of Ulster Protestants, that at the level of community dreamwork, the foundering of the ship and the founding of Northern Ireland were intertwined, that the ship *became* Northern Ireland, a statelet that invited the pride in which it was fashioned, but was always in danger of being sunk by the chilling impersonal 'iceberg dynamics' of Irish nationalism.[76]

It is a long way, conceptually, from Sarajevo to Stormont, or indeed from iceberg to terrorist (which does seem to be the common denominator in these two analogies). As Hawthorn points out, something about the *Titanic* disaster 'encourages such searches for minutely differentiated symbolic clues, as if the *Titanic*'s loss were a highly coded Renaissance painting or piece of medieval church architecture'.[77] But in the midst of these heady similes lurks a sensitive cultural issue: the modernity which for Foster was being enacted in Belfast in the building of the *Titanic*, and the modernity that brought about changing perceptions of space and time for Kern, can have both positive and negative connotations. In Ulster, negativity has tended to dominate attitudes: in Mary Costello's *Titanic Town*, the *Titanic* does not represent a modernizing project; rather, the title of the book links Belfast with disaster, casts the city, like the ship, as 'ill-fated', as it also expresses her sense of marginalization in a Protestant city.[78] The modernity which brought about the *Titanic* ('God Himself could not sink this ship') was also part of the attempted scientific domination of nature that enabled, but was travestied by, the First World War, when machines dominating nature

---

[75] *The Culture of Time and Space 1880–1918* (Cambridge, Mass.: Harvard University Press, 1983), 268–9.

[76] 'Imagining the *Titanic*', 333.

[77] *Cunning Passages*, 108.

[78] Mary Costello, *Titanic Town: Memoirs of a Belfast Girlhood* (London: Mandarin, 1993), 26.

altered to machines dominating man (nature) at appallingly high cost to human life. With such a view now commonplace, pride in the *Titanic* is, for Ulster Protestants, as difficult to sustain in the post-war years as pride in their achievements at the Somme. The tide of opinion turned against any such emotion: in the modern and modernizing world, the *Titanic* points the dangers of hubris; the Somme is the final tragedy.

John Wilson Foster, in 'Imagining the *Titanic*', points beyond sectarianism to the modernizing achievements of Belfast, and thus tries to rehabilitate the *Titanic* in its Ulster Protestant context: whatever one's reading of modernity, the city does at least, he claims, require a more sophisticated cultural analysis than it has yet received. Like Hawthorn, he also concentrates on the ways in which the *Titanic* was imagined before and after the disaster actually happened, and, more particularly, on the imaginative response to the event in Ireland. That he titles his essay 'Imagining the *Titanic*' is not unambiguous. Referring to the fact that the *Titanic*'s fate was, unlike the war which followed it, eerily imagined in various fictional works before the ship was even built, he is also perhaps implicitly saying something about his own imaginative potential as an East Belfast Protestant within a community which, so the stereotype goes, while it might have been capable of *building* the *Titanic*, certainly could not have 'imagined' it.

Hawthorn, when he considers the 'Irish Connection' of the *Titanic*, never really lifts the debate beyond the Orange–Green fault-lines that for Foster have prevented proper appreciation of the 'modernism being enacted' in the shipyards. Outlining the historical context in a way which elides the political (and cultural) importance of Ulster Protestantism within the Empire—'Technically, the ship was built in what was, and formally remains, a part of Britain: the northern-Irish town of Belfast'— Hawthorn misses some of the implications behind the *Titanic*'s 'posthumous literary life...in Irish—and especially Northern Irish literature', suggesting that 'the more specifically Irish associations of the *Titanic*—cultural and political—are passed over in silence' by Robert Johnstone and Derek Mahon. In Mahon's 'Bruce Ismay's Soliloquy' (retitled 'After the Titanic'), it is, he writes, 'the view of Ismay as victim' which is 'Central to the poem'.[79] Perhaps, taking this further, one could instead see Ismay as the representative figure for a collective guilt which is as unacknowledged as it is irrational as it is also perceived to be

<hr/>

[79] *Cunning Passages*, 152, 155–7.

a characteristic of the Ulster Protestant community. The poem does not, as Hawthorn assumes, post-date Frank McGuinness's 1986 *Observe the Sons of Ulster*, where the sense of guilt is implicit in Anderson's line 'We weren't to blame. No matter what they say'. It appeared under the title 'As God is my Judge', a title more evocative of the evangelical tradition of those who built the ship, in Mahon's first collection, *Night Crossing*, in 1968. And Mahon's 'A Refusal to Mourn', often missed by collectors of *Titanic* poems, is, as Edna Longley points out, 'not only an elegy for his boiler-making grandfather but a requiem for the Titanic and for Belfast as a shipbuilding city'.[80]

Instead, it is McGuinness's *Observe the Sons of Ulster* which, like a gift from the gods, provides a 'good example' for Hawthorn of 'the way in which the more local symbolic associations of the ship and its fate could be tapped in a literary work'. McGuinness uses *Titanic* folklore to create a web of guilt, pride, lost pride, superstition, and premonition—the *Titanic* forewarns of the Somme: 'Every nail we hammered into the *Titanic*, we'll die the same amount in this cursed war'. In the play, the *Titanic* offers itself, as Hawthorn points out, as a 'perfect symbol' for a 'doomed generation of Ulster Protestants, going down in the Battle of the Somme as helplessly as those passengers and crew in the ship which represented their pride'.[81] But perhaps a caveat, or at least a reminder, is sometimes necessary in relation to *Observe the Sons of Ulster*: the *Titanic* in the play is, it is made clear, a fiction, whose 'life in popular myth' does not necessarily equate with the ship that sank, but so too is the Ulster Protestant generation in the play that it symbolizes.

It is impossible, of course, to locate, once and for all, the significance of the *Titanic* in an Irish context. It does not possess innate significance: it was a ship which, like numerous other ships, sailed and sank. Any significance attributed to it seems to carry its own agenda. So perhaps one *could* offer it as a symbol of the Ulster Protestant community, not because of its perceived connection with war, modernity, hubris, class structure, or imperialism, but because the *Titanic* and the Ulster Protestant community can both, in terms of cultural preoccupations, become the victims of 'improper' expectations. The desire for the *Titanic* to 'mean' something, or for the Ulster Protestant community to 'say' something (witness the critical over-dependence on a play which seems to do exactly that), are desires which, even if they presuppose essential

---

[80] *The Living Stream*, 99.   [81] *Cunning Passages*, 153–5.

or innate qualities, reveal little about their objects and more about the politics of interpretation.

IV

This is not to denigrate McGuinness's play itself, but to point out that it is neither the first, nor the most complex, imaginative exploration of aspects of Irish involvement in the Great War. (It is preceded by, amongst other things, Jennifer Johnston's account of cross-barrier friendship in the trenches in *How Many Miles to Babylon?*.) The negative perceptions of Ulster Protestantism's culture, and its politically determined, reductive self-perceptions, which the reception of McGuinness's play reveals to be still current, have, in one sense, been invalidated in the work of, amongst others, Michael Longley and Derek Mahon. In other words, the tongue-tied, at one time artistically cornered Ulster Protestant community has already 'said' several things. Remembrance gives way in Mahon and Longley to a more painful form of remembering, and their poetry contains, at times, self-exhortations not to allow the latter to collapse into the former. (Mahon's 'Once more, as before, I remember not to forget' ('The Spring Vacation'), redirects and rehabilitates Ulster Protestantism's own self-exhortation, 'Lest We Forget'.) Mahon has engaged with aspects of *Titanic* and war mythology in relation to Protestant memory; Longley with the story of the Ulster Division at the Somme, and with the consequent politicization of remembrance North and South. For both, it is an engagement which pre-dates the renewal of interest in Ireland and the Great War among historians and literary critics, and one whose role in stimulating that renewal is sometimes overlooked.

Edna Longley notes that the 1966 commemoration of the Easter Rising 'revived a waning piety'.[82] Remembering and revisiting Easter 1916 in literature has been a thriving industry: the Rising is anthologized, analysed, and revised to an extent that bears comparison with the Great War industry in England. But at the time of that revival in piety, poetry in Northern Ireland also addressed the question of First World War remembrance, already felt to be problematical, and prompted in part by the fiftieth anniversary of the Armistice. It is worth noting that it began to do so before the Troubles, and before any explicit or journalistic

---

[82] *The Living Stream*, 70.

connection of a war-torn Northern Ireland with the landscape of the Great War. In *Room to Rhyme*, a 1968 anthology of poems by Seamus Heaney and Michael Longley and ballads collected by David Hammond, Longley included a poem, 'Remembrance Day', which pondered the betrayal and possibility of poetic redemption of 'Our godforsaken heroes, || Outlandish dead beneath whose | Medals memory lies bruised.'[83] 'Remembrance Day' poems appeared in the *Honest Ulsterman* in 1968/9. John Montague's *The Rough Field* projects back to the immediate aftermath of the Great War as a way of understanding, and revising understandings of, his home ground. In John Hewitt's recollections of a 'Belfast Boyhood', he revisits the aftermath of the Great War, the discrepancy between pre-war enthusiasms and post-war actualities—'our cheering then my memory often mocks'.[84] Seamus Heaney's first collection, *Death of a Naturalist* in 1966, is heavily influenced by the English Great War poets, and brings Great War imagery to Co. Derry. The preoccupation with the First World War is also apparent in the recent work of a younger generation of Northern Irish poets—in, for example, Tom Paulin's concern with the relationship between art and war, and with Yeats's response to the Great War in *Walking a Line*; in Ciaran Carson's projection back through contemporary Northern Irish violence in *Belfast Confetti* to the Home Rule crisis, and his vision of the streets of Belfast, a city 'built on mud', as continually shifting, a cityscape reminiscent of the trench world, with its transience, its 'street names'; in Medbh McGuckian's exploration in *Captain Lavender*, sometimes through familiar war-poetry images, of the nexus between war, sexuality, creativity, and death.

More so than any of his contemporaries, Michael Longley, as will be seen, evinces in his work an almost overwhelming concern with remembering and memorializing the dead, offering poetry as a possible vehicle in which to combine 'The cure and the remembrance'.[85] To elegize the dead is also to redeem them from the narrow perspectives which have dominated politicized forms of remembrance. But this is not an exercise

---

[83] Subsequently collected in *No Continuing City* (London: Macmillan, 1969), 44. The first half of the poem, quoted from here, was cut in *Poems 1963–1983* (1985; London: Secker & Warburg, 1991), and the revised poem retitled 'Aftermath'.

[84] See 'The YCVs and the Ulster Division' and 'Portstewart, July 1914', *The Collected Poems of John Hewitt*, ed. Frank Ormsby (Belfast: Blackstaff Press, 1991), 295–6.

[85] Don Shriver, quoted in Michael Longley, *Tuppenny Stung: Autobiographical Chapters* (Belfast: Lagan Press, 1994), 76.

which has been confined to those writing in the 'Protestant' tradition, in spite of Longley's almost intimidating example, and in spite of the prominence, in contemporary Northern Irish politics, of Protestantism's association with the Great War. (On the contrary, perceptions of Ulster Protestantism's character and history have complicated both the terms and the evaluation of its literary response.) For Longley, Mahon, and Heaney, addressing the Great War has been, with varying degrees of success, a means of destabilizing reductive histories; for all three, it has involved a break with communal silences, whether Catholic or Protestant. This is ultimately to shift the emphasis away from Terence Brown's view that Heaney's 'dar[ing] to speak . . . of Catholic nationalist Ireland's part in the Great War' is 'an . . . even more audacious break with tribal silences' than is found in Longley's work.[86] Audacity rather depends on what you say. The unionist Great War package is no less ideologically determined than the nationalist one; as a consequence, imaginative engagement with the war and its effect, approached from either tradition, may involve transgression of political as well as canonical codes.

Some of those codes are simultaneously transgressed and restated in what is, with the possible exception of Michael Longley's 'Wounds', the best-known contemporary poem concerned with Ireland and the Great War, Heaney's 'In Memoriam Francis Ledwidge'.[87] The poem stands, therefore, as an example of subversion *and* perpetuation of historical and cultural myths. It is one of a series of elegies for artists, friends, and relatives in *Field Work*, but is also a poem overtly concerned, not just with remembering the dead, but with the politics of remembrance in Northern Ireland. In the latter sense, it both undermines and reinforces problems surrounding perceptions of Irish involvement in the Great War. Its starting point is the Portstewart war memorial, 'The bronze soldier . . . forever craned | | Over Flanders'. The memorial, with its 'loyal, fallen names' establishes the Great War as an apparently Protestant phenomenon, something felt, initially, to be of little relevance to the poet-figure, the 'worried pet . . . in nineteen forty-six or seven' walking 'Along the Portstewart prom'. ('[L]oyal' 's connotation is loyalist; 'fallen' reminds of Laurence Binyon's 1914 poem 'For the Fallen', that staple of

[86] Terence Brown, 'Who Dares to Speak? Ireland and the Great War', in Robert Clark and Piero Boitani (eds.), *English Studies in Transition: Papers from the ESSE Inaugural Conference* (London: Routledge, 1993), 235.
[87] Seamus Heaney, *Field Work* (London: Faber, 1979), 59–60.

British Remembrance Day ceremonies.) But Francis Ledwidge is a figure who connects the speaker to that war: Ledwidge is 'Literary, sweet-talking, countrified', belonging with 'the May altar of wild flowers, | Easter water . . . Mass-rocks', a Great War soldier who is, he states explicitly (in case the point has not already been grasped from the preceding images), a 'haunted Catholic'. The divided psychic landscape is implicit in place itself: the poem ranges rural, pacifist, and Catholic on one side; Protestant, urban, and militaristic on the other. Ledwidge, displaced from the former, 'Ghost[s] the trenches with a bloom of hawthorn'. One objection to the poem might be that it reinforces certain stereotypes even as it breaks the tribal taboos: it opposes pastoral to war, and in doing so follows a long tradition of English and Irish poetic practice, but it also appropriates pastoral for a Catholic or nationalist tradition: the opposition mirrors the sectarian fault-lines. Equally, though, in writing nationalist Ireland back into the Great War, it also challenges some of the myths through which those fault-lines have been sustained. The poem enacts remembrance which public memorializing obscures. '[L]oyal', while it casts those named on the memorial as Protestant, is also redefined by the emergence of Ledwidge in the poem: the Protestant myth that only Protestants were capable of loyalty in 1914–18 is revealed as false by Ledwidge's own 'loyalty' that has no loyalist connotations. The claim that Heaney's poem 'fully addresses the questions Ledwidge's death raises' is slightly extravagant;[88] but the poem does at least raise those questions, and acknowledges the failure in language that it also enacts:

> In you, our dead enigma, all the strains
> Criss-cross in useless equilibrium
> And as the wind tunes through this vigilant bronze
> I hear again the sure confusing drum
>
> You followed from Boyne water to the Balkans
> But miss the twilit note your flute should sound.
> You were not keyed or pitched like these true-blue ones
> Though all of you consort now underground.

Ledwidge is given the title Tom Kettle, another nationalist casualty of the Great War, also earns from his biographer—'enigma'. The phrase 'our dead enigma' points to Heaney's awareness that Ledwidge distorts the stereotypical perceptions of the role of a nationalist Irishman in

---

[88] Thomas C. Foster, *Seamus Heaney* (Dublin: O'Brien Press, 1989), 89.

1914–18. But it simultaneously highlights the non-existence of any terms of reference outside those stereotypes. If 'all the strains | Criss-cross in useless equilibrium', they do so (hence 'useless') at a point beyond definition. The wind 'tun[ing] through this vigilant bronze' evokes loyalist rhetoric ('eternal vigilance') as well as military defensiveness, leading to the 'sure confusing drum', and the enlistment described in terms reminiscent of an Orange parade: the drum, the Boyne, the flutes. From such a perspective on Great War involvement, a perspective which has dominated in the North, Ledwidge's 'twilit note' is inevitably absent, though in pointing up the omission, the poem itself resounds that note. In doing so, it risks reducing one version of history in order to restore another, simplifying perceptions of the 'other'— 'these true-blue ones' who, by implication, had some certainty about their motives, and were not out of place in the trenches—in order to introduce, through Ledwidge, a new complexity. In this sense, the poem is unable to escape from a version of history that consists of two competing versions of history. The last line of the poem evokes Owen's 'Strange Meeting', as it also recalls the aspirations (naiveties) of those Irish politicians who hoped that consorting underground might, in the longer term, exercise a beneficial effect on the surface. The 'Balkans' remind one of the earlier time of confusion in Irish political and military history; the more recent Serbian wars also project that confusion into the present: as Terence Brown notes, while the Troubles in Northern Ireland have forced it back on its own history, 'the map of early twentieth-century Europe [has] re-emerge[d] like a prior print in a palimpsest'.[89]

The poem's struggle with reductive histories and inadequate language makes it in some ways paradigmatic of the wider struggle in Northern Ireland to confront difficult aspects of the past, and to redefine the present through that confrontation, to shift the emphasis from 'Lest We Forget' to how we remember. At the close of *The Great War and Modern Memory*, Fussell turns to Frye's claim in *Anatomy of Criticism* that

The culture of the past is not only the memory of mankind, but our own buried life, and study of it leads to a recognition scene, a discovery in which we see, not our past lives, but the total cultural form of our present life. It is not only the poet but his reader who is subject to the obligation to 'make it new'.[90]

[89] 'Who Dares to Speak? Ireland and the Great War', 237.
[90] Northrop Frye, *Anatomy of Criticism* (1957; London: Penguin, 1990), 346 (see Fussell, *The Great War and Modern Memory*, 335).

To 'make it new', in Frye's sense, is to understand the implications of repetition. The most effective and affecting poetry in Northern Ireland also understands those implications: the tendency to 'remove the products of culture from our own sphere of influence' is as deceptive as the appropriation of past art merely 'to support a cause or thesis in the present'.[91] Paul Fussell presents 'recognition scenes' from the Great War on the grounds that 'what we recognize in them is a part, and perhaps not the least compelling part, of our own buried lives'.[92] The quest in Northern Irish poetry for a voice to uncover repression, to articulate a 'cultural form' beyond simple antithesis, makes a return to the buried past of the Great War as compelling and as prevalent as it is in the English modern memory Fussell explores.

[91] *Anatomy of Criticism*, 346.
[92] *The Great War and Modern Memory*, 335.

CHAPTER SIX

A Dying Art: Derek Mahon's Solving Ambiguity

'Somehow Ulster Protestants are expected to be ironical. This is a way of explaining the liberal Ulster Protestant and apologizing for him ... By being ironical, we somehow escape culpability.'

Derek Mahon[1]

I am saying that there seems to be one dominating form of modern understanding; that it is essentially ironic; and that it originates largely in the application of mind and memory to the events of the Great War.

Paul Fussell[2]

all ironies, in fact, are probably unstable ironies.

Linda Hutcheon[3]

I

One of the problems of MacNeicean criticism has been a tendency to judge MacNeice's poetry according to English history and literary tradition, rather than according to the complex relations between Irish and English history and tradition. The same has been true in relation to Derek Mahon, whose response to the Troubles is criticized by Stan Smith as being anachronistic, one of 'shell-shocked Georgianism'.[4] Edna Longley offers a corrective in her essay 'The Singing Line: Form in Derek Mahon's Poetry': 'That Irish history does not march with

[1] 'Q & A with Derek Mahon', interview by James J. Murphy et al., *Irish Literary Supplement*, 10/2 (Fall 1991), 28.
[2] *The Great War and Modern Memory* (London: OUP, 1975), 35.
[3] *Irony's Edge: The Theory and Politics of Irony* (London: Routledge, 1994), 195.
[4] *Inviolable Voice: History and Twentieth-Century Poetry* (Dublin: Gill and Macmillan, 1982), 189.

English history, or in certain respects stands still, does not render obsolescent the *poetry* which grows out of it.'[5] In making his criticism, Stan Smith gestures towards, yet misses, a crucial point about Mahon's imagination and Ulster's history: the role of the First World War in shaping both, and the continuing relevance of the years 1914–1918 to Ulster's cultural and political development. Smith is right that the poet's response to the Northern Ireland Troubles evokes a memory of the Great War, and the problem of the poetic response to that war, but he is wrong to assume that such an evocation equates with the Great War's position in English modern memory. Ironically, the anachronism here is Smith's, who in claiming that Mahon's tone might be 'mistaken for indifference before the ugly realities of life, and death, in Ulster', seems to be making a call to poetic arms (as others did before him in the First and Second World Wars), suggesting that Mahon should rise to the occasion in a recognizable role of war poet, instead of keeping his hands 'indubitably clean'.[6]

It is a call which Mahon, like MacNeice, Graves, and Yeats, writing 'in times like these' before him, resists: 'we're supposed to write about the Troubles; a lot of people expect us to act as if it were part of our job— it's not, unless we choose to make it so.'[7] But, as with Yeats, resistance to a type of war writing is not *ipso facto* an evasion of war, its consequences, or its place in cultural memory. It may even be the opposite. Mahon's poetic response to violence has been 'learned' from the memory of the Great War, from his predecessors, and from his own experience of Ulster in the Troubles. He shares with MacNeice a tendency to approach the earlier conflict as a means of understanding Ulster Protestantism, Ulster's relations with England, and his own place within the 'community'. At no point in his work does Mahon explicitly approach the problematic subject of Ulster's remembrance of the Great War, but he considers England's remembrance of that war in relation to his own position as 'enlightened alien', as someone who regards English pieties with a perspective informed by his experience of Ulster. While the Troubles in Northern Ireland engage his attention, and although he writes in a post-Second World War context, he is drawn, obliquely, to the Great War as a means of understanding contemporary events.

---

[5]   *Poetry in the Wars* (Newcastle: Bloodaxe, 1986), 171.
[6]   *Inviolable Voice*, 189.
[7]   Mahon, 'A Very European Poet', interview by Eileen Battersby, *Irish Times*, 10 Nov. 1992, 12.

Mahon's role as a poet in relation to violence is therefore more complex, in response to his context, than the ones Smith attributes and prescribes. Deane perceptively describes him as 'dazzlingly sophisticated', an urbane and civilized figure with perfect formal control, and yet one who within that sophistication gives an unparalleled sense of apocalypse, 'abysmal chaos', 'wild formlessness':[8] as such, he stands not in opposition to Ulster Protestantism, but as inheritor of both its self-control and its fear. '[W]hat is alive', as Longley points out, *'cannot be* anachronistic. The creative baton changes hands throughout the English speaking world and the compost of poetry accrues unpredictably.'[9] Reactions to the First World War in England and Ireland are paradigmatic of this unpredictability. The cultural effect of the Great War in England, rather than in the English-speaking world, and the influential studies of that effect by Fussell, Hynes, Silkin, and others, can lead to an interpretative exclusivity (for English-speaking read English) that posits some Irish writers as out of touch. Similarly, the Ulster Protestant community finds itself castigated for its failure to develop politically in line with England, in other words its failure to 'keep up' with England's post-war, post-imperial developments. Tom Paulin describes loyalist terrorism as issuing partly 'from a cultural quality which might be described as a trapped and backward-looking anger—the Protestant working class is unique in Europe "in that it is the only working class not to have been radicalised by World War I"'. He continues: 'UVF terrorists... were prepared to torture and kill in order to remain in their chosen imperial time-warp'.[10]

Paulin is looking here at an extremist faction within Ulster's loyalist community. He does note the crucial point about Ulster Protestantism's response to the Great War and the imperial breakdown consequent upon that war, that is, its *difference* from the English response. But 'time-warp' is still potentially reductive and misleading. To perceive Northern Ireland as existing within a 'time-warp' is to ascribe to an alternative, in this case English, culture an impossible role as objective guardian of time, historical truth, and progress. It is not so much that 'Ulster is what England (or Europe) was', or that this apparent stagnation is mirrored in its literature and culture. It is, rather, that Ulster and England, with

---

[8] 'Celebrant of Lost Lives and the Sublime', review of *Selected Poems* by Derek Mahon, *Irish Times*, 22 Dec. 1990, Weekend 8.

[9] *Poetry in the Wars*, 171.

[10] *Ireland and the English Crisis* (Newcastle: Bloodaxe, 1984), 138.

different goals in mind, predicate identity on differing social and cultural codes after 1918. Attempts (and self-attempts) to dissociate Mahon from his working-class, Protestant Ulster background—to view him as exile, an outsider with an 'urbane perspective'—implicitly pass judgement on the community from which he is apparently detached. Such urbanity and self-reflexivity, these attempts suggest, cannot exist within the Protestant community. In a curious mixture of perception and prejudice, Seamus Deane writes:

It would be possible to write of Mahon's poetry as though it enacted a drama of belonging and not belonging to a country itself isolated from world history, divided within itself, obsessed by competing mythologies, Northern and Southern, ambiguously ensnared in the subtle politics of colonialism and independence, a central void with violent peripheries. Terence Brown has written eloquently on these themes and it is right to admit their force and the bearing they have on this ultimately 'protestant' poetry. *For Mahon does not enjoy or seek to have a sense of community with the kind of Ireland which is so dominant in Irish poetry.* All his versions of community depend on the notion of a disengagement from history achieved by those whose maverick individuality resisted absorption into the official discourses and decencies. [my italics][11]

The drama of belonging and not belonging is, as Deane implies, operating on the level of intention as well as interpretation, for reasons which will be explored later. But he also implies that Mahon oscillates between the two poles of belonging and not belonging because the 'belonging' available is to different mythologies of history, which are designed to serve certain political ends, those of colonizer and colonized. And one is, according to Deane's reading, more worth having than the other: Mahon does not 'seek' it, but, and the value judgement is inherent in this, neither is he privileged to 'enjoy' it. '[W]orld history' in this view is somehow detached from this internal struggle; Mahon is doubly displaced in apparently seeking detachment from both world history *and* competing Irish mythologies.

More productively, to locate Mahon within the community and within history can expand the notion of what the community is. His poetry enacts the struggle between simplified mythologies and complex historical circumstances, a struggle which has been characteristic of Ulster Protestant memory, perhaps of 'modern memory' more generally,

---

[11] 'Derek Mahon: Freedom from History', *Celtic Revivals* (London: Faber, 1985), 159–60.

in the twentieth century, and a struggle which has also been character-ized by repression. It is, in this sense, a poetry which is 'ambiguously ensnared' (between what is said and unsaid, also between what is sayable and unsayable), but one which need not function within Deane's dual framework of Northern colonialism and Southern post-colonialism, nor one which is caught between a time-warped Ulster and a progressive, post-imperial England. Neither anachronistic nor escapist, Mahon en-gages with problems of Ulster Protestantism's post-First World War historical sensibility: the relationship between Protestantism and vio-lence; the concept of empire; cultural relations with England; the implications for an Ulster Protestant of the attenuation of religious belief in England and elsewhere.

Terence Brown suggests that 'the contemporary northern protest-ant's history...seems impoverished by comparison with nationalist historical awareness...because that history has had to perform fewer functions and is necessarily simpler'.[12] Further, 'Only a community with very simple historical needs could maintain such an extraordinary, near-unanimous reticence about the complications of its past'.[13] As discussed previously, that reticence is apparent in the Northern Irish reaction to the First World War, 'reflecting...the reluctance of some Ulster people to confront with honesty their own place in history and, in particular, to question the true nature of their link with Britain'.[14] Mahon addresses imperial breakdown through an evocation of England and Northern Ireland which points up their different response to the decline of the British Empire, and therefore the failure in understanding between the two. When Orr suggests Ulster Protestants are reluctant to confront the 'true nature of [the] link with Britain', his concern is, implicitly, their reluctance to accept that Ulster is no longer the 'Imperial Province'. But the disappearance of one link does not preclude the existence of a close cultural link which is not necessarily bound up with the Empire. Mahon's relationship to the English tradition simultaneously invalidates as it acknowledges a breakdown in understanding: he restructures the relationship in terms which recognize English and Ulster anxieties. Traditionally, as has been seen in the cases of Matthew Arnold, Robert

---

[12] *The Whole Protestant Community: The Making of a Historical Myth* (Field Day Pamphlet No. 7; Derry: Field Day, 1985), 8.

[13] Ibid. 10.

[14] Philip Orr, *The Road to the Somme: Men of the Ulster Division Tell Their Story* (Belfast: Blackstaff Press, 1987), 227.

Graves, and others, Ireland can be used poetically to interrogate the values of imperial England. In Mahon's case, as with MacNeice, an England in imperial decline, with its own mythical simplicities, can serve to illustrate Ulster or Ireland.

'Afterlives' exemplifies both the dependency and misunderstandings which can characterize the Ulster–England relationship. Structurally, parts I and II of the poem are mutually dependent: the return to Ulster is informed by the experience of England; the second Ulster section forces a retrospect on the English opening. The liberal intellectuals of part I believe in progress and education, have 'faith' that war will be a thing of the past, will become merely an aspect of history to

> ...amaze the literate children
> In their non-sectarian schools
> And the dark places be
> Ablaze with love and poetry
> When the power of good prevails.[15]

There is, in the poem, a reaction against this complacency: it is a misconception based on self-aggrandizement and a form of irresponsibility—'What middle-class cunts we are | To imagine for one second | That our privileged ideals | Are divine wisdom . . .'. The 'orators' and 'guns . . . in a back street' disrupt, or should disrupt, certain pieties sustainable in England if not in Northern Ireland. Yet it is this reaction, in part I, that makes the return home in part II more complex than it might have appeared from the vantage point of London. There are no simple oppositions based on experience; instead, every understanding attained falls short of reconciliation. In spite of the reaction against liberal intelligentsia, on the return to Belfast, he can 'scarcely recognize | The places I grew up in'. The 'I' never finally locates itself, but splits imaginatively ('I' who might have stayed; 'I' who left). This split self questions the possible virtue of direct experience of the Troubles, and ponders the possible changes in perception that experience would have engendered:

> Perhaps if I'd stayed behind
> And lived it bomb by bomb
> I might have grown up at last
> And learnt what is meant by home.[16]

---

[15] Mahon, *The Snow Party* (London: OUP, 1975), 1. Unless otherwise indicated, quotations are taken from the earliest collected versions of the poems.
[16] Ibid. 2.

Significantly, the thought remains speculative. On the one hand, the poet might be seen as succumbing to a belief—implicit in the aesthetic of some of the Great War poets—that direct experience gives a poetic mandate to speak as well as a responsibility to do so. On the other, the movement of part I finds its echo in part II, from the 'moon-splashed waves exult' to the recognition of alienation: the 'dim | Forms that kneel at noon | In the city' are and, in the end, are not 'ourselves'. While he might have 'learnt what is meant by home', the experience of part I does allow for the possibility that such understanding could be as illusory as the 'bright | Reason on which we rely | For the long-term solutions'.

II

Mahon, like MacNeice, negotiates several different contexts and traditions—English, American, Irish, and Northern Irish—drawing on all of them to avoid 'idol or idea, creed or king'. If he inherits Fussell's 'dominating form of modern understanding', he does so through the mediation of Yeats, the war poets, and MacNeice, and also through Eliot, Lowell, and the American tradition. 'England', as it appears in his fourth collection, *The Hunt by Night*, is a place bewildered by an influx of 'alternative' culture and nostalgic for its pre-1914 certainties, a place where a huge gap yawns between generations, but where there is still comfort to be found in recycling the old myths (as in 'One of these Nights'): 'traditional' and 'modern' sometimes conspire, but more often coexist uneasily. It is also an England imagined in relation to New England, resulting in a complex intertextuality between American, English, and Irish literary traditions, and an exploration of imperialist culture outside Deane's Anglo-Irish framework.

The collection as a whole is indebted to Lowell's neocolonial exposé in his 1967 collection, *Near the Ocean*. Lowell's connection with Heaney has frequently been noted: Raban's description of Lowell's language—'the vocabulary is clotted, syntax and metre buckle under the pressure of experience'[17]—strikes an immediate chord with what Hobsbaum describes as 'Heaneyspeak', and with Heaney's desire to 'take the English lyric and make it eat stuff that it has never eaten before'.[18] Hobsbaum, in fact, draws the lines of influence from Yeats to Eliot to Lowell, and from

[17] Introduction to *Robert Lowell's Poems: A Selection*, ed. Jonathan Raban (London: Faber, 1974), 16.
[18] Heaney, 1973, quoted in Neil Corcoran, *Seamus Heaney* (London: Faber, 1986), 95.

Lowell to Hughes, Hill, and the Belfast Group (in other words, Heaney).[19] But if *Near the Ocean* marks a shift for Lowell—for Axelrod it is the point where he 'became a public poet in earnest'[20]—it is also the volume which illustrates Mahon's thematic and stylistic links with the earlier poet. The 'quarrel' with Puritan ancestors; the poetic struggle under the weight of the 'Faith of our Fathers', an oppressive Calvinist theology; the apocalyptic sensibility; the 'agonised whirl of tradition and modernity';[21] the protest against war in its imperial forms; urban elegy— Mahon is, predictably, drawn to all these aspects of Lowell's writing. *The Hunt by Night* not only picks up the tone and mood of Lowell's poems, but also structurally and thematically has much in common with *Near the Ocean*. Lowell's concern in *Near the Ocean* is with the dubious policies of a neocolonialist America, 'Hammering military splendor, | top-heavy Goliath in full armour'.[22] The translations in the volume are, Lowell writes in the preface, connected thematically by 'Rome, the greatness and horror of her Empire'. 'America' itself, he argues, '*is* something immense, crass and Roman'.[23]

Mahon's 'Courtyards in Delft' and 'Another Sunday Morning', both in some ways responses to Lowell's 'Waking Early Sunday Morning' and 'Central Park' in *Near the Ocean*, explore war and imperialism. The first displaces Ulster's militant Protestantism into a seventeenth-century Dutch painting; the second adapts England's twentieth-century imperial decline as a metaphor for the endings of all civilizations. In both the poet tentatively proposes that art itself has a Yeatsian answer to violence, decline, and fall. In 'Courtyards in Delft', the 'chaste | Precision of the thing and the thing made' is perfect but limited.[24] As Terence Brown points out, the composure is achieved only by the exclusion of 'music, eroticism, lust, politics and the imperial adventurism which was the source of that wealth which made Dutch society so stable and secure but which…became the cause of "fire | And sword upon parched veldt"'.[25] This is empire which simplifies its self-presentation

[19] Hobsbaum, *A Reader's Guide to Robert Lowell* (London: Thames and Hudson, 1988), 7–8.

[20] *Robert Lowell: Life and Art* (Princeton: Princeton UP, 1978), 177.

[21] Raban, introduction to *Robert Lowell's Poems*, ed. Raban, 21.

[22] 'Waking Early Sunday Morning', *Near the Ocean* (London: Faber, 1967), 15.

[23] Quoted in Axelrod, *Robert Lowell: Life and Art*, 190.

[24] *The Hunt by Night* (Oxford: OUP, 1982), 9.

[25] 'Derek Mahon: The Poet and Painting', *Irish University Review* 24/1 (Spring/Summer 1994), 46.

to preserve its own stability, and its own provinciality. It is, for the poet, a concept with which he is familiar—'I lived there as a boy...'— and one whose 'chaste | Precision' is undermined whenever his own imagery comes into contact with the 'benighted' Antrim coast. Stephen Kern points out that the use of arboreal imagery to express the expansion of the nation was frequent in the late nineteenth century, when the British Empire was at its height.[26] It is also imagery which was for ever changed by the experience of the Great War, with its shattered branches, burnt-out tree-stumps, bits of men stuck in trees, and vice versa. For writers in the Great War, trees become parallels for the mutilated human condition: Henri Barbusse describes 'a row of excoriated willow trunks, some of wide countenance, and others hollowed and yawning, like coffins on end'; for Blunden, Thiepval Wood is an 'apparition', 'a black vapour of smoke and naked tree trunks or charcoal'.[27] In Mahon's 'Courtyards in Delft', 'No breeze | Ruffles the trim composure of those trees'. They stand for stability, uniformity, nature perfectly controlled. In an earlier poem, 'The Return' (later retitled 'Going Home'), there is, instead, a 'stubborn growth | Battered by constant rain | And twisted by the sea wind', which symbolizes Ulster Protestantism's besieged mentality as well as the poet's conception of his own role, but is also reminiscent of the landscape destroyed in the Great War:

> Its worn fingers scrabbling
> At a torn sky, it stands
> On the edge of everything
> Like a burnt-out angel
> Raising petitionary hands.
>
> Grotesque by day, at twilight
> An almost tragic figure
> Of anguish and despair,
> It merges into the funeral
> Cloud-continent of night
> As if it belongs there.[28]

---

[26] *The Culture of Time and Space 1880–1918* (Cambridge, Mass.: Harvard University Press, 1983), 239.

[27] Henri Barbusse, *Under Fire* (1916), trans. Fitzwater Wray (London and Toronto: J. M. Dent & Sons, 1929), 272; Edmund Blunden, *Undertones of War* (1928; London: Penguin, 1982), 90.

[28] *Poems 1962–1978* (Oxford: OUP, 1979), 99–100.

If 'Courtyards in Delft' sees what is there in terms of what is missing, 'The Return' inserts that unsaid, or unseen, into his vision of a post-war and 'troubled' Ulster. The poet in 'Courtyards' is 'lying low in a room there, | A strange child with a taste for verse, | While my hard-nosed companions dream of war . . .'. While 'lying low' may be read simply as keeping out of the way, it also allows for the possibility that the poet's low profile, his apparent uselessness, is in fact a conscious waiting for the right moment, for fulfilment of his subversive role (a sentiment also articulated in 'Rage for Order'), a role which, it might be said, is already fulfilled in 'Going Home'.

Fredric Jameson suggests that the 'problem of imperialism' has been restructured since the Second World War:

in the age of neo-colonialism, of decolonisation . . . it is less the rivalry of the metropolitan powers among each other that strikes the eye . . . rather, contemporary theorists . . . have been concerned with the internal dynamics of the relationship between First and Third World countries, and in particular the way in which this relationship—which is now very precisely what the word 'imperialism' means for us—is one of necessary subordination or dependency, and that of an economic type, rather than a primarily military one. This means that in the period from World War I to World War II the axis of otherness has as it were been displaced: it first governed the relationship of the various imperial subjects among each other; it now designates the relationship between a generalised imperial subject . . . [and] its various others or objects.[29]

In 'Courtyards in Delft', Jameson's displacement appears in reverse: the poem projects forwards to contemporary Ulster but approaches the problem of imperialism in its phase of military rivalry, anticipating the potential destructiveness, and self-destructiveness, of a culture which will 'punish nature in the name of God'. 'Another Sunday Morning', set in the heart of a former imperial power, views that destruction, with subversive humour, as almost complete. In Jameson's terms, the poem must articulate post-post-imperialism, where: 'Black diplomats with stately wives, | Sauntering by, observe the natives | Dozing beside the palace gates—'.[30] Who can tell the colonizer from the colonized? The age reverses itself, becomes its own opposite in true Yeatsian fashion. The latter half of the poem echoes MacNeice's opening to *Autumn Journal*, where 'summer is . . . Ebbing away down ramps of

---

[29] *Modernism and Imperialism* (Field Day Pamphlet No. 14; Derry: Field Day, 1988), 9.
[30] *The Hunt by Night*, 29.

shaven lawn where close-clipped yew | Insulates the lives of retired generals and admirals'. Mahon's 'old ladies' who remember Kitchener are 'Exhausted now | By decades of retrenchment' and 'Wait for the rain at close of play'.[31] 'Retrenchment' operating somewhat maliciously in several different ways—the gradual erosion of the Empire's territory; the decline in individual fortunes; the slowly decreasing numbers of those who *do* remember—also locates the source of decline in the trenches of the Great War. It is also the war which invalidates the code of conduct—playing the game—by which the 'natives' were trained to live, leaving nothing to wait for but death.

The poem reassesses MacNeice's claim in *Autumn Journal*, I, that 'no river is a river which does not flow'; it is also in part a response to his 'Sunday Morning', where the attempt to 'abstract this day and make it to the week of time | A small eternity, a sonnet self-contained in rhyme' fails because there is 'no...Escape from the weekday time. Which deadens and endures'.[32] Mahon's 'old ladies', and his 'old man...Making dreadnoughts out of matches' are caught in a time warp of their own creating, but one which is also an illusion, since the flow of time simultaneously denies it: 'So many empires come and gone...'. They are, in this sense, no more or less time-locked than the new age strollers in the park: 'Rastafarians...provincial tourists, Japanese | Economists, Saudi families'. In both cases, a failure of recognition is implied: 'now' is as transitory as 'then':

> Asia now for a thousand years—
> A flower that blooms and disappears
> In a sand-storm...[33]

Another Sunday morning is as much another millennium as it is the mere passing of one week. If the poet is a 'chiliastic prig', complacent in the possession of a particular metaphysical world-view, he is also self-aware in that there was an Asiatic pre-Christian civilization no more or less valid than his own. 'Another' implies that there may always be 'another'. Operating within the frame of reference this civilization gives, the poet delivers his own Sunday morning sermon, and flies:

> The private kite of poetry—
> A sort of winged sandwich board
> El-Grecoed to receive the Lord;

---

[31] Ibid.   [32] MacNeice, *CP*, 23.   [33] *The Hunt by Night*, 29.

An airborne, tremulous brochure
Proclaiming that the end is near.[34]

The poet is here both the prophet of doom, making his proclamation, and the powerless figure whose art, by its nature, and regardless of intention, is inherently indicative of the approaching end of civilization. Yet the feeling of helplessness, while it might be an inevitable consequence of the argument of the poem, is no more felt as helpless than the Yeatsian poetic which, if true to its 'Vision', works on the assumption of its own ultimate destruction in a cyclical process. In this sense, Mahon takes the bleakness, sometimes despair, of Robert Lowell's poetic, and recasts it in terms which rely for strength on acknowledgement of its own frailty—its transience. Lowell's 'Waking Early Sunday Morning' (challenging the latent optimism of Wallace Stevens's 'Sunday Morning') mourns the loss of certainty, of the 'Faith of our Fathers'—'Each day, He shines through darker glass'—and the resulting chaos of imperial tragedy: 'a million foreskins stacked like trash'. While Christianity is not to be regretted of itself, the void it leaves is just that—a void: 'Pity the planet, all joy gone . . .'.[35] Mahon's 'Another Sunday Morning' begins in light: 'the sun make[s] bright | The corners of our London flat'; Lowell's dawn is a 'daily remorseful blackout'. 'Central Park' has been described as an 'urban apocalypse', with its 'images of despair': 'a grounded kite . . . The stain of fear and poverty', the 'life-term in jail', 'a snagged balloon'.[36] Within this bleak context, 'All wished to leave this drying crust, | borne on the delicate wings of lust . . .'. Lowell's image of escape is 'a single, fluttery, paper kite' which 'sailed | where the light of the sun had failed';[37] but one senses that the poetry, like the poet, is left in the dark, grounded and yearning. Mahon takes this image in his own Lowellian prowl around the park in 'Another Sunday Morning', and makes of it an aesthetic principle: 'The private kite of poetry'.

Like Lowell, Mahon can be, as Brown points out, 'an elegist for a vanishing civility, a pessimist of the present moment'.[38] But, in terms of Mahon's own comments about Beckett—'Sometimes I have a curious sense that Beckett is almost a sentimental writer, and if he's a sentimental writer I don't know who isn't. Having hit rock bottom as you do with

---

[34] Ibid. 28.   [35] *Near the Ocean*, 15–16.
[36] See Axelrod, *Robert Lowell: Life and Art*, 190–1.   [37] *Near the Ocean*, 23–4.
[38] 'Derek Mahon: The Poet and Painting', 46.

him, you know there's nowhere to go but up'[39]—the elegist and pessimist is also, in recognizing the transitional nature of human achievement, a latent optimist. Hence, in 'Another Sunday Morning', the 'locked heart, so long in pawn | To steel', to the building and destroying of empires, may be redeemed by the 'pure, self-referential' act, even when that act will not outlast its own civilization. The illusion of creation and progress in empire-building is countered with the act of creation that reaches to nothing outside itself, that rises above what he describes in 'The Globe in North Carolina' as the now commonplace 'harsh refusal to conceive | A world so different from our own'.[40] 'A good poem', Mahon famously stated, 'is a paradigm of good politics—of people talking to each other, with honest subtlety, at a profound level.'[41] The 'harsh refusal' to do so leads to political stalemate—a militaristic single-mindedness or a bewildered nostalgia, neither of which are open to the diversity which would at once prove their undoing and their virtue. So Mahon, while elegizing a civilization, also elegizes the elegy itself:

> You will tell me that you have executed
> A monument more lasting than bronze;
> But even bronze is perishable.
> Your best poem, you know the one I mean,
> The very language in which the poem
> Was written, and the idea of language,
> All these things will pass away in time.[42]

III

Edna Longley suggests that 'the contrasting effect of Yeats on Mahon and Philip Larkin... seems to follow the lines of Anglo-Irish/English difference'. Mahon, 'in the light—or dark—of his Ulster Protestant background lacks Larkin's attachment to "customs and establishments". He takes certain Yeatsian modes for a further walk on the wild side, and into renewed tension between the imagination's "rage for order" and historical convulsions.'[43] Mahon shares with Larkin a profound

[39] 'Each Poem for Me is a New Beginning', interview by Willie Kelly, *Cork Review*, 2/3 (June 1981), 11.

[40] *The Hunt by Night*, 62.

[41] 'Poetry in Northern Ireland', *Twentieth Century Studies*, 4 (Nov. 1970), 93.

[42] 'Heraclitus on Rivers', *Poems 1962–1978*, 107.

[43] Edna Longley, 'Where a Thought Might Grow', review of *Selected Poems* by Derek Mahon, *Poetry Review*, 81/2 (Summer 1991), 7.

understanding of the way in which England has remembered the First World War, and has dealt with its imperial past. To understand, however, is not to collude, and Mahon also pushes what in Larkin can appear as nostalgia for the pre-1914 idyll and recognition of its disappearance a further step down the road to cultural reflexivity. Larkin's 'MCMXIV' captures images of the lines of recruits, the commercialized imperial paraphernalia, as they appear in memory. It is less a poem about August 1914 than it is about the mythicized remembrance of 1914. Geoff Dyer points out that 'there is a sense in which, for the British at least, the war helped to preserve the past even as it destroyed it.... The past *as past* was preserved by the war that shattered it.'[44] Larkin's poem contains awareness, and is implicitly a critique, of this version of history, of an 'innocence' that 'changed itself to past | Without a word'.[45] It does not create but explores an existing historical myth, one whose power does not seem to have diminished even with recognition of its inaccuracies. (That the final phrase, 'never such innocence', was used as the title for an anthology of First World War poems nearly thirty years after the poem appeared only reaffirms the currency of the 1914 myth.) Mahon also writes, in 'Homecoming':

> we cannot start
> at this late date
> with a pure heart,
> or having seen
> the pictures plain
> be ever in-
> nocent again.[46]

But in 'MCMXIV' it is not only 1914 that is 'innocent': the post-war vision of 1914 is also (deliberately) innocent. Its existence in memory becomes, in the poem, a ceremonious and stylized remembrance rather than a disturbing remembering. Perhaps remembrance of 1914 is itself a peculiar way of not remembering the war that followed.

Mahon, in 'A Kensington Notebook', locates the end of an era not in 1914, though he plays on the 1914 myth, but in the retrospective judgements of the post-war years. Tom Nairn suggests that 'resistance

---

[44] *The Missing of the Somme* (London: Penguin, 1995), 5.
[45] Larkin, *Collected Poems* (1988), ed. Anthony Thwaite (London: Faber and the Marvell Press, 1990), 127.
[46] *Lives* (London: OUP, 1972), 1.

to modernity is in reality not separable from the senility of the old imperialist state'.[47] 'A Kensington Notebook' challenges the assumption that modernity necessarily leads forward from the old state by tracing the marginalization by the modern state of three figures at one time representative of its modernist movement. The poem is a restrained, sometimes ambiguous tribute to three literary figures of pre-war London (Ford Madox Ford, Ezra Pound, and Wyndham Lewis), a series of quirky biographical sketches, and an elliptical overview of a period of literary history from 1914 to the Second World War. On another level, it engages with the question of artistic responsibility, and its consequences. Ford, Mahon hints, made an aesthetic compromise in the face of war (writing commissioned patriotic poetry and prose), setting out his 'toy soldiers on the | Razed table of art'.[48] Robert Lowell speculates along similar lines in 'Ford Madox Ford' (to which poem Mahon's 'A Kensington Notebook', part I is partially indebted):

> Was it war, the sport of kings, that your *Good Soldier*,
> the best French novel in the language, taught
> those Georgian Whig magnificoes at Oxford,
> at Oxford decimated on the Somme?[49]

In 'A Kensington Notebook', Mahon parodies, with a deliberate tonal naivety, the supposed realities of 1914, echoing Rupert Brooke's 1914 sonnets ('swimmers into cleanness leaping' and so on) and also the pastoral idyll of the English countryside, with its untamed beauty:

> There was a great good place
> Of clean-limbed young men
> And high-minded virgins,
> Cowslip and celandine...[50]

The poem questions, not just the failure of idealism, but the illusion of free will, of chosen destiny, held by those who fought the war (those who survived it and those who did not), the extent to which they were victims as well as creators of their moment in history:

[47] *The Break-Up of Britain: Crisis and Neo-Nationalism* (2nd edn., London: Verso, 1981), 45.
[48] *Antarctica* (Dublin: Gallery Press, 1985), 9.
[49] *Life Studies* (London: Faber, 1959), 63.
[50] *Antarctica*, 9.

What price the dewy-eyed
Pelagianism of home
To a lost generation
Dumbfounded on the Somme?[51]

Ford's departure from England in the poem coincides with this destruction of 'England': ' "The last of England" | Crumbles in the rain | As he embarks for | Paris and Michigan'. The Ford at the centre of London's literary activity becomes, after fighting in the war, an 'old cod' (playing on Lowell's description of him in 'Ford Madox Ford' with 'mouth pushed out | fish fashion') rejected by a 'land | Unfit for heroes',[52] forced into exile, and devoting his declining years to love and love poetry. Mahon approaches 1914–18 from an unusual and subversive perspective, evoking a survivor of the war who colluded in encouragement of that war, and found himself something of an anachronism in a new world that dismissed 1914 as for ever vanished. He also evokes the war artist who rejected conventional representations and depicted 'The death-throes of an era',[53] and yet who, anything but an anachronism (Orpen takes that role),[54] turns on post-war culture and is also, like Ezra Pound, (self-)exiled for fascist affiliations. 'The last of England' is, then, a complex and ironic phrase: subversively, it may be Ford himself (who at one time attempted to obtain German nationality); or it may be the generation dying in the trenches, for those who died came to represent England in a way the survivors did not; it may also be the post-war culture Ford leaves behind to 'crumble'; alternatively, the line evokes the end of England as an infinitely recurring event, since Ford Madox Brown's painting of that title depicted the artist/immigrant, disillusioned with the old world, leaving for the colonies some seventy years earlier. Any consideration of Mahon's Kensington artists suggests that England consisted of something more complex than the idea of 'dewy-eyed | Pelagianism' which it perpetuates in its own 1914 myth. Ford, as exemplar of this, may be the uncomplicated patriot of the early war years; he is also one of those who, in the 1914 *Blast*, attacked the smugness of English culture, and in the post-war years interrogated patriotic values in *Parade's End*. The war, in effect, serves to simplify England's conceptions of its own cultural history, and homogenize diverse opinion into the 1914 enlistment queues. Lewis, Pound, and Ford all find themselves in

---

[51] *Antarctica*, 9.   [52] Ibid. 10.   [53] Ibid. 12.
[54] An Irishman who was also an official British war artist.

one way or another rejected by or rejecting post-war society: they exist as cultural influences who are sometimes sidelined by a cultural norm. Mahon's tribute to them, albeit cast in the negative, does nevertheless credit them with survival as artists in spite of marginality, self-condemnation, or treason:

> ... 'available
> Reality' was increased,
> The sacred flame kept alive,
> The Muse not displeased;
>
> And if one or two
> Were short on ἀγάπη,
> What was that to the evil
> Done in their day?[55]

At some level, the inability of society to accommodate its 'outsiders' (those drawn, like Pound, to extremist positions) and aspects of its own history may bring about its own downfall, more than, in the case of England in the Great War, the mass slaughter of its 'innocent' troops in the trenches. The moral, with regard to Ulster's repressive, Calvinist culture, at one time, if not still, unfriendly to its artists, is sufficiently pointed. Mahon is habitually drawn to those who spoke for and of their time, but were still unaccommodated by it: Ovid, Lowry, Van Gogh, de Hooch, De Quincey, Nerval, Graves. Ford, Lewis, and Pound are not usually considered part of Mahon's 'tribe'; nevertheless, the questing and solitary individuals of 'A Kensington Notebook' do have something in common with those other 'tempest-torn' figures who appear throughout his work. The concept of a lost tribe is an adaptable and encompassing one: it may apply to those who fail to comprehend the limitations of the historical simplicities (to go back to Brown's formula for Ulster Unionist history) by which they live; or, alternatively, it may apply to those who in recognizing them, 'depict[s] | The death-throes of an era', and are, metaphorically or literally, expelled from the city gates.

Tom Nairn suggests that,

Trapped ... between past and future, Ulster Protestantism was unable to formulate the normal political response of threatened societies: nationalism. Instead, what one observes historically is a lunatic, compensatory emphasis of the two ideologies already strongly present in its community: militant Protestantism

---

[55] *Antarctica*, 13.

and imperialism. It is as aberrant substitutes for nationalism that these idea-systems have to be understood[56]

To some extent, Nairn, like others, implies that Ulster has failed to formulate the 'correct' response. England, hardly a threatened society in Nairn's sense of the word here, resorts to the nationalism which helped to form the Empire as a response to the loss of empire. Nationalism engenders a security within borders which can then override loss of territory elsewhere. Ironically, the two ideologies Nairn detects as strongly present in the Ulster Protestant community were also, up to 1914, strongly present in England. If loss of empire constitutes a threat to society, then repression of those ideologies—militant Protestantism and imperialism—may be England's own, 'lunatic', compensatory measure. Ulster and England have, in other words, dealt with the First World War in ways which not only differ but can conflict. The impact of modern warfare and consequent attenuation of religious belief in England—Orwell describes the 'slump in religious beliefs' in England at the end of the Great War as 'spectacular'[57]—make the Ulster writer from a background of militant Protestantism impossible to explain in an English context, in spite of the many aspects of shared history—for example, the experience of fighting in the Great War itself. Mahon's 'Brighton Beach' reminisces about the 'rough sectarian banter | Of Lavery's back bar' in Belfast, but describes Brighton as indicative of 'Decline', 'the spirit of empire | Fugitive as always'.[58] 'Brighton Beach' is, as Colin Graham points out, Mahon's 'Dover Beach' scenario, 'the spirit of place', like the 'sea of faith' in decline.[59] Like 'Afterlives', the poem works on a two-part structure where, ironically in view of Deane's comments quoted earlier, it is England which seems 'isolated from world history'; Ireland which is given the images of life and activity.

IV

If both Mahon and Larkin mourn the end of civilizations, Mahon 'preaches' from a more extreme position. He does so because, for the

---

[56] *The Break-Up of Britain*, 236.

[57] 'Inside the Whale', in *The Collected Essays, Journalism and Letters of George Orwell*, ed. Sonia Orwell and Ian Angus, i (London: Penguin, 1970), 553.

[58] *The Hunt by Night*, 34–5.

[59] See 'Derek Mahon's Cultural Marginalia', in Eve Patten (ed.), *Returning to Ourselves: Second Volume of Papers from the John Hewitt International Summer School* (Belfast: Lagan Press, 1995), 246.

Ulster Protestant, the apocalyptic quality of Protestant writing is bound up with the disintegration of empire, in contrast to the nostalgia which feeds into the English self-image. Ulster's militant Protestantism might proclaim its struggle as being 'For God and Ulster'; but in the First World War, the popular sentiment was also 'Ulster will strike for England—and England will not forget'. To make this connection is problematical: political betrayal, as a consequence, can be formulated in religious rather than secular terms. Loyalist nostalgia would be an admission of political and religious defeat: Ulster Protestantism's rhetoric did not shift its ground in the twentieth century because a wistful yearning for a pre-1914 era would imply that the informing principles behind that era—the faith, the union—have disappeared. The past is therefore a continuous present. Contrastingly, in England, the acceptance that the historical continuum is irrevocably broken means that the past is de-problematized in its relation to the present. It has an 'irreversible pastness' conducive to nostalgia. Nostalgia can thus be symptomatic of a culture which accepts the insecurity and breakdown of the current condition and is thereby able to sentimentalize or idealize a secure past. Apocalypse, in contrast, is the language of insecurity but the product of a culture which resists breakdown, which holds itself 'eternally vigilant' on the edge of contemporary chaos. Anticipation of apocalypse holds the present moment intact.

Both these categories collapse in, and into, Mahon's poetry: he subscribes neither to an obsolete ideology, nor to a complacent sense of 'newness' affirmed against a fixed sense of the past. Poetry displaces ideology to become the holding operation (as in 'The Studio') as it also points the dangers, in 'The Sea in Winter' and elsewhere, of reductive historical interpretation—'history | ignores those who ignore it, not | the ignorant whom it begot'.[60] His vision has been described as 'neither revolutionary nor utopian', but 'nostalgic': 'Rather than re-imagine history, he takes refuge in a nostalgic vision in which we can find neither a "usable past" nor a "usable future"'.[61] Characteristic of Mahon's nostalgia is its yearning for a pre-historical, pre-linguistic, pre-civilized world; 'post' is interchangeable with 'pre' for it can also be nostalgia for an imagined future—'the lives we might have led'. But since nostalgia

---

[60] *Selected Poems* (London: Viking; Oldcastle; Gallery Press, 1991), 117. (These lines do not appear in the earlier version of the poem in *Poems 1962–1978*.)

[61] Patricia Horton, 'Romantic Intersections: Romanticism and Contemporary Northern Irish Poetry', doct. diss., Queen's University, Belfast, 1996, 100.

can idealize history—'Cowslip and celandine'—then Mahonesque nostalgia for what is imagined is less of a disengagement from history, or a refuge, than it might at first appear. It is, in some ways, a nostalgia for what has not been, a history reimagined: what might have been, or might be, is no more or less fictional than versions of past or present. When life and art collide in his poetry, the vision is not only nostalgic, it is also apocalyptic, and within that vision he plays havoc with the illusions of security in the very language in which, for a Calvinist culture, a form of security is found.

In this aspect of his work, his connection to, and inherited strategies from, First World War writing are particularly apparent. The war poets, as they spoke in apocalyptic terms of the ending of a Western system of Christian morality, tended to abandon one notion of the sacred, but often only to replace it with another—in Graves's case his White Goddess—one which was freed from the doctrines which had led them to the trenches. Owen's comment is as pertinent to Mahon's poetry as it is to the trench poets: 'There is a point where prayer is indistinguishable from blasphemy. There is also a point where blasphemy is indistinguishable from prayer'.[62] For Jay Winter, apocalypse in First World War writing is the last gasp of a nineteenth-century way of thinking, which demonstrates the Great War to be a 'nineteenth-century war' provoking literature 'touching on an ancient set of beliefs about revelation, divine justice, and the nature of catastrophe'.[63] He argues that such literary imagery grew 'out of date' and became 'unusable' after 1945:

Apocalypse is predicated on divine justice; where was justice after the gas chambers? The literary metaphor of the Apocalypse could accommodate virtually every human catastrophe except the ultimate one. The archaic quality of this language was a link with the past; it drew the mind back to older visions and older certainties.[64]

The apocalypse metaphor, however, is not one necessarily predicated on the existence of any Christian 'justice'. (The Book of Revelation has always occupied an uneasy and disputed place in the New Testament of forgiveness and justice, in part because its Old Testament links are

---

[62] Quoted in Robert A. Hinde (ed.), *The Institution of War* (New York: St Martin's Press, 1992), 97.

[63] *Sites of Memory, Sites of Mourning: The Great War in European Cultural History* (Cambridge: Cambridge UP, 1996), 178.

[64] Ibid. 203.

stronger than in any other Christian book.) Perhaps, more simply, it provided a set of images for the wasteland in which the poets found themselves which, because of their familiarity, could, with different handling, point, deliberately, to the extent to which 'older visions and older certainties' had disappeared. It is on that level that language functions most effectively to criticize and subvert in the Great War: to work imagery in terms of what is 'known' can also show how unknown it has become. Rosenberg's 'Break of Day in the Trenches' is, in Fussell's view, the greatest poem of the war 'partly...because it is a great traditional poem', which 'while looking back on literary history...also acutely looks forward'.[65] (As will be seen, Keith Douglas and, later, Michael Longley, also work this technique in the contexts of different wars in their responses to Rosenberg's poem.)

This is also Mahon's strategy for elucidating Ulster Protestant cultural memory, and simultaneously allowing the poetry to stand as testimony to the ways that memory can alter. He thus fulfils an ambiguous dual role as preacher or prophet who sets out to demonstrate what cannot be preached or prophesied. An early poem, 'Ecclesiastes', is paradigmatic of this ambiguity. The poem rests on the ultimate irony that while Ulster's evangelical Protestantism might promise 'nothing under the sun', in another way, that is also precisely what the prophet of Ecclesiastes claims himself: 'all is vanity...The sun also ariseth, and the sun goeth down, and hasteth to the place where he arose...the work that is wrought under the sun is grievous unto me: for all is vanity and vexation of spirit'.[66] The poet criticizes the emptiness at the centre of the 'God-chosen' society which itself preaches that emptiness to draw its people to repentance. The absent 'I' in the poem—the one who feels called upon to 'understand and forgive'—attacks the 'You', the embryo preacher who does not, with all the vengeance of a prophet. The backward-looking movement—to 'the heaped graves of your fathers'—is shown to be a repressed communal ego through a parody of the exhortation to repression—'Bury that red | Bandana and stick, that banjo'—an exhortation which states unequivocally what the communal ego never could, that it sustains itself through wilful blindness: 'close one eye and be king'.[67]

---

[65] *The Great War and Modern Memory*, 250.
[66] Ecclesiastes (King James Version) 1: 2–5; 2: 17.
[67] *Lives*, 3.

Northrop Frye writes of Ecclesiastes that

Those who have unconsciously identified a religious attitude either with illusion or with mental indolence are not safe guides to this book, although their tradition is a long one. Some editor with a 'you'd better look out' attitude seems to have tacked a few verses on to the end suggesting that God trusts only the anti-intellectual, but the main author's courage and honesty are not to be defused in this way. He is 'disillusioned' only in the sense that he has realized that an illusion is a self-constructed prison. He is not a weary pessimist tired of life: he is a vigorous realist determined to smash his way through every locked door of repression in his mind. Being tired of life is in fact the only mental handicap for which he has no remedy to suggest.[68]

In some ways, this critique of the preacher is a blueprint for understanding Mahon's role as poet. 'Ecclesiastes', in offering a harsh critique of Ulster Protestantism's own 'self-constructed prison'—its denial of pleasure, its economic and religious stagnation, 'the shipyard silence, the tied-up swings'—is also a return to origins, a rewriting that rejects centuries of misreading. The poet displaces the preacher by his assertion that the repressed communal ego is fundamentally flawed because it distorts truth; in doing so, the absent 'I', almost by default, *becomes* the original preacher. With the stylistic repetition that is a characteristic of the source text, as much as it is indicative of a self-constructed prison (Ulster Protestantism has sustained itself politically in the twentieth century by simple reiteration of its 'truths'), the use of 'God' in the poem to cover the spectrum of belief, pride, disillusionment, blasphemy, contempt, points to the potential insecurity of this rhetorical style.

It is, Jameson points out, now 'a commonplace that transgressions, presupposing the laws or norms or taboos against which they function, thereby end up precisely reconfirming such laws'. Echoing Wilfred Owen, he continues: 'blasphemy not only requires you to have a strong sense of the sacred quality of the divine name, but may even be seen as a kind of ritual by which that strength is reawakened and revitalized'. The problem, however, with this interpretation is, he argues, that it places desire

outside of time, outside of narrative: it has no content, it is always the same in its cyclical moments of emergence, and the event in question takes on historicity only to the degree that the context of the explosion, the nature of that particular and historical repressive apparatus, knows specification.

---

[68] *The Great Code: The Bible and Literature* (1983; London: Penguin, 1990), 123.

What is more damaging...is that desire...remains locked into the category of the individual subject, even if the form taken by the individual in it is no longer the ego or self, but rather the individual body...[T]he need to transcend individualistic categories and modes of interpretation is in many ways the fundamental issue for any doctrine of the political unconscious, of interpretation in terms of the collective or associative.[69]

Seamus Deane describes Mahon's prophetic and ironic tone as 'rooted in the one desire—to have done with history...to imagine its disappearance in a moment of doom'.[70] If Mahon's transgressions challenge Ulster Protestantism's capitalist, patriarchal, and middle-class values, it could be argued that the 'elsewhere' he sets up in the poetry disables or limits that transgressive potential.[71] The position may be more complicated than this. Both these views imply that Mahon is, in effect, trying to do two different and mutually exclusive things: transgress and transcend. (Deane, inevitably, finds difficulty accommodating 'A Disused Shed in Co. Wexford' into Mahon's oeuvre, since this poem very evidently pleads for release *into* history.) Mahon's 'elsewhere', his 'desiring' sometimes, maybe even usually, avoids specificity. But specificity, while it might on one level demonstrate historicity, is not a necessary precondition for it. Transgression and transcendence may instead be mutually dependent. Jameson contends that 'all literature must be read as a symbolic meditation on the destiny of community'.[72] Mahon, in other words, cannot be in and of the community, transgressing its codes, and simultaneously outside the community, outside history, in a narrative that has no 'content'. The existence of desire may be by its nature transgressive: it might aspire to the unattainable 'cold dream', but it is simultaneously a desire rooted in history, recognizable only as desire because it comes from within the community.

That contradiction is confronted by Mahon in his revisions and re-revisions of 'Courtyards in Delft'. The poem exists in three versions: in the first, in *Courtyards in Delft*, an interim collection published in 1981, it has four stanzas; the year after, in *The Hunt by Night*, it has five; in the

[69] Jameson, *The Political Unconscious: Narrative as a Socially Symbolic Act* (London: Routledge, 1989), 68.
[70] *Celtic Revivals*, 157.
[71] See Horton, 'Romantic Intersections: Contemporary Northern Irish Poetry and Romanticism', 100.
[72] *The Political Unconscious*, 70.

Selected Poems, the poem appears again with four stanzas and slight alterations to the ending. Mahon describes the alteration as 'I tried to be too explicit with a fifth stanza and succeeded only in being inept'.[73] The fifth stanza, which caused the problem, is, in a way, Mahon's attempt to find the transcendent solution he is sometimes credited with (and criticized for) offering:

> For the pale light of that provincial town
> Will spread itself, like ink or oil,
> Over the not yet accurate linen
> Map of the world which occupies one wall
> And punish nature in the name of God.
> If only, now, the Maenads, as of right,
> Came smashing crockery, with fire and sword,
> We could sleep easier in our beds at night.[74]

Here, the problem of militant Protestantism's imperialist destruction is countered by simple assertion of the female principle absent from Protestantism's patriarchal ideology. Mahon hankers after the 'Womanly Times' exemplified in Robert Graves's aesthetic: Graves's 'poetic personality', Mahon writes, 'provides the perfect paradigm of a maleness which, by submitting itself to the female principle, *enhances* its own nature'. Crucially, he also views that personality as subversive and transgressive: 'Graves had spoken in *The White Goddess* of "the irreligious improvidence with which man is exhausting the earth", and he clearly feels that human folly and wickedness are enjoying exponential growth. Those who still dismiss him as an ivory-tower poet might ponder the implications of his work.'[75] The fundamental difficulty with the additional stanza in 'Courtyards in Delft' is that the conflict in the previous stanzas between the poetic personality 'lying low' who misses 'the dirty dog, the fiery gin' and the 'hard-nosed companions' who 'dream of war' is already the assertion of a Gravesian poetic. Longley argues that 'one way in which Mahon addresses the nexus of religion and history is by transmuting its constrictions within his own artistic structures. Thus relegated to the unconscious, "lying low", poetry is well placed to

---

[73] 'Derek Mahon Interviewed' by William Scammell, *Poetry Review*, 81/2 (Summer 1991), 6.
[74] *The Hunt by Night*, 10.
[75] Mahon, 'Womanly Times', review of *Between Moon and Moon: Selected Letters of Robert Graves*, ed. Paul O'Prey, *Literary Review*, 75 (Sept. 1984), 8.

subvert.'[76] Transgressive desire is implicit in the poem's first four stanzas: the insertion of extraneous Maenads in the fifth compromises an internal quarrel, and simplifies Graves, by proposing too easy an external answer.

In this context, certain Mahon poems can look like two sides of the same coin: 'The Last of the Fire Kings' expresses the desire to be 'through with history', to escape from 'the barbarous cycle';[77] 'A Disused Shed in Co. Wexford' desires release into history from the barbarous cycle. 'The Last of the Fire Kings' is not so much Mahon's agenda for escapism, but a poem which holds a middle ground somewhere between a rock and a hard place, recognizing two obligations—to escape the barbarous cycle, but to inhabit the world of those who perpetuate it. Both obligations are predicated on an ambiguous sense of responsibility for, belonging to, and (self-)alienation from, a community. That community is, the poem makes explicit, a Northern Irish one, with its 'Sirens, bin-lids | And bricked-up windows'.[78] 'A Disused Shed' is a poem cast in more general terms which seems (like Yeats's 'The Second Coming') to have encouraged very specific interpretations. Heaney's is one of them:

> [Mahon] makes the door of a shed open so that an apocalypse of sunlight blazes onto an overlooked, unpleasant yet pathetic colony of mushrooms. What they cry out, I am bold to interpret, is the querulous chorus that Mahon hears from the pre-natal throats of his Belfast ancestors, pleading from the prison of their sectarian days with the free man who is their poet descendent.[79]

The poem does not limit its historical scope to something less than history, but instead projects its mushrooms/victims back and forward, to natural and 'manmade' disasters: 'Lost people of Treblinka and Pompeii!'[80] In thus widening its scope, it allows for readings informed by the concerns of different times and/or cultures. Heaney's response to the poem—mushrooms as Protestant ancestors—elides recognition of the fact that 'A Disused Shed' responds to one of his own poems, 'Bye Child': the child's 'frail shape, luminous | Weightless... stirring the

[76] Edna Longley, 'Derek Mahon: Extreme Religion of Art', in Michael Kenneally (ed.), *Poetry in Contemporary Irish Literature* (Gerrards Cross: Colin Smythe, 1995), 287.

[77] *The Snow Party*, 9.

[78] Ibid. 10.

[79] Heaney, *The Place of Writing* (Atlanta, Ga.: Scholar's Press, 1989), 49.

[80] *The Snow Party*, 37.

dust'[81] is Heaney's rather more self-reflexive conception of embryo poet transformed by Mahon into ethically questioning prototype mushroom. Having said that, Heaney's reading of 'A Disused Shed' is still quirky: those in a sectarian prison are, in one sense, 'lost people', but the poem's energies are directed primarily at the issue of forgetfulness, the victimization which results from reductive historical memory, a crime of which those trapped in a sectarian mindset have themselves been culpable. Heaney's mushrooms, self-aware victims of their own nature, are made to jump one step ahead by demonstrating an understanding which the poem itself condemns 'us' for not yet possessing. The poem's concern is, as its epigraph makes clear, with what has been forgotten. In a way, it is a natural heir to Mahon's earlier self-exhortations in 'The Spring Vacation', where, confronted by 'the unwieldy images of the squinting heart', he consciously affirms 'Once more, as before, I remember not to forget'.[82] Memory is not without responsibility; neither, therefore, should it be an unquestioned or unquestionable 'given'.

Insofar as Mahon does temporally locate 'A Disused Shed', he dates the mushrooms back to Ireland's 'civil war days', and the poem's imagery encourages a perception of the mushrooms as war victims. That perception draws, in part, on the horrors of the trenches; with men buried alive, shell-shocked, sharing their underground prison with the decomposing bodies of their companions, drowning in seas of mud, breathing poisoned air, and convinced the war would last for ever:

> There have been deaths, the pale flesh flaking
> Into the earth that nourished it;
> And nightmares, born of these and the grim
> Dominion of stale air and rank moisture.
> Those nearest the door grow strong—
> Elbow room! Elbow room!
> The rest, dim in a twilight of crumbling
> Utensils and broken pitchers, groaning
> For their deliverance, have been so long
> Expectant that there is left only the posture.[83]

Like Eliot's *The Waste Land*, 'A Disused Shed', though its focus is not the First World War in particular, is more profoundly a memory of war than

[81]   Heaney, *Wintering Out* (London: Faber, 1972), 71–2.
[82]   *Night-Crossing* (London: OUP, 1968), 6. The poem was originally titled 'In Belfast'.
[83]   *The Snow Party*, 37.

one might initially suspect. Probably at no other time in the twentieth century except in the Great War has the imagery of these lines been so literally true of the human condition. The way in which war victims, in Ireland and elsewhere, were and are manipulated by conflicting ideologies serves to make 'Let not our naïve labours have been in vain' particularly poignant. And as with Yeats's 'The Second Coming', while the poem is open to interpretation in a European context, it is also implicitly a critique of colonial (and post-colonial) relationships. The 'flaking flesh' evokes a memory of the victims of the Irish famine, the people 'groaning for deliverance' from colonial servitude and poverty. The poem shares some of its imagery with Kavanagh's *The Great Hunger*, which connects a forgotten and misrepresented people—the Irish peasantry—with famine victims: Maguire, the peasant ploughman, is 'half a vegetable', 'in a mud-walled space . . . unknown and unknowing', 'hungry for life' and light, peering, after death, 'Through a crack in the crust of the earth'.[84]

In 'The Last of the Fire Kings' and 'A Disused Shed', the issue addressed is that of historical memory. The community he exhorts to remember in the latter poem may be the community that pressurizes the poet in the former. 'Who lives by the sword | | Dies by the sword'[85] is an indictment of the way in which the past is remembered, or rather not remembered. So if 'The Last of the Fire Kings' resists the pressure to subscribe to historical myth, 'A Disused Shed' looks for a release into cultural memory that transcends the repressions by which such myths function. It is, in this sense, the 'break with tradition' that 'Last of the Fire Kings' reaches towards.

V

Jay Winter suggests that the 'vigorous mining of eighteenth and nineteenth-century images and metaphors to accommodate expressions of mourning is one central reason why it is unacceptable to see the Great War as the moment when "modern memory" replaced . . . "tradition" '.[86] Although he attributes the phrase 'modern memory' to Paul Fussell, he takes it to mean 'modernism . . . the work of elites', so, in pointing out

---

[84] Kavanagh, *The Complete Poems* (1972), ed. Peter Kavanagh (Newbridge, Ireland: Goldsmith Press, 1984), 86, 96, 101–3.
[85] *The Snow Party*, 9.
[86] *Sites of Memory, Sites of Mourning*, 5.

that the modern and traditional intersect, he restates what Fussell's study
of this, under the title of 'modern memory', already assumes. For
Fussell, remembering, conventionalizing, and mythologizing the war
meant a reliance on 'inherited myth' but it also generated 'new myth'
which became 'part of the fiber of our own lives'.[87] Where traditional
literary motifs—prolific in First World War writing—are adapted to
a new and subversive function, the semi-paradox of modern memory is
formed. And it is because of the coexistence of conflictual elements (the
complacencies inherited; the reality confronted) that irony has become,
as Fussell points out, the 'one dominating form of modern understand-
ing'. It enables the writer to traverse the distance between the familiar,
the reassuring, and the incomprehensible which demands expression. It
offers the illusion of critical distance from the events it describes, and it
presupposes the author to be no longer 'deceived'. If a death was
significant pre-1914, it acquires significance in the war years only when
it makes an ironic point, because only then, as Fussell suggests, is it
sufficiently 'memorable'.[88] Further, 'The irony which memory associ-
ates with the events, little as well as great, of the First World War has', he
claims, 'become an inseparable element of the general vision of war in
our time'.[89]

One reason why this ironic strategy is not confined to the war years,
or the soldier poets, may be that if one can now be undeceived about
pre-war pieties, they have not been written out of existence. Fussell
writes:

In 1918, the Somme area now cleared of the enemy, someone in authority in
the Durham Light Infantry erected an elaborate twenty-foot-tall memorial
cross atop the notorious Butte of Warlencourt... [Painted on the cross] in
a circle around the intersection—it is a Celtic cross—[are] the words '*Dulce
et decorum est pro patria mori*'. Did Owen ever see this cross? No, he wrote his
poem a year before it was put up. Did those who set up the cross see his
poem? No, it was not published until two years later. This is to suggest the
unlikelihood, then and now, of the chivalric and the antichivalric taking
much notice of each other. Despite the shock of the Somme and a thousand
subsequent disillusions, the chivalric tradition, enfeebled and compromised
though it may be, remains one of the attendants of social and political con-
servatism. For its part, the antichivalric impulse takes off in the opposite

---

[87] *The Great War and Modern Memory*, p. ix.
[88] Ibid. 31.   [89] Ibid. 33.

direction, its rude skepticisms helping to consolidate the gains of Modernism and Post-Modernism.[90]

The Ulster Unionists can, without irony, publish a pamphlet celebrating the Ulster Division's achievements at the Somme entitled 'Rather be an Ulsterman'. Recent evidence of social and political conservatism is not confined to Northern Ireland. The cross to which Fussell refers was brought back from the Somme in 1926 and now holds pride of place in the military chapel of Durham Cathedral, where irony is neither intended nor understood by its presence, and this in spite of the by now familiar Owen poem.

The point of this is to suggest that irony, while it may be redemptive for the poet, is an interpretative as well as, perhaps even more than, an intentional act, and one which depends for its effect on the notion of a community which can grasp it. In the case of Derek Mahon, irony is the single most noticed yet unchallenged factor in his poetry: 'a poet of ironically long-term perspectives'; a 'terminal ironist'; 'an ironic conscience at one minute to midnight'.[91] For Mahon, as for the First World War poets, irony enables the poet to travel the distance between political conservatism and what Longley terms 'historical convulsions'. It is a means of dealing with the way in which his poetry is 'ambiguously ensnared', and it also helps to sustain that ambiguity as a dialectical strength. In cultivating this ambiguity, between the said and unsaid, Mahon crosses boundaries, and breaks culturally repressive codes of silence using irony as a means of assuming critical distance. 'Politically speaking', Linda Hutcheon points out, 'the ironist is extremely hard to assail precisely because it is impossible to fix his or her text convincingly'.[92] Irony can function as 'a way to avoid the single and dogmatic'.[93] Hence Mahon's 'By being ironical, we somehow escape culpability'. But the claim is more complex than this. Linda Hutcheon starts from the premiss that 'nothing is ever guaranteed at the politicized scene of irony':[94] intentionality, as declared by Mahon, cannot control interpretation. Further, irony, in intention and interpretation, can

[90] Fussell, *Thank God for the Atom Bomb* (1988), repr. as *Killing in Verse and Prose* (London: Bellew, 1990), 232.

[91] These few examples are taken from blurbs and article titles. It would be difficult to find any critical study of Mahon that does not mention his ironic perspective.

[92] *Irony's Edge*, 16.

[93] Ibid. 44.

[94] Ibid. 15.

'invoke[s] notions of hierarchy and subordination, judgement and perhaps even moral superiority'.[95] Hutcheon writes:

From the point of view of the intending ironist, it is said that irony creates hierarchies: those who use it, then those who 'get' it and, at the bottom, those who do not. But from the perspective of the interpreter, the power relations might look quite different. It is not so much that irony *creates* communities or in-groups: instead … irony happens because what could be called 'discursive communities' already exist and provide the context for both the deployment and attribution of irony.[96]

'Mahon's poetry', Edna Longley writes, 'starts from the premise of its repudiation by the tribe'.[97] It is also in danger of operating on the level of repudiation of the tribe in the way in which it deals with that premiss. To apply terminology such as 'exile' or 'ironist' to Mahon may be to take at face value the construction of Ulster Protestantism in the poetry as the whole picture, when the whole picture must also include the poetry that claims to stand outside it. He is, therefore, treading a fine line: the irony that could redeem the community might also, in positing its stereotypical existence as actual, simultaneously damn that community. Ironic self-awareness, which Mahon possesses in abundance (of what should he be 'culpable', and does he really believe in an 'escape'?), gives the poet a status at the top of Hutcheon's hierarchy; attribution of the irony does likewise. In both cases, there may be a sense in which the Ulster Protestant community is made to work as the discursive community that doesn't 'get' the irony.

Instead, it is more illuminating to see Mahon's irony as operating, not as the 'escape' from the Ulster Protestant community he proclaims it as, but as indicative of 'something in flux', an oscillation 'between the said and the unsaid',[98] between hope and despair, that resists black and white categorization. 'Irony', Fussell suggests, 'is the attendant of hope, and the fuel of hope is innocence'.[99] Mahon's irony both understands the community, in the sense that it is 'innocent' and unironic—a community with 'simple historical needs'—and projects into that community a new form of understanding. In 'Craigvara House', the poet, like Yeats before

---

[95]   Chamberlain, quoted in Hutcheon, *Irony's Edge*, 17.

[96]   *Irony's Edge*, 17–18.

[97]   'An Ironic Conscience at One Minute to Midnight', review of *The Hunt by Night* by Derek Mahon, *Fortnight*, 211 (Dec. 1984), 17.

[98]   Hutcheon, *Irony's Edge*, 60.

[99]   *The Great War and Modern Memory*, 18.

him in 'Meditations in Time of Civil War', and MacNeice in *Autumn Journal*, XVI, envies those who possess the certainty that comes from a form of historical innocence:

> I stared each night
> at a glow of yellow light
> over the water where the interned sat tight
>
> (I in my own prison
> envying their fierce reason,
> their solidarity and extroversion)[100]

But also, like Yeats ('I turn away and shut the door...'), he finds a different 'frequency' in the poem, and 'crossed by night | a dark channel'. 'Craigvara House' places the poet's anxieties at the centre of the poem; the earlier 'Rage for Order' does not. Nevertheless if 'Rage for Order' does not find a different frequency in the course of the poem, it still validates the notion that to do so is the poet's role. In 'Rage for Order', the fictive 'I' displaces the poet in time of war, and mocks his 'dying art'. It ranges the revolutionary and the 'people' on one side, and alienates the poet on the other. That the poet is 'indulging' his rage for order implies that he should, instead, take action. But 'dying art' is, from its first appearance in the poem, laden with irony and ambiguity: while the poet's art may be a 'dying' one, less and less useful as time progresses, it is, in fact, the embattled speaker of this poem who is involved in, literally, a 'dying art', that of war. If war has had, at times, an almost aesthetic appeal, 'art' mocks that perspective by adding 'dying' to make a cliché which, MacNeicean-style, works to subvert when it is read literally. But there is another sense in which the poet's art is a 'dying art', and that is as elegy. Following on from MacNeice, Mahon implies that if poetry appears to be temporarily displaced by war, it is not thereby disproved. Its final word leaves the different frequency—the poet's 'Germinal ironies'—waiting in the wings:

> Now watch me
> As I make history,
> Watch as I tear down
>
> To build up
> With a desperate love,
> Knowing it cannot be

[100] *Antarctica*, 16.

> Long now till I have need of his
> Germinal ironies.[101]

The early poem, 'In Carrowdore Churchyard', appears to ascribe a much more positive role to the poet, one which in 'Rage for Order', at least on the surface, is untenable. But if 'Rage for Order', written, unlike 'In Carrowdore Churchyard', in time of war, is reluctant to centralize the poet, it allows only a temporary, almost time-serving displacement: the revolutionary speaker might choose to need the poet only after the battle, but the timing is not prescriptive. The 'Germinal ironies' in 'Rage for Order' and the 'fragile, solving ambiguity' of 'In Carrowdore Churchyard' are not unconnected. From different vantage points, one might see these poems as defending or attributing the same poetic capability: in other words, the assumption is that what the poet in 'Rage for Order' will do, MacNeice, the inspiration behind 'In Carrowdore Churchyard', has done. In 'In Carrowdore Churchyard', when the poet is no longer displaced by the 'fierce reason' or 'intransigence' of the tribe, he is the figure who, metaphorically at least, records change and complexity, ends as well as elegizes war, and speaks for and to the tribe. It is a poem in which Mahon, like MacNeice before him, conflating images from both world wars, argues for a world in colour:

> This, you implied, is how we ought to live—
>
> The ironical, loving crush of roses against snow,
> Each fragile, solving ambiguity. So
> From the pneumonia of the ditch, from the ague
> Of the blind poet and the bombed-out town you bring
> The all-clear to the empty holes of spring,
> Rinsing the choked mud, keeping the colours new.[102]

[101] *Lives*, 23.   [102] *Night-Crossing*, 3.

CHAPTER SEVEN

The End of Art: Seamus Heaney's Apology for Poetry

What do I say if they wheel out their dead?

Seamus Heaney (1972)[1]

The question, as ever, is 'How with this rage shall beauty hold a plea?' And my answer is, by offering 'befitting emblems of adversity'.

Seamus Heaney (1974)[2]

I

'[C]elebrity', Wilfred Owen wrote, 'is the last infirmity I desire'.[3] Unique though the pressures upon Owen may have been, they did not include overt pressure from a public to provide, in his poetry, an adequate response to war—adequate, that is, in terms of social or political rather than aesthetic expectations. Owen does not appear to have been in doubt about what those expectations would have been—his draft preface conducts a quarrel with an imagined readership ('This book is not about heroes...nor...about glory, honour, might, majesty...these elegies are...in no sense consolatory') which, though it may be seen as social commentary, is primarily a defence of aesthetic freedom. But he remained free, during his lifetime, from critical commentary upon his work, and from pressure, as a public figure, to find for an audience hungry for answers 'befitting emblems of adversity'. Those pressures were brought to bear upon Owen posthumously. As a result his reputation has, as Mahon points out, 'been fought over by critics as

---

[1] 'A Northern Hoard: 3. Stump', *Wintering Out* (London: Faber, 1972), 41.
[2] *Preoccupations: Selected Prose 1968–1978* (London: Faber, 1980), 57.
[3] 'To Susan Owen', 25 May 1918, *Collected Letters*, ed. Harold Owen and John Bell (London: OUP, 1967), 553.

much as Vimy Ridge by the opposing armies, and there is little left to say'.[4]

Celebrity, in this sense, is an 'infirmity' from which Seamus Heaney has not been immune. If he shares with Owen a dilemma that causes a genuine crisis of response in the poetry to contemporary conditions— as Owen wrote, 'am I not myself a conscientious objector with a very seared conscience?'[5]—he has also both succumbed to, and been a victim of what Edna Longley terms 'improper expectations'.[6] As with Owen, his reputation has been fought over in debates about feminism, post-colonialism, Marxism, and so forth, which have reverberated in critical schools of thought in the United States, Britain, and Ireland. Heaney has been castigated, variously, for being too political, or not political enough, praised on the one hand for finding 'befitting emblems of adversity', for crossing boundaries, damned on the other for writing poetry at once 'damagingly gendered', disingenuous, dangerously emotive, and finally tendentious.[7]

Critical views have often been at odds not just with each other but also with the representation of Heaney in the press. The extremes

---

[4] 'Break of Day in the Trenches', review of *Out of Battle: The Poetry of the Great War* by Jon Silkin, *Irish Times*, 20 Feb. 1988, Weekend 9.

[5] 'To Susan Owen', ?16 May 1917, *Collected Letters*, 461.

[6] *Poetry in the Wars* (Newcastle: Bloodaxe, 1986), 185.

[7] Desmond Fennell attacks Heaney's poetry for its 'nothing saying and its poverty of meaning'. See *Whatever You Say, Say Nothing: Why Seamus Heaney is No. 1* (Dublin: ELO Publications, 1991). Edna Longley questions whether the partisanship of some of Heaney's poems may have a 'petrifying effect on poetic life'. See ' "Inner Emigré" or "Artful Voyeur"? Seamus Heaney's *North*', in *Poetry in the Wars*, 140 ff. Ciaran Carson condemns Heaney for a potentially dangerous mythologizing of Northern Irish history ('Escaped from the Massacre?', review of *North* by Seamus Heaney, *Honest Ulsterman*, 50 (Winter 1975)). Sidney Burris, on the other hand, praises Heaney for his subversive yet compensatory mythologies (*The Poetry of Resistance: Seamus Heaney and the Pastoral Tradition* (Athens, Ohio: Ohio UP, 1990)). David Lloyd describes Heaney as a 'minor Irish poet' unnaturally elevated because he reinforces rather than challenges 'imperial ideology'. (' "Pap for the Dispossessed": Seamus Heaney and the Poetics of Identity', in Elmer Andrews (ed.), *Seamus Heaney*, (London: Macmillan, 1992), 87–116). For Arthur McGuinness, Heaney is an oppressed Irish native who successfully reclaims his language from the (colonial) oppressor. See 'Politics and Irish Poetry: Seamus Heaney's Declaration of Independence', *Études Irlandaises*, 15/2 (Dec. 1990), 75–82. Patricia Coughlan argues that Heaney's poetry is 'insistently and damagingly gendered': ' "Bog Queens": The Representation of Women in the Poetry of John Montague and Seamus Heaney', in Michael Allen (ed.), *Seamus Heaney* (London: Macmillan, 1997), 185–205. Others have praised the unifying 'female thematic elements' in Heaney's poetic. See Jacqueline McCurry, 'The Female in Seamus Heaney's Prose Poetics and the Poetry of *The Haw Lantern*', *Éire-Ireland*, 23/4 (Winter 1988), 114–24.

became most apparent when he was awarded the Nobel prize for literature in 1995. The Swedish Academy press release stated the award was given 'for works of lyrical beauty and ethical depth, which exalt everyday miracles and the living past'. Heaney was acclaimed in the national press in Britain as 'the Irishman without frontiers', who deserved the prize because of his 'insights into Ireland and the Irish— a quasi-political responsibility which transcends the normal vocation of the poet'. Harking back to the First World War aesthetic and the expectations placed on poets in wartime, the leading article in *The Times* continues: 'A writer who had nothing adequate to say about the violence and hatred of those years would not deserve to be honoured at home, let alone abroad'.[8] Roy Foster and James Fenton, on the other hand, referred, diplomatically but more reservedly, to his 'place in Irish national life that no poet since Yeats has enjoyed' (note 'life' not 'literature') and his 'extraordinary ability to inspire affection in his audience' respectively.[9] Heading the case for the prosecution, Robert McLiam Wilson argued, in the Belfast-published magazine *Fortnight*, that the Nobel praise-fest was fundamentally misguided. Heaney cannot be praised for 'ethical depth' because he has not 'straddled and spoken to both traditions in this divided island', 'he has largely avoided writing a great deal about political violence in Northern Ireland... he has left out that unpoetic stuff, that very actual mess'.[10] In other words, far from having something 'adequate to say', Heaney has spoken of, to, and for only one side of a dispute, promoting a reductive version of Irishness and thereby claiming his laurels while resting on them. Michael Parker attempts a corrective to Wilson's polemic in *Fortnight*, arguing that the presentation of Heaney as 'an insular, banal, peat-and-potatoes pastoralist... is highly reductive', that Wilson's critique of Heaney fails to engage in any way with the poetry itself, and that many other critiques of Heaney do not give sufficient, if any, consideration to 'the *specific* historical/political circumstances appertaining when the poet's texts were produced'.[11]

Peter McDonald points out that, in one sense, 'the Nobel prize is entirely beside the point... a matter of mere "finish"'. '[A]s Yeats was well aware', he continues, '"the finished man" in poetry has to remain something other than a man who is finished, and whose voice responds

[8] *The Times*, 6 Oct. 1995, 21.   [9] Ibid. 5.
[10] Wilson, 'The Glittering Prize', *Fortnight*, 344 (Nov. 1995), 24.
[11] 'Levelling with Heaney', *Honest Ulsterman*, 103 (Spring 1997), 103–4.

only to its own public resonances'. But, he also suggests, one con-
sequence of the Nobel prize is that 'Heaney's understanding of the plight
of the "authoritative public poet"... is now more likely to be regularly
tested'.[12] The critical debates about Heaney, brought to the fore by the
award, centre, ultimately, on three connected issues: how Heaney has
responded to the Troubles in Northern Ireland; whether that response is
'adequate' (and what determines the notion of adequacy); and, lastly,
whether those two questions are themselves an adequate way of evalu-
ating a poetry. Heaney, under pressure, as Edna Longley notes, as 'the
popular standard-bearer of "Ulster Poetry" '[13] is caught in the crossfire
of an argument about the function of poetry in the present, troubled
times. He is caught there, not just because of celebrity, but because he
himself has centred his work within that debate through what Michael
Allen describes as 'his bid to influence the climate of taste in which his
poems will be read'.[14] What the debate about Heaney has in common at
all levels, whether in the press, in criticism, in self-criticism, and in the
poetry, is the question of poetry as ethical or unethical, adequate or
inadequate, 'the need to be both socially responsible and creatively
free'.[15] Within Heaney's oeuvre, the argument itself goes on at different
levels—in his critical prose (Heaney as Heaney); in some of the poetry
glossed in that prose and intended to be read alongside it (Heaney as
standard-bearer); and in the resolutely irresolute aesthetic which in
various poems contradicts the other two (Heaney as poet).

There is an element of déjà vu in the Heaney debate, hence the
suggestion of Wilfred Owen as progenitor. The conflict in Northern
Ireland has prompted re-evaluation of questions that have dominated
discussions of First World War poetry. With an echo of Owen's 'seared
conscience' sensibility, the *Irish Times*, in August 1970, ran a series of
articles by Eavan Boland concerning 'the Northern Writers' crisis of
conscience' in the face of political crisis: what to write; how to write it;
how to evaluate what was being written. Whether or not the Great War
poets found answers to these questions has long been disputed. John H.
Johnstone's 1964 study of Great War poetry argues that most of the war

[12] 'The Poet and "The Finished Man": Heaney's Oxford Lectures', *Irish Review*, 19
(Spring/Summer 1996), 98–9.
    [13] 'Stars and Horses, Pigs and Trees', in Mark Patrick Hederman and Richard Kearney
(eds.), *The Crane Bag Book of Irish Studies*, (Dublin: Blackwater Press, 1982), 480.
    [14] Introduction to Allen (ed.), *Seamus Heaney*, 1.
    [15] Heaney, *The Redress of Poetry: Oxford Lectures* (London: Faber, 1995), 193.

poets were 'hampered in their efforts to depict or evaluate their experiences' of war by 'their almost exclusive reliance on the contemporary lyric response and on the attitudes and techniques inherent in that response'.[16] The experience of the Great War meant that 'The "static lyric" had suddenly been forced to accommodate a flood of experience too vast for it to assess, too various for it to order, and too powerful for it to control'.[17] Johnstone quotes Synge's well-known comment from 1908 that 'before verse can be human again it must learn to be brutal',[18] a sentiment later echoed and adapted in Heaney's desire to 'take the English lyric and make it eat stuff that it has never eaten before'.[19] The epic is, in the end, Johnstone suggests, the best way to deal with the subject of war, and the modern war poet found epic unworkable because he was 'deprived of the aesthetic advantages of temporal remoteness'.[20] Arthur Lane challenges this assumption, arguing that the lyric response in Owen and Sassoon was an adequate response, 'both as art and as statement'.[21] He claims that theirs was a protest poetry which radically redefined imagery and style and thus altered perceptions of the capability of the lyric poem to deal with the experience of mechanized warfare.[22] And he defends Owen against the epithet sometimes applied of 'minor'—Bergonzi, for example, suggests that Owen's 'conscious restriction of range...count[s] against him if he is being considered as a claimant for absolute greatness'[23]—arguing instead for the virtues of what he describes as a 'Poetics of Responsibility'.[24]

One reason for connecting Heaney's dilemma with that of the Great War poets is the ghostly presence of the Great War and its poetry in Heaney's work, never explored or confronted directly as in Michael Longley's poetry, but indirectly dictating the terms of response in and to the poetry. The idea of a 'poetics of responsibility' is one with which Heaney has engaged throughout his critical writings, and an idea which

---

[16] *English Poetry of the First World War: A Study in the Evolution of Lyric and Narrative Form* (Princeton: Princeton UP, 1964) p. x.

[17] Ibid. 13

[18] Ibid. 8.

[19] Heaney quoted in Neil Corcoran, *Seamus Heaney* (London: Faber, 1986), 95.

[20] *English Poetry of the First World War*, 12.

[21] *An Adequate Response: The War Poetry of Wilfred Owen and Siegfried Sassoon* (Detroit: Wayne State UP, 1972), 7.

[22] Ibid. 7–27.

[23] *Heroes' Twilight: A Study of the Literature of the Great War* (London: Constable, 1965), 124.

[24] *An Adequate Response*, 128 ff.

has undergone subtle mutations from the early *Preoccupations* to his recent Nobel lecture, *Crediting Poetry*. In an interview with Thomas Foster in 1987, Heaney, echoing Yeats's *A Vision*, describes the first demand placed on the writer as being to 'deal somehow with truth and justice' and the second

that you beware of the fallout of your words, and perhaps I've been unduly aware of that, of the relationship between lyric and life, of the responsibility for what you say. Geoffrey Hill has three lines in *The Mystery of the Charity of Charles Peguy*, 'Must men stand by what they write/as by their camp-beds or their weaponry/or shell-shocked comrades while they sag and cry?'. In other words, do you have to take responsibility for the effect of your work? And in the North of Ireland, I think the answer is yes.[25]

The 'crisis of conscience' of the Northern writer is connected explicitly, through Hill's lines, to the crisis of the Great War poets. Heaney's entire critical endeavour may be seen as an attempt to offer an 'apology for poetry'. It is, for the trench poets, an endeavour which became, under extreme circumstances, a moral imperative, hence Owen's question to Sassoon about 'Spring Offensive': 'Is this worth going on with? I don't want to write anything to which a soldier would say No Compris!'.[26]

The trenches are, to some extent, Heaney's own metaphorical starting point, but on the whole, the implications of the proliferation of Great War imagery in Heaney's poetry have not been explored. Several critics, including Thomas Foster and Neil Corcoran, remark upon the militaristic imagery of *Death of a Naturalist*, and attribute this to excessive Ted Hughes influence. They do not, however, connect the imagery specifically to the Great War. If anything, it is likely that such imagery, and the stylistic inheritance from the First World War lyricists, have, implicitly, helped to fuel the criticisms sometimes made of Northern Irish poetry of inadequate neo-Georgianism, of stylistic anachronism. (Great War references do not need to be explicated if they are merely symptomatic of a 'time-warped' condition.) Despite his fame, his phenomenal sales, and his apparently established position in the Western canon, Heaney is often misrepresented in relation to English literary tradition, a victim, albeit a best-selling one, of the same criticisms that have plagued Mahon and Longley. One reason why the references to the First World War, the indebtedness to Owen, Hughes, and an English tradition of war writing

---

[25]   Quoted in Thomas C. Foster, *Seamus Heaney* (Dublin: O'Brien Press, 1989), 6.
[26]   Quoted in Lane, *An Adequate Response*, 141.

are elided or overlooked in Heaney's work is, understandably, that he stems from a community with a highly problematical relationship to the First World War. But the pantheon of father figures—Yeats, Joyce, Kavanagh, Montague—which Heaney suggests liberated his own voice should not obscure connections with an English literary tradition—the work of Hughes, Hill, the Great War poets, Keith Douglas—that also effected some kind of liberation. Conversely, Heaney does not stand or fall according to the word of English history and tradition. Far from working in an either/or straitjacket (in terms both of literary traditions—English or Irish—or versions of history—grounded in, say, the Rising or the Somme), the poetry, as much as recent historical research, reveals those distinctions as arbitrary.

To some extent, Heaney is caught in a no-win situation: the expectations placed upon him are reminiscent of those placed on the Georgian poets in 1914; the accusation of neo-Georgianism thus fails to recognize the culpability of criticism in attributing the need for the quality which it subsequently finds wanting. John Wilson Foster's 1985 essay 'Post-War Ulster Poetry' explores some of the inconsistencies in 'the tangled relations between English and Irish writers', the 'odd mixture of envy and admiration, respect and condescension' that characterizes the English writer's attitude towards his Irish counterpart, and the desire of Irish writers to 'avail themselves of the hospitality of English readers' but also 'maintain the refuge of difference against the day when the critical going gets rough'.[27] In view of Foster's acute exposé of some of these inconsistencies, 'concentrated' in Northern Ireland, a place 'geographically Irish but constitutionally British',[28] it is surprising to find criticisms of Heaney recycled on the grounds which Foster points to as fallacious. Antony Easthope's attempted demolition job on Heaney and the English empirical tradition risks collapsing distinctions between English poetry and poetry in English—indeed, it has to collapse such distinctions for the analysis to work. The only fundamental problem he perceives which needs to be overcome in that tradition in order to 'continue the series which runs: Shakespeare and Milton and Wordsworth and…Hardy and…Seamus Heaney' is Modernism.[29] (*Pace* Yeats?) On one level, he objects to the way in which Heaney has been

[27] *Colonial Consequences: Essays in Irish Literature and Culture* (Dublin: Lilliput Press, 1991), 61.

[28] Ibid.

[29] 'How Good is Seamus Heaney?', *English*, 46/184 (Spring 1997), 22.

read; Heaney is thus the victim of a critical 'conspiracy' that wants to place 'an old-fashioned poetic empiricism' at the heart of the English canon. But Easthope's final judgement on Heaney is that he is a 'back-ward-looking Neo-Georgian' (shades of Stan Smith's criticism of Mahon here), and that for British culture to honour him 'is not a symptom of vitality'.[30] Heaney's Northern Irish background means that his 'pastoralism could make a claim to political discourse', but for Easthope, 'Terrible as the situation has been in Northern Ireland, it has staged something backward-looking and atavistic, not a genuinely con-temporary politics [*sic*]'. As a consequence, since 'things have moved on' elsewhere in the world, Heaney can draw on the subject matter of Northern Ireland, can 'sound very serious and authoritative without treading on anyone's toes'.[31] Easthope's argument is concerned with reception, with canon-building, but it also, and finally, blames the poet: Heaney is atavistic and backward-looking, therefore the Establishment is culpable for praising him; his atavism is itself symptomatic of his place of origin. The alleged Northern Ireland time warp rears its head again.

In effect, both those involved in the English praise-fest, and those, like Easthope, who criticize it, ignore some of the contexts and implica-tions of Heaney's work in order either to accommodate or condemn him. In so doing, they lay him open to the charge of 'atavism', robbing Peter to pay Paul in the placing, or displacing, of him in certain versions of the canon.[32] If Northern Ireland is perceived as atavistic and back-ward-looking, this is an indictment, not of the place (or, consequently, of its poets), but of an attitude which assumes itself, its politics, and its literary developments to be a quantifiable 'norm' against which atavism can be recognized and measured. To connect Heaney's aesthetic with the Great War poets is not to suggest that Northern Ireland's culture, along with its politics, would look more at home in 1914 than 1999. Rather it is to illustrate that, although Heaney relates his dilemma, his search for 'images and symbols adequate to our predicament'[33] to the

---

[30] 'How Good is Seamus Heaney?', *English*, 46/184 (Spring 1997), 35.
[31] Ibid. 30.
[32] The charge of conservatism which may be brought against Heaney differs from that of atavism, in that it has less to do with style, the New Critical idiom, the anti-modernist empirical preoccupations, the born-again Romanticism, and the political nothing-saying that Easthope and others object to, than with the form of political 'saying' and the implications of a world-view that many, notably American, critics find radical and forward-looking and others find static, or resistant to change.
[33] *Preoccupations*, 56.

First World War poets (and in that sense, neo-Georgianism should not be a derogatory term), and although Northern Ireland still confronts unresolved political questions stemming from the Great War era, neither of these factors in themselves warrants a charge of anachronism, in terms of literature or politics. On the contrary, Paul Fussell demonstrates that the Great War has permeated modern memory to the extent that it is often impossible to conceive of experience in terms *other* than those brought about by the Great War. To look backwards can be a way of looking forwards. As in the case of Mahon, the call for Heaney to produce an adequate war poetry, to come up with something 'new' in a time of crisis, may be where the only anachronism lies.

Like Longley, Heaney has linked an imagined Great War landscape to his perception of Ulster, and has done so on two different, but interdependent, levels: first, by 'borrowing' Great War imagery in order to construct his own Ulster landscape; second, and more importantly, by utilizing Great War landscapes and terminology as metaphors for the condition of poetry, and the poet, in the Northern Ireland Troubles. The purpose here, then, is not so much to question the 'adequacy' of Heaney's response to the Troubles, but to consider, first, how effectively the Great War functions as a metaphor for Heaney's own engagement with that question, and second, to explore some of the broader implications behind the use of the metaphor as Heaney develops his own 'Apology for Poetry'. A highly self-conscious poet, even when that self-consciousness is transmuted into the mystical, the epiphanic, Heaney reveals a more acute insecurity than either Mahon or Longley about the pressure to respond to the Troubles in some tangible way, for poetry to make something happen, to legitimate its function in the world. At different points in his career, he gives way to this pressure, engages with it in order to try and transcend it, or transcends it entirely on his own terms. Through the various mutations of Heaney's poetry, the Great War metaphor functions as a kind of barometer, measuring self-doubt, crisis, resolution, and the Great War poets, particularly Owen, as a means of evaluating a poetics of responsibility.

II

Heaney's first collection, *Death of a Naturalist*, is littered with Great War debris. The imagery is less prevalent in *Wintering Out*, but intensified when it does appear by its connection to an Owenesque aesthetic questioning. In *North*, the First World War is not accommodated in Heaney's mythologized view of history, his claimed discovery of 'befitting emblems of adversity', though, as will be seen, it works as a subtext to the movement of that volume. By the time of *Field Work*, the Great War is again a focal point for Heaney (and it is only in this volume that he explicitly approaches the subject of Irish involvement in the war, in 'In Memoriam Francis Ledwidge'). After *Field Work*, the Great War largely disappears as a subject or metaphor for poetry, or as a way of 'explaining' Northern Ireland. Side by side with this development in the poetry is Heaney's developing conception, in his prose criticism, of the Great War aesthetic as exemplified by Wilfred Owen, and his growing consciousness of the importance of East European poets, notably Osip Mandelstam, gradually replacing Owen et al. as dominating influences. One might, therefore, risk the suggestion that as Heaney finds, in the 1980s, a point of resolution in his criticism about the function of poetry, particularly in relation to the Northern Irish situation, he ceases to engage, in the poetry itself, with the earlier war that had originally both sparked and grounded his aesthetic questioning.

Death of a Naturalist, Thomas Foster points out, does not contain 'poetry for agrarian sentimentalists'. It 'testifies throughout to the small-scale violence of rural life'.[34] Heaney's early poems mark out a difference between pastoral and what might be described as 'country sentiment': the former has the capacity to challenge or subvert because it sees the landscape itself as under threat, bound within limits, and defined only through awareness of its 'other'. As Stallworthy notes, the poems 'praised for their loving evocation of the natural world...abound in images of man-made violence'.[35] Heaney, attempting retrospectively to account for the proliferation of military metaphors in that volume, writes:

Denis Donoghue probably got to the heart of the matter when he suggested, in a review, that I had seen too many war films when I was a youngster. But two other explanations occur to me (for I was not conscious of planting mines at the time). First, that Ted Hughes's poetry was a strong influence in releasing me, and the habit of explosive diction may have been caught from him. And second—a more tentative, perhaps mystifying thought—when I set about

---

[34] Foster, *Seamus Heaney*, 14.
[35] 'The Poet as Archaeologist: W. B. Yeats and Seamus Heaney', in Robert F. Garratt (ed.), *Critical Essays on Seamus Heaney* (New York: G. K. Hall; London: Prentice Hall International, 1995), 175.

a poem in those days, I was tensed and triggered within myself. I usually wrote at a sitting and generated a charge within me: the actual writing was an intense activity, battened down. So maybe that state reflected itself in the diction and imagery.[36]

The Yeatsian sense of creativity he describes, of energy reined down, elevates the use of such imagery to the mystical, even the prophetic—the 'slightly aggravated young Catholic male part'[37] of Heaney anticipating, unwittingly, the war-torn landscape of the future, with writing itself almost a form of military activity that pre-dates conflict. Heaney's first explanation—Hughesian influences—is limited: the centrality of the First World War to Hughes's aesthetic vision makes slightly too easy the view that Heaney merely picked up elements of style and imagery, and applied them, randomly and unconsciously, to farming life in Co. Derry. His second verges on the inexplicable.

The truth is somewhere in between. Neil Corcoran writes that

some of Hughes's stylistic devices are obviously a direct, indeed an overwhelming influence, on some of the poems of *Death of a Naturalist*: on the trick of eliding title into first line in 'The Diviner' and 'Trout'; on the almost absurd range of military metaphors in 'Trout' itself ... and on the similar metaphors and portentously over-insistent anthropomorphisms in 'Turkeys Observed' ... These poems have their eyes so eagerly trained on *The Hawk in the Rain* and *Lupercal* ... that trout and cow and turkeys disappear unrecognizably into pale imitation and pastiche.

It is possible to feel, however, that something more subtle and complex has been learned from Hughes in 'Digging'[38]

The stylistic devices Heaney has absorbed also have something to do with the preoccupations that dominate later collections, notably *Wintering Out* and *North*, where they are used to much greater effect. Heaney inherits, at least partly from Ted Hughes, a sense of landscape as something for ever tainted and violated by the wars of the twentieth century, a landscape which acts as conscience and custodian of memory. Ted Hughes, describing his home ground, writes:

Everything in West Yorkshire is slightly unpleasant. Nothing ever quite escapes into happiness. The people are not detached enough from the stone, as if they

---

[36] 'To Jon Stallworthy', 6 Mar. 1980, quoted ibid. 176.
[37] Heaney, 'Unhappy and at Home', interview by Seamus Deane, in Hederman and Kearney (eds.), *Crane Bag Book of Irish Studies*, 66.
[38] Corcoran, *Seamus Heaney*, 45.

were only half-born from the earth, and the graves are too near the surface. A disaster seems to hang around in the air there for a long time. I can never escape the impression that the whole region is in mourning for the First World War.[39]

This perspective is not one that Heaney adapts with unqualified success in *Death of a Naturalist*. He turns his home ground into a Great War battlefield of sorts in order to construct an image of the self as embattled (soldier) poet, but the internal struggle, such as it is, does not really justify the framework. From the initial connection, in 'Digging', of soldier with poet, pen with gun, Heaney moves into a world which at times looks like Co. Derry crossed with Passchendaele: the 'flax-dam festered…rotted…weighted down by huge sods', frogs 'Poised like mud-grenades'; 'an armoury | Of farmyard implements', 'great blind rats'; 'large pottery bombs'; the 'Trout…a fat gun-barrel'; 'bombarded by the empty air'.[40] There are more rats in this book than in most Great War memoirs. They function, in 'An Advancement of Learning', as the focus of childhood and sexual fears—'This terror, cold, wet-furred, small-clawed'—which are overcome en route to adulthood: 'I stared him out…I walked on and crossed the bridge'.[41] It is probably also impossible now to put a rat in a poem without evoking an imagined memory of war (as mediated partly through Orwell): the rat has come to represent the survival of the barbaric in a 'civilized' world, a result partly of the fact that it was, in the First World War, often the only tangible enemy the soldier, in his fight for 'civilization' ever saw. The poet, pen (gun) in hand, undergoes pseudo-trench-trials.

The Great War metaphor is at its most extreme and its most ineffective in 'Dawn Shoot'. The early morning shooting expedition becomes a First World War 'over the top' dawn-attack scenario:

> Clouds ran their wet mortar, plastered the daybreak
> Grey…
>
> .   .   .   .
>
> …A corncrake challenged
> Unexpectedly like a hoarse sentry
> And a snipe rocketed away on reconnaissance.
> Rubber-booted, belted, tense as two parachutists,

[39] Quoted in Keith Sagar (ed.), *The Achievement of Ted Hughes* (Manchester: Manchester UP, 1983), 10.
[40] See 'Digging', 'Death of a Naturalist', 'The Barn', 'Churning Day', 'Storm on the Island', in Seamus Heaney, *Death of a Naturalist* (London: Faber, 1966).
[41] Ibid. 7.

We climbed the iron gate and dropped
Into the meadow's six acres of broom, gorse and dew.

A sandy bank, reinforced with coiling roots,
Faced you, two hundred yards from the track.
Snug on our bellies behind a rise of dead whins,
Our ravenous eyes getting used to the greyness,
We settled, soon had the holes under cover.

.   .   .   .

The cock would be sounding reveille
In seconds.[42]

Although the poem deploys its imagery with some fidelity to the details of an original dawn 'push'—the sentry, the snipe(r), the barbed wire ('coiling roots'), shell holes, funk-holes, the tense moments waiting for the signal to attack, the lines diminishing at the countdown—it does not rework the imagery either to illuminate the poetic process, or to cast new light on the events it describes, and is, in the final analysis, factitious. But it is noteworthy partly because, as will be explored later, it experiments with an idea used to greater effect in 'Exposure', from *North*, partly because it illustrates more comprehensively than the other poems in Heaney's first volume his indebtedness not just to Ted Hughes, but also to Wilfred Owen. Heaney's Great War allusions are, in part, drawn from Hughes—whose first collection, *The Hawk in the Rain*, is preoccupied with memory of that war—but 'Dawn Shoot' shows Owen to be the figure standing behind Hughes. The lines quoted above owe something to Owen's 'Exposure'—

Dawn massing in the east her melancholy army
Attacks once more in ranks on shivering ranks of grey.

.   .   .   .

We cringe in holes, back on forgotten dreams, and stare, snow-dazed
Deep into grassier ditches. So we drowse, sun-dozed,
Littered with blossoms trickling where the blackbird fusses...[43]

—though they lack the insistent questioning, the irony, and the pastoral subversion that inform Owen's poem.

The outbreak in 1968–9 of the current Troubles in Northern Ireland triggers that questioning for Heaney. His second collection, *Door into the*

---

[42] Ibid. 16–17.
[43] *The Poems of Wilfred Owen*, ed. Jon Stallworthy (London: Chatto & Windus, 1990), 162.

Dark, published in 1969, is, in many ways, a continuation of *Death of a Naturalist*, its title indicating its role as sequel to the earlier collection, whose final poem, 'Personal Helicon', states 'I rhyme | To see myself, to set the darkness echoing'.[44] But between 1969 and 1972, when the poems which comprise *Wintering Out* were written, the resurgence of violence in the North gives a new dimension to the work in that it brings to the surface the 'seared conscience' which Heaney has spent his subsequent career trying to appease. He attributes to the poet an extra responsibility in relation to Northern Ireland (as revealed in his comments to Thomas Foster quoted earlier—'in the North of Ireland, I think the answer is yes'; no claims are made for those writing outside that framework), even as he simultaneously resists what he later describes as the 'expectation that you would speak for your own crowd, your own "tradition"...using that chance to air grievances and so forth'.[45] In the 1974 essay 'Feeling into Words', discussing the outbreak of violence in August 1969, Heaney writes that

From that moment the problems of poetry moved from being simply a matter of achieving the satisfactory verbal icon to being a search for images and symbols adequate to our predicament. I do not mean liberal lamentation that citizens should feel compelled to murder one another...I do not mean public celebration or execrations of resistance or atrocity—although there is nothing necessarily unpoetic about such celebration, if one thinks of Yeats's 'Easter 1916'. I mean that I felt it imperative to discover a field of force in which, without abandoning fidelity to the processes and experience of poetry as I have outlined them, it would be possible to encompass the perspectives of a humane reason and at the same time to grant the religious intensity of the violence its deplorable authenticity and complexity.[46]

This is the first, and most explicit, articulation of the notion of adequacy upon which Heaney is still brooding twenty years later in *The Redress of Poetry*, where he writes: 'Seferis...found in [poetry] an adequate response to conditions in the world at a moment when the world was in crisis and Greece *in extremis*. And that idea of poetry as an answer, and the idea of an answering poetry as a responsible poetry...that...has been one of my constant themes.'[47] '[O]ur

---

[44] *Death of a Naturalist*, 44.
[45] Heaney, 'Calling the Tune', interview by Tom Adair, *Linen Hall Review*, 6/2 (Autumn, 1989), 5.
[46] *Preoccupations*, 56–7.
[47] *The Redress of Poetry*, 191.

predicament', in 'Feeling into Words', is that of the people, caught up in a violent struggle, and also that of the poet who is both of the people and seeking a perspective beyond communal identity. It is a restatement of the desire for a contented duality, for soul and sense (art and life) to lie down together. Owen and Sassoon, perhaps even more than Yeats, are precursors in this by reason of circumstances. 'One cannot be a good soldier and a good poet at the same time', Sassoon writes.[48] Nevertheless, he expresses the desire to be a good soldier, 'to get a good name in the Battalion for the sake of poetry and poets'.[49] Owen too outlines a dual role for himself: 'I came out in order to help these boys—directly by leading them as well as an officer can; indirectly, by watching their sufferings that I may speak of them as well as a pleader can. I have done the first.'[50] Both make only tentative claims for their achievements as poets; both leave the aesthetic in a state of permanent instability; and yet both admit that one of the reasons for participating in the war is to enable their poetry. In Owen's case particularly, the poetry is in the apology for poetry that the war provokes.

That sensibility—a self-critical rather than self-indulgent questioning—appears in *Wintering Out*. If Ted Hughes's sense of England as a mass grave for First World War victims does not translate effectively into Heaney's early perceptions of Ulster, the later view of a troubled Northern Ireland that evokes memories of the Western Front is more effective: it is a way of explaining Northern Ireland to the outside world, at a time when some of the horrors of the Troubles equalled scenes associated with the Great War in their barbarity, their physical and emotional mutilation, if not in their death toll. It is also to follow the tradition of explaining one war in terms of another. As in *Death of a Naturalist*, the poet ventures out into a war-torn landscape, but in *Wintering Out* that landscape functions to contextualize the poet's dilemma in the face of atrocities.

Eric J. Leed writes that for veterans of the Great War, the war experience, 'through the metaphors derived from it, became something that could encompass everything'. He goes on to suggest that 'any claustrophobic situation, be it political, sexual, or psychic, can call up

[48] *Siegfried Sassoon Diaries 1915–1918*, ed. Rupert Hart-Davis (London: Faber, 1983), 271.
[49] Ibid. 51.
[50] 'To Susan Owen', 4/5 Oct. 1918, *Collected Letters*, 580.

the image of the trench labyrinth'.[51] Once those war images have been
called up, or have imposed themselves on a situation, a modern con-
sciousness makes a judgement on a contemporary situation through
ironic contrast or comparison with the events and images of the First
World War. There are certain Great War images which now carry so
much cultural baggage they inevitably conjure up what Vernon Scannell
describes as a 'deathscape'. His poem 'The Great War' deliberately, and
conveniently, encapsulates most of them: the 'grey militia' matching the
grey landscape, 'shells' opening 'fans | Of smoke and earth', 'rosettes of
fire' in the sky, 'Candles in dug-outs, | Duckboards, mud and rats',
'Crosses and flares, tormented wire…crimson flowers'. Everybody
knows what this landscape looks like without ever having seen it: the
poet remembers 'not the war I fought in | But the one called Great |
Which ended in a sepia November | Four years before my birth'.[52]

Descriptions of the Western Front have become parallels for the
human condition. Even at the time of the First World War, people were
puzzled by the fact that the 'narrow…strip of ground' on which the war
was being fought seemed 'too narrow for its gigantic significance'.[53]
That strip of ground represents in post-war imaginations the clash of
past and future, the development from innocence to experience, anti-
pastoral versus pastoral, the imposition of technology in the most
ruthless way imaginable on the natural world. A violated landscape is
a theme which occurs again and again in literature of the Great War. It is
not an idea which originates with that war. Rather it indicates a general
tendency, when thinking of war, to think in terms of a suffering land-
scape, whereas the reality, of course, is that people not the land are
bleeding and dying. Suffering is projected onto the land as something
which transcends time, which bears scars and memories long after any
veterans have died. But what is peculiar to the Great War, and what
lends it particularly to this kind of expression, is the visual absence of
any people on the battlefield. As Leed points out, 'The invisibility of the
enemy, and the retirement of troops underground, destroyed any notion
that war was a spectacle of contending humanity'.[54] The war represents

---

[51] *No Man's Land: Combat and Identity in World War I* (Cambridge: Cambridge UP,
1979), 76–7.
[52] 'The Great War', in Martin Stephen (ed.), *Poems of the First World War: 'Never Such
Innocence'* (London: J. M. Dent, 1993), 311–12.
[53] Herbert Weisser, quoted in Leed, *No Man's Land*, 132.
[54] Ibid. 19.

the birth of the modern age: its battlefields also provide images of the worst possibilities of that modern age, images which can seemingly be used *in perpetuum* in the quest for understanding the new age engendered by the technological advances of the twentieth century. The war landscape symbolizes the ambivalence informing perceptions of almost any landscape—literal or psychic: it is both one's home and the source of a hidden, ever-present threat; it is, paradoxically, a landscape destroyed by machinery in the interests of what is often seen as a kind of pastoral quest—as Edmund Blunden puts it, 'Greenness...was our dream scenery. There was to have been green country on the victorious far side of the Somme battlefield.'[55]

The ambivalence is articulated by David Jones in the preface to *In Parenthesis*: 'Even while we watch the boatman mending his sail,' he writes, 'the petroleum is hurting the sea. So did we in 1916 sense a change.'[56] If, as Fussell suggests, 'the opposite of experiencing moments of war is proposing moments of pastoral',[57] one moment does not exist anymore without awareness of the other informing the vision. And if the pastoral concept of 'home' is designed to counterbalance the effect of wars fought on someone else's ground (as is usually the case in English history), the Northern Irish poet would appear to have an almost impossible task confronting him or her: the landscape of war is also the landscape of home; the front line is perpetually shifting and always intangible. The Great War is, however, also the setting where landscapes of peace and war merge: Blunden, in *Undertones of War*, slips in and out of pastoral, in and out of the front line. Trenches themselves are pastoral or 'not so pastoral'; a 'pretty landscape' can be noticed amidst a bombardment of shells. Equally, the pastoral retreat away from the front line is, for Blunden in 1917, 'visited at night by aircraft well accustomed to the art of murdering sleep if not life'. Slipping into the present tense and writing ten years after the war is over, he continues 'Out of the line was out of the line in 1916, but we are older now'.[58] If war leads initially to an idealization of home, return home often leads to an idealization of at least some aspects of war. What remains to be idealized in the end is neither front nor home, but what a survivor of the Great War called the 'rainbow of yearning' between the two.[59]

[55] *Undertones of War* (1928; London: Penguin, 1982), 143.
[56] *In Parenthesis* (1937; London: Faber, 1963), p. ix.
[57] *The Great War and Modern Memory* (London: OUP, 1975), 231.
[58] *Undertones of War*, 206.   [59] Quoted in Leed, *No Man's Land*, 189.

The crossover between a sense of a landscape of war and, simultaneously, of pastoral (home) informs much of Heaney's 1970s poetry. In the sequence 'A Northern Hoard', he no longer has his eyes 'eagerly trained' on Hughes's first two books (although he has absorbed influences from Hughes's *Wodwo*, notably from 'Heptonstall', 'The Warriors of the North', and the Great War sequence 'Out'), but is engaged on a quest to find his own apology for poetry through negotiation with the conflict in which Hughes is also imaginatively involved. In the first poem in the sequence, 'Roots', 'the fault is opening', the inner space is invaded by 'gunshot, siren and clucking gas' even as they are resisted. To resist violence from the outside is also to perpetrate an act of violence against the self, to be culpable in violating the land even in departing it. The poem disallows an easy answer to the question of responsibility:

> We petrify or uproot now.
>
> I'll dream it for us before dawn
> When the pale sniper steps down
> And I approach the shrub.
> I've soaked by moonlight in tidal blood
>
> A mandrake, lodged human fork,
> Earth sac, limb of the dark;
> And I wound its damp smelly loam
> And stop my ears against the scream.[60]

The poet is caught between, on the one hand, the fear of rigid, archaic postures, the acceptance that might seem to condone—petrifaction— and on the other, the potentially fatal effects of uprooting the self, implicit in the mandrake's scream. The next poem in the sequence, 'No Man's Land', articulates the same dilemma, the same crisis of conscience: 'I deserted . . . Must I crawl back now . . .'. It visualizes Derry in terms of a preconceived image of No Man's Land in the Great War: it is the place where the poet must crawl 'abroad between | shred-hung wire and thorn | to confront my smeared doorstep'.[61] Pastoral and mechanical are compressed into the same image here, playing on the juxtaposition of the two in First World War literature, where 'iron thickets'[62] existed on either side of No Man's Land. The sense of helplessness characteristic of those caught in the ubiquitous mud of

---

[60] *Wintering Out*, 39.   [61] Ibid. 40.   [62] Blunden, *Undertones of War*, 159.

the First World War battlefields relates to the speaker's position as a poet
in Northern Ireland:

> Why do I unceasingly
> arrive late to condone
> infected sutures
> and ill-knit bone?[63]

As 'spirochete' he is also self-accusing; a part of, perhaps even a cause
of, the infection he arrives late to condone. (The image also looks
forward to the 'long-haired...wood-kerne' of 'Exposure' in *North*.)
He is indicted, the embattled tone of the poem suggests, and indicts
himself, for a failure to act.

In 'Stump', the self-questioning reaches its unanswerable climax:

> I am riding to plague again.
> Sometimes under a sooty wash
> From the grate in the burnt-out gable
> I see the needy in a small pow-wow.
> What do I say if they wheel out their dead?
> I'm cauterized, a black stump of home.[64]

The ambivalence of the landscape becomes the ambivalence of his
position in that landscape: the poet himself is, like Mahon's 'last stub-
born growth', the wounded pastoral, a 'black stump' of war, or, as in the
poem, of 'home'. The poem also looks back to the sixteenth and
seventeenth centuries—'riding to plague', bringing out the dead, the
burnings. Its imagery owes something to Ted Hughes's 'The Martyrdom
of Bishop Farrar', where

> ...she seized
> And knotted him into this blazing shape
> In their eyes, as if such could have cauterized
> The trust they turned towards him, and branded on
> Its stump her claim, to outlaw question.[65]

The question, in 'The Martyrdom of Bishop Farrar', is how events
themselves validate words—not so much 'what do I say?' but 'how

[63] *Wintering Out*, 40.
[64] Ibid. 41.
[65] *The Hawk in the Rain* (London: Faber, 1957), 58–9. Hughes's epigraph to the poem
reads: 'Burned by Bloody Mary's men at Caermarthen. "If I flinch from the pain of the
burning, believe not the doctrine that I have preached." (His words on being chained to
the stake.)'

will I be believed?'. Heaney's feeling of helplessness in 'Stump' puts him in the opposite position to the earlier martyr, even though both are felt as victims. The poet in 'Stump' falls into the 'as if such could have cauterized' that in Hughes's poem is derided. Farrar's transcendence of horror at the end of the poem, the triumph of the doctrine preached— 'out of his eyes, | Out of his mouth, fire like a glory broke . . . '—has no equivalent in 'A Northern Hoard'. The martyr is burned but unsilenced; the speaker of Heaney's poem is effectively silenced, 'cauterized', rendered numb and powerless, freed from the 'infection' of the previous poem perhaps, but helpless as a result. He is, in a way, shell-shocked into insensitivity by the events around him, with an echo of Owen's well-known comments, 'My senses are charred. I shall feel again as soon as I dare, but now I must not. I don't take the cigarette out of my mouth when I write Deceased over their letters.'[66] The sequence ends in confusion about the past, the future, and the poet's role, as he faces a desolate landscape irreversibly changed and irreparably damaged by war and revolution:

> What could strike a blaze
> From our dead igneous days?
>
> Now we squat on cold cinder,
> Red-eyed, after the flames' soft thunder
> And our thoughts settle like ash.[67]

III

Robert Buttel's study of Heaney's poetry, which pre-dates publication of *North*, notes the impatience of reviewers with *Wintering Out*: 'they want Heaney to "move on" to what they see as more urgent subjects'. Stephen Spender's review of *Wintering Out*, for example, assumes that Heaney's poetry will, in the future, 'enlarge' from 'deep personal feelings' to 'a much wider subject matter, especially since he comes from Northern Ireland, and the Irish situation must be boiling in him'.[68] If it is not, such reviews are designed to make it so. Desmond Fennel suggests that with *North*, in 1975, Heaney 'delivered the "war book"

---

[66] Owen, 'To Siegfried Sassoon', 10 Oct. 1918, *Collected Letters*, 581.

[67] *Wintering Out*, 43–4.

[68] See Buttel, *Seamus Heaney* (Lewisburg: Bucknell University Press; London: Associated University Presses, 1975), 69.

that London was waiting for'.[69] It was greeted, Blake Morrison writes, with 'an almost audible sigh of relief that at last a poetry of stature had emerged from the "troubles"'.[70] Ciaran Carson reiterates this feeling— 'Everyone was anxious that *North* should be a great book'—though he qualifies it—'when it turned out that it wasn't, it was treated as one anyway and made into an Ulster '75 Exhibition of the Good that can come out of Troubled Times'.[71]

Elmer Andrews notes that there are two temptations for a writer in wartime: the first is to become 'a mouthpiece for opinion and dogma'; the second is 'to exploit a situation of brutal factionalism for a kind of aestheticism which the poet indulges in for its own sake and without committing himself'. 'In the poems in *North*', he concludes, 'there are times when Heaney succumbs to both these temptations'.[72] In *North*, Heaney comes close to claiming he has found 'befitting emblems of adversity' from P. V. Glob's *The Bog People*, that he has something to say 'if they wheel out their dead'. The victims of 'ritual sacrifices to the Mother Goddess', he writes, 'blended in my mind with photographs of atrocities, past and present, in the long rites of Irish political and religious struggle'. They create for him an 'archetypal pattern'.[73] He offers, Graves-fashion, a 'romantic mythology' as an explanation of Northern Irish violence. It is a mythology which, unlike Graves's, has proved extremely contentious, and has attracted a vast amount of critical attention, both positive and negative. That debate is not primarily the issue here, but Heaney's indebtedness to the systems both Yeats and Graves formulated in wartime sheds light on both his purpose in constructing an 'archetypal pattern', and on the reasons for his only very limited success. Yeats's *A Vision* and Graves's *The White Goddess* are, as discussed earlier, mythologies designed to accommodate conflict and division, in the poet and in the world. Yeats projects his 'system' as a symbolic one, a way of ordering experience not dictating it, and thus retains a high degree of flexibility in the way in which it appears in the poetry. Graves, on the other hand, derives flexibility from the denial of symbolic status altogether. His claim to the actuality of the goddess insists, by default, on arbitrariness: to acknowledge the system as

[69] *Whatever You Say, Say Nothing: Why Seamus Heaney is No.1*, 27.
[70] Quoted ibid. 27.
[71] 'Escaped from the Massacre?', 186.
[72] *The Poetry of Seamus Heaney: All the Realms of Whisper* (London: Macmillan, 1988), 82.
[73] *Preoccupations*, 57–8.

constructed might restrict freedom; to avow its status as the only truth and the only story is to project all other freedoms as illusory. In *North*, Heaney tends to fall between these two stools. In 'Kinship', the speaker 'stand[s] at the edge of centuries | Facing a goddess', 'the goddess swallows | our love and terror';[74] in 'Strange Fruit' he outstares 'What had begun to feel like reverence'.[75] He reaches towards a pre-Christian mythology, only to establish within that mythology contemporary lines of sectarian division. In effect, he adopts a kind of Yeatsian symbolism which he then attempts to treat with Graves-style devotion.[76] He is consistent only in his indecisiveness about whether he is sacrificing or sacrificed, bridegroom or bride, archetypal product or liberal humanist.

'Punishment' encapsulates this indecisiveness. The poem has become, as Michael Allen points out, 'a *locus classicus* of Heaney criticism'.[77] Its fluctuation between empathy and voyeurism translates into passive collusion in the atrocities it simultaneously wants to condemn: 'I can feel...I can see...I almost love...I who have stood dumb...who would connive...yet understand...'.[78] Edna Longley queries whether the poet 'can...run with the hare...and hunt with the hounds'.[79] Paul Stanfield, answering in the affirmative, praises the 'double perspective' of the poem, its refusal to privilege 'the voice of the individual reason over that of the community's instinct, instead letting these two voices co-exist, interact, contend without declaring a victor'.[80] For Longley, however, the poem's 'artistic...fence-sitting' is unacceptable precisely because of the absence of any interaction and contention: 'The conclusion' of the poem, she suggests, 'states, rather than dramatises, what

[74] *North* (London: Faber, 1975), 42–5.

[75] Ibid. 39.

[76] Like Yeats, he is, for a time, seduced by the mythology he constructs. But also, like Yeats, his 'reason' recovers (though he finds no use for the 'mythology' as a purely symbolic system). '[A]t that time', Heaney says, 'I was, I suppose, in the grip of what is a romantic mythology...and then a moment came when I got a salutary reminder of what I was into.... One afternoon we went across the waters of a famous clearwater lake to an island which had the most entrancing Byzantine churches...[A Danish poet] said to me "This is you, isn't it? you aren't really black bogs and sacrificial Iron Age creatures." In a way he was right.' ('Between North and South: Poetic Detours', interview by Richard Kearney, *Visions of Europe: Conversations on the Legacy and Future of Europe* (Dublin: Wolfhound Press, 1992), 84).

[77] Introduction to Allen (ed.), *Seamus Heaney*, 17 n.

[78] *North*, 37–8.

[79] *Poetry in the Wars*, 154.

[80] 'Facing *North* Again: Polyphony, Contention', *Éire-Ireland*, 23/4 (Winter 1988), 138, 143.

should be profound self-division'.[81] Running with the hare and hunting with the hounds is, of course, exemplified in the life of Wilfred Owen, who made poetry out of condemning the atrocities of a war in which he also participated. Or, as Heaney puts it, 'He connived in what he deplored so that he could deplore what he connived in'.[82] ('Connive' is not wholly appropriate to a junior officer, and has rather more to do with Heaney's self-perceptions at the end of 'Punishment' than with Owen.) It is a contradiction apparent in Owen's correspondence, as well as in the poetry: 'When I looked back and saw the ground all crawling and wormy with wounded bodies, I felt no horror at all, but only an immense exultation...';[83] 'I lost all my earthly faculties and fought like an angel';[84] 'Passivity at any price! Suffer dishonour and disgrace; but never resort to arms'.[85] The poem which stands as a precursor to the divided loyalties Heaney attempts to expound in 'Punishment' is Owen's 'Strange Meeting', with its famous paradox: 'I am the enemy you killed, my friend'. But there is a fundamental difference between the sentiments of 'Punishment' and the dilemma confronted by Owen every day in the trenches. In 'Strange Meeting', the feeling of enmity is shown to be illusory even before the word 'enemy' is mentioned; although the killing has taken place, Owen does not claim to 'understand' killing as an underlying, somehow genuine impulse which has a validity of its own. Nor, therefore, does he excuse the life in the work. Heaney, on the other hand, later describes the 'half-acknowledged supposition' underlying the mythologies of *North*, as 'that the nativist, the barbaric, is as authentic if not more authentic than the civilised'.[86] 'Punishment' does not offer voices in contention. Instead, one is shown as a civilized veneer (false) imposed on the communal instinct which underlies it (true):

> I who have stood dumb
> when your betraying sisters,
> cauled in tar,
> wept by the railings,
>
> who would connive
> in civilized outrage

[81] *Poetry in the Wars*, 154.
[82] *The Government of the Tongue* (London: Faber, 1988), p. xv.
[83] 'To Colin Owen', 14 May 1917, *Collected Letters*, 458.
[84] 'To Susan Owen', 4/5 Oct. 1918, ibid. 580.
[85] 'To Susan Owen', ?16 May 1917, ibid. 461.
[86] 'Between North and South: Poetic Detours', 84.

> yet understand the exact
> and tribal, intimate revenge.[87]

Consequently, the language is that of the tribe even as he claims to be dumb—'betraying' not betrayed, the ironically protective 'cauled'.

The critical attention devoted to the Bog/Viking element of the volume and Heaney's subsequent move away from those mythologies has detracted attention from the continued engagement of Heaney's aesthetic with the Great War; indeed, it is the revision of his approach to his war-poet predecessors, which begins in *North* and is consolidated through *Field Work*, that distinguishes the later from the earlier volumes as much as the abandonment of the bog people. *North* marks the beginning of a process whereby Heaney commends Owen's aesthetic, but gradually distances it from his own understanding of an adequate poetry. In qualifying Owen's achievement he sets up a different concept of the term 'war poet' as it relates to himself and Ireland.

The landscape of *North*, like that of *Wintering Out*, is reminiscent of Great War battlefields, though in *North* the association is incidental rather than central. The poet is 'skull-handler...smeller of rot'; the land is a graveyard of drowned bodies, dead moles, a 'skull-capped ground'.[88] The volume itself moves from entrenchment, or collusion, to exposure and isolation. Much of what gives No Man's Land its mythical status in the Great War is the experience of going 'over the top', the move from safe burial in the earth to exposure on the surface. In the famous push of 1 July 1916, 'the innocent army fully attained the knowledge of good and evil'.[89] Wilfred Owen, describing such an attack, writes: 'There was an extraordinary exultation in the act of slowly walking forward, showing ourselves openly.'[90] It is an escape from the troglodyte world (a 'door into the light'?) in which the knowledge acquired seems to be understood most readily in sexual terms. Eksteins describes the soldier's experience as follows:

Physical nakedness is the first sensation. The body is now exposed, tense, expectant, awaiting direct violence upon it. Even if one is to follow the 'creeping barrage'...of one's own artillery towards the enemy trenches, that first moment

---

[87] *North*, 38.

[88] Ibid. 23–4. Cf. Blunden's description of Festubert: 'At some points in the trench, bones pierced through their shallow burial, and skulls appeared like mushrooms.' (*Undertones of War*, 25).

[89] Fussell, *The Great War and Modern Memory*, 29.

[90] 'To Colin Owen', 14 May 1917, *Collected Letters*, 458.

of exposure reduces him to innocence. 'A man who stepped out of the trenches at that moment and lived through has never in all the ensuing years faced such a climax,' wrote a survivor.[91]

Heaney's 'Exposure' in the context of *North* in some ways parallels this movement; from being 'cradled in the dark that wombed me... nurtured in every artery' of the earth in 'Antaeus',[92] the poet ventures out in 'Exposure' to the surface. As with Wilfred Owen's 'Exposure', the act of doing so has made of him an exile, has turned him into a tormented shadow of a former self. But in fact, the opposite position is held by Heaney. Owen puts it as rejection or abandonment *by* the world: 'Shutters and doors, all closed: on us the doors are closed,—│We turn back to our dying.'[93] In Heaney's 'Exposure', the isolation comes from rejection *of* that world: 'Escaped from the massacre'. If the poet in Heaney's 'Exposure' is initially reduced to innocence in exposure, 'Taking protective colouring│From bole and bark', it is only because in that reduction he is then open to knowledge of 'Every wind that blows'.[94] In the poem, Heaney's is, finally, a privileged individual position that translates Owen's experience of battle into his own, artistic terms. The early poem, 'Dawn Shoot', is true to the details of a Great War experience, if not to the poet's experience; *North* reworks second-hand images of the Great War to help articulate the poet's wartime dilemma but does not simultaneously illuminate the Great War experience from the Northern Ireland perspective. Heaney is faithful to his perception of Northern Ireland, but not faithful to the past he trawls for images to convey that perception. Too often, he is unable to combine these two things—truth to the image from the past, and to the present context created in the poem by that image. The imaginatively powerful idea of exposure in the Great War is, in a way, the original Fall reiterated, where the earth itself is cursed by the knowledge of evil attained. The knowledge, with the First World War, as with the Fall, has been perceived as permanent because hereditary: 'Never such innocence again', Larkin writes of the pre-war condition. And as Ted Hughes puts it when contemplating the photograph of 'Six Young Men' killed in the war:

[91] *Rites of Spring: The Great War and the Birth of the Modern Age* (1989; New York: Anchor-Doubleday, 1990), 141.
[92] *North*, 12.
[93] 'Exposure', *The Poems of Wilfred Owen*, 162.
[94] *North*, 73.

> To regard this photograph might well dement,
> Such contradictory permanent horrors here
> Smile from the single exposure and shoulder out
> One's own body from its instant and heat.[95]

The ending of Hughes's poem serves to illustrate the fundamental difference between Heaney's and Longley's uses of the Great War. For Heaney, that war can be used to express his position and dilemma as poet; it is also an 'image-bank' that helps him to articulate his vision of the Northern Irish landscape in the Troubles. For Longley, an imagined Great War landscape and engagement with the Great War poets do both these things, but also, as with Hughes and unlike Heaney, draw him back into history and serve to interpret the past in terms of the present as well as the other way round. The lack of historical imagination in Heaney's treatment of the Great War means that, on the whole, it resonates in his Northern Ireland only as a metaphor for finding an 'apology for poetry'.

If 'Exposure' acknowledges, obliquely, that the poet will not follow the western soldier poet's example, that he is not the 'hero' whose 'gift' is 'Whirled for the desperate', it also marks the entrance of Mandelstam as an equally traumatized but more congenial replacement: 'weighing' his 'responsible *tristia*', the poet describes himself as 'neither internee nor informer | An inner émigré, grown long-haired | And thoughtful'.[96] *Tristia* is the title of Mandelstam's second collection, published in 1922; 'inner émigré' was the description of Mandelstam current in Moscow in the 1930s, at a time when, as David McDuff explains, 'a writer with such a label could confidently suppose himself doomed'.[97] The accusatory self-questioning followed by self-assessment in 'Exposure' finds a precedent in the work of the Great War soldier poets, but also in Osip Mandelstam:

> Who am I? No forthright stonemason,
> no roofer or shipbuilder:
> I am a double dealer, with a double-dealing soul.
> I am a friend of night, a pioneer of day.[98]

---

[95] 'Six Young Men', *The Hawk in the Rain*, 54–5.
[96] *North*, 73.
[97] Introduction to Osip Mandelstam: *Selected Poems*, trans. David McDuff (Cambridge: Rivers Press, 1973), pp. xi–xii.
[98] Mandelstam, 'Slate Pencil Ode', *Selected Poems*, 85–7.

IV

Owen and Mandelstam embody, for Heaney, two kinds of response to violence, which start by negotiating, and end with the elision of one into the other.[99] In *Field Work*, that elision is, at times, already apparent before its articulation in the prose criticism, most notably in *The Government of the Tongue*. Heaney describes the shift from *North* to *Field Work* as 'a shift in trust: a learning to trust melody, to trust art as reality'.[100] The sequence of ten Glanmore sonnets at the heart of the volume attempts to establish that trust, to create a realm which cannot be violated, even if it is a realm perfected only in memory: 'art a paradigm of earth new from the lathe...'; the desire 'to raise | A voice... That might continue, hold, dispel, appease'.[101] Those moments are still phrased only as possibilities, a kind of wish-fulfilment: 'the good life could be...'; 'I...hoped'; 'I...would crouch | Where small buds shoot...'.[102] (That realm is later attained without tentativeness in the 'Clearances' sonnet sequence of *The Haw Lantern*.)

'*Field Works*' are 'defensive or protective works, or temporary fortifications, made by an army to strengthen its position'.[103] Oddly, the return to a more tranquil evocation of the natural world in *Field Work*, the renewed contact with nature outside the mythologies of *North*, and the foregrounding of Wordsworth's influence, particularly in the Glanmore sonnets, have led to an overemphasis of one aspect of a double-edged phrase, to the extent that Elmer Andrews perceives as inherent in the volume's title 'a conscious scaling down of Heaney's vision. His imaginative parameters are now those of a field, not the international time-warps of *North*.'[104] (The Return of the Naturalist?) But Heaney's field is also a field of war from which respite is gained only with difficulty. Sonnets VIII and IX look back to the division within the

---

[99] Bernard O'Donoghue, in 'Heaney's *Ars Poetica*: Mandelstam, Dante and *The Government of the Tongue*', in *Seamus Heaney and the Language of Poetry* (London: Harvester Wheatsheaf, 1994), 135–52, offers an illuminating discussion of the centrality of Mandelstam, and through him, Dante, to Heaney's aesthetic. He does not, however, mention the role of Owen in facilitating Heaney's use of Mandelstam, since he takes his discussion from a point after the negotiation and elision discussed in this chapter.

[100] Quoted in Corcoran, *Seamus Heaney*, 127.

[101] Heaney, *Field Work* (London: Faber, 1979), 33–4.

[102] Ibid. 37.

[103] E. C. Brewer and Ivor H. Evans, *Dictionary of Phrase and Fable* (1970; London: Wordsworth, 1994) 409.

[104] *The Poetry of Seamus Heaney*, 116.

poet which begins in 'A Northern Hoard', an aspiration towards tran-
scendence compromised by memory of war:

> This morning when a magpie with jerky steps
> Inspected a horse asleep beside the wood
> I thought of dew on armour and carrion.
> What would I meet, blood-boltered, on the road?
> How deep into the woodpile sat the toad?
> What welters through this dark hush on the crops?[105]

More subtle, and reminiscent of the First World War, is the imagery
pervading Sonnet IX, where 'a black rat | Sways on the briar' (with its
connotation of 'wire').[106] The 'fault . . . opening' in 'A Northern Hoard',
where there is 'No Sanctuary' and no escape, is revisited in this poem. As
with 'Roots', it sets up an opposition between what is going on 'out
there' in the world, and inside for the individual. Unlike the earlier poem,
it translates this opposition into one between beauty and truth. But
despite the 'burnished bay tree at the gate', there is not really an 'out of
the line' here, any more than in 'A Northern Hoard': 'Did we come to
the wilderness for this? . . . Blood on a pitch-fork . . . Rats speared in the
sweat and dust of threshing'.[107] Attuned to the implications of his
imagery, the poet wonders 'What is my apology for poetry?' (harking
back to the question in 'A Northern Hoard', 'What do I say if they wheel
out their dead?', but rephrasing it away from such specificity). He is,
unconsciously or otherwise, echoing here, amongst other things,
Owen's 'Apologia Pro Poemata Meo':

> I have perceived much beauty
>> In the hoarse oaths that kept our courage straight;
>> Heard music in the silentness of duty;
>> Found peace where shell-storms spouted reddest spate.
>
> Nevertheless, except you share
>> With them in hell the sorrowful dark of hell
>> Whose world is but the trembling of a flare
>> And heaven but as the highway for a shell,
>
> You shall not hear their mirth:
>> You shall not come to think them well content
>> By any jest of mine.[108]

---

[105] *Field Work*, 40.   [106] Ibid. 41.   [107] Ibid.
[108] *The Poems of Wilfred Owen*, 101–2.

For Owen, beauty is compromised, to the extent that it is no longer beauty, if it serves to ease a guilty conscience. It is this aspect of Owen's aesthetic which Heaney, finally, resists, though he reformulates it prior to rejection. Osip Mandelstam is, as Corcoran notes, 'a hidden presence' in the Glanmore sonnets.[109] And Mandelstam becomes, for Heaney, a poet who, under difficult circumstances, attains a new kind of beauty in transcendence that Owen rejects, within which is implicit a new kind of freedom: 'The reign of the four elements is favorable to us, | but free man has made a fifth . . . the three dimensions' bonds are burst | the seas of all the world revealed.'[110]

In *The Government of the Tongue*, Heaney sets up a conflict of sorts between these two precursors, already implicit in his poetry, in order to be able to resolve it. The 'opposition' is based on a slanted reading of Owen's aesthetic, and on the deliberate polarization of terms, in order to be able to 'discover' afresh the middle ground as an arena at once subversive and radical but ultimately quite safe. 'The artist', he says elsewhere, 'can refuse history as a category', and to do so is a 'disruptive activity' because 'It is a refusal of the terms'.[111] Heaney's influential role as critic and self-critic does make it possible for him to set up the terms which he then 'disruptively' refuses. Thus, in the introduction to *The Government of the Tongue*, he redefines 'Art and Life' as 'Song and Suffering'.[112] In doing so, Edna Longley argues that he polarizes the two 'as if history were only suffering and poetry were only song'; then, 'having set up an antithesis rather than an antinomy (the aesthetic *versus* the empathetic)', he 'bridges it with an oxymoron, "radical witness", which tries to fuse the activist and the static-spectatorial'.[113]

Owen and Mandelstam are similarly polarized. Pondering the dangers of 'a complacency and an insulation from reality in some song and some art', Heaney returns to the First World War and the example of Wilfred Owen:

it is from this moment in our century that radiant and unperturbed certitudes about the consonance between the true and the beautiful become suspect. The *locus classicus* for all this is in the life and poetry of Wilfred Owen . . . In a preface

---

[109] See Corcoran, *Seamus Heaney*, 144.
[110] Mandelstam, 'The Admiralty Building', *Selected Poems*, 39.
[111] 'Between North and South: Poetic Detours', 88.
[112] *The Government of the Tongue*, p. xii.
[113] 'The Aesthetic and the Territorial', in Elmer Andrews (ed.), *Contemporary Irish Poetry* (Basingstoke: Macmillan, 1992), 77.

which would not see the light until after his own death ... Owen affirmed that his poems would have nothing to do with this complacent, acceptable version of the beautiful which he contemptuously calls 'Poetry' ... His poems have the potency of human testimony, of martyr's relics, so that any intrusion of the aesthetic can feel like impropriety. They so opt for truth that the beauty consideration is made to seem irrelevant.[114]

In Owen, he goes on to argue, 'the truth-telling urge and the compulsion to identify with the oppressed becomes necessarily integral with the act of writing itself'.[115] He is a poet whose impulse is to 'elevate truth above beauty, to rebuke the sovereign claims which art would make for itself'.[116] Against this 'type of poet', Heaney sets the example of Osip Mandelstam,

singing in the Stalinist night, affirming the essential humanism of the act of poetry itself against the inhuman tyranny which would have had him write odes not just to Stalin but to hydro-electric dams[?] As opposed to these prescribed and propagandist themes, the essential thing about lyric poetry, Mandelstam maintained, was its unlooked-for joy in being itself ... Unlike Chekhov, who wrote on behalf of the prisoners explicitly, and unlike Owen, who had a messianic and socially redemptive message to impart, Mandelstam had no immediate social aim. *Utterance itself was self-justifying and creative, like nature. ... For him, obedience to poetic impulse was obedience to conscience; lyric action constituted radical witness. ...* [my italics] So if Owen sponsors an art which seems to rebuke beauty in favour of truth, Mandelstam, at an equally high price, sponsors all over again the Keatsian proposition that beauty *is* truth, truth beauty.[117]

This essay has been quoted at some length because, in effect, it constitutes Heaney's own apology for poetry which, cast in these terms, apparently leaves him in the enviable position of writing a responsible poetry which has no responsibilities, a Romantic (with a rather Yeatsian distaste for the industrial world) whose work is, by default, infused with the traumas of the twentieth century.

To reach this resolution, the opposition has to be faked. The First World War is, as Heaney notes, the point where the beauty-truth consonance, as it had been understood, is questioned, but it is also the point where, in the aesthetics of Owen and others, the synonymity of 'beauty' and 'truth' is itself a 'truth' which becomes fully apparent, if retrospectively, perhaps for the first time. Hence, Rupert Brooke's 1914 sonnets might appear to fall on the side of 'beauty' if one is to separate the terms, but in fact what has made these poems 'ugly', or inadequate, to a later generation, is that they rely, as MacNeice points out, on a 'falsehood to life'.[118] Ronald Sharp argues that what Keats means by beauty is 'that which is life-affirming' and 'consolatory', and that 'Since metaphysical truth cannot be certainly known, this human truth, beauty, is really the only truth there is for man': the 'radical identification of beauty and truth that Keats makes at the end of "Ode on a Grecian Urn" is', he suggests, 'to be taken quite literally once we understand that he is not referring to metaphysical categories'.[119] The real focus of the poem is not the tension between art and life, but 'the function of art in life'.[120] In this sense, Keats's famous statement that 'with a great poet the sense of Beauty overcomes every other consideration, or rather obliterates all consideration' could be applied to Owen with the synonym 'truth' inserted instead. Owen's draft preface may be seen, not as a radical departure from the Keats aesthetic, but as a restatement of it, a restatement necessary because of the transcendental associations traditionally drawn in Keatsian criticism. Of Graves and Sassoon he writes, 'are they not already as many Keatses?'.[121] For Owen, to tell the 'truth' *is* to affirm the value of life, at a time when it was treated by the authorities as expendable commodity. Although his elegies, he claimed, were not intended to 'console', in the sense that they were not designed to make continuation of the war acceptable to the public, they do console because the work of art is itself an affirmation of life. In that sense they are, as he suggested they would be, 'consolatory' to the next generation. 'Strange Meeting', which at first sight seems to deny the Keatsian conjunction, in fact reaffirms it. The real tragedy of the poem is the 'truth' which is left, through death, 'untold'. The poetic aspirations of the poet's 'enemy'—the pre-war search for 'the wildest beauty in the world'; the unfulfilled post-war desire to wash away blood 'with truths that lie too deep for taint'—are invalidated not so much by war, as by the early death, literally, of the speaker himself, who has 'poured [his] spirit without stint' in the wrong place—on the battlefield not the page.[122] It is

[118] *PWBY*, 29.
[119] *Keats, Skepticism, and the Religion of Beauty* (Athens, Ga.: University of Georgia Press, 1979), 30–4.
[120] Ibid. 151.
[121] 'To Susan Owen', 25 May 1918, *Collected Letters*, 553.
[122] *The Poems of Wilfred Owen*, 125–6.

hard to see, with Heaney, that Owen 'seemed almost to obliterate the line between art and life' by sheer force of 'truthfulness',[123] when in fact Owen, like Keats, worries constantly over 'the function of art in life'.

Corcoran's comparison of Heaney's 'The Harvest Bow' with Keats's 'Ode on a Grecian Urn' finds Heaney's motto to be 'cautious', offered 'not as discovery and advice ("Beauty is truth, truth beauty") but as frail aspiration'. Heaney affirms an art 'which, in the face of human loss and diminishment, still presumes to offer a model of pacific reconciliation', but the presumption is only 'tentative'.[124] The comparison is, however, slightly misleading. Keats's own conclusion is tentative if one reads 'all | Ye know on earth' as, literally, all one is capable of knowing, and while art may have a consolatory function, this is not quite the claim which Heaney makes.[125] 'The Harvest Bow' is a poem which has been read as if it were a blueprint for understanding Heaney's poetic:

> *The end of art is peace*
> Could be the motto of this frail device
> That I have pinned up on our deal dresser—
> Like a drawn snare
> Slipped lately by the spirit of the corn
> Yet burnished by its passage, and still warm.[126]

Henry Hart describes the poem as both 'confession' and 'aesthetic treatise'.[127] For Elmer Andrews, the creation of the bow is 'a paradigm

---

[123]   *The Government of the Tongue*, p. xiv.

[124]   Corcoran, *Seamus Heaney*, 150. Thomas Foster also makes this comparison, drawing the same inference as Corcoran. See Foster, *Seamus Heaney*, 87.

[125]   Henry Hart also reads the poem as a Keatsian revision, and suggests that Heaney 'is hardly as sanguine about art's ability to reconcile opposites as his early sponsor'. 'Truth and beauty' in Heaney, he writes, 'are at violent odds' (*Seamus Heaney: Poet of Contrary Progressions* (New York: Syracuse UP, 1992), 129). This is to read 'beauty' as transcendent aspiration rather than human truth, to suggest that one is attainable only at the expense of the other, and to categorize Heaney as a poet of conflict in a Yeatsian sense (see also ibid. 130). While agreeing that Heaney, in contrast to Keats, puts the terms in opposition to each other, redefining them in order to do so, 'The Harvest Bow' does not appear to me to encapsulate this particular conflict, though the Keatsian imagery of the poem has encouraged the connection. Nor does it seem entirely accurate to suggest that the two elements are 'at violent odds' in Heaney. On the contrary, Heaney's privileging of one over the other has led to some arbitrary readings of other poets, notably Larkin, in *The Redress of Poetry*, where, Roger Caldwell points out, Heaney 'would seem to demand that the claims of poetry be set apart from those of telling the truth'. See Caldwell, 'Heaney, Larkin and the Grim Reaper', *Honest Ulsterman*, 103 (Spring 1997), 109.

[126]   *Field Work*, 58.

[127]   *Seamus Heaney: Poet of Contrary Progressions*, 129.

of artistic activity'; it is 'woven without conscious effort, just as poetry should spring naturally and inevitably from deep wells of being'.[128] Partly the poem may be read in this way because Heaney's own critical explication of the poetic process encourages the interpretation: 'The achievement of a poem . . . is an experience of release' and 'A plane is—fleetingly—established where the poet is intensified in his being and freed from his predicaments'.[129] Effectively, Heaney reaches a point—the creative misreading of Owen and the lauding of Mandelstam form part of the progression towards this point—where the early question 'What do I say if they wheel out their dead?' is not so much answered as found to be unnecessary. Through a somewhat convoluted argument, he reaches the conclusion that 'the artistic endeavour . . . is not obliged to have any intention beyond its own proper completion'.[130] In such a formula, it is possible to be a war poet without writing about or from a position of conflict. Heaney writes:

[Francis Ledwidge] keeps the nest warm and the lines open for a different poetry, one that might combine tendermindedness towards the predicaments of others with an ethically unsparing attitude towards the self. Indeed, it is because of this scruple, this incapacity for grand and overbearing certainties, and not because of the uniform he wore, it is for this reason that Ledwidge can be counted as a 'war poet' in the company of Wilfred Owen and Siegfried Sassoon.[131]

It is difficult to resist the thought that the different poetry for which the lines were kept open is Heaney's own, that he has, therefore, both implicitly defined himself as a war poet of the ethically committed soldier-poet variety, and simultaneously distanced himself from those who have specific social aims in view.

In his prose, Heaney's apology for poetry is rehearsed through a game of eternal return, a constant brooding on the question of what makes an 'adequate' (the word appears time and time again in *The Redress of Poetry*) poetry allied with constant reaffirmation of poetry's transcendence of any preordained considerations of adequacy. What appears on the surface as resolution is, ultimately, more akin to a state of chronic poetic

[128] *The Poetry of Seamus Heaney*, 123–4.
[129] *The Government of the Tongue*, p. xxii.
[130] *Place and Displacement: Recent Poetry of Northern Ireland* (Grasmere: Trustees of Dove Cottage, 1984), 8.
[131] Introduction to Francis Ledwidge: *Selected Poems*, ed. Dermot Bolger (Dublin: New Island Books, 1992), 20.

schizophrenia. Hence, he writes that 'There is nothing extraordinary about the challenge to be in two minds', then goes on to say that 'within our individual selves we can *reconcile* two orders of knowledge [my italics]'.[132] Heaney's quest for reconcilement, for poetry as 'a source of truth and at the same time a vehicle of harmony',[133] is akin to, but not the same as, Yeats's desire to 'hold in a single thought reality and justice'.[134] In Yeats they are held in conflict; in Heaney's criticism, the conflict is not always recognized as conflict. '[I]t is dangerous', Heaney writes in *Preoccupations*, 'for a writer to become too self-conscious about his own processes'.[135] Lucy McDiarmid, discussing 'Exposure', points out that 'Heaney's position is a position' in this poem, 'even though he is "neither internee nor informer"'.[136] Consciousness of his public role as standard-bearer for poetry sometimes, though not always, inclines Heaney-as-critic towards the suppression of acknowledgement of the virtue in holding the position at once tenable, contradictory, *and* unstable that is felt in much of his poetry. Peter McDonald rightly suggests that the fact that the 'distinction between the sources of authority and the satisfactions of reputation . . . is liable to break down' in Heaney's poetry is one reason why 'it is important that Heaney carries on the process of intellectual *work* in thinking about poetry'.[137] The work advocated here is in contrast to the too easy resolution Heaney sometimes asserts: 'If one aspect of [his] public voice is growing more sure of its significance in promoting "the central, epoch-making role that is always available in the world to poetry and the poet", another is starting to see in the process of poetry a more complex, involved and paradoxical encounter with choice and inevitability'.[138] An excessive desire on Heaney's part to define his position and his responsibilities has perhaps obscured the fact that, in the final analysis, the only effective apology for poetry lies in the poetry itself, that the question 'What is my apology for poetry?' is answered as completely as it can be in the asking.

[132]   *The Redress of Poetry*, 202–3.
[133]   Ibid. 193.
[134]   *AV*, 25.
[135]   *Preoccupations*, 52.
[136]   'Heaney and the Politics of the Classroom', in Garratt (ed.), *Critical Essays on Seamus Heaney*, 117.
[137]   'The Poet and "The Finished Man"', 107.
[138]   Ibid. 107–8.

CHAPTER EIGHT

Michael Longley: Poet in No Man's Land

For here the lover and killer are mingled

Keith Douglas[1]

I have written...in a kind of space between—
I don't know between quite what—

David Jones[2]

...in No Man's Land
What is there to talk about but difficult poems?

Michael Longley[3]

I

'I am still of [the] opinion', Yeats writes, 'that only two topics can be of the least interest to a serious and studious mind—sex and the dead'.[4] Echoing this attitude, Longley states: 'My concerns continue to be Eros and Thanatos, the traditional subject-matter of the lyric', concerns that are focused for him by 'the natural world' and by 'the catastrophe of the First World War, the influence of that catastrophe on subsequent Irish and European history and politics'.[5] Those two things—the war and the natural world—like love and death, impinge upon each other throughout his work; both inform a psychic landscape that, Yeatsian-style, is always characterized by awareness of its dual possibilities. Paul Durcan,

---

[1] 'Vergissmeinnicht', *The Complete Poems*, ed. Desmond Graham (Oxford: OUP, 1987), 111.

[2] Preface to *In Parenthesis* (1937; London: Faber, 1963), p. xv.

[3] 'No Man's Land', *Poems 1963–1983* (1985; London: Secker & Warburg, 1991), 199.

[4] 'To Olivia Shakespear', 2 Oct. 1927, *The Letters of W. B. Yeats*, ed. Allan Wade (London: Rupert Hart-Davis, 1954), 730.

[5] 'The Future is Behind Us', interview by Pat Boran, *Books Ireland*, 187 (Summer 1995), 147.

in his review of *The Echo Gate*, perceptively noted the grounding of Longley's aesthetic in the landscape, literal and metaphorical, of the Great War, a grounding which has coloured all his collections from the early *No Continuing City* to the recent *The Ghost Orchid*: 'Longley's themes: Of Love and War. The First World War (which was the beginning of the Irish tragedy as indeed it was the beginning of every other convulsion in the western world in the 20th century) has been the primal landscape of Longley's poetry from the start'.[6]

The dual possibilities, the ambivalence informing that landscape are inherent in, and originate in, the No Man's Land of the Great War. Consequently, No Man's Land resonates both literally and symbolically in Longley's poetry. His engagement with the Great War begins with the familial, expands to encompass a sense of poetic ancestry, and, more recently, has led to a conscious redefinition and rehabilitation of the politics—in the broadest sense of the word—of remembrance, all three strands working in the elegiac mode. And elegy is, he notes, one side of a coin of which the love poem is the other.[7] The sense of belonging in No Man's Land that resonates through his poetry is both symptomatic of, and a cause of, this engagement. No Man's Land, with its universal significance, begins, in some ways, as a private and literal ground for Longley, which gradually expands within his aesthetic to become an all-encompassing, sometimes intangible, imaginative space, potentially and simultaneously redemptive and threatening, a place of infinite possibility and infinite regret. As it does so, it moves away from its specific historical location in 1914–18, but, in another sense, reaches back to those origins through a developing understanding in the poetry of the inherent ambiguities of the original Great War landscape, and the ways in which those ambiguities have persisted through the century.

During the Great War itself, No Man's Land was perceived both as actual and metaphorical space. The setting for the now legendary fraternization with the enemy on 25 December 1914, and for the carnage of 1 July 1916, it was, in myth and in fact, both the place of greatest danger in the war and the only place where enemies met without enmity. It was the setting for some of the most anomalous events in trench life:

---

[6] 'Poetry and Truth', review of *The Echo Gate* by Michael Longley and *The Strange Museum* by Tom Paulin, *Irish Press*, 20 Mar. 1980, 6.

[7] See Longley, quoted in Tom Adair, 'Of Flock and Fold: A Consideration of the Poetry of Michael Longley', *Linen Hall Review*, 4/1 (Spring 1987), 17.

In certain sectors there were extraordinary agreements that provided for the safe removal of the wounded, the repair of trenches and wire, sunbathing on the first days of spring, and the cutting of grass and the harvesting of fruit in No Man's Land. . . . [In one sector] the French had . . . established a peaceful co-existence with the Germans, to such a point that they shared the shelter of undestroyed houses in No Man's Land . . . [8]

If No Man's Land works here as an ironic parody of the original concept of 'anyone's land' in the pre-enclosure Open Field system of agriculture, it also travestied that concept as the site of some of the most horrific experiences of the Great War: men drowning in shell-holes already filled with decaying flesh; wounded men, beyond help from behind the wire, dying over a number of days, their cries audible, and often unbearable, to those in the trenches; sappers buried alive beneath its surface. At its most appalling, it was almost beyond language, beyond description. Wilfred Owen, trying to explain No Man's Land to his mother, resorts to an apocalyptic mode of language, a heightened rhetoric that struggles, in one image after another, to convey what can only be approximated:

It is like the eternal place of gnashing of teeth; the Slough of Despond could be contained in one of its crater-holes; the fires of Sodom and Gomorrah could not light a candle to it—to find the way to Babylon the Fallen.

It is pock-marked like a body of foulest disease and its odour is the breath of cancer. . . .

No Man's Land under snow is like the face of the moon chaotic, crater-ridden, uninhabitable, awful, the abode of madness.[9]

Yet he writes elsewhere that 'Christ is literally in no man's land. There men often hear His voice'.[10] It is, paradoxically, the place of eternal damnation and of redemption.

Unsurprisingly, No Man's Land became the focus of war myths—notably the belief that an army of deserters lived beneath its surface, scavenging off corpses—and it did so because it remained, to the end, an unknown quantity, an unconquerable space, at least in human terms. Eric Leed notes that for many Great War veterans, it persisted in the post-war years as 'their most disturbing and lasting image' of the war.[11]

[8]   Eric J. Leed, *No Man's Land: Combat and Identity in World War I* (Cambridge: Cambridge UP, 1979), 108.

[9]   'To Susan Owen', 19 Jan. 1917, *Collected Letters*, ed. Harold Owen and John Bell (London: OUP, 1967), 429.

[10]   'To Susan Owen', ?16 May 1917, ibid. 461.

[11]   *No Man's Land*, 15.

'No-man's-land fascinates me', Sassoon wrote in 1916, 'with its jumble of wire-tangles and snaky seams in the earth',[12] to the extent that he took huge risks exploring it. Another veteran writes:

> In fifty years I have never been able to rid myself of this obsession with no man's land and the unknown world beyond it. On this side of our wire everything is familiar and every man is a friend, over there, beyond the wire, is the unknown, the uncanny.[13]

No Man's Land was, Leed points out, 'the very image of the marginal, the liminal, the "betwixt-and-between"'; as a term, it 'captured the essence of an experience of having been sent beyond the outer boundaries of social life, placed between the known and the unknown, the familiar and the uncanny'.[14] The existence of a No Man's Land indicates perpetuation of a war of attrition; it is also a landscape where resolution of the problem is deceptively and tantalizingly possible. (The 'resolution' is the point where it is written out of existence.)

In the post-war years, 'No Man's Land' has become a dominating metaphor for what David Jones calls the 'space between', for anything and everything which falls between or beyond reductive social, linguistic, political, literary, and other categories. It can, in contemporary metaphorical usage, carry positive connotations—a realm beyond reductive categorization. But it was also, in the Great War, a 'deathscape' which implicitly questioned the value of writing as it also made the act of writing more difficult. '[I]t is impossible now to work', Rosenberg complained in 1916, 'and difficult even to think of poetry';[15] but, he also noted, 'if poetry at this time is no use it certainly won't be at any other'.[16] No Man's Land is, therefore, both the area which must be challenged if the poet is to find his own aesthetic space, and a metaphor which can create that space. It is the image of war which, perhaps more than any other, still dominates memory in the western world; it is the place where the question 'what is the use or function of poetry?' resurfaced with a new energy and new resonance to worry the century's poets.

---

[12] *Siegfried Sassoon's Diaries 1915–1918*, ed. Rupert Hart-Davis (London: Faber, 1983), 51.
[13] Charles Edmund Carrington, quoted in Leed, *No Man's Land*, 14–15.
[14] Ibid.
[15] 'To Laurence Binyon', Autumn 1916, in *The Collected Works of Isaac Rosenberg: Poetry, Prose, Letters, Paintings and Drawings*, ed. Ian Parsons (London: Chatto & Windus, 1979), 249.
[16] 'To Edward Marsh', 30 June 1916, ibid. 237.

Both Mahon and Heaney, while they have to some extent articulated their aesthetic questions through negotiation with the landscape and poetry of the First World War, perhaps a now inescapable inheritance, also began their careers, Longley suggests, with what he himself lacked, 'recourse to solid hinterlands—Heaney the much publicized farm in County Derry, Mahon his working-class background and the shipyards'. In contrast, Longley, who as a child 'walked out of an English household on to Irish streets', felt himself to be more obviously 'schizophrenic on the levels of nationality, class and culture'.[17] As a result, No Man's Land is a landscape which does not simply inform Longley's own poetic locale, rather it becomes that poetic locale: it is adapted and adopted as a kind of schizophrenic hinterland which, in acknowledging the contradictory nature of its origins, challenges as it enables the poetry. It offers a 'solid' ground whose solidity depends, paradoxically, on its fluidity, on its 'betwixt-and-between' quality.

Significantly, the evolution of that hinterland is also entwined with the evolution of a distinctive poetic 'voice', and a growing awareness of identity as ultimately unquantifiable. Longley himself notes: 'I was slow to find a voice, much slower than Mahon or Heaney'.[18] In retrospect, a poem in his first collection, *No Continuing City*, has become, for critics, particularly noteworthy: the elegy for his father, 'In Memoriam'. Conor Kelly writes that it has 'a depth and a sympathetic imaginative understanding which raises it far above the other poems in the book';[19] Peter McDonald describes it as 'enormously powerful'.[20] It stands, in some ways, as a precursor to an aesthetic developed with greater effectiveness and wider resonance in subsequent collections. In 'In Memoriam', the poet's father and, by implication, the poet, narrowly escape death in No Man's Land:

> Between the corpses and the soup canteens
> You swooned away, watching your future spill.
> But, as it was, your proper funeral urn
> Had mercifully smashed to smithereens,
> To shrapnel shards that sliced your testicle.

[17] Longley, 'Strife and the Ulster Poet', *Hibernia* (7 Nov. 1969), 11.
[18] Quoted in Adair, 'Of Flock and Fold', 16.
[19] 'Keeping the Faith', review of *Poems 1963–1983* by Michael Longley, *Magill* (21 Mar. 1985), 47.
[20] 'From Ulster With Love', review of *Poems 1963–1983* by Michael Longley, *Poetry Review*, 74/4 (Jan. 1985), 14.

> That instant I, your most unlikely son,
> In No Man's Land was surely left for dead,
> Blotted out from your far horizon.[21]

The poet exists in two places—in life here and now, and in an imaginative realm of non-existence. He is, therefore, indebted to the past, but exists in spite of the past, since No Man's Land is as much the land of what might have been as of what is. The poet projects back to meet the vision of the future, the 'far horizon', at the moment when it is under threat: his own far horizon recedes into the past to make present into future possibility. No Man's Land, both literally and metaphorically, is seen as his ground of inception as man and poet. Longley suggests elsewhere that 'Somehow my father's existence, and his experience, the stories he passed on to me, gave me a kind of taproot into the war'.[22] The speaker of the poem, as well as his father, is a survivor of the Great War, if only by virtue of the poem he has written. And, by implication, since he was held secure by history, history will be secure with him: 'As your voice now is locked inside my head, | I yet was held secure, waiting my turn'. The poem simultaneously finds a voice for the present as it enacts the finding of a voice in the past: from the words written 'in memory' (and from memory) of the father's 'anecdote rehearsed and summarised', the narrative is appropriated imaginatively as an authentic telling—'Now I see in close-up . . .'. The 'last confidence' spoken by the father—'You hunted down experimental lovers, | Persuading chorus girls and countesses'—enables the poet's own last confident resurrection of 'those lost wives', in a voice that can 'summon' and 'materialise', as consolation at the end of the poem: 'They lift their skirts like blinds across your eyes.'[23]

In a way, the poem is inadvertently prophetic: 'old wounds woke | As cancer' resonates now in the wider context of Northern Ireland, and the resurfacing of the Troubles in 1968. If the father's experience of the Great War is technically separated from the son's experience of Northern Ireland, the poem offers both the first connection between the two and the last distinction. In subsequent collections, his father is elegized again and again, sometimes directly, as in 'Wounds' or 'Last Requests',

---

[21] *Poems 1963–1983*, 48.
[22] 'Making Some Kind of Sense', interview by Fintan O'Toole, *Sunday Tribune*, 17 Mar. 1985, 17.
[23] *Poems 1963–1983*, 49.

sometimes more obliquely, as in 'The Linen Workers'. He is elegized because he is the subject of private grief, but also because he is representative of a generation who survived the trenches, and, more broadly, of twentieth-century war victims. An almost symbolic figure, he provides not merely a 'taproot into the war' of the past, but also a taproot into the present. In a two-way process, the Great War offers a way into writing about Northern Ireland, as Northern Ireland prompts an eternal imaginative return to the earlier conflict. Alan Peacock discusses the 'analogical processes' in Longley's poetry which 'provide a generalised context for treating particularized, local experience', concluding that a pattern of 'wide-ranging cultural parallelisms' is discernible throughout his career.[24] That pattern also incorporates a development: if the strength of the early 'In Memoriam' lies in the way in which it expresses private grief through public utterance, a progression that is self-referential and heavily coded enables public utterance in the later poems to be mediated through what is felt as private grief.

Longley describes 'In Memoriam' as 'some kind of descent from the ivory tower'; it confirmed for him the view that 'You have got to bring your personal sorrow to the public utterance' to avoid the 'deadly danger of regarding the agony of others as raw material for your art, and your art as a solace for them in their suffering'.[25] 'Wounds', from his second collection, *An Exploded View*, is itself an exploded view of the earlier 'In Memoriam'. In 'Wounds', the Great War becomes, as Fussell notes, both an 'archetype for subsequent violence—as well as a criticism of it'.[26] The poem is notable, in the first instance, for being one of the few, and earliest, imaginative evocations of the unionist experience of the Great War, an evocation which, in linking that experience with personal suffering, and with sectarian killing in contemporary Northern Ireland, breaks tribal taboos 'kept...like secrets', sets memory in opposition to society. The poem was misread by one reviewer as a 'fine tribal Orange poem', a straightforward celebration of the Ulster Division's achievement.[27] Instead, it is an elegy for (sometimes misguided) innocence in

[24] 'Michael Longley: Poet between Worlds', in Michael Kenneally (ed.), *Poetry in Contemporary Irish Literature* (Gerrards Cross: Colin Smythe, 1995), 274, 279.
[25] 'An Interview with Michael Longley', by Dermot Healy, *Southern Review*, 31/3 (July 1995), 560.
[26] *The Great War and Modern Memory* (London: OUP, 1975), 324.
[27] Thomas McCarthy, 'Northern Voices', review of *The Echo Gate* by Michael Longley, *Irish Times*, 9 Feb. 1980, 13.

whatever shape or form that might take: its sympathies encompass the
Ulster Division and the 'boy about to die, | Screaming "Give 'em one for
the Shankill!"', the teenage soldiers in Northern Ireland, 'bellies full
of | Bullets and Irish beer', the murdered bus-conductor and his family,
and the 'shivering boy' who pulls the trigger in front of 'the children', the
'bewildered wife'.[28] Against the youth of those suffering and causing
suffering in the poem is set the death of the father, a delayed result of
violence that revises, or at least offers a retrospective perspective on, the
passionately held beliefs that inspire violent action. '[I]t seems to me',
Longley writes, 'important...to imagine how one can be so brain
washed or so angry or in a sense perhaps even so innocent that one
can drive in a car and go into somebody's house and shoot that person
stone dead'.[29] The 'shivering boy', the 'teenage soldiers', the innocent
civilian victim—all these things are, unexpectedly, redolent of the now-
notorious 'innocence' that characterized the 1914 generation, that led to
the inspired, futile attacks on the Somme in 1916. 'Bewilderment' in both
stanzas unites the actions if only in their incomprehensibility. The
attempt to make sense of events, to balance consequence against mo-
tivation—his father's words '"I am dying for King and Country,
slowly"'—is central to the poem. 'Slowly' adds to a well-known, now
sometimes trite, sentiment, turns cliché to tragedy through a self-aware
irony redolent of the disillusion that damaged the concept itself, while
the death simultaneously serves to dignify the concept. The 'landscape
of dead buttocks', over which his father followed for 'fifty years', is
a permanent condition: past and present, like the war and the consequ-
ent death(s), are not so much paralleled as telescoped into a seamless
continuity. 'Wounds', as a title, thus encompasses more than the obvious
wounds in the poem—the cancer, the bullet-holes. It looks back to the
'old wounds' of 'In Memoriam'; it expands to include emotional as well
as literal wounding, the open wounds of history aggravated in Northern
Ireland in the early 1970s, the wounding of the innocent, the invisible
scars left on society. (Shell-shocked soldiers in the Great War were
described as 'wounded without wounds'.)[30] Longley's elegies reveal
not only the short-term, tangible damage caused by violence, but also
the long-term effects not immediately, or possibly ever, readily apparent.

[28] *Poems 1963–1983*, 86.
[29] 'Q & A with Michael Longley', interview by Dillon Johnston, *Irish Literary Supple-
ment*, 5/2 (Fall 1986), 20.
[30] Leed, *No Man's Land*, 177.

The modern elegy, Ramazani writes, 'resembles not so much a suture as "an open wound"'.[31] It exists, in one sense, in the space between its author and its subject matter, to the extent that the subject matter itself may become the impossibility of crossing that space. Ramazani suggests that

Owen states only half of his paradoxical aesthetic when he writes: 'My subject is War, and the pity of War. The Poetry is in the pity'. 'Pity' is Owen's term for emotional identification with the victims of war. But Owen's poetry suggests that 'pity' cannot erase the boundary that separates victim from onlooker.... His subject is also the incomprehensibility of war; the poetry is also in the alienation. Having roused pity, Owen often forces the reader back, warning that pity cannot bridge the chasm separating spectator and victim.[32]

In effect, he concludes, 'the poet inhabits a terrible no-man's-land between victim and reader'.[33] Longley's poetry, like that of the Great War poets, exists 'in the pity'. But, as with Owen, it exists also in the alienation, in its helpless awareness of the impossibility of reaching its own subject matter. In 'Last Requests', that alienation is imaged as a tangible barrier:

> I thought you blew a kiss before you died,
> But the bony fingers that waved to and fro
> Were asking for a Woodbine, the last request
> Of many soldiers in your company,
> The brand you chose to smoke for forty years
> Thoughtfully, each one like a sacrament.
> I who brought peppermints and grapes only
> Couldn't reach you through the oxygen tent.[34]

It is also intangible, in the failure in understanding, and in the inability of love to counteract death: the 'Heart contradicting...epitaph' in part I does not do so metaphorically in part II. The last request is also a last rite, one rehearsed again and again through a life that, after the experience of the Great War, is no longer taken for granted. Longley attributes to his father a sense of 'unexpected bonus' which 'pervaded all the ordinary aspects of life'.[35] It is a sense which he has imaginatively

---

[31] *Poetry of Mourning: The Modern Elegy from Hardy to Heaney* (Chicago: University of Chicago Press, 1994), 4.

[32] Ibid. 80.

[33] Ibid. 82.

[34] *Poems 1963–1983*, 150.

[35] *Tuppenny Stung: Autobiographical Chapters* (Belfast: Lagan Press, 1994), 19.

inherited, hence his belief that 'the artist . . . has a duty to celebrate life in all its aspects'.[36] But the reverse side to a celebration of life—the awareness of death—is implicit in the 'sacramental' nature of celebration: each moment held as if it were both the first and the last. That sensibility forms what Fussell describes as 'the Great War theme— already mastered by Hardy even before the war broke out—of the ironic proximity of violence and disaster to safety, to meaning, and to love'.[37] The persistence of that theme in Longley's work means that the effective elegies are those which are anti-elegiac. They do not impose meaning or consolation on the inconsolable and incomprehensible, but instead point up the inadequacy of traditional elegiac resources. They do so as a way of finding a voice for, rather than an answer to, grief. Their hallmark, as with many of Owen's poems, is sometimes one of guilt. It is there at the end of 'Last Requests' for the failure to 'reach' his father; it is implicit in 'Kindertotenlieder', which, rejecting Friedrich Rückert's original, consolatory elegizing, opts instead for a Dylan Thomas 'Refusal to Mourn', mourns the fact that it can no longer mourn, but still creates, though rhythmic repetition, the song it will not create: 'There can be no songs for dead children . . . No songs for the children . . .'.[38] As with Mahon, as, perhaps, with every modern elegist, 'every elegy is an elegy for elegy'.[39]

II

Fussell's Great War theme is a theme peculiarly pertinent to Northern Ireland, where the redemptive ground is also, in Keith Douglas's phrase, 'the nightmare ground', where 'proximity' collapses into synonymy.[40] The private, domestic space, which in the Great War was idealized by the soldier at the Front, is no longer inviolate: the domestic details in 'Wounds', the invasion of violence 'Before they could turn the television

---

[36] Introduction to Michael Longley (ed.), *Causeway: The Arts in Ulster* (Belfast: Arts Council of Northern Ireland; Dublin: Gill and Macmillan, 1971), 9.

[37] *The Great War and Modern Memory*, 69.

[38] *Poems 1963–1983*, 87.

[39] Ramazani, *Poetry of Mourning*, 8.

[40] 'Vergissmeinnicht', *Complete Poems*, 111. Longley uses Douglas's lines from this poem—'returning over the nightmare ground | we found the place again . . .'—as epigraph to the 'Letters' sequence in *An Exploded View* where his own ground has become a nightmare ground reminiscent of Yeats's 'Nineteen Hundred and Nineteen': 'Blood on the kerbstones . . . The pity, the terror' (see *Poems 1963–1983*, 76–8).

down | Or tidy away the supper dishes',[41] hint at what is explored more comprehensively in the later 'The Civil Servant', from the sequence 'Wreaths':

> He was preparing an Ulster fry for breakfast
> When someone walked into the kitchen and shot him:
> A bullet entered his mouth and pierced his skull,
> The books he had read, the music he could play.[42]

'I will not', Rosenberg insisted in the trenches, 'leave a corner of my consciousness covered up'.[43] In the face of random domestic killing, Longley implies, it is, in any case, impossible to do so. As Edmund Blunden eventually discovered in the Great War, there is no such thing as 'out of the line'.[44] More completely than Heaney, Longley has absorbed the 'hereditary' knowledge from the First World War that colours all subsequent perceptions. That he writes with the sense of 'pervasive, latent war' may be one reason why the title 'war poet' is attributed to him perhaps even more frequently than to Heaney, even if Heaney, as the more popular figure, has been exposed to greater 'war poet' pressures from the public. It may also be something to do with the fact that a poet in Ireland is known partly by the ancestry he keeps. The family ghosts who habitually walk Longley's poetry are rarely separated from the war which he perceives as a turning point for western civilization, and in which they were intimately and destructively involved: from his father, to 'Uncle Lionel' who 'good for nothing except sleep-walking to the Great War ... Collected littered limbs' in a sack until 'His head got blown off in No Man's Land',[45] (and whose 'vanishing act', Longley writes, 'haunted my childhood'),[46] to his mother, elegized in 'The Third Light' as making the transition from life to death, to remarry her husband, on a Great War battlefield: 'Waiting to scramble hand in hand with him | Out of the shell hole ... ',[47] and his grandmother with 'second sight' and 'Flanders ... at the kitchen window— | The mangle rusting in No Man's Land, gas | Turning the antimacassars yellow'.[48]

[41] *Poems 1963–1983*, 86.
[42] Ibid. 148.
[43] 'To Laurence Binyon', Autumn 1916, in *Collected Works of Isaac Rosenberg*, 248.
[44] Blunden, *Undertones of War* (1928; London: Penguin, 1982), 206.
[45] *Poems 1963–1983*, 133.
[46] 'Interview with Michael Longley', by Dermot Healy, 558.
[47] *Poems 1963–1983*, 200.
[48] Ibid. 151.

His sense of the Great War as a political and social crisis from which Europe is still recovering is also allied to his sense of literary antecedents:

Modernism in English writing came about to some extent because two generations were decimated in the first and second world wars and certain American theorists, i.e., Eliot and Pound, moved in and filled a vacuum. And then a brilliant generation of poets in the thirties—mainly MacNeice and Auden—showed by their practice that the lyric tradition was not exhausted. They went back via Edward Thomas and Wilfred Owen, both of whom were killed in the trenches, to Hardy and Keats and Donne. I see myself as doing that in a humble way as well.[49]

To a greater extent than any other contemporary Northern Irish poet, Longley's aesthetic measures itself against the war poets associated with the First and Second World Wars: Owen, Douglas, Thomas, Rosenberg. Longley describes his 'proper reluctance to cash in on the troubles',[50] a feeling shared by his contemporaries. To 'engage' with the situation in Northern Ireland, Muldoon notes, can lead to the accusation of being 'on the make, almost, cashing in'.[51] '[W]e cannot be unaware', Heaney writes, 'of the link between the political glamour of the place (Ulster), the sex-appeal of violence, and the prominence accorded to the poets'.[52] It is, as previously discussed, the problem first confronted by the Great War soldier poets, whose popularity (even if, perhaps especially if, posthumous) is not unconnected to the now almost romantic mystique surrounding the Great War, and who sensed at the time the paradoxical nature of their engagement in and with the war. Allied to this sense of a moral dilemma was a stylistic one: how to write an experience for which nothing in their cultural background appeared to provide a precedent.

On the whole, the soldier poets resolved both dilemmas on their own terms, and in similar ways; not by abandoning a tradition, or through conscious decisions to compromise 'Poetry', but by working with a literary inheritance (sometimes parodically), and by opting to live with, rather than resolve, the paradox. In that sense, their influence, as has been noted, pervades much contemporary poetry. Those terms are ones which Longley has absorbed, consciously or unconsciously, to the

[49] 'The Longley Tapes', interview by Robert Johnstone, *Honest Ulsterman*, 78 (Summer 1985), 23.
[50] 'Making Some Kind of Sense', 17.
[51] Quoted in Edna Longley, *Poetry in the Wars* (Newcastle: Bloodaxe, 1986), 13.
[52] 'Calling the Tune', interview by Tom Adair, *Linen Hall Review*, 6/2 (Autumn 1989), 5.

extent that, more than most contemporary poets, his reflections on poetry are virtually interchangeable with those of other earlier twentieth-century war poets. His first reaction to the Troubles, the 'burgeoning nightmare', was, he suggests, a feeling of inadequacy, that he and his contemporaries 'didn't have the equipment as lyric poets to deal with it',[53] a reaction partially conditioned by the critical judgements of in-adequacy sometimes passed on the trench lyrics, and, in fairness, by the failure of some war poetry, in both the First and Second World Wars, and in Northern Ireland, to hold its own against propagandist expecta-tions. '[W]e ourselves', he writes, 'represented, or our families came from, one side or the other'.[54] Hence the ever-present danger of suc-cumbing under political pressure to what Fussell describes as the 'simple antithesis' that dominated thinking in the failed poems of the Great War.

But as Longley's introduction to *Causeway* in 1971 makes clear, Owen et al. stand as an example of resistance to such pressures. In 1916, Rosenberg wrote: 'You know the conditions I have always worked under . . . You know how earnestly one must wait on ideas, (you cannot coax real ones to you) and let as it were, a skin grow naturally round and through them.'[55] He reiterates the idea some months later: 'I will . . . saturate myself with the strange and extraordinary new conditions of this life, and it will all refine itself into poetry later on.'[56] Echoing this view, Longley writes:

Too many critics seem to expect a harvest of paintings, poems, plays and novels to drop from the twisted branches of civil discord. They fail to realise that the artist needs time in which to allow the raw material of experience to settle to an imaginative depth where he can transform it and possibly even suggest solutions to current and very urgent problems by reframing them according to the dictates of his particular discipline. He is not some sort of super-journalist commenting with unfaltering spontaneity on events immediately after they have happened. Rather, as Wilfred Owen stated over fifty years ago, it is the artist's duty to warn, to be tuned in before anyone else to the implications of a situation.[57]

---

[53] 'Making Some Kind of Sense', 17.

[54] Ibid.

[55] 'To Edward Marsh', 4 Aug. 1916, *Collected Works of Isaac Rosenberg*, 239. Cf. Long-ley's comments in the long gap between his collections *The Echo Gate* and *Gorse Fires*: 'I believe that my present silence is part of the impulse and sooner silence than forgery. I've enough technique now to be quite a good forger.' ('The Longley Tapes', 27.)

[56] 'To Laurence Binyon', Autumn 1916, in *Collected Works of Isaac Rosenberg*, 248.

[57] Introduction to Longley (ed.), *Causeway: The Arts in Ulster*, 8.

Inevitably, to share Owen's view is also to share the frustration: 'Warnings generally go unheeded. Art seldom changes things.'[58] But it is also to work on the assumption that although an assertion of art's transformative function cannot be made, that does not preclude the possibility of its having a transformative effect.[59] '[O]ne is shamed by the example of ... Wilfred Owen', Longley suggests, since 'in the front line, [he] just sat down and wrote poems'.[60] It is not, of course, as simple as it sounds, in that Owen fought and killed even as he offered the 'pity of war' as his subject. But it does recognize that the answer to the dilemma—as it was also Owen's answer—is to write the dilemma. It is perhaps for this reason that Brendan Kennelly describes Longley as 'probably the most confident poet writing in Ireland today ... the one who most successfully resists the temptation to explain himself or his work'.[61] The 'apologia', either for one's political activities, or inactivities, is not made to facilitate poetry; rather it constitutes the poetry:

I accept, as I must, the criticism of the slogan 'Malone Road fiddles while the Falls Road burns', the implication that the still and heartless centre of the hurricane is the civic inactivity of liberals like myself. Nevertheless, I have to insist that poetry is an act which in the broadest sense can be judged political, a normal human activity[62]

As Longley's embattled feeling makes clear here, the 'crisis of conscience' is not necessarily limited to those directly involved in war: it may, in fact, be the opposite. Northern Irish poetry has helped to extend perceptions of 'war poetry' away from the narrow view, still prevalent in England, that it is experiential and occasional—a combatant art form.

---

[58]   *Causeway: The Arts in Ulster*, 9.

[59]   MacNeice's response to Auden's 'The Public v. the Late Mr W. B. Yeats' also works in these terms: the 'fallacy' of Auden's argument, MacNeice suggests, 'lies in thinking that it is the *function* of art to make things happen and that the effect of art upon actions is something either direct or calculable' (*PWBY*, 192). In 1970, Longley suggests: 'I'm not saying that something I might write might save lives, but there's always a chance that it will', quoted in Eavan Boland, 'The Northern Writers' Crisis of Conscience: 3: Creativity', *Irish Times*, 14 Aug. 1970, 12. By 1997, the idea is not couched as transparently as this, but the formulation is essentially unchanged: 'I don't ... agree with Auden when he said "Poetry makes nothing happen" ... I actually think it stops things from getting worse.' ('"Walking forwards into the past": An Interview with Michael Longley', by Fran Brearton, *Irish Studies Review*, 18 (Spring 1997), 39.)

[60]   Quoted in Boland, 'Northern Writers' Crisis of Conscience: 3: Creativity', 12.

[61]   'Wonder and Awe', review of *Gorse Fires* by Michael Longley, *Fortnight*, 295 (May 1991), 24.

[62]   Longley, 'Strife and the Ulster Poet', 11.

If the Great War offered a challenge to the poet in terms of perceptions of his role as artist, as man of action, as voice of conscience, or as social commentator, it also offered a stylistic challenge, one which was met by redirecting and rejuvenating the resources of a tradition. Rosenberg's feeling, quoted above, that poetry must still be of some use in the trenches, also reverberates in the issue of poetic form. 'Simple *poetry*,' Rosenberg writes, 'that is where an interesting complexity of thought is kept in tone and right value to the dominating idea so that it is understandable and still ungraspable'.[63] The preoccupation with the possibilities of lyric form in the trenches is not indicative of stagnation in an inadequate mode of writing; rather it suggests a desire, Yeatsian-fashion, to push out the boundaries of the lyric tradition.[64] In doing so, the act of writing becomes self-justifying. Heaney notes that Longley's poetry should 'enforce a realization that the sweetness of achieved forms is a good in itself'.[65] In effect, it is also a realization forced upon Longley (and his contemporaries Heaney and Mahon) by the example of poets writing in earlier wars. Keith Douglas writes: 'my object (and I don't give a damn about my duty as a poet) is to write true things, significant things in words each of which works for its place in a line.'[66] This assertion, itself a response to the aesthetic preoccupations of the Great War poets, is also echoed by Longley: 'every word has to earn its place'.[67] Poets in both world wars (and in the Northern Ireland Troubles) resist the notion that the scale of a poem reflects the magnitude of events, or, conversely, that the magnitude of the subject can of itself make the poem. As Edward Thomas points out: 'Anything, however small, may make a poem; nothing, however great, is certain to.'[68] Longley, following on from this, argues that 'A poem's weight and seriousness should not ... be measured by its subject matter alone.'[69]

For Longley, the war poets serve to prove the point that the lyric tradition is alive and kicking, and potentially inexhaustible. Crucially, his

---

[63] 'To George Bottomley', 23 July 1916, in *Collected Works of Isaac Rosenberg*, 238.

[64] In a letter to Wilfred Owen, Robert Graves writes: 'I don't want to lose sight of you—You must help S. S. and R. N. and R. G. to revolutionize English Poetry—So outlive this War' *c.* 22 Dec. 1917, in *Collected Letters of Wilfred Owen*, app. C, p. 596.

[65] Blurb to *Poems 1963–1983*, by Michael Longley (King Penguin Series; London: Penguin, 1985).

[66] 'To J. C. Hall', 10 Aug. 1943, in *The Complete Poems of Keith Douglas*, 124.

[67] 'The Longley Tapes', 27.

[68] Quoted in Edna Longley, *Poetry in the Wars*, 12.

[69] 'A Tongue at Play', in Tony Curtis (ed.), *How Poet's Work* (Bridgend: Seren Books, 1996), 120.

own sense of a literary tradition is validated not so much because it is formed in No Man's Land, but because it survives *and* precedes it. The 'nightmare ground' of the twentieth century precipitates doubt and self-questioning, but the sense of tradition serves to validate for Longley an underlying assumption that 'the equipment as lyric poets' to deal with conflict is lyric poetry. In a retrospect on the reasons behind the stylistic inheritance of the Ulster 'tight-assed trio'—the description applied, with a negative charge, to Heaney, Longley, and Mahon—he suggests that

the poets here needed some kind of shape with which to deal with the emerging nightmare of the Troubles. Some kind of tact was required; some kind of order was required, which meant that all of the resources of the native tradition were required. And that meant looking to what had happened at an earlier time of disturbance and menace[70]

To be a 'war poet' may simply be, in the broadest definition, to assert the inherent value and potential possibilities of poetry at a time when they appear to be proscribed, whilst simultaneously destabilizing the text by opening it up to the very context in which it is threatened.

III

Since that context—a psychic landscape which is also a landscape of war—is seen by Longley (as, also, by Ted Hughes) as the essential condition of the twentieth century—'Looked at from the next century, we will be thinking in terms of the fifty or sixty years war that began in 1914'[71]—the war poet 'ancestors' are also appropriated, imaginatively, as ghostly contemporaries: in 'Second Sight', the poet himself is, in a traditional as well as familial sense, a 'ghost among ghosts…Who crowd around me to give directions' in the troglodyte trench-world of the London Underground.[72] Notably in the two late 1970s collections, *Man Lying on a Wall* and *The Echo Gate*, the war poets become subjects as well as precursors: Edward Thomas, Keith Douglas, and Isaac Rosenberg are obliquely elegized in a way which casts the subject of elegy as the ghostly self-elegizer. 'Edward Thomas's War Diary' undertakes the task that Thomas himself, killed in 1917, was largely unable to fulfil, or even begin—to write the experience of the Front into his

---

[70] ' "Walking forwards into the past": An Interview with Michael Longley', 37.
[71] 'Q & A with Michael Longley', 20.
[72] *Poems 1963–1983*, 151.

poetry. It does so almost entirely through quotation rearranged so that it comes at what Douglas Dunn calls 'an imagined angle to reality'.[73] Thomas's diary, unlike Sassoon's consciously literary and self-reflexive narrative (which perhaps had at least one eye to publication), is a series of sense impressions, notes for poems, the time progression marked only by observance of seasons and animals, the landscape gradually changing from white to green. In Longley's poem, images are lifted and restructured to create a narrative dream world which is, in a way, the other dream Thomas himself, on waking, could not remember.[74] It recreates the scene with a fidelity to original details that is also testimony to Thomas's own attention to the minutiae of the landscape around him. The diary is, like much Great War writing, a conjunction of war and the natural world: one which makes for some anomalous observations: 'Owls on Dainville Road. Machine guns and hanging lights above No-Man's-Land'; 'Chaffinch sang once.... Sordid ruin of Estaminet'; and so on.[75] Thomas's 'eye on what remained' in Longley's poem is an eye on the ruins of the landscape and towns caused by the war, the remains of the pre-war civilization; it is also an awareness of what can still be seen of the natural world within that ruination.[76] 'Mole', the companion piece to 'Edward Thomas's War Diary', also fills in the blanks, responding to Thomas's original question—'Does a mole ever get hit by a shell?'[77]—with its own further question, a question that encompasses the whole poem and in doing so turns Thomas's original question into its own answer:

> Who bothers to record
> This body digested
> By its own saliva
> Inside the earth's mouth
> And long intestine,
>
> Or thanks it for digging
> Its own grave, darkness

[73] 'The Poetry of the Troubles', review of *Selected Poems 1963–1980* by Michael Longley, *Times Literary Supplement* (31 July 1981), 886.

[74] See *The Diary of Edward Thomas 1 January–8 April 1917*, ed. Roland Gant and Myfanwy Thomas (Gloucestershire: The Whittington Press, 1977), 28. The diary, which was not discovered until the late 1960s, first appeared in the *Anglo-Welsh Review* in Autumn 1971.

[75] *Diary of Edward Thomas*, 16.

[76] See 'Edward Thomas's War Diary', *Poems 1963–1983*, 134.

[77] *Diary of Edward Thomas*, 17.

> Growing like an eyelid
> Over the eyes, hands
> Swimming in the soil?[78]

The poem's anthropomorphism serves to elegize the dead of the war (including Thomas himself)—the soldiers lost in a communal grave; the men who were drowned in the mud of No Man's Land; more generally, those forgotten by history: the 'vanishing act[s]'. The lines also reverberate in a Northern Irish context, with its own unrecorded or unremembered vanishing acts.[79]

Tjebbe Westendorp categorizes Longley's 'Bog Cotton', 'Mole', 'The War Poets', and 'Edward Thomas's War Diary' as poems about war poets, and finds it odd that 'Longley is full of compassion with the soldier poets of the Great War, while at the same time he does not make a single allusion to the men and the boys involved in the contemporary violence of Northern Ireland'.[80] The allusion is more subtle and, consequently, more elusive than Westendorp recognizes. In 'The War Poets', the poet looks back through MacNeice to the Great War poets in order to cast light upon his own situation in Northern Ireland. The 'Irish implications' are, as Terence Brown points out, 'suggested by a buried allusion to Louis MacNeice's poem of a First World War childhood, "Carrickfergus", where the Irish boy at school...thinks the "war would go on for ever"'. Thus, 'the sense of the endlessness of the First World War is made a metaphor for the interminable nature of the Irish troubles'.[81] The soldier poets' deaths are a rebirth into darkness, into obliteration within the element from which they came: 'shrapnel opened up again the fontanel | Like a hailstone melting towards deep water...'.[82] In death, there is no armistice: as with

---

[78] *Poems 1963–1983*, 135.

[79] 'Concepts such as "a clean slate" and "drawing a line" are', Longley writes, 'offensive. If we are not ever to know who bombed Enniskillen, Birmingham, Dublin and Monaghan, we can at least go on asking "Where are all the missing bodies of the last twenty-five years? Where have they been buried?" In the ghastly paramilitary argot these are the "bog jobs".' ('Memory and Acknowledgement', *Irish Review*, 17/18 (Winter 1995), 158.)

[80] 'The Great War in Irish Memory: The Case of Poetry', in Geert Lernout (ed.), *The Crows behind the Plough: History and Violence in Anglo-Irish Poetry and Drama* (Amsterdam: Rodopi, 1991), 135–7.

[81] 'Who Dares to Speak? Ireland and the Great War', in Robert Clark and Piero Boitani (eds.), *English Studies in Transition: Papers from the ESSE Inaugural Conference* (London: Routledge, 1993), 234.

[82] *Poems 1963–1983*, 168.

MacNeice's 'Carrickfergus', the poem reaches into a never-ending, essentially static, future:

> ...darkness streamed into the dormitory
> Where everybody talked about the war ending
> And always it would be the last week of the war.[83]

In the poem which, in *The Echo Gate*, immediately precedes 'The War Poets'—'Bog Cotton'—different historical and geographical perspectives also work to illuminate the poet's home ground. 'Bog Cotton' is an Irish pastoral which is connected in the poem to a tradition of pastoral images associated with war. It rewrites Keith Douglas's 'Desert Flowers', itself a response to Rosenberg's 'Break of Day in the Trenches'. Paul Fussell notes that red flowers in the Great War 'became fixtures of experience because they had already attained an indispensable place in pastoral elegy, where red and purple flowers...are traditional'.[84] Hence, Rosenberg's 'Break of Day in the Trenches' draws on, and redirects, traditional pastoral elegy, with its 'Poppies whose roots are in man's veins', as it is also a response to one of the most popular poems of the war, John McCrae's 'In Flanders Fields' ('If ye break faith with us who die | We shall not sleep, though poppies grow | In Flanders fields.'). Douglas, in 'Desert Flowers', acknowledges, ironically, the 'tautological' nature of the war poet's enterprise:

> Living in a wide landscape are the flowers—
> Rosenberg I only repeat what you were saying—
> the shell and the hawk every hour
> are slaying men and jerboas, slaying
>
> the mind: but the body can fill
> the hungry flowers and the dogs who cry words
> at nights, the most hostile things of all.
> But that is not new.[85]

All the Great War elements are here: the flowers, the rats, the quenching of human spirit as well as life, the enemy (the opposing army) that is not really felt as the true enemy (lice, rats, etc.). The first stanza of

---

[83] Ibid.

[84] *Thank God for the Atom Bomb* (1988), repr. as *Killing in Verse and Prose* (London: Bellew, 1990), 188. For an extended discussion of Rosenberg's 'Break of Day in the Trenches' and its relation to English pastoral, see Fussell, *The Great War and Modern Memory*, 250–53.

[85] *Complete Poems*, 102.

Longley's 'Bog Cotton' stylistically imitates 'Desert Flowers', but with a difference:

> Let me make room for bog cotton, a desert flower—
> Keith Douglas, I nearly repeat what you were saying
> When you apostrophised the poppies of Flanders
> And the death of poetry there...[86]

The poem evokes images of the First and Second World Wars, but the 'flower' on his Irish landscape does not feed on dead men. He acknowledges the war landscapes evoked by his poetic predecessors, but attempts to make instead a 'hospital' of his own. To 'make room' is a tentative endeavour, against the odds, that takes place entirely in parentheses. The parentheses extend through the second and third stanzas to become the substance of the poem, pushing outwards to create, literally and metaphorically, the 'space between': '(It hangs on by a thread, denser than thistledown, | Reluctant to fly...And useless too, though it might well bring to mind | The plumping of pillows, the staunching of wounds...)'. It is a healing pastoral which, with awareness of the ambiguous nature and function of pastoral in the wars, makes no such grandiose claims for itself. As with Douglas's own 'Desert Flowers', fine detail is rewarded with a far horizon: the two, in fact, become inseparable. Douglas, in his final stanza, writes:

> I see men as trees suffering
> or confound the detail and the horizon.
> Lay the coin on my tongue and I will sing
> of what the others never set eyes on.

Longley's tribute to Douglas's vision works with the same technique: it sees beyond the Second to the First World War, and does so from the perspective of his own ground:

> You saw that beyond the thirstier desert flowers
> There fell hundreds of thousands of poppy petals
> Magnified to blood stains by the middle distance
> Or through the still unfocused sights of a rifle—
> And Isaac Rosenberg wore one behind his ear.[87]

The 'hundreds of thousands of poppy petals' evoke the poppy petal shower of Remembrance Day ceremonies, realized fully in the poem, in

---

[86] *Poems 1963–1983*, 167.   [87] Ibid.

the context of another war, as deaths—'Magnified to blood stains'. The last line, while it looks back to Rosenberg's poem, also looks to his death.[88]

Longley's family and literary ghosts, hitherto never explicitly connected in the poems, converge on 'No Man's Land'. The first half of the poem appeared in *Man Lying on a Wall* entitled 'Granny'. An elegy for his 'jewish granny', the poem redresses the neglect of her memory, gives her substance within the family history—'I shall give skin and bones | To my jewish granny . . .'—and obliquely indicts the anti-Semitism of the twentieth century: 'A terrible century, | A circle of Christian names'.[89] It was subsequently rewritten to become part I of 'No Man's Land', included in the 'New Poems' of *Poems 1963–1983*. The poem is a culmination of the preoccupations that colour the first four collections; it also points towards the themes which dominate the later two:

I

Who will give skin and bones to my Jewish granny?
She has come down to me in the copperplate writing
Of three certificates, a dog-eared daguerreotype
And the one story my grandfather told about her.

He tossed a brick through a rowdy neighbour's window
As she lay dying, and Jessica, her twenty years
And mislaid whereabouts gave way to a second wife,
A terrible century, a circle of Christian names.

II

I tilt her head towards you, Isaac Rosenberg,
But can you pick out that echo of splintering glass
From under the bombardment, and in No Man's Land
What is there to talk about but difficult poems?

Because your body was not recovered either
I try to read the constellations of brass buttons,
Identity discs that catch the light a little.
A shell-shocked carrier pigeon flaps behind the lines.[90]

The 'vanishing act[s]' in his family history are connected here to both world wars and the issue of remembering the century's dead. On one

[88] Rosenberg's red poppy, 'white with the dust', implicitly connects images of the Great War with the Irish landscape's white bog cotton. Those colours—white and red—dominate Longley's later collection, *The Ghost Orchid*, and, to a lesser extent, *Gorse Fires*.

[89] *Man Lying on a Wall* (London: Gollancz, 1976), 36.

[90] *Poems 1963–1983*, 199.

level, Longley's poem is a Holocaust poem: less confident than the earlier version—opening assertion modified to question—the attempt in 'No Man's Land' to give tragic status and human dignity to his 'Jewish granny' loses its significance in a 'terrible century' simply by reason of numbers. It returns to the Great War as, in a way, the origin of a 'terrible century', the first calamity in which the sheer scale of suffering seemed to disallow space for individual tragedy ('can you pick out that echo...?'). While the 'mislaid whereabouts' of Jessica may be literal— as it is with Rosenberg, whose 'body was not recovered'—it refers also, and in both cases, to a mislaid whereabouts in history: those for whom public remembrance has obscured remembering; those whose deaths themselves are unrecorded; the deaths whose numbers are not even known. Connecting the two deaths also evokes the concept of the lost generation—Jessica's 'twenty years' serving as an ironic counterpoint to the 'granny' of conventional expectation and one which offers a parallel with the soldier poets killed prematurely in the Great War.

If the place in which the poet is writing is in some respects a No Man's Land, he is implicitly passing judgement on a society which forces poetry into the margins (a society which has also permitted much of its own history to founder there). It is also an implicit judgement on the political violence of his own country where, as Falkenhayn said of the First World War, 'The first principle...[is]...to yield not one foot of ground'.[91] Sassoon wrote of the Great War:

While exploring my way into the War I had discovered the impermanence of its humanities. One evening we could all be together in a cosy room in Corbie, with Wilmot playing the piano...A single machine-gun or a few shells might wipe out the whole picture within a week. Last summer the First Battalion had been part of my life; by the middle of September it had been almost obliterated.... And now there was a steel curtain down between April and May. On the other side of the curtain, if I was lucky, I should meet the survivors, and we should begin to build up our little humanities all over again.[92]

In 'No Man's Land', Longley writes from a poetic landscape that is designed to make the survival of poetry as evidently problematic as it is felt to be within the poetic tradition of war poets that he constructs in his own verse. But the poem simultaneously searches, through part II,

---

[91]   Quoted in Modris Eksteins, *Rites of Spring: The Great War and the Birth of the Modern Age* (1989; New York: Anchor-Doubleday, 1990), 144.
[92]   *The Complete Memoirs of George Sherston* (1937; London: Faber, 1972), 421.

for a way of hearing, articulating, and visualizing that which is in danger of obliteration—not only Sassoon's 'humanities', but, more specifically, poetry itself. In the rhetorical question 'in No Man's Land | What is there to talk about but difficult poems?', Adorno's suggestion that to write poetry after Auschwitz is 'barbaric' is up for interrogation, as it is also countered. 'Perhaps', Longley states elsewhere, Adorno was 'suggesting that there would have to be distortions, that art would have to contort and hurt itself before it could face a nightmare like that'.[93] The rhetorical question in 'No Man's Land' both recognizes the distortion and asserts the value of poetry (inherent in its difficulty) within that distorted and traumatized context. Famously, Owen wrote in his draft preface: 'if the spirit of [this book] survives—survives Prussia—my ambition...will have achieved fresher fields than Flanders'.[94] If, at first glance, this seems to suggest that the war landscape can be erased from memory, or at least contained in the Western Front, it is obvious now (as it was to Owen then) that it cannot. It is as much a psychic condition as it was a geographical entity. But Owen still implies what Sassoon explicitly asserts: 'The only effective answer that a poet can make to barbarism is poetry, for the only answer to death is the life of the spirit. Explosives cannot destroy the immaterial or dumbfound the utterance of inspiration.'[95] In the final stanza of 'No Man's Land', when the poet tries to read 'the constellations of brass buttons', he attempts to find his way in a landscape where, the previous stanza implies, poetry itself might founder, a No Man's Land strewn with dead bodies in quantities like the stars.[96] Longley's poetic hinterland is always qualified by the 'shell-shocked carrier pigeon' flapping behind the lines of the verse. But in the ebb and flow of what can or cannot be heard, seen, or created under the bombardment, the desire to build up what Sassoon describes as 'humanities' is consistently present. '[T]o admit any hope of a better world', Keith Douglas wrote, 'is criminally foolish, as foolish as it is to stop working for it',[97] and it is an awareness of the validity of this

---

[93] ' "Walking forwards into the past": An Interview with Michael Longley', 39.

[94] *The Poems of Wilfred Owen*, ed. Jon Stallworthy (London: Chatto & Windus, 1990), 192.

[95] Sassoon, *Siegfried's Journey 1916–1920* (London: Faber, 1945), 193.

[96] The image also looks back, or forwards, through Rosenberg's No Man's Land to Keith Douglas's 'The Offensive 2': 'The stars are dead men in the sky' (*Complete Poems*, 94).

[97] 'To J. C. Hall', 10 Aug. 1943, *Complete Poems*, 124.

274 Michael Longley: Poet in No Man's Land

contradiction that informs the landscape of Longley's poetry, as it informs the Great War itself.

IV

Gorse Fires, which appeared in 1991 after a twelve-year silence, was, rightly, hailed as a volume which signalled a new energy in Longley's writing. And *The Ghost Orchid*, as Ian Duhig points out, 'continues where *Gorse Fires*...left off'.[98] The two volumes negotiate both with each other, and with Longley's previous collections. The poems work in the fine dividing line between memory and remembrance, birth and death, love and war, barbarity and civility. The Great War is less a direct subject for elegy than in the earlier poems, but No Man's Land remains a poetic locale, a paradigm of the 'betwixt and between'. That sensibility dominates the poems in *Gorse Fires*: 'Between now and one week ago...'; 'Between hovers and not too far from the holt'; 'the otter, on wet sand in between, | Engraves its own reflection and departure'; 'travelling from one April to another. | It is the same train between the same embankments'; 'I lie awake between the two sleeping couples'; 'Between the bells and prayers...'; 'harmonics, | A blackbird fluttering between electrified fences'. The sense of No Man's Land as poetic hinterland expands in these later collections to become an all-encompassing hinterland as secure in its indeterminacy as Heaney's specific geographical locale. The Great War elegies of *Poems 1963–1983* feed into the elegies of *Gorse Fires*. 'Between Hovers', an elegy for Joe O'Toole, looks back to 'Third Light': the dead badger in the poem is 'a filament of light our lights had put out'. (It also evokes the guilt and love of Othello's tormented 'Put out the light, and then put out the light'.) The ghosts of 'Second Sight' who collapse distinctions between past and future, life and death, metamorphosize into the 'dying otter' who 'gaze[d] right through me...as though it were only | Between hovers'.[99] Edward Thomas's 'eye on what remained' is also the poet's sense in 'Sea Shanty' that 'I am making do with what has been left me'.[100] The poet's relationship with his father, and through his father, the world wars, is rehearsed again in the Homeric translations that also reflect on violence in Northern Ireland. Odysseus is 'the master-craftsman...love-poet,

---

[98] Review of *The Ghost Orchid* by Michael Longley, *Fortnight*, 340 (June 1995), 33.
[99] *Gorse Fires* (London: Secker & Warburg, 1991), 5.   [100] Ibid. 1.

carpenter',[101] the compassionate custodian of memory who (looking
back to the voice 'held secure', 'locked inside my head' of the early
'In Memoriam') 'drew the old man fainting to his breast and held
him there | And cradled like driftwood the bones of his dwindling
father'.[102] If Odysseus is the lover, he is also the killer who, in 'The
Butchers', 'made sure there were no survivors in his house | And that
all the suitors were dead, heaped in blood and dust', and who 'hanged
the women', the 'disloyal housemaids'.[103] The poem returns to an
Irish context at the end: their souls 'came to a bog-meadow full of
bog-asphodels | Where the residents are ghosts or images of the
dead', an image that in 'Bog Cotton' is connected with victims of
both world wars and the Northern Ireland Troubles. The moments of
poignant healing are counterbalanced by acts of butchery, and vice
versa, ad infinitum, or, in effect, for as long as one requires the
other: the poems traverse the distance between the two as they also
acknowledge their mutual dependence. Selected poems by Robert
Graves were published in two companion volumes—*Poems about Love*
and *Poems about War*. In Graves's work the distinction is arbitrary, since
the Gravesian notion of the Muse is in part a response to war and
violence. In Longley's work, the distinction becomes logistically imposs-
ible. As Odysseus is a double-sided figure—'lover and killer...
mingled'—so too the love poems of the later volumes are also the war
poems. In 'The Kilt', a poem reminiscent of 'Third Light', the father's
march into battle, to kill 'in real life', is accompanied, in the final stanza,
by an act of love:

> You pick up the stitches and with needle and thread
> Accompany him out of the grave and into battle,
> Your arms full of material and his nakedness.[104]

Longley writes: 'I suppose that my love poetry is addressed to what
I grandiosely call the female principle, to the Gravesian notion of the
Muse'.[105] If he is a Muse poet, he is also a war poet and a political poet in
a sense that Graves, Longley's 'kindred spirit', would, Mahon notes,
have recognized. Longley protests against the 'ruin' wrought by what
Graves, in *The White Goddess*, describes as the 'capricious experiments in

[101] 'Tree-House', *Gorse Fires*, 25. [102] 'Laertes', ibid. 33. [103] Ibid. 51.
[104] Longley, *The Ghost Orchid* (London: Jonathan Cape, 1995), 35.
[105] 'Q & A with Michael Longley', 21.

philosophy, science and industry'.[106] Set against those capricious experiments is the act of naming, a technique which reaches its apotheosis in *Gorse Fires*, notably in 'The Ice-Cream Man' and 'Ghetto'. It is a technique which was also a mainstay of First World War writing, a ritualistic assertion of sanity, or, in T. S. Eliot's phrase, 'These fragments I have shored against my ruins'.[107] It is present, not merely because it was a Georgian poetic convention, but because it offers at least a form of response to that which cannot be contained within a coherent narrative; in the last analysis, naming means something to write, the sounding of a voice. Edward Thomas's perceptions of a ruined estaminet are recorded in his diary as 'wet, mortar, litter, almanacs, bottles, broken glass, damp beds, dirty paper, knife, crucifix, statuette, old chairs'.[108] Sassoon habitually listed the belongings taken out to France after each leave; he also devotes two pages of his wartime diary to listing fifty-seven 'Birds seen in Judaea'.[109] Hemingway writes of the Great War:

I had seen nothing sacred, and the things that were glorious had no glory and the sacrifices were like the stockyards at Chicago if nothing was done with the meat except to bury it. There were many words that you could not stand to hear and finally only the names of places had dignity. Certain numbers were the same way and certain dates and these with the names of places were all you could say and have them mean anything. Abstract words such as glory, honour, courage, or hallow were obscene beside the concrete names of villages, the numbers of roads the names of rivers[110]

John Lyon's illuminating study of Longley's lists notes that 'their *recoverable* literary origins [are] in the epic lists of Homer', but that the 'attractions of naming, classifying and cataloguing also manifest themselves early in the poet's own biography'.[111] The breakdown of the relationship between word, concept and experience in the Great War, the failure of language, and yet, paradoxically, the refuge of words, might also be added to this analysis, as an origin which combines the biographical and intertextual. In 'Laertes':

---

[106] Mahon, 'An Enormous Yes', review of *Poems 1963–1983* by Michael Longley, *Literary Review*, 80 (Feb. 1985), 55.

[107] 'The Waste Land', *Collected Poems 1909–1962* (London: Faber, 1974), 79.

[108] *Diary of Edward Thomas*, 16.

[109] *Siegfried Sassoon's Diaries 1915–1918*, 233–4.

[110] *A Farewell to Arms* (1929; London: Penguin, 1935), 144.

[111] 'Michael Longley's Lists', *English*, 45/183 (Autumn 1996), 234.

Odysseus sobbed in the shade of a pear-tree for his father
So old and pathetic that all he wanted then and there
Was to kiss him and hug him and blurt out the whole story,
But the whole story is one catalogue and then another[112]

Listing, then, is a form in which the inaccessibility of the subject matter and the inadequacy of language is turned into the subject matter. 'Laertes' has Gravesian echoes: 'There is one story and one story only' which is told and retold. The one story in Longley—or rather the 'whole story'—is itself the problem of telling. In this sense, 'The Ice-Cream Man', is, understandably, as Lyon notes, 'currently acquiring the status of a poetic touchstone'.[113] Every word in the poem 'works for its place', and does so with awareness of its own inadequacy. It imitates a traditional Georgian form of pastoral—naming as many flora as possible in one poem—with the naming an almost 'religious' incantation, an attempted stay against violence which, in contrast to Georgian pastoral, is aware of itself as such not only within history but within the context of the poem:

Rum and raisin, vanilla, butter-scotch, walnut, peach:
You would rhyme off the flavours. That was before
They murdered the ice-cream man on the Lisburn Road
And you bought carnations to lay outside his shop.
I named for you all the wild flowers of the Burren
I had seen in one day: thyme, valerian, loosestrife,
Meadowsweet, tway blade, crowfoot, ling, angelica,
Herb robert, marjoram, cow parsley, sundew, vetch,
Mountain avens, wood sage, ragged robin, stitchwort,
Yarrow, lady's bedstraw, bindweed, bog pimpernel.[114]

The poem incorporates the violence which implicitly tries to unravel the list even as it is formed. The list is felt to be never-ending, a sense which is illustrative of its limitations—one might list for ever, but the death still occurred. It is also implicitly an indictment of the ongoing violence which prompted the list, and an acknowledgement that the effects of that violence are not finite. 'A catalogue like this one', Longley writes, 'is meant to go on forever'.[115] Lyon points out that the poem's power 'derives from the opposition of the composed coherence to be seen and heard *within* the list, and the *in*coherence of the context in which that list

---

[112] *Gorse Fires*, 33.   [113] 'Michael Longley's Lists', 242.
[114] *Gorse Fires*, 49.   [115] 'A Tongue at Play', 115.

is placed'.[116] The two lists of flavours and flowers within the poem, as Michael Allen notes, also parallel each other as 'equally inadequate anecdotes to the "murder"'.[117] They exist on either side ('before' and after) of the short sentence—the killing—which neither of them reaches: structurally, the poem embodies the impossibility of traversing the psychological distance between then and now—pre- and post-violent interruption. The once inspiring and consolatory concepts of sacrifice, glory, and honour no longer hold meaning after the Great War. In 'The Ice-Cream Man', the catalogue itself becomes the 'in memoriam', rather than any abstract ideals embodied within it: the flower names, in Longley's own phrase, are turned into 'a wreath of words'.[118]

For Longley, the idea of poetry as a gesture of remembrance, a 'wreath', is a way of redirecting the traditional forms of remembrance that have sometimes served to obscure rather than illuminate history. 'The Remembrance Day ceremony', he argues, 'encourages us *not* to remember how shrapnel and bullets flay and shatter human flesh and bones, how continuous bombardment destroys minds as well as bodies'. The recitation of Binyon's 'We will remember them' from 'For the Fallen' is, he suggests, used as a 'mind-numbing narcotic'. In opposition to this, he places the work of Owen, Sassoon, Rosenberg, Sorley, and Gurney, work which undermines the 'cult of remembrance' which has developed over the years.[119] To oppose, as Sorley did, 'mind-numbing' consolations—the forms of remembrance that are akin to, and as culpable as, forgetfulness—is also the driving force behind Longley's 1995 collection, *The Ghost Orchid*. A volume concerned with memory, it is dominated by the colours and symbols of remembrance, those associated with the wars of the twentieth century—snow, white feathers; red poppies, blood—colours that also evoke the sacrament (sacrifice) of the Eucharist. 'We Irish', Longley writes, 'are good at claiming a monopoly on human suffering. We are good at resurrecting and distorting the past in order to evade the present. In Ireland we must break the mythic cycles and resist unexamined, ritualistic forms of commemoration.'[120] One of the strengths of *The Ghost Orchid* is that it uses the images of 'mythic

---

[116] 'Michael Longley's Lists', 240.
[117] 'Letter to the Editor', *Thumbscrew*, 4 (Spring 1996), 44.
[118] 'A Tongue at Play', 114.
[119] Longley, 'Say Not Soft Things', in Gordon Lucy and Elaine McClure (eds.), *Remembrance* (Armagh: Ulster Society (Publications) Ltd., 1997), 122.
[120] 'Memory and Acknowledgement', 158.

cycles' in order to break or disrupt them: traditional symbolism is redirected in order to interrogate the values (or evasions) behind it. Thus, in 'Poppies', the poppy is the wound itself; but it also inflicts wounds in a controversial remembrance that has little to do with the dead and everything to do with versions of history:

> Some people tried to stop other people wearing poppies
> And ripped them from lapels as though uprooting poppies
> From Flanders fields, but the others hid inside their poppies
> Razor blades and added to their poppies more red poppies.[121]

The poem describes events in Ireland, notably in Belfast, in the post-war years: it also indicts what becomes a self-perpetuating blood feud, from war to remembrance to war. Two histories compete: one which would 'uproot' its past from any connection with 'Flanders fields', the other which wears its historical wounding on the Western Front as a weapon.

If the poppy is seen here as a tool manipulated by competing and reductive mythologies, in 'Buchenwald Museum' it is rehabilitated as a symbol of that which it is both difficult and painful to remember—the history that is forgotten by, because it complicates, political 'bias':

> Among the unforgettable exhibits one
> Was an official apology for bias. Outside
>
> Although a snowfall had covered everything
> A wreath of poppies was just about visible.
>
> No matter how heavily the snow may come down
> We have to allow the snow to wear a poppy.[122]

The poem's imagery, as with others in the collection, also looks to MacNeice, Eliot, Wallace Stevens. To 'allow the snow to wear a poppy', however difficult that conjunction might be, incorporates a veiled allusion to MacNeice's 'Snow': 'the great bay-window ... | Spawning snow and pink roses against it | Soundlessly collateral and incompatible'.[123] Longley's snow is influenced by Mahon's 'Snow Party': both owe something to Eliot's *The Waste Land*, where the painful awakening and remembering associated with 'the cruellest month' is set in opposition to the 'Winter' which, insulating the mind, covers 'Earth in forgetful snow'.[124] The 'snowscape' of poems in *The Ghost Orchid* and *Gorse Fires* is an inherently ambiguous and dualistic landscape, one which may be

[121] *The Ghost Orchid*, 40.   [122] Ibid. 41.   [123] MacNeice, *CP*, 30.
[124] T. S. Eliot, *Collected Poems 1909–1962*, 63.

both a healing and a cover-up; it may symbolize death or disguise it, obscure images or freeze them. Thus, one side of the image—'the snowscape of the big double-bed'; snow as 'feathers from the wings of Icarus', an imaginary fountain of poetry—is compromised by awareness of its other—'the need for whitewash and disinfectant'; the obliteration of voice, 'as if snow had fallen . . .'. The child in 'Ghetto' who is fixed in memory—'He turns into a little snowman and refuses to melt'—and who lingers on into *The Ghost Orchid* ('the melting snowman was some-body's child'), also reminds of the paradoxical nature of elegizing in Wallace Stevens's 'The Snow Man', with its anti-elegiac striving after a 'mind of winter . . . not to think | Of any misery'.[125] In *Tuppenny Stung*, Longley quotes Don Shriver's 'The cure and the remembrance are co-terminous'.[126] 'Remembrance' itself, though, the experience of Northern Ireland makes clear, is a double-edged sword, one which can harden into what Mahon calls 'the *rigor mortis* of archaic postures, political and cultural' or melt into the 'fluidity of a possible life'.[127] For Longley, writing from a hinterland informed by both, the 'cure' is in the balance of opposing forces, the potentiality of the space between: 'The wind-farmer's small-holding reaches as far as the horizon. | Between fields of hailstones and raindrops his frost-flowers grow'.[128]

V

'[T]he world wars', Edna Longley writes, 'divide imaginations [in Irish writing], if more subtly than the way Remembrance Day every Novem-ber divides Dublin'.[129] They would seem also to divide reputations in Northern Ireland. 'Being misrepresented, swindled, short-changed is', Michael Longley is aware, 'the perpetual risk all poets have to take'.[130] Those comments, made in relation to MacNeice as part of a process whereby MacNeice's misrepresentation has slowly been redressed, have become, ironically enough, and for some of the same reasons, not irrelevant in terms of the critical reception of Longley's own work. If his poetic hinterland is a 'No Man's Land', it is also the case that his

[125] Wallace Stevens, *Collected Poems* (London: Faber, 1955), 9–10.
[126] *Tuppenny Stung*, 76.
[127] 'Poetry in Northern Ireland', *Twentieth Century Studies*, 4 (Nov. 1970), 93.
[128] 'Wind-Farmer', *The Ghost Orchid*, 50.
[129] *The Living Stream* (Newcastle: Bloodaxe, 1994), 156.
[130] 'Louis MacNeice: A Misrepresented Poet', *Dublin Magazine*, 6/1 (Spring 1967), 68.

reputation has sometimes foundered there. Some of the terms in which Edna Longley points up 'The Importance of Keith Douglas' also apply in part to Longley:

What Geoffrey Hill, twenty years ago, called his [Douglas's] 'ambivalent status—at once "established" and overlooked' remains unresolved.... Nor can all sins of omission be explained by Douglas's half-shunting into the 'war poetry' siding; although perhaps only in England would Michael Hamburger's point not be taken: 'In the era of total politics...war poetry has become continuous, ubiquitous and hardly distinguishable from any other kind of poetry.' Roger Garfitt...implies a deeper reason why English criticism and poetry lack the 'catholic belly' to digest Douglas: 'Critics have mistaken his masterly verse control for a cerebral detachment.'[131]

The neglect is, Edna Longley suggests, indicative of an aesthetic conflict in England 'between the style-faction and the content-faction', with Ulster poets 'sniped at in No Man's Land for not keeping their enviable raw material raw enough'.[132]

In its most extreme form, as has been seen, canon-building in Ireland has not so much sidelined 'war poetry' as it has sidelined the whole experience of the world wars. Hence MacNeice's struggle to assert both his Irish identity and the impact on his writing of the First and Second World Wars. Michael Longley's early and consistent engagement with those wars *before* the recent resurgence of interest in the Irish involvement in them has led to misrepresentation of his work, a misrepresentation that causes him to fall between English and Irish versions of their literary heritage. In the late 1970s, when the centrality of the Great War to his poetry was acknowledged by reviewers, some confusion about the significance of that presence is also in evidence. In a review of *The Echo Gate*, Thomas McCarthy describes Longley's voice as 'a benign unionist voice', one which is characterized by 'continuous references to *England*'s experience of the war, to the First World War in particular. One mourns so that one may belong.'[133] Two assumptions hover behind these remarks: first, that to be unionist means to want to be English, that unionism is in sympathy with an English perception of history (when in fact it has been, if anything, out of sympathy with it); second, and connected, that the Great War references can have little, if anything, to do with Ireland. It is a misconception that has also dogged MacNeice,

---

[131] Edna Longley, *Poetry in the Wars*, 94.   [132] Ibid.
[133] 'Northern Voices', review of *The Echo Gate*, 13.

who, James Liddy states, 'was in Ireland, in the South, when the war against Hitler was declared' but 'was swept with the natural jingoism of the Loyalist...when the reality of the conflict materialized'.[134] On the contrary, Longley's imaginative engagement with the Great War, through the experience of his English father, is, like MacNeice's, extended to encompass both English and Irish (and other) experiences of war.

If the choice of subject has been seen to place Longley (and Mac-Neice) outside the 'Irish' tradition, so too has his style. In fact, between style-faction and content-faction, Longley seems at times to be in a no-win situation, wrong-footed in relation to English and Irish versions of the canon both for his choice of subject matter and for the supposed lack of it. The 'tight-lipped quality' of the verse 'lead[s] one to think of it as Protestant';[135] Longley is seen as an adherent of the Movement's style, an adept at producing the 'well-made poem', whose formalism is indicative of a refined Anglicanism. In Philip Hobsbaum's review of *The Ghost Orchid*, he claims that 'one misses in Longley...the urgency of an inner life', that 'One finds oneself speaking of style rather than subject, as though manner itself were the poet's material'.[136] As Michael Allen demonstrates, Hobsbaum makes this claim only because 'the significance of [the] poems' he discusses 'escapes [him] so completely'.[137] But Hobsbaum's review, though unhelpful in all other respects, does at least serve to illustrate, since it is one of the more explicit formulations of the position, the perpetuation of value judgements within which poetic technique can be a suspect element in poetry, and size has a virtue all its own.[138] As with Douglas, Longley's style has been associated with 'cerebral detachment'. Brian McIlroy sees Longley as lacking the 'understanding of victims' that Heaney has in 'Punishment' and 'The Grauballe Man'. In Longley, he suggests, 'there is a greater sense of secularization, of scientificity, of dehumanization'.[139] As evidence, he

---

[134] 'Ulster Poets and the Protestant Muse', *Éire-Ireland*, 14/2 (Summer 1979), 121.

[135] Colin Folk, quoted ibid. 123.

[136] ' "Growing like a coral among shadows": Literary Life Respectable', review of *The Ghost Orchid* by Michael Longley, *Thumbscrew*, 3 (Autumn/Winter 1995), 58.

[137] See 'Letter to the Editor', 44–5.

[138] Hobsbaum's response to Michael Allen's 'Letter to the Editor' challenges Allen's reading of 'The Ice-Cream Man' as, amongst other things, a comment on ecological threat on the grounds that the poem is only ten lines long. See *Thumbscrew*, 4 (Spring 1996), 45–7.

[139] 'Poetic Imagery as Political Fetishism: The Example of Michael Longley', *Canadian Journal of Irish Studies*, 16/1 (July 1990), 61.

notes the prevalence of body parts in Longley's poems, but in disembodying the images themselves from the poems in which they appear, misses the understanding of victimization that reveals itself through minute detail. Thus, his reading of 'Master of Ceremonies'—'the park attendant's job appears to be that of collecting littered limbs until his sack is heavy'—overlooks the fact that the 'park' is No Man's Land, and the 'attendant', the 'retarded uncle', is himself the victim killed whilst undertaking one of the most barbaric tasks necessary on the Western Front. Dismemberment and disembodiment in Longley poetry are, McIlroy argues, indicative of 'Protestant consciousness [as] one of synecdoche, always a part for a slippery whole'.[140] The reason itself, however, may be rather less cerebral than this: not so much 'morbid curiosity' and political displacement as McIlroy claims, as imaginative engagement with a century of war in which those images were literally present.

Connected to such misrepresentations is the fact that Longley's work has also been, in a more literal sense, 'short-changed' in terms of the still only very slight critical response to it, certainly in comparison with the (sometimes excessive) ink spillage on the subject of Heaney's poetry. Several reasons have been put forward to explain why Longley's poetry suffers critical neglect. One may be the agreement between Edna Longley and Michael Longley that, as Michael Longley puts it, 'she won't write about my work'.[141] The effect of this is, of course, impossible to quantify. But Edna Longley's formidable critical presence in the field of contemporary British and Irish poetry is one which engenders a high level of response. Since the example of Longley's poetry is excluded from the content (although not the terms) of her criticism, it is not always addressed by critics who respond directly to her work. Tom Adair attributes the neglect to the fact that both Heaney and Mahon 'were perceived to have evolved their own stance and idiom, to have created a poetic identikit intelligible to critics'.[142] Peter McDonald probes further into some of the implications of this last perception:

the critical boom in Ulster poetry . . . was a far from unmixed blessing; for the poets themselves, the opportunity to write for a large audience has brought with it the problems of having to satisfy the demand for a public, responsible voice

---

[140] Ibid. 61–2.   [141] 'Q & A with Michael Longley', 21.
[142] Adair, 'Of Flock and Fold', 16.

of the kind proper to war-poets. Of course the responsibility game is one that can be played profitably: full-blown mythologizing, as in *North* or *The Rough Field*, is only one approach; there are also Paulin's rasping, strident Ulsterisms, Mahon's self-conscious cosmopolitan exile or Muldoon's oblique parables, all of these leading back to the ever-fertile dilemma of Being A Poet From Northern Ireland. Michael Longley's poetry doesn't fit into this scheme quite so easily[143]

In effect, Longley's work, like MacNeice's, disrupts both the stereotypes of an 'Irish poet' and a 'Poet From Northern Ireland'. Consequently, as is also the case with MacNeice, his place within critical debates is often either non-existent or anomalous. Some of the criticism that does exist is offered solely as tribute, is rarely contentious, and all too often apologizes, paradoxically, both for its own existence and for the critical neglect of the poet.[144] It seems at times, with regard to Longley, that even angels fear to tread. As with Graves, critical neglect may be, amongst other things, symptomatic of a refusal to acknowledge the implications of the poetry in question. Hence, as Peter McDonald notes, he is too often given 'vague praise for the integrity of his craftsmanship, his accomplishment as a "nature-" or "love-" poet, but too little real attention as an artist whose work is "responsible", not in any self-congratulating or grandiose way'.[145] And this in spite of the fact that, as Robert Johnstone points out, Longley 'has so consistently, so directly and so effectively written about the actual human damage of the past twenty years in Northern Ireland'.[146]

Seamus Heaney's high profile, notably (however misleadingly) as poet of the Troubles, and the fact that he and Longley are contemporaries, can lead to comparisons between them which are, McDonald suggests, unhelpful, since 'Heaney is working in a different direction'.[147] But comparing the critical reception of the two does illustrate some of the anomalies through which Longley's achievement is sidelined. For Hobsbaum, in the early days of the Belfast 'Group', Heaney is a traditionalist stick with which to beat emerging structuralist agendas,

---

[143] 'From Ulster with Love', 14.

[144] Mark Storey's 'Michael Longley: A Precarious Act of Balancing', *Fortnight*, 194 (May 1983), illustrates this sensibility: 'With some trepidation . . . I offer some reflections at a distance' (21).

[145] 'From Ulster with Love', 14.

[146] Johnstone, 'Harmonics between Electrified Fences', review of *Gorse Fires* by Michael Longley, *Honest Ulsterman*, 92 (1991), 79.

[147] 'From Ulster with Love', 16.

a poet who adapts and rejuvenates a British empirical tradition.[148] Twenty-five years later, Heaney is, for the Field Day enterprise, the poet with European orientation, an orientation which, Richard Kirkland argues, is indicative of a desire 'to escape from British empirical paradigms'.[149] Either way, Longley, less user-friendly for critics than Heaney, is sometimes adopted as the 'other' who serves to illustrate what the 'Irish' tradition is not. In the introduction to the 'Contemporary Irish Poetry' section of the *Field Day Anthology*, Declan Kiberd writes that Heaney's poetry is characterized by 'A sustained attempt... to locate the northern violence in wider patterns of universal history'.[150] Likewise, Seamus Deane's recent poetry 'has evinced a strong sense of European history and a desire to locate the Irish experience as part of that wider pattern'.[151] In contrast, Kiberd writes that

> Longley may have more in common with the semi-detached suburban muse of Philip Larkin and post-war England than with Heaney or Montague. His self-effacing courtesy, his dry good humour, and his addiction to off-key closures, all align him with British post-modernism... And yet the very fact that he should apply these techniques to the Belfast of the 'Troubles' indicates also his sustained attempt to widen the traditions of modern Irish poetry.[152]

The difference between these two views of poetic activity is significant: Longley, according to Kiberd, brings British techniques into Ireland (or tries to); Deane and Heaney reach out from Ireland (and for Ireland) to a European context. The comments also incorporate a judgement: Deane and Heaney work within a recognizably Irish tradition, exploring new contexts for that tradition; Longley, implicitly, works outside that tradition, a British suburban poet. One might go so far as to say that one is intended to suggest a post-colonial activity; the other is redolent of a lingering colonialism. Kiberd's notes to Longley's poems in the anthology attempt to contextualize them within English lower middle-class culture and in northern English landscapes. Derek Mahon's comments, in 1973, that the suburbs of Belfast are 'the final anathema for the

---

[148] For a discussion of Hobsbaum's 'agenda' for the Belfast Group see Richard Kirkland, *Literature and Culture in Northern Ireland since 1965: Moments of Danger* (London and New York: Longman, 1996), 80–1.

[149] Ibid. 139.

[150] 'Contemporary Irish Poetry', in Seamus Deane (gen. ed.), *The Field Day Anthology of Irish Writing*, (Derry: Field Day, 1991), iii. 1364.

[151] Ibid. 1377.

[152] Ibid. 1375.

traditional Irish imagination', are still pertinent here. Mahon continues, 'A lot of people who are regarded as important in Irish poetry cannot accept that the Protestant suburbs in Belfast are a part of Ireland, you know. At an aesthetic level they can't accept that'.[153] Antimacassars, and all they represent, seem to be, for Kiberd, fundamentally un-Irish:

The influence of Auden on Mahon, Longley and Montague is at least as extensive as that of Kavanagh...And there is good reason for this. Auden was, along with Philip Larkin, the artist of post-imperial England, a land of anticlimax and antimacassars[154]

'I must...listen to a lecture on Trench Warfare, and discuss yesterday's Field Day', Sassoon complained in 1918: 'No peace for poets'.[155] The comment is not without its prophetic resonances. The revival of interest in the Irish experience of the First World War points up the former neglect, or denial, of aspects of Irish history and culture, by Field Day and others, a denial in evidence when imaginative engagement with the war is viewed as an enterprise that takes place primarily outside the 'Irish' tradition, at best in a No Man's Land between English and Irish traditions. As neglect of the memory of Ireland's Great War involvement is gradually redressed, it should become apparent, if it was not before, that Longley's poetry, in its placing of the 'Irish experience' in the context of the European wars of the twentieth century deserves, ironically enough, the encomiums Kiberd reserves for Heaney's poetry: that it is characterized by 'ethical as well as aesthetic probing', and that it makes a 'sustained attempt...to locate the northern violence in wider patterns of universal history'.[156]

---

[153] 'Harriet Cooke Talks to the Poet Derek Mahon', *Irish Times*, 17 Jan. 1973, 10.
[154] 'Contemporary Irish Poetry', 1311–12.
[155] *Siegfried Sassoon's Diaries 1915–1918*, 260.
[156] 'Contemporary Irish Poetry', 1364.

Bibliography

I. POETRY

Blunden, Edmund, *Selected Poems*, ed. Robyn Marsack (Manchester: Carcanet Press, 1982).

Boas, F. S., *Songs of Ulster and Balliol* (London: Constable and Company Ltd., 1917).

Brooke, Rupert, *The Poetical Works*, ed. Geoffrey Keynes (London: Faber, 1970).

Carson, Ciaran, *Belfast Confetti* (1989; Oldcastle: Gallery Press, 1991).

Douglas, Keith, *The Complete Poems*, ed. Desmond Graham (Oxford: OUP, 1987).

Eliot, T. S., *Collected Poems 1909–1962* (London: Faber, 1974).

Graves, Robert, *Poems 1914–1926* (London: Heinemann, 1927).

—— *Collected Poems 1959* (London: Cassell, 1959).

—— *Collected Poems* (London: Cassell, 1975).

—— *Selected Poems*, ed. Paul O'Prey (London: Penguin, 1986).

—— *Poems about War*, ed. William Graves (London: Cassell, 1988).

—— *Complete Poems*, ed. Beryl Graves and Dunstan Ward, 2 vols. (Manchester: Carcanet Press, 1995, 1997).

Heaney, Seamus, *Death of a Naturalist* (London: Faber, 1966).

—— *Door into the Dark* (London: Faber, 1969).

—— *Wintering Out* (London: Faber, 1972).

—— *North* (London: Faber, 1975).

—— *Field Work* (London: Faber, 1979).

—— *Station Island* (London: Faber, 1984).

—— *The Haw Lantern* (London: Faber, 1987).

—— *Seeing Things* (London: Faber, 1991).

—— *The Spirit Level* (London: Faber, 1996).

Hewitt, John, *Collected Poems*, ed. Frank Ormsby (Belfast: Blackstaff Press, 1991).

Hughes, Ted, *The Hawk in the Rain* (London: Faber, 1957).

—— *Lupercal* (London: Faber, 1960).

—— *Wodwo* (London: Faber, 1967).

—— *Selected Poems 1957–1981* (London: Faber, 1982).

Jones, David, *In Parenthesis* (1937; London: Faber, 1963).

Kavanagh, Patrick, *The Complete Poems* (1972), ed. Peter Kavanagh (Newbridge, Ireland: Goldsmith Press, 1984).

Kettle, T. M., *Poems and Parodies* (Dublin: The Talbot Press, 1916).

Kipling, Rudyard, *Rudyard Kipling's Verse: Inclusive Edition 1885–1918*, i (London: Hodder & Stoughton, 1919).

Larkin, Philip, *Collected Poems* (1988), ed. Anthony Thwaite (London: Faber and the Marvell Press, 1990).

Ledwidge, Francis, *The Complete Poems*, ed. Alice Curtayne (London: Martin Brian & O'Keefe, 1974).

—— *Selected Poems*, ed. Dermot Bolger (Dublin: New Island Books, 1992).

Lewis, C. S., *The Collected Poems of C. S. Lewis*, ed. Walter Hooper (London: Fount Paperbacks, 1994).

Longley, Michael, *No Continuing City* (London: Macmillan, 1969).

—— *An Exploded View* (London: Gollancz, 1973).

—— *Man Lying on a Wall* (London: Gollancz, 1976).

—— *The Echo Gate* (London: Secker & Warburg, 1979).

—— *Poems 1963–1983*, King Penguin Series (London: Penguin, 1985).

—— *Poems 1963–1983* (1985; London: Secker & Warburg, 1991).

—— *Gorse Fires* (London: Secker & Warburg, 1991).

—— *The Ghost Orchid* (London: Jonathan Cape, 1995).

Lowell, Robert, *Life Studies* (London: Faber, 1959).

—— *Near the Ocean* (London: Faber, 1967).

—— *Robert Lowell's Poems: A Selection*, ed. Jonathan Raban (London: Faber, 1974).

MacGill, Patrick, *The Navvy Poet: The Collected Poetry of Patrick MacGill* (Dingle, Co. Kerry: Brandon, 1984).

MacGreevy, Thomas, *Collected Poems*, ed. Thomas Dillon Redshaw (Dublin: New Writers' Press, 1971).

—— *Collected Poems of Thomas MacGreevy: An Annotated Edition*, ed. Susan Schriebman (Dublin: Anna Livia Press, 1991).

McGuckian, Medbh, *Captain Lavender* (Oldcastle: Gallery Press, 1994).

MacNeice, Louis, *Collected Poems*, ed. E. R. Dodds (London: Faber, 1966).

—— *Selected Poems*, ed. Michael Longley (London: Faber, 1988).

Mahon, Derek, *Night-Crossing* (London: OUP, 1968).

—— *Lives* (London: OUP, 1972).

—— *The Snow Party* (London and New York: OUP, 1975).

—— *Poems 1962–1978* (Oxford: OUP, 1979).

—— *Courtyards in Delft* (Dublin: Gallery Press, 1981).

—— *The Hunt by Night* (Oxford: OUP, 1982).

—— *A Kensington Notebook* (London: Anvil Press Poetry, 1984).

—— *Antarctica* (Dublin: Gallery Press, 1985).

—— *Selected Poems* (London: Viking; Oldcastle: Gallery Press, 1991).

—— *The Hudson Letter* (Oldcastle: Gallery Press, 1995).

Mandelstam, Osip, *Selected Poems*, trans. David McDuff (Cambridge: Rivers Press Ltd., 1973).

Midgley, Harry, *Thoughts from Flanders* (Belfast: n.p., 1924).

Montague, John, *The Rough Field* (1972; 4th ed., Dublin: Dolmen Press, 1984).

Muldoon, Paul, *Why Brownlee Left* (London: Faber, 1980).

Owen, Wilfred, *The Poems of Wilfred Owen*, ed. Jon Stallworthy (London: Chatto & Windus, 1990).

Paulin, Tom, *Walking a Line* (London: Faber, 1994).

Pearse, Padraic, *Rogha Dánta; Selected Poems*, ed. Dermot Bolger (Dublin: New Island Books, 1993).

Read, Herbert, *Collected Poems* (London: Sinclair-Stevenson Ltd., n.d).

Rosenberg, Isaac, *The Collected Works of Isaac Rosenberg: Poetry, Prose, Letters, Paintings and Drawings*, ed. Ian Parsons (London: Chatto & Windus, 1979).

Sassoon, Siegfried, *The War Poems* (London: Faber, 1983).

Spender, Stephen, *Poems* (London: Faber, 1933).

—— *Collected Poems 1928–1985* (London: Faber, 1985).

Thomas, Edward, *The Collected Poems of Edward Thomas*, ed. R. George Thomas (Oxford: OUP, 1981).

Tynan, Katherine, *The Poems of Katherine Tynan*, ed. Monk Gibbon (Dublin: Allen Figgis, 1963).

Yeats, W. B., *Collected Poems* (London: Macmillan, 1950).

—— *The Variorum Edition of the Poems of W. B. Yeats*, ed. Peter Allt and Russell K. Alspach (New York: Macmillan, 1957).

II.   POETRY ANTHOLOGIES

Gardner, Brian (ed.), *Up the Line to Death: The War Poets 1914–1918*, with foreword by Edmund Blunden (1964; London: Methuen, 1986).

Graves, Alfred Perceval (ed.), *The Book of Irish Poetry* (Dublin: Talbot Press; London: T. Fisher Unwin, n.d).

Kinsella, Thomas (ed.), *The New Oxford Book of Irish Verse* (Oxford: OUP, 1986).

Lloyd, Bertram (ed.), *The Paths of Glory: A Collection of Poems written during the War 1914–1919* (London: George Allen and Unwin Ltd., 1919).

Mahon, Derek (ed.), *The Sphere Book of Modern Irish Poetry* (London: Sphere Books, 1972).

—— and Fallon, Peter (eds.), *The Penguin Book of Contemporary Irish Poetry* (London: Penguin, 1990).

Montague, John (ed.), *The Faber Book of Irish Verse* (London: Faber, 1974).

Muldoon, Paul (ed.), *The Faber Book of Contemporary Irish Poetry* (London: Faber, 1986).

Parsons, I. M. (ed.), *Men Who March Away: Poems of the First World War* (London: Chatto and Windus, 1965).

Paulin, Tom (ed.), *The Faber Book of Political Verse* (London: Faber, 1986).

Poems of the Great War 1914–1918 (London: Penguin, 1998).

Reeves, James (ed.), *Georgian Poetry* (London: Penguin, 1962).

Reilly, Catherine (ed.), *Scars upon My Heart: Women's Poetry and Verse of the First World War* (London: Virago, 1981).

Roberts, David (ed.), *Minds at War: Essential Poetry of the First World War in Context* (Burgess Hill: Saxon Books, 1996).

Room to Rhyme, an anthology of poems by Seamus Heaney and Michael Longley and of ballads collected by David Hammond (Belfast: Arts Council, 1968).

Royle, Trevor (ed.), *In Flanders Fields: Scottish Poetry and Prose of the First World War* (Edinburgh: Mainstream Publishing Co., 1990).

Silkin, Jon (ed.), *The Penguin Book of First World War Poetry* (2nd edn., London: Penguin, 1981).

Skelton, Robin (ed.), *Poetry of the Thirties* (London: Penguin, 1964).

Stephen, Martin (ed.), *Poems of the First World War: 'Never Such Innocence'* (London: J. M. Dent, 1993).

Yeats, W. B. (ed.), *The Oxford Book of Modern Verse* (Oxford: Clarendon, 1936).

III.   WAR MEMOIRS AND DIARIES

Barbusse, Henri, *Under Fire* (1916), trans. Fitzwater Wray (London and Toronto: J. M. Dent & Sons, 1929).

Blunden, Edmund, *Undertones of War* (1928; London: Penguin, 1982).

Brittain, Vera, *Testament of Youth* (1933; London: Fontana, 1979).

Gibbon, Monk, *Inglorious Soldier* (London: Hutchinson, 1968).

Graves, Robert, *Goodbye to All That* (1929; 2nd edn., 1957; London: Penguin, 1960).

Hemingway, Ernest, *A Farewell to Arms* (1929; London: Penguin, 1935).

MacGill, Patrick, *The Red Horizon* (1916; London: Caliban Books, 1984).

—— *The Great Push* (1916; London: Caliban Books, 1984).

Remarque, E. M., *All Quiet on the Western Front* (1929), trans. A. W. Wheen (London: Mayflower Books, 1963).

Sassoon, Siegfried, *The Complete Memoirs of George Sherston* (1937; London: Faber, 1972).

—— *Siegfried's Journey, 1916–1920* (London: Faber, 1945).

—— *Siegfried Sassoon's Diaries 1915–1918*, ed. Rupert Hart-Davis (London: Faber, 1983).

Thomas, Edward, *The Diary of Edward Thomas 1 January–8 April 1917*, ed. Roland Gant and Myfanwy Thomas (Gloucestershire: The Whittington Press, 1977).

Vaughan, Edwin Campion, *Some Desperate Glory: The Diary of a Young Officer, 1917* with foreword by John Terraine (London: Macmillan, 1994).

IV.   OTHER PRIMARY SOURCES

Graves, Robert, *Poetic Unreason and Other Studies* (London: Cecil Palmer, 1925).

—— *The English Ballad: A Short Critical Survey* (London: Ernest Benn Ltd., 1927).

—— *I, Claudius* (1934; London: Penguin, 1953).

—— *The Common Asphodel: Collected Essays on Poetry 1922–1949* (London: Hamish Hamilton, 1949).

—— *Oxford Addresses on Poetry* (London: Cassell, 1962).

—— *The White Goddess*, ed. Grevel Lindop (1948; 4th edn., London: Faber and Faber, 1999).

—— *In Broken Images: Selected Letters of Robert Graves 1914–1946*, ed. Paul O'Prey (London: Hutchinson, 1982).

—— *Between Moon and Moon: Selected Letters of Robert Graves 1946–1972*, ed. Paul O'Prey (London: Hutchinson, 1984).

—— and Hodge Alan, *The Long Weekend: A Social History of Great Britain 1918–1939* (2nd edn., London: Faber, 1950).

—— and Riding, Laura, *A Survey of Modernist Poetry* (London: Heinemann, 1927).

Heaney, Seamus, *Preoccupations: Selected Prose 1968–1978* (London: Faber, 1980).

—— 'Unhappy and at Home', interview by Seamus Deane, in Mark Patrick Hederman and Richard Kearney (eds.), *The Crane Bag Book of Irish Studies* (Dublin: Blackwater Press, 1982), 66–72.

—— *'Among Schoolchildren': A John Malone Memorial Lecture* (Belfast: John Malone Memorial Committee, 1983).

—— *Place and Displacement: Recent Poetry of Northern Ireland* (Grasmere: Trustees of Dove Cottage, 1984).

—— 'Envies and Identifications: Dante and the Modern Poet', *Irish University Review*, 15/1 (Spring 1985), 5–19.

—— 'The Sense of the Past', *Ulster Local Studies*, 9/20 (Summer 1985), 109–15.

—— 'The New Poet Laureate', *Belfast Review*, 10 (Mar.–May 1986), 6.

—— *The Government of the Tongue* (London: Faber, 1988).

—— *The Place of Writing* (Atlanta, Ga.: Scholar's Press, 1989).

—— 'Calling the Tune', interview by Tom Adair, *Linen Hall Review*, 6/2 (Autumn, 1989), 5–8.

—— 'Between North and South: Poetic Detours', interview by Richard Kearney, in *Visions of Europe: Conversations on the Legacy and Future of Europe* (Dublin: Wolfhound Press, 1992), 81–9.

—— *The Redress of Poetry: Oxford Lectures* (London: Faber, 1995).

Longley, Michael, 'Louis MacNeice: A Misrepresented Poet', *Dublin Magazine*, 6/1 (Spring 1967), 68–74.

—— 'Strife and the Ulster Poet', *Hibernia* (Nov. 1969), 11.

—— 'The Northerner', *Sunday Independent*, 26 Sept. 1976.

—— 'Lisburn Road (Belfast)', *Fortnight*, 207 (1984), 21.

—— 'Making Some Kind of Sense', interview by Fintan O'Toole, *Sunday Tribune*, 17 Mar. 1985, 17.

—— 'The Longley Tapes', interview by Robert Johnstone, *Honest Ulsterman*, 78 (Summer 1985), 13–31.

—— 'Q & A with Michael Longley', interview by Dillon Johnston, *Irish Literary Supplement*, 5/2 (Fall 1986), 20–2.

Longley, Michael, *Tuppenny Stung: Autobiographical Chapters* (Belfast: Lagan Press, 1994).

—— 'An Interview with Michael Longley', by Dermot Healy, *Southern Review*, 31/3 (July 1995), 557–61.

—— The Future is Behind Us', interview by Pat Boran, *Books Ireland*, 187 (Summer 1995), 147–8.

—— ' "Walking forwards into the past": An Interview with Michael Longley', by Fran Brearton, *Irish Studies Review*, 18 (Spring 1997), 35–9.

—— (ed.), *Causeway: The Arts in Ulster*, (Belfast: Arts Council of Northern Ireland; Dublin: Gill and Macmillan, 1971).

MacNeice, Louis, *Modern Poetry* (1938; 2nd edn., Oxford: Clarendon Press, 1968).

—— *The Poetry of W. B. Yeats* (1941; 2nd edn., London: Faber, 1967).

—— *The Strings are False* (London: Faber, 1965).

—— *Selected Literary Criticism of Louis MacNeice*, ed. Alan Heuser (Oxford: Clarendon Press, 1987).

—— 'Broken Windows or Thinking Aloud', *Poetry Review*, 78/2 (Summer 1988), 4–6.

—— *Selected Prose of Louis MacNeice*, ed. Alan Heuser (Oxford: Clarendon Press, 1990).

Mahon, Derek, 'Poetry in Northern Ireland', *Twentieth Century Studies*, 4 (Nov. 1970), 89–93.

—— 'Harriet Cooke Talks to the Poet Derek Mahon', *Irish Times*, 17 Jan. 1973, 10.

—— 'Mother Tongue', review of John Montague (ed.), *The Faber Book of Irish Verse*, *New Statesman*, 29 Mar. 1974, 451–2.

—— 'Elgy Gillespie talks to Derek Mahon', *Irish Times*, 2 Dec. 1978, 14.

—— 'Un Beau Pays, Mal Habité', *Magill* 2/5 (Feb. 1979), 18–22.

—— 'Each Poem for Me is a New Beginning', interview by Willie Kelly, *Cork Review*, 2/3 (June 1981), 10–12.

—— 'Womanly Times', review of *Between Moon and Moon: Selected Letters of Robert Graves 1946–1972*, ed. Paul O'Prey, *Literary Review*, 75 (Sept. 1984), 7–8.

—— 'An Enormous Yes', review of *Poems 1963–1983* by Michael Longley, *Literary Review*, 80 (Feb. 1985), 55–7.

—— 'An Interview with Derek Mahon', by Terence Brown, *Poetry Ireland Review* 14 (Autumn 1985), 11–19.

—— Review of *Across a Roaring Hill*, ed. G. Dawe and E. Longley, *Celtic Revivals* by Seamus Deane, *Lady Gregory* by Mary Lou Kohlfeld, *Literary Review*, 89 (Nov. 1985), 52–3.

—— 'Uncle Robert', review of *The Assault Heroic* by Richard Perceval Graves, *Irish Times*, 20 Sept. 1986, 4.

—— 'The Other Ship', review of *A Titanic Myth: The Californian Incident* by Leslie Harrison, *Irish Times*, 3 Jan. 1987, Weekend 7.

—— 'Our Proper Dark', review of *We Irish* by Denis Donoghue, *Irish Times*, 31 Jan. 1987, Weekend 5.

—— 'An Ulster Blackthorn', review of *Selected Literary Criticism of Louis MacNeice*, ed. Alan Heuser, *Irish Times*, 11 Apr. 1987, Weekend 5.

—— 'A Parcel of Earth, a Handful of Dust', review of *The Lost Voices of World War I*, ed. Tim Cross, *Irish Times*, 21 Jan. 1988, Weekend 8.

—— 'Break of Day in the Trenches', review of *Out of Battle: The Poetry of the Great War* by Jon Silkin, *Irish Times*, 20 Feb. 1988, Weekend 9.

—— 'Made in Belfast', interview by Eileen Battersby, *Sunday Tribune*, 25 Aug. 1990, 26.

—— 'Derek Mahon Interviewed', by William Scammell, *Poetry Review*, 81/2 (Summer 1991), 4–6.

—— 'Q & A with Derek Mahon', interview by James J. Murphy, Lucy McDiarmid, and Michael J. Durkan, *Irish Literary Supplement*, 10/2 (Fall 1991), 27–8.

—— 'A Very European Poet', interview by Eileen Battersby, *Irish Times*, 10 Nov. 1992, 12.

——*Journalism: Selected Prose 1970–1995*, ed. Terence Brown (Oldcastle: Gallery Press, 1996).

Yeats, W. B., *Mythologies* (London: Macmillan, 1952).

——*Autobiographies* (London: Macmillan, 1955).

—— *Essays and Introductions* (Dublin: Gill and Macmillan, 1961).

——*A Vision* (1937; 2nd edn. London: Macmillan, 1962).

—— *Explorations* (London: Macmillan, 1962).

—— *The Letters of W. B. Yeats*, ed. Allan Wade (London: Rupert Hart-Davis, 1954).

—— *Letters on Poetry from W. B. Yeats to Dorothy Wellesley*, introd. Kathleen Raine (London: OUP, 1964).

—— *W. B. Yeats and T. Sturge Moore: Their Correspondence*, ed. Ursula Bridge (Westport Conn.: Greenwood Press, 1978).

—— *The Collected Letters of W. B. Yeats 1901–1904*, ed. John Kelly and Ronald Schuchard, iii (Oxford: Clarendon, 1994).

V.   NEWSPAPERS

Belfast Newsletter
Belfast Telegraph
Guardian
Independent
Irish Independent
Irish News
Irish Times
Newtownards Chronicle
Northern Whig
Observer
The Times

VI.   SECONDARY SOURCES

Adair, Tom, 'Of Flock and Fold: A Consideration of the Poetry of Michael Longley', *Linen Hall Review*, 4/1 (Spring 1987), 16–19.

Agee, Chris, 'Chinese Whispers, Epic Recensions', review of *The Ghost Orchid* and *Tuppenny Stung* by Michael Longley, *Poetry Ireland Review*, 49 (Spring 1996), 72–9.

Allen, Michael, 'Options: The Poetry of Michael Longley', *Éire-Ireland*, 10/4 (Winter 1975), 129–35.

—— 'Derek Mahon: The "Protestant Community" and "The North"', (Seminar paper: Queen's University, Belfast, 1993).

—— *Michael Longley* (British Council: Contemporary Writers Pamphlet, 1993).

—— 'Letter to the Editor', *Thumbscrew*, 4 (Spring 1996), 44–5.

—— (ed.), *Seamus Heaney* (London: Macmillan, 1997).

Anderson, Nathalie F., 'Queasy Proximity: Seamus Heaney's Mythical Method', *Éire-Ireland*, 23/4 (Winter 1988), 103–13.

Andrews, Elmer, *The Poetry of Seamus Heaney: All the Realms of Whisper* (London: Macmillan, 1988).

—— (ed.), *Contemporary Irish Poetry* (Basingstoke: Macmillan, 1992).

—— (ed.), *Seamus Heaney* (London: Macmillan, 1992).

Armour, W. S., *Ulster, Ireland, Britain: A Forgotten Trust* (London: Duckworth, 1938).

Arnold, Matthew, *On the Study of Celtic Literature* (London: Macmillan, 1903).

Auden, W. H., *The English Auden: Poems, Essays, and Dramatic Writings 1927–1939*, ed. Edward Mendelson (London: Faber, 1977).

Axelrod, Stephen Gould, *Robert Lowell: Life and Art* (Princeton: Princeton UP, 1978).

Bardon, Jonathan, *A History of Ulster* (Belfast: Blackstaff Press, 1992).

Beaver, Patrick (ed.), *The Wipers Times* (London: Peter Davies, 1973), (1st pub. on the Western Front in newspaper form 1916–18).

Bell, Geoffrey, *The Protestants of Ulster* (London: Pluto Press, 1976).

Bergonzi, Bernard, *Heroes' Twilight: A Study of the Literature of the Great War* (London: Constable, 1965).

Bew, Paul, *Conflict and Conciliation in Ireland 1890–1920: Parnellites and Radical Agrarians* (Oxford: Clarendon, 1987).

Bew, Paul, and Gillespie, Gordon, *Northern Ireland: A Chronology of the Troubles 1968–1993* (Dublin: Gill and Macmillan, 1993).

The Bible: King James Version.

Birmingham, George, *The Red Hand of Ulster* (London: Smith, Elder & Co., 1912).

Bloom, Harold, *The Anxiety of Influence: A Theory of Poetry* (Oxford: OUP, 1973).

—— *Yeats* (New York: OUP, 1970).

—— *The Western Canon* (London: Macmillan, 1995).

Boland, Eavan, 'The Northern Writers' Crisis of Conscience: 1: Community', *Irish Times*, 12 Aug. 1970, 12.

—— 'The Northern Writers' Crisis of Conscience: 2: Crisis', *Irish Times*, 13 Aug. 1970, 12.

—— 'The Northern Writers' Crisis of Conscience: 3: Creativity', *Irish Times*, 14 Aug. 1970, 12.

—— 'Compact and Compromise: Derek Mahon as a Young Poet', *Irish University Review*, 24/1 (Spring/Summer 1994), 61–6.

Bolger, Dermot (ed.), *16 on 16* (Dublin: Raven Arts Press, 1988).

Bourke, Joanna, ' "Irish Tommies": The Construction of a Martial Manhood 1914–1918', *Bullán*, 3/2 (Winter 1997–Spring 1998), 13–30.

Bowman, Timothy, 'The Irish at the Somme', *History Ireland*, 4/4 (Winter 1996), 48–52.

Boyce, D. George, *Nineteenth-Century Ireland: The Search for Stability* (Dublin: Gill and Macmillan, 1990).

—— *The Sure Confusing Drum: Ireland and the First World War* (Swansea: University College of Swansea, 1993).

Brewer, E. C., and Evans, Ivor H., *Dictionary of Phrase and Fable* (1970; London: Wordsworth, 1994).

Brown, George Mackay, 'Poetry Without Obstacles', review of *Man Lying on a Wall* by Michael Longley, *Scotsman*, 4 Sept. 1976.

Brown, Terence, *Louis MacNeice: Sceptical Vision* (Dublin: Gill and Macmillan, 1975).

—— *Northern Voices: Poets from Ulster* (Dublin: Gill and Macmillan, 1975).

—— *The Whole Protestant Community: The Making of a Historical Myth* (Field Day Pamphlet No. 7; Derry: Field Day, 1985).

—— *Ireland: A Social and Cultural History 1922–1985* (London: Fontana Press, 1985).

—— 'Who Dares to Speak? Ireland and the Great War', in Robert Clark and Piero Boitani (eds.), *English Studies in Transition: Papers from the ESSE Inaugural Conference* (London: Routledge, 1993), 226–37.

—— 'Derek Mahon: The Poet and Painting', *Irish University Review*, 24/1 (Spring/Summer 1994), 38–50.

—— and Grene, Nicholas (eds.), *Tradition and Influence in Anglo-Irish Poetry* (Basingstoke: Macmillan, 1989).

—— and Reid, Alec (eds.), *Time Was Away: The World of Louis MacNeice* (Dublin: Dolmen Press, 1974).

Buchan, John, *The Three Hostages* (1924; London: Penguin, 1953).

Bunyan, John, *The Pilgrim's Progress* (1684; London: Penguin, 1987).

Burris, Sidney, *The Poetry of Resistance: Seamus Heaney and the Pastoral Tradition* (Athens, Ohio: Ohio University Press, 1990).

Buttel, Robert, *Seamus Heaney* (Lewisburg: Bucknell University Press; London: Associated University Presses, 1975).

Byrne, John, 'Derek Mahon: A Commitment to Change', *Crane Bag*, 6/1 (1982), 62–72.

Caldwell, Roger, 'Heaney, Larkin and the Grim Reaper', *Honest Ulsterman*, 103 (Spring 1997), 106–9.

Carson, Ciaran, 'Escaped from the Massacre?', review of *North* by Seamus Heaney, *Honest Ulsterman*, 50 (1975), 183–6.

Casey, Patrick J., 'Irish Casualties in the First World War', *The Irish Sword*, 20/81 (Summer 1997), 193–206.

Chilman, Eric, 'W. B. Yeats', *Poetry Review* (Jan.–June 1914), 70.

Clausewitz, Carl von, *On War* (1832), trans. J. J. Graham, and ed. Anatol Rapoport (London: Penguin, 1982).

Clifford, Brendan, and O'Donnell, Charles James, *Ireland in the Great War: The Irish Insurrection of 1916 set in its Context of the World War* (Belfast: Athol Books, 1992).

Cohen, J. M., *Robert Graves* (London and Edinburgh: Oliver and Boyd Ltd., 1960).

Connolly, Peter (ed.), *Literature and the Changing Ireland* (Gerrards Cross: Colin Smythe, 1982).

Corcoran, Neil, 'Last Words: Michael Longley's Elegies', *Poetry Wales*, 24/2 (n.d), 16–18.

——*Seamus Heaney* (London: Faber, 1986).

——'Ovid in Ulster', review of *The Ghost Orchid* by Michael Longley, *Times Literary Supplement*, 7 July 1995, 13.

——(ed.), *The Chosen Ground: Essays on the Contemporary Poetry of Northern Ireland* (Bridgend: Seren Books, 1992).

Corkery, Daniel, *Synge and Anglo-Irish Literature* (1931; Dublin: Mercier Press, 1966).

Costello, Mary, *Titanic Town: Memoirs of a Belfast Girlhood* (London: Mandarin, 1993).

Cullingford, Elizabeth, *Yeats, Ireland and Fascism* (London: Macmillan, 1981).

Curran, Stuart, *Poetic Form and British Romanticism* (Oxford: OUP, 1986).

Curtayne, Alice, *Francis Ledwidge: A Life of the Poet (1887–1917)* (London: Martin Brian and O'Keefe, 1972).

——'Francis Ledwidge, Who Fought in Another Man's War', *Éire-Ireland*, 15/i (Spring 1980), 114–27.

Curtis, Tony (ed.), *How Poets Work* (Bridgend: Seren Books, 1996).

Davie, Donald, *Thomas Hardy and British Poetry* (London: Routledge, 1973).

Davis, Dick, 'King Image', review of *The Echo Gate* by Michael Longley, *The Listener*, 31 Jan. 1980, 157–8.

Dawe, Gerald, review of *Poems 1963–1983* by Michael Longley, *Poetry Ireland Review*, 14 (Autumn 1985), 54–9.

——and Foster, J. (eds.), *The Poet's Place: Ulster Literature and Society* (Belfast: Queen's University Institute of Irish Studies, 1991).

Deane, Seamus, *Civilians and Barbarians* (Field Day Pamphlet No. 3; Derry: Field Day, 1983), repr. in *Ireland's Field Day* (Notre Dame, Ind.: University of Notre Dame Press, 1986), 33–42.

—— *Heroic Styles: The Tradition of an Idea* (Field Day Pamphlet No. 4; Derry: Field Day, 1984) repr. in *Ireland's Field Day* (Notre Dame, Ind.: University of Notre Dame Press, 1986), 45–58.

—— *Celtic Revivals* (London: Faber, 1985).

—— *A Short History of Irish Literature* (London: Hutchinson, 1986).

—— 'Celebrant of Lost Lives and the Sublime', review of *Selected Poems* by Derek Mahon, *Irish Times*, 22 Dec. 1990, Weekend 8.

—— (gen. ed.), *The Field Day Anthology of Irish Writing*, 3 vols. (Derry: Field Day, 1991).

Denman, Peter, 'Know the One? Insolent Ontology and Mahon's Revisions', *Irish University Review*, 24/1 (Spring/Summer 1994), 27–37.

Denman, Terence, *Ireland's Unknown Soldiers: The 16th (Irish) Division in the Great War, 1914–1918* (Dublin: Irish Academic Press, 1992).

Devine, Kathleen (ed.), *Modern Irish Writers and the Wars* (Gerrard's Cross: Colin Smythe, 1999).

—— and Peacock, Alan J. (eds.), *Louis MacNeice and his Influence* (Gerrard's Cross: Colin Smythe, 1998).

Di Nicola, Robert, 'Time and History in Seamus Heaney's "In Memoriam Francis Ledwidge"', *Éire-Ireland*, 21/4 (Winter 1986), 45–51.

Doherty, Richard, *The Sons of Ulster: Ulstermen at War from the Somme to Korea* (Belfast: Appletree Press, 1992).

Donnelly, Brian, 'The Poetry of Derek Mahon', *English Studies*, 60/1 (Feb. 1979), 23–34.

Donoghue, Denis, *We Irish: Essays on Irish Literature and Society* (Berkeley and Los Angeles: University of California Press, 1986).

Dooley, Thomas P., 'Southern Ireland, Historians and the First World War', *Irish Studies Review*, 4 (Autumn 1993), 5–9.

—— *Irishmen or English Soldiers?: The Times and World of a Southern Catholic Irish Man (1876–1916) Enlisting in the British Army during the First World War* (Liverpool: Liverpool UP, 1995).

Duhig, Ian, Review of *The Ghost Orchid* by Michael Longley, *Fortnight*, 340 (June 1995), 33–4.

Dungan, Myles, *Irish Voices from the Great War* (Dublin: Irish Academic Press, 1995).

—— *They Shall Grow Not Old: Irish Soldiers and the Great War* (Dublin: Four Courts Press, 1997).

Dunn, Douglas, 'The Poetry of the Troubles', review of *Selected Poems 1963–1980* by Michael Longley, *Times Literary Supplement*, 31 July 1981, 886.

—— (ed.), *Two Decades of Irish Writing* (Cheadle: Carcanet Press, 1975).

Durcan, Paul, 'Poetry and Truth', review of *The Echo Gate* by Michael Longley and *The Strange Museum* by Tom Paulin, *Irish Press*, 20 Mar. 1980, 6.

Dyer, Geoff, *The Missing of the Somme* (London: Penguin, 1995).

Eagleton, Terry, 'The Commitment of our Forms: New Political Poetry', review of *The Snow Party* by Derek Mahon, *Stand*, 17/2 (Spring 1976), 76–80.

Easthope, Antony, 'How Good is Seamus Heaney?', *English*, 46/184 (Spring 1997), 21–35.

Edwards, Owen Dudley, and Pyle, Fergus (eds.), *1916: The Easter Rising* (London: MacGibbon and Kee Ltd., 1968).

Eisenstadt, S. N. (ed.), *The Protestant Ethic and Modernization: A Comparative View* (New York and London: Basic Books Inc., 1968).

Eksteins, Modris, *Rites of Spring: The Great War and the Birth of the Modern Age* (1989; New York: Anchor-Doubleday, 1990).

Ellmann, Richard, *The Identity of Yeats* (London: Macmillan, 1954).

—— *Yeats: the Man and the Masks* (2nd edn. 1979; London: Penguin, 1987).

Encounters, Channel 4, 5 May 1996.

English, Richard, and Walker, Graham (eds.), *Unionism in Modern Ireland* (Dublin: Gill and Macmillan, 1996).

Ervine, St John G., *Changing Winds* (1917; London: George Allen & Unwin Ltd., 1930).

Falls, Cyril, *The History of the 36th (Ulster) Division* (1922; Belfast: The Somme Association, 1991).

Featherstone, Simon, *War Poetry: An Introductory Reader* (London: Routledge, 1995).

Fennell, Desmond, *Whatever You Say, Say Nothing: Why Seamus Heaney is No. 1* (Dublin: ELO Publications, 1991).

Fitzgerald, F. Scott, *Tender is the Night* (1934; London: Penguin, 1986).

Fitzgerald, J., Deane, Seamus, Fowler, Joan, and McGuinness, Frank, 'The Arts and Ideology', *Crane Bag*, 9/2 (1985), 60–9.

Fitzpatrick, David (ed.), *Ireland and the First World War* (Dublin: Trinity History Workshop, 1986).

Ford, Ford Madox, *The Good Soldier* (1915; London: Penguin, 1972).

—— *Parade's End* (1924–1928; London: Penguin, 1982).

Foster, John Wilson, *Colonial Consequences: Essays in Irish Literature and Culture* (Dublin: Lilliput Press, 1991).

—— *The Titanic Complex: A Cultural Manifest* (Vancouver: Belcouver Press, 1997).

Foster, R. F., *Modern Ireland 1600–1972* (London: Allen Lane, 1988).

—— *Paddy & Mr Punch: Connections in Irish and English History* (1993; London: Penguin, 1995).

—— *W. B. Yeats: A Life, i. The Apprentice Mage* (Oxford: OUP, 1997).

—— 'Writing a Life of W. B. Yeats', *Irish Review*, 21 (Autumn/Winter 1997), 92–101.

Foster, Thomas C., *Seamus Heaney* (Dublin: O'Brien Press, 1989).

Foy, Michael, 'Ulster Unionist Propaganda against Home Rule 1912–1914', *History Ireland*, 4/1 (Spring 1996), 49–53.

Fraser, T. G., and Jeffery, Keith (eds.), *Men, Women and War* (Dublin: Lilliput Press, 1993).

Frye, Northrop, *Anatomy of Criticism* (1957; London: Penguin, 1990).

—— *The Great Code: The Bible and Literature* (1983; London: Penguin, 1990).

Fussell, Paul, *The Great War and Modern Memory* (London: OUP, 1975).

—— *Thank God for The Atom Bomb* (1988), repr. as *Killing in Verse and Prose* (London: Bellew, 1990).

—— (ed.), *The Bloody Game: An Anthology of Modern War* (London: Scribners, 1991).

Gardner, Brian, *The Big Push: The Somme 1916* (London: Sphere Books, 1968).

Garratt, Robert F., 'Two from Wake Forest', review of *Selected Poems 1963–1980* by Michael Longley and *Why Brownlee Left* by Paul Muldoon, *Irish Literary Supplement*, 1/2 (Fall 1982), 15.

—— *Modern Irish Poetry: Tradition and Continuity from Yeats to Heaney* (Berkeley and Los Angeles: University of California Press, 1986).

—— (ed.), *Critical Essays on Seamus Heaney* (New York: G. K. Hall; (London: Prentice Hall International, 1995).

Genet, Jacqueline (ed.), *Studies on Seamus Heaney* (Caen: Centre de Publications de Caen 147, 1987).

—— 'W. B. Yeats and W. H. Auden', in Wolfgang Zach and Heinz Kosok (eds.), *Literary Interrelations: Ireland, England and the World*, ii. *Comparison and Impact* (Tübingen: Gunter Narr Verlag, 1987), 95–110.

Gibbon, Monk, 'Q & A with Monk Gibbon', interview by Geoffrey Inverarity, *Irish Literary Supplement*, 6/2 (Fall 1987), 29–30.

Goldring, Maurice, 'On Top of That', *Fortnight*, 259 (Feb. 1988), 25.

Graham, Desmond, *The Truth of War* (Manchester: Carcanet Press, 1984).

Graves, Alfred Perceval, *To Return to All That* (London: Jonathan Cape, 1930).

Graves, Richard Perceval, *Robert Graves: The Assault Heroic 1895–1926* (London: Papermac-Macmillan, 1987).

—— *Robert Graves: The Years with Laura 1926–1940* (London: Papermac-Macmillan, 1991).

—— *Robert Graves and the White Goddess 1940–1985* (London: Weidenfeld and Nicolson, 1995).

Gray, John, Review of *The Road to the Somme: Men of the Ulster Division Tell Their Story*, by Philip Orr, *Linen Hall Review*, 4/4 (Winter 1987), 34.

Greacen, Robert, *Patrick MacGill: Champion of the Underdog* (Glentries: Glentries Development Association Pamphlet, 1991).

The Great War: A Tribute to Ulster's Heroes (Belfast Citizen's Committee, 1919; Belfast: Pretani Press, 1991).

Gregory, Lady Augusta (ed.), *Ideals in Ireland* (1901; New York: Lemma, 1973).

Grennan, Eamon, 'Mortal Lights', review of *Courtyards in Delft* by Derek Mahon, *Irish Times*, 28 Mar. 1981, 13.

Haberstroh, Patricia Boyle, 'Poet, Poetry, Painting, and Artist in Seamus Heaney's *North*', *Éire-Ireland*, 23/4 (Winter 1988), 124–33.

Hall, Michael, *Sacrifice on the Somme* (Antrim: Island Publications Pamphlet, 1993).

Hamilton, Ernest W., *The Soul of Ulster* (2nd edn., London: Hurst and Blackett Ltd., 1917).

Hamilton, Paul, *Historicism* (London: Routledge, 1996).

Harmon, Maurice, Review of *Courtyards in Delft* by Derek Mahon, *Irish University Review*, 21/1 (Spring 1982), 101–7.

Harmon, Maurice (ed.), *The Irish Writer and the City* (Gerrards Cross: Colin Smythe, 1984).

Hart, Henry, *Seamus Heaney: Poet of Contrary Progressions* (New York: Syracuse UP, 1992).

Harte, Liam, 'Louis MacNeice: An Irish Nomad', review of *Louis MacNeice* by Jon Stallworthy, *Irish Studies Review*, 10 (Spring 1995), 38–40.

Hartley, L. P., *The Go-Between* (1953; London: Penguin, 1958).

Hawthorn, Jeremy, *Cunning Passages: New Historicism, Cultural Materialism and Marxism in the Contemporary Literary Debate* (London: Arnold, 1996).

Henn, T. R., *The Lonely Tower* (2nd edn. London: Methuen, 1965).

——*Last Essays* (Gerrards Cross: Colin Smythe, 1976).

Hennessey, Thomas, *Dividing Ireland: World War I and Partition* (London: Routledge, 1998).

Hewitt, John, *Ancestral Voices: The Selected Prose of John Hewitt*, ed. Tom Clyde (Belfast: Blackstaff Press, 1987).

Hibberd, Dominic, *Owen the Poet*, (London: Macmillan; Athens, Ga.: University of Georgia Press, 1986).

Hinde, Robert A. (ed.), *The Institution of War* (New York: St Martin's Press, 1992).

Hobsbaum, Philip, *A Reader's Guide to Robert Lowell* (London: Thames and Hudson, 1988).

——'"Growing like a coral among shadows": Literary Life Respectable', review of *The Ghost Orchid* by Michael Longley, *Thumbscrew*, 3 (Autumn/Winter 1995), 54–61.

——Response to 'Letter to the Editor', *Thumbscrew*, 4 (Spring 1996), 45–7.

Hoffman, Daniel, *Barbarous Knowledge: Myth in the Poetry of Yeats, Graves and Muir* (New York: OUP, 1967).

Holdridge, Jefferson, 'Heart's Victim and its Torturer: Yeats and the Poetry of Violence', *Irish University Review*, 27/1 (Spring/Summer 1997), 111–29.

Hone, Joseph, *W. B. Yeats 1865–1939* (London: Macmillan, 1942).

Horton, Patricia, 'Romantic Intersections: Romanticism and Contemporary Northern Irish Poetry', doct. diss., Queen's University, Belfast, 1996.

Howard, Michael, *War and the Liberal Conscience* (London: OUP, 1981).

——— *The Causes of Wars and Other Essays* (1983; London: Unwin, 1984).

Hutcheon, Linda, *Irony's Edge: The Theory and Politics of Irony* (London: Routledge, 1994).

Hynes, Samuel, *The Auden Generation: Literature and Politics in England in the 1930s* (London: Bodley Head, 1976).

———*A War Imagined: The First World War and English Culture* (New York: Atheneum, 1991).

Jackson, Alvin, 'Unionist History (I)', *Irish Review*, 7 (Autumn 1989), 58–65.

——— 'Unionist Myths 1912–1985', *Past and Present*, 136 (Aug. 1992), 166–85.

Jameson, Fredric, *The Political Unconscious: Narrative as a Socially Symbolic Act* (1981; London: Routledge, 1989).

———*Modernism and Imperialism* (Field Day Pamphlet No. 14; Derry: Field Day, 1988).

Jeffery, Keith, 'Irish Culture and the Great War', *Bullán*, 1/2 (Autumn 1994), 87–96.

——— (ed.), *'An Irish Empire'? Aspects of Ireland and the British Empire* (Manchester: Manchester UP, 1996).

John, Brian, 'The Achievement of Michael Longley's *The Ghost Orchid*', *Irish University Review*, 27/1 (Spring/Summer 1997), 139–51.

Johnston, Dillon, *Irish Poetry after Joyce* (Notre Dame, Ind.: University of Notre Dame Press, 1985).

Johnston, Jennifer, *How Many Miles to Babylon?* (1974; London: Penguin, 1988).

Johnstone, John H., *English Poetry of the First World War: A Study in the Evolution of Lyric and Narrative Form* (Princeton: Princeton University Press, 1964).

Johnstone, Robert, 'Harmonics between Electrified Fences', review of *Gorse Fires* by Michael Longley, *Honest Ulsterman*, 92 (1991), 78–82.

Johnstone, Tom, *Orange, Green and Khaki: The Story of the Irish Regiments in the Great War 1914–1918* (Dublin: Gill and Macmillan, 1992).

Jusdanis, Gregory, *Belated Modernity and Aesthetic Culture: Inventing National Literature* (Minneapolis: University of Minneapolis Press, 1991).

Kearney, Richard, *Myth and Motherland* (Field Day Pamphlet No. 5; Derry: Field Day, 1984), repr. in *Ireland's Field Day* (Notre Dame, Ind.: University of Notre Dame Press, 1986), 61–80.

Kearney, Timothy, 'The Poetry of the North: A Post-Modernist Perspective', in Mark Patrick Hederman and Richard Kearney (eds.), *The Crane Bag Book of Irish Studies*, (Dublin: Blackwater Press, 1982), 465–73.

Keegan, John, *The Face of Battle: A Study of Agincourt, Waterloo and the Somme* (1976; London: Pimlico, 1991).

Kelly, Conor, 'Keeping the Faith', review of *Poems 1963–1983* by Michael Longley, *Magill*, 21 Mar. 1985, 47–8.

Kenneally, Michael (ed.), *Cultural Contexts and Literary Idioms in Contemporary Irish Literature* (Gerrards Cross: Colin Smythe, 1988).

Kenneally, Michael (ed.), *Poetry in Contemporary Irish Literature* (Gerrards Cross: Colin Smythe, 1995).

Kennelly, Brendan, 'Lyric Wit', review of *Poems 1962–1978* by Derek Mahon, *Irish Times*, 22 Dec. 1979, 11.

——'Wonder and Awe', review of *Gorse Fires* by Michael Longley, *Fortnight*, 295 (May 1991), 24.

Kern, Stephen, *The Culture of Time and Space 1880–1918* (Cambridge, Mass.: Harvard University Press, 1983).

Kettle, T. M., *The Day's Burden: Studies Literary and Political* (Dublin: Maunsel & Co., 1910).

Kiberd, Declan, Review of *Poems 1962–1978* by Derek Mahon, *Irish University Review*, 21/1 (Spring 1982), 108–9.

——'Culture and Barbarism: Heaney's Poetry and its Recent Critics', *Poetry Ireland Review*, 27 (1989), 29–37.

——*Inventing Ireland: The Literature of the Modern Nation* (London: Jonathan Cape, 1995).

Kinsella, Thomas, and Yeats, W. B., *Davis, Mangan, Ferguson: Tradition and the Irish Writer* (Dublin: Dolmen Press, 1970).

Kirkham, Michael, *The Poetry of Robert Graves* (London: Athlone Press, 1969).

Kirkland, Richard, *Literature and Culture in Northern Ireland since 1965: Moments of Danger* (London and New York: Longman, 1996).

Lane, Arthur E., *An Adequate Response: The War Poetry of Wilfred Owen and Siegfried Sassoon* (Detroit: Wayne State UP, 1972).

Leed, Eric J., *No Man's Land: Combat and Identity in World War I* (Cambridge: Cambridge UP, 1979).

Lernout, Geert (ed.), *The Crows behind the Plough: History and Violence in Anglo-Irish Poetry and Drama* (Amsterdam: Rodopi, 1991).

Lewis, C. S., *Surprised by Joy* (1955; London: Fount Paperbacks, 1977).

Liddy, James, 'Ulster Poets and the Protestant Muse', *Éire-Ireland*, 14/2 (Summer 1979), 118–27.

Lojek, Helen, 'Myth and Bonding in McGuinness's *Observe the Sons of Ulster Marching towards the Somme*', *Canadian Journal of Irish Studies*, 14/1 (1988), 45–53.

Longenbach, James, *Stone Cottage: Pound, Yeats and Modernism* (New York and Oxford: OUP, 1988).

Longley, Edna, 'Snow-Parties', review of *The Snow Party* by Derek Mahon, *Irish Times*, 26 Aug. 1975, Weekend 8.

——'Fire and Air', review of *The Snow Party* by Derek Mahon, *Honest Ulsterman*, 50 (1975), 179–83.

——'Stars and Horses, Pigs and Trees', in Mark Patrick Hederman and Richard Kearney (eds.), *The Crane Bag Book of Irish Studies* (Dublin: Blackwater Press, 1982), 474–80.

——'Sweet Dreams or Rifles', review of *The Liberty Tree* by Tom Paulin, *Fortnight*, 196 (Aug. 1983), 19–21.

—— 'An Ironic Conscience at One Minute to Midnight', review of *The Hunt by Night* by Derek Mahon, *Fortnight*, 211 (Dec. 1984), 17–18.

—— *Poetry in the Wars* (Newcastle: Bloodaxe, 1986).

—— 'Opening Up: A New Pluralism', *Fortnight* (Nov. 1987), 24–25.

—— 'MacNeice and After', *Poetry Review*, 78/2 (Summer 1988), 6–10.

—— *Louis MacNeice: A Study* (London: Faber, 1988).

—— 'Where a Thought Might Grow', review of *Selected Poems* by Derek Mahon, *Poetry Review*, 81/2 (Summer 1991), 7–9.

—— *The Living Stream: Literature and Revisionism in Ireland* (Newcastle: Bloodaxe, 1994).

—— and Dawe, Gerald (eds.), *Across a Roaring Hill: The Protestant Imagination in Modern Ireland* (Belfast: Blackstaff Press, 1985).

Lucy, Gordon (ed.), *The Ulster Covenant: A Pictorial History of the 1912 Home Rule Crisis* (The Ulster Society: New Ulster (Publications) Ltd., 1989).

—— and McClure, Elaine (eds.), *The Twelfth: What it Means to Me* (Armagh: Ulster Society (Publications) Ltd., 1997).

—— (ed.), *Remembrance* (Armagh: Ulster Society (Publications) Ltd., 1997).

Lundy, Jean, and MacPóilin, Aodán (eds.), *Styles of Belonging: The Cultural Identities of Ulster* (Belfast: Lagan Press, 1992).

Lyon, John, 'Michael Longley's Lists', *English* 45/183 (Autumn 1996), 228–46.

Lyons, F. S. L., *Ireland since the Famine* (1971; London: Fontana, 1973).

—— *Culture and Anarchy in Ireland 1890–1939* (1979; Oxford: OUP, 1982).

Lyons, J. B., *The Enigma of Tom Kettle* (Dublin: Glendale Press, 1983).

McBrien, Richard, *Catholicism* (3rd edn. London: Geoffrey Chapman, 1994).

McCarthy, Thomas, 'Northern Voices', review of *The Echo Gate* by Michael Longley, *Irish Times*, 9 Feb. 1980, 13.

McCormack, W. J., *From Burke to Beckett: Ascendancy and Betrayal in Literary History* (1985; rev. edn., Cork: Cork UP, 1994).

McCurry, Jacqueline, 'The Female in Seamus Heaney's Prose Poetics and the Poetry of *The Haw Lantern*', *Éire-Ireland*, 23/4 (Winter 1988), 114–24.

McDaniel, Denzil, *Enniskillen: The Remembrance Sunday Bombing* (Dublin: Wolfhound Press, 1997).

McDiarmid, Lucy, *Saving Civilization: Yeats, Eliot and Auden between the Wars* (Cambridge: Cambridge UP, 1984).

MacDonagh, Michael, *The Irish on the Somme*, introd. by John Redmond, MP (London: Hodder and Stoughton, 1917).

McDonald, Lyn, *Somme*, (London: Papermac-Macmillan, 1984).

McDonald, Peter, 'From Ulster with Love', review of *Poems 1963–1983* by Michael Longley, *Poetry Review*, 74/4 (Jan. 1985), 14–16.

—— *Louis MacNeice: The Poet in his Contexts* (Oxford: Clarendon, 1991).

—— 'The Poet and "The Finished Man": Heaney's Oxford Lectures', *Irish Review*, 19 (Spring/Summer 1996), 98–108.

—— *Mistaken Identities: Poetry and Northern Ireland* (Oxford: Clarendon, 1997).

McDonald, Peter 'Yeats and Remorse', Chatterton Lecture on Poetry 1996, *Proceedings of the British Academy*, 94: 173–206.

McGuinness, Arthur E., 'Politics and Irish Poetry: Seamus Heaney's Declaration of Independence', *Études Irlandaises*, 15/2 (Dec. 1990), 75–82.

——*Seamus Heaney: Poet and Critic* (New York: Peter Lang, 1994).

McGuinness, Frank, *Observe the Sons of Ulster Marching Towards the Somme* (London: Faber, 1986).

——'In the Forefront of Irish Writing', review of *Poems 1963–1983* by Michael Longley, *Irish Literary Supplement*, 5/1 (Spring 1986), 23.

McHugh, Roger (ed.), *Dublin 1916: An Illustrated Anthology* (London: Arlington Books, 1976).

McIlroy, Brian, 'Poetic Imagery as Political Fetishism: The Example of Michael Longley', *Canadian Journal of Irish Studies*, 16/1 (July 1990), 59–64.

McIntosh, Gillian, *The Force of Culture: Unionist Identities in Twentieth-Century Ireland* (Cork: Cork University Press, 1999).

McIvor, Peter K., 'Regionalism in Ulster: An Historical Perspective', *Irish University Review*, 13/2 (Autumn 1983), 180–8.

McNeill, Ronald, *Ulster's Stand for Union* (London: John Murray, 1922).

Mahony, Christina Hunt, 'London Meets Laredo: Louis MacNeice's Irish War', *Irish University Review*, 25/2 (Autumn/Winter 1995), 204–14.

Matthews, Aidan C., 'Winter Quarters for a Poet-exile', review of *The Hunt by Night* by Derek Mahon, *Irish Times*, 19 Feb. 1983, 12.

Middlebrook, Martin, *The First Day on the Somme: 1 July 1916* (London: Allen Lane, 1971).

Miller, David, *Queen's Rebels: Ulster Loyalism in Historical Perspective* (Dublin: Gill and Macmillan, 1975).

Mole, John, 'A Question of Balance', review of *The Echo Gate* by Michael Longley, *Times Literary Supplement*, 8 Feb. 1980, 138.

Moloney, Ed, 'The Most Expensive Own Goal', *Fortnight* (Dec. 1987), 6–7.

Montague, John, *The Figure in the Cave and Other Essays* (New York: Syracuse University Press, 1989).

Motion, Andrew, 'Burning Snow', review of *The Echo Gate* by Michael Longley, *New Statesman*, 11 Jan. 1980, 61.

Mullaney, Kathleen, 'A Poetics of Silence: Derek Mahon "At One Remove"', *Journal of Irish Literature*, 18/3 (Sept. 1989), 45–54.

Murphy, Patrick, 'Nudity and Nakedness: Jack B. Yeats and Robert Graves', *Éire-Ireland*, 10/2 (Summer 1975), 119–23.

Naiden, James, review of *Selected Poems 1963–1980* by Michael Longley, *Éire-Ireland*, 18/1 (Spring 1983), 146–9.

Nairn, Tom, *The Break-Up of Britain: Crisis and Neo-Nationalism*, (2nd edn., London: Verso, 1981).

Newsnight, BBC2, 1 Feb. 1995.

Ní Dhonnchadha, Máirín, and Dorgan, Theo, (eds.), *Revising the Rising* (Derry: Field Day, 1991).

Nijinsky, Romola, *Nijinsky* (1933; London: Sphere Books, 1970).

North, Michael, *The Political Aesthetic of Yeats, Eliot and Pound* (Cambridge: Cambridge UP, 1991).

O'Casey, Sean, *Collected Plays*, ii (London: Macmillan, 1949).

O'Donnell, C. J., *Outraged Ulster: Why Ireland is Rebellious, by An Ulster Catholic* (London: Anglo-Eastern Publishing Co. Ltd., 1932).

O'Donoghue, Bernard, *Seamus Heaney and the Language of Poetry* (London: Harvester Wheatsheaf, 1994).

O'Dowd, J. J., review of *The Living Stream* by Edna Longley, *Books Ireland*, 184 (Mar. 1995), 49–50.

O'Faoláin, Seán, 'A Portrait of the Artist as an Old Man', *Irish University Review*, 6/1 (Spring 1976), 10–18.

Officer, David, 'Re-presenting War: The Somme Heritage Centre', *History Ireland*, 3/1 (Spring 1995), 38–42.

O'Halloran, Clare, *Partition and the Limits of Irish Nationalism: An Ideology under Stress* (Dublin: Gill and Macmillan, 1987).

O'Neill, Michael, and Reeves, Gareth, *Auden, MacNeice, Spender: The Thirties Poetry* (London: Macmillan, 1992).

Orr, Philip, *The Road to the Somme: Men of the Ulster Division Tell Their Story* (Belfast: Blackstaff Press, 1987).

—— 'The Somme Legacy', *Linen Hall Review*, 4/4 (Winter 1987), 5–7.

—— 'Lessons of the Somme for an Era of Change', *Causeway* (Summer 1996), 14–18.

Orwell, George, *The Collected Essays, Journalism and Letters of George Orwell*, ed. Sonia Orwell and Ian Angus, i (London: Penguin, 1970).

—— *The Road to Wigan Pier* (1937; London: Penguin, 1979).

—— *Nineteen Eighty-Four* (1949; London: Penguin, 1989).

Owen, Wilfred, *Collected Letters*, ed. Harold Owen and John Bell (London: OUP, 1967).

Parker, Michael, Review of *The Ghost Orchid* by Michael Longley, *Irish Studies Review*, 14 (Spring 1996), 50–2.

—— 'Levelling with Heaney', *Honest Ulsterman*, 103 (Spring 1997), 101–5.

Patten, Eve (ed.), *Returning to Ourselves: Second Volume of Papers from the John Hewitt International Summer School* (Belfast: Lagan Press, 1995).

Paulin, Tom, 'A Rare and Extraordinary Imagination', review of *Poems 1962–1978* by Derek Mahon, *Honest Ulsterman*, 65 (1980), 64–9.

—— *Ireland and the English Crisis* (Newcastle: Bloodaxe, 1984).

Peacock, Alan J., 'Prolegomena to Michael Longley's Peace Poem', *Éire-Ireland*, 23/1 (Spring 1988), 60–74.

—— Review of *Gorse Fires* by Michael Longley, *Linen Hall Review*, 9/1 (Spring 1992), 44–5.

Powell, Anne, *A Deep Cry: A Literary Pilgrimage to the Battlefields and Cemeteries of First World War Soldier Poets Killed in Northern France and Flanders* (Aberporth: Palladour Books, 1993).

Prior, Robin, and Wilson, Trevor, 'Paul Fussell at War', *War in History*, 1/1 (1994), 63–80.

A Question of Union, Channel 4, 1 Feb. 1995.

Ramazani, Jahan, *Yeats and the Poetry of Death: Elegy, Self-Elegy, and the Sublime* (New Haven and London: Yale University Press, 1990).

—— *Poetry of Mourning: The Modern Elegy from Hardy to Heaney* (Chicago: University of Chicago Press, 1994).

Report on the Loss of the S.S. 'Titanic': The Official Government Enquiry (1912; Belfast: Blackstaff Press, 1991).

Robinson, Peter, *Their Cry was 'No Surrender'*, with foreword by Ian Paisley (Belfast: Crown Publications, 1988).

Roulston, Stewart, 'Past Tense, Present Tension: Protestant Poetry and Ulster History', *Eire-Ireland*, 18/3 (Fall 1983), 100–23.

Sagar, Keith, *The Art of Ted Hughes* (2nd edn., Cambridge: Cambridge UP, 1978).

—— (ed.), *The Achievement of Ted Hughes*, (Manchester: Manchester UP, 1983).

Said, Edward, *Culture and Imperialism*, (London: Vintage, 1994).

Seymour, Miranda, *Robert Graves: Life on the Edge*, (London and New York: Doubleday, 1995).

Sharp, Ronald A., *Keats, Skepticism, and the Religion of Beauty* (Athens, Ga.: University of Georgia Press, 1979).

Shields, Kathleen, 'Derek Mahon's Poetry of Belonging', *Irish University Review* (Spring/Summer 1994), 67–79.

Silkin, Jon, *Out of Battle: The Poetry of the Great War*, (1972; London: Ark, 1987).

Simmons, James, 'Two Talented Friends', review of *The Echo Gate* by Michael Longley and *Poems 1962–1978* by Derek Mahon, *Books Ireland*, 40 (Jan.–Feb. 1980), 21–2.

—— 'Profile: Michael Longley', *Fortnight*, 4 Dec. 1970, 20.

Smith, Stan, *Inviolable Voice: History and Twentieth-Century Poetry* (Dublin: Gill and Macmillan, 1982).

—— 'Writing a Will: Yeats's Ancestral Voices in "The Tower" and "Meditations in Time of Civil War"', *Irish University Review*, 13/1 (1983), 14–37.

—— *The Origins of Modernism: Eliot, Pound, Yeats and the Rhetorics of Renewal* (London: Harvester Wheatsheaf, 1994).

Smythe, Colin (ed.), *Robert Gregory 1881–1918: A Centenary Tribute* (Gerrards Cross: Colin Smythe, 1981).

Snow, Jon, 'End of an Unseemly Era', *Fortnight*, 332 (Oct. 1994), 25.

The Soldiers' Pilgrimage, BBC2 11 Nov. 1998.

The Somme Association, 'Commemoration of the 75th Anniversary of the Battle of the Somme: Northern Ireland Pilgrimage to the Ulster War Memorial at Thiepval, Somme, Official Souvenir Programme.'

—— *Battle Lines: The Journal of the Somme Association.*

Stallworthy, Jon, *Between the Lines: Yeats's Poetry in the Making* (Oxford: Clarendon, 1963).

—— 'W. B. Yeats and Wilfred Owen', *Critical Quarterly*, 11/3 (Autumn 1969), 199–214.

—— *Wilfred Owen* (Oxford: OUP, 1977).

—— *Louis MacNeice* (London: Faber, 1995).

Stanfield, Paul Scott, 'Facing *North* Again: Polyphony, Contention', *Éire-Ireland*, 23/4 (Winter 1988), 133–44.

Stevens, Wallace, *The Necessary Angel: Essays on Reality and the Imagination* (London: Faber, 1960).

Stewart, A. T. Q., *The Ulster Crisis* (London: Faber, 1967).

Storey, Mark, 'Michael Longley: A Precarious Act of Balancing', *Fortnight*, 194 (May 1983), 21–2.

Taylor, A. J. P., *The First World War: An Illustrated History* (London: Penguin, 1966).

—— 'Distressful Country', review of *Political Violence in Ireland: Government and Resistance since 1848* by Charles Townshend, *Observer*, 12 Feb. 1984.

Thomas, Edward, *A Language Not to be Betrayed: Selected Prose of Edward Thomas*, ed. Edna Longley (Manchester: Carcanet New Press, 1991).

Thompson, W. I., *The Imagination of an Insurrection: Dublin, Easter 1916* (New York: OUP, 1967).

Tinley, Bill, 'International Perspectives in the Poetry of Derek Mahon', *Irish University Review*, 21/1 (Spring/Summer 1991), 106–17.

—— ' "Harmonies or Disharmonies": Derek Mahon's Francophile Poetics', *Irish University Review*, 24/1 (Spring/Summer 1994), 80–95.

The Trouble with Peace, Channel 4, 30 Aug. 1995.

Tylee, Claire M., *The Great War and Women's Consciousness: Images of Militarism and Womanhood in Women's Writings, 1914–1964* (Iowa City: University of Iowa Press, 1990).

Vansittart, Peter, *Voices from the Great War* (1981; London: Pimlico, 1998).

Vincent, Andrew, *Modern Political Ideologies* (Oxford: Blackwell, 1992).

Viney, Michael, 'Requiem for a Badger', *Irish Times*, 1 Nov. 1986, Weekend 11.

Walker, Graham S., *The Politics of Frustration: Harry Midgley and the Failure of Labour in Northern Ireland* (Manchester: Manchester University Press, 1985).

Watson, George, 'Heaney at the Top of His Form', review of *The Haw Lantern* by Seamus Heaney, *Irish Literary Supplement*, 6/2 (Fall 1987), 35.

Weber, Max, *The Protestant Ethic and the Spirit of Capitalism* (1930); with introduction by Anthony Giddens (London: George Allen & Unwin Ltd., 1976).

Welch, Robert (ed.), *The Oxford Companion to Irish Literature* (Oxford: Clarendon, 1996).

Whyte, John, *Interpreting Northern Ireland* (Oxford: Clarendon, 1990).

Wilcox, Angela, 'The Temple of the Lord is Ransacked: McGuinness's *Observe the Sons of Ulster Marching towards the Somme* and *Baglady*', *Theatre Ireland*, 8 (Winter 1984), 87–9.

Williams, David E., 'The Poetry of Derek Mahon', *Journal of Irish Literature*, 13/3 (Sept. 1984), 88–99.

Wilson, Robert McLiam, 'The Glittering Prize', *Fortnight*, 344 (Nov. 1995), 23–5.

Winter, Jay, *Sites of Memory, Sites of Mourning: The Great War in European Cultural History* (Cambridge: Cambridge UP, 1996).

Yeats, J. B., *Letters to his Son W. B. Yeats and Others 1869–1922*, ed. Joseph Hone (London: Secker & Warburg, 1983).

Index